Worried About the Wrong Things

The John D. and Catherine T. MacArthur Foundation Series on Digital Media and Learning

Worried About the Wrong Things

Youth, Risk, and Opportunity in the Digital World

Jacqueline Ryan Vickery

The MIT Press
Cambridge, Massachusetts
London, England

Set in ITC Stone Sans Std and ITC Stone Serif Std by Toppan Best-set Premedia Limited. Printed and bound in the United States of America.

Library of Congress Cataloging-in-Publication Data

Names: Vickery, Jacqueline Ryan, author.
Title: Worried about the wrong things : youth, risk, and opportunity in the digital world / Jacqueline Ryan Vickery ; foreword by S. Craig Watkins.
Description: Cambridge, MA : The MIT Press, 2017. | Series: The John D. and Catherine T. MacArthur Foundation series on digital media and learning | Includes bibliographical references and index.
Identifiers: LCCN 2016038045 | ISBN 9780262036023 (hardcover : alk. paper)
Subjects: LCSH: Information society--United States. | Digital media--Social aspects--United States. | Information technology--Social aspects--United States. | Internet and teenagers--United States. | Internet--Safety measures. | Internet--Security measures.
Classification: LCC HM851 .V527 2017 | DDC 303.48/33--dc23
LC record available at https://lccn.loc.gov/2016038045

10 9 8 7 6 5 4 3 2 1

for Mom and Dad—Thanks for believing that a silly story about a bunny could lead to bigger dreams.

Contents

Series Foreword

In recent years, digital media and networks have become embedded in our everyday lives and are part of broad-based changes to how we engage in knowledge production, communication, and creative expression. Unlike the early years in the development of computers and computer-based media, digital media are now *commonplace* and *pervasive*, having been taken up by a wide range of individuals and institutions in all walks of life. Digital media have escaped the boundaries of professional and formal practice, and of the academic, governmental, and industry homes that initially fostered their development. Now they have been taken up by diverse populations and non-institutionalized practices, including the peer activities of youth. Although specific forms of technology uptake are highly diverse, a generation is growing up in an era when digital media are part of the taken-for-granted social and cultural fabric of learning, play, and social communication.

This book series is founded upon the working hypothesis that those immersed in new digital tools and networks are engaged in an unprecedented exploration of language, games, social interaction, problem solving, and self-directed activity that leads to diverse forms of learning. These diverse forms of learning are reflected in expressions of identity, in how individuals express independence and creativity, and in their ability to learn, exercise judgment, and think systematically.

The defining frame for this series is not a particular theoretical or disciplinary approach, nor is it a fixed set of topics. Rather, the series revolves around a constellation of topics investigated from multiple disciplinary and practical frames. The series as a whole looks at the relation between youth, learning, and digital media, but each contribution to the series might deal with only a subset of this constellation. Erecting strict topical boundaries would exclude some of the most important work in the field. For example, restricting the content of the series only to people of a certain age would mean artificially reifying an age boundary when the phenomenon demands otherwise. This would become particularly problematic with new forms of online participation where one important outcome is the mixing of participants of different ages. The same goes for digital media, which are increasingly inseparable from analog and earlier media forms.

The series responds to certain changes in our media ecology that have important implications for learning. Specifically, these changes involve new forms of media *literacy* and developments in the modes of media *participation*. Digital media are part of a convergence between interactive media (most notably gaming), online networks, and existing media forms. Navigating this media ecology involves a palette of literacies that are being defined through practice but require more scholarly scrutiny before they can be fully incorporated pervasively into educational initiatives. Media literacy involves not only ways of understanding, interpreting, and critiquing media, but also the means for creative and social expression, online search and navigation, and a host of new technical skills. The potential gap in literacies and participation skills creates new challenges for educators who struggle to bridge media engagement inside and outside the classroom.

The John D. and Catherine T. MacArthur Foundation Series on Digital Media and Learning, published by the MIT Press, aims to close these gaps and provide innovative ways of thinking about and using new forms of knowledge production, communication, and creative expression.

Foreword

Today, some things about teens and their digital and connected lives are given. We expect that teens will be active on social media, performing the aspirational self, sharing their lives with peers, and commenting on the latest episode in a pop culture universe that plays out like a reality TV show. While the platforms continue to change, teens' enthusiasm for constructing their own identities and aspirations, sharing their lives, and connecting with peers via digital media remains steadfast. But we have also come to expect something else, as Jacqueline Vickery meticulously details in this wonderful book—we have come to "expect harm."

The very fact that we expect that teens will inflict pain on each other, will only be interested in viewing content that adults find objectionable (and that sometimes is), and will suffer immeasurably from their engagement with digital media says a lot about the world that adults have both imagined and, unfortunately, realized for young people. The "risk discourse," as we learn in this book, is a regime of institutionalized power and a flourishing industry that shapes distinct policy formations, school-based approaches to digital media and learning, parenting practices, and a media industry that turns teens' adoption of technology into primetime scripts of despair, doom, and even death. If we are to believe what we are repeatedly told by the risk industry, young people are a generation at risk and need the adults in their lives—parents, teachers, mentors, and politicians—to protect them from themselves and the harm that awaits them in the digital media world.

But Vickery pulls a jujitsu maneuver in this fascinating inquiry into the digital media lives of teens. Rather than ask "How do the risks that kids encounter through their engagement with digital media promote harm?" she asks "What if we see risk as an opportunity?" It is a brave question and one that resonates throughout this meticulous study of young people's digital media practices.

What really stands out about her analysis is the degree to which it is punctuated by the voices and lived experiences of young people who rarely figure in public discourses about teens, technology, and risk. Think about it. Whose voices and life experiences inform policy decisions related to teens, technology, and risk? As you read this book it is clear that youth labeled "at risk" or "disadvantaged" are seldom if ever genuinely considered in the policy prescriptions advocating risk avoidance and protection.

In a carefully woven ethnography and cultural critique, Vickery focuses her knack for detailed research and nuanced analysis on the lives of our most vulnerable youth. This, quite frankly, is a revelation. It is also a break-through perspective that has much to offer those who consider her ideas and provocations. What happens when we think about risk, harm, and opportunity from the perspective of young people often marginalized by society? How does the risk discourse suddenly shift and compel us to rethink the very terms, norms, and expectations that power the risk indus-try? In Vickery's account the lives and voices of these young people ring loud and clear. We learn about their aspirations and their frustrations. We see how their social and media ecologies have been transformed by the adoption of social and mobile media. Even though disparities in the digital world persist, we also see how young people bring ingenuity and aspira-tions to their digital media practices. In this book we see how educational and digital disparities as well as restrictive policies related to digital media continue to matter, but in ways that educators and policy makers seldom think about.

As she maneuvers expertly around a conventional wisdom that is often guided by sensational headlines and adult-driven fears rather than empiri-cal evidence and youth-driven experiences, Vickery asks us to think about the unintended consequences of the risk discourse on non-dominant youth. Much of the risk discourse, by default, imagines privileged youth. As a result, educators, policy makers, and media industries seldom think about the implications of the "risk equals harm" perspective for young people on the margins. And yet, as Vickery reminds us, these young people stand the most to lose in current formulations of risk.

This book is a provocation that challenges our very notion of youth and digital media culture and, consequently what is really at stake as young people struggle to find dignity and opportunity in the world. While reading this book you are likely to ask yourself questions that have either remained dormant or simply not been articulated for far too long: What are the unin-tended consequences of "protecting" young people from participation in the digital world? How do discourses of risk and the risk avoidance regime reproduce social and educational inequalities? How can schools empower young people to leverage technology as agents of change rather than exist as passive victims of the technologies they use?

Our schools are built almost entirely on the idea of technologies as risk. This explains why our schools block social media, offer technology courses that are more vocational than educational, and do very little to support learning opportunities that promote higher-order digital literacy and civic agency. It explains why our schools invest in curricula that restrict young people's engagement with technology instead of curricula that would empower their engagement with the digital world. It is hard to believe, but more than twenty years after the Internet first came into our classrooms we still look at the technology through a lens of suspicion and stress rather than trust and courage.

The risk discourse is a pervasive narrative and gives shape to a regime of power, influence, and control that is dispersed across many fields, including schools, the policy-making apparatus, and media and pop culture. The risk discourse from this view emerges as controlling, class-biased, and likely injurious to many of the children and teens it purports to protect. The risk industry is dangerous because it encourages us to worry about some things (i.e., addiction, porn, harm) and not other things (i.e., digital literacy, equity, and opportunity). After reading this book you are likely to think that the risk industry is an enterprise that, in the end, may be doing more harm than good. We learn from Vickery that the real risk, indeed the ultimate risk, is the reproduction of social, economic, and digital inequality. A generation of young people are coming of age in schools and a society that, in the name of protecting them, may actually be limiting their prospects for developing the skills, competences, and networks that are the true currencies of opportunity in a knowledge-driven culture and economy. What do we really block when we block children's and teens' access to networked media? What harm do we inflict when we build institutions that fail to build young people's confidence and competence in the digital world? Answers to these questions represent the most profound and enduring risks to our children, and by extension, our ability to create what Vickery envisions: a safer, healthier, more equitable digital future.

If you are a parent, an educator, a media maker, or a policy maker, you would do well to heed Vickery's call to think about these questions and about the harm that the risk industry is causing our kids and our culture. Harm-driven expectations do not just inspire fear. These expectations also provoke the design of spaces, practices, and policies that rob young people of their agency and disables their capacity to develop vital skills for a world gone digital. By contrast, Vickery explains how "opportunity-driven expectations" and the discursive possibilities that they inspire can provoke the design of spaces, practices, and policies that enable young people to develop the agency and skills that will serve them well in the digital age.

After you have read this book, the very framework that you use to think about teens, technology, and risk will likely be transformed. You are almost certain to ask how our schools, families, communities, and civic sphere would be different if digital media were to be treated as a "technology of opportunity" rather than a "technology of risk." You will ask yourself "What are we overlooking in terms of risk and opportunity?" More important, this book also compels you to ask "Who are we overlooking?" This is the question that our institutions—schools, families, policy, and pop culture—must begin to ask and courageously address if we are to ever establish a social framework for thinking in more nuanced ways about what is at stake for young people and about the ongoing struggle to create more equitable forms of agency and participation in our world.

S. Craig Watkins

Acknowledgments

Above all, I want to thank the high school students who opened up their lives to me and made this book possible. I also want to thank the teachers for opening up their classrooms and the parents and grandparents for opening up their homes. I wish I could thank all of you by name, because you deserve more credit than I publicly can give to you. You are the reason this book is here, and I will forever be grateful for your willingness to share your lives with me and for your commitment to this project. Thank you—we all have much to learn from the experiences and perspectives that you shared.

Importantly, I want to thank my advisor, Craig Watkins, for developing this project and allowing me the privilege to be a part of it. Thank you for being a dedicated mentor and teaching me how to respectfully research the lives of youth with awareness and care. I owe a big thanks to the entire Digital Edge team as co-collaborators of this research. Your insights were a priceless part of this project. Thank you Alex Cho, Vivian Shaw, Jennifer Noble, Andres Lombana Bermudez, and Adam Williams. Our times together at FHS were some of my most valuable experiences in grad school. And thank you Lauren Weinzimmer for carefully helping code our hundreds of transcripts.

I had the privilege of incredible mentors and advisors at the University of Texas who indirectly contributed to this project and directly contributed to my approach as a youth ethnographer and scholar. Mary Kearney, thank you for teaching me how to practice and teach my feminist values, which have influenced this book and all of my research. Joe Straubhaar, your ethnography course offered much-needed guidance on how to conduct ethnographic research, how to take effective field notes, and how to code and interpret hours of transcriptions. Laura Stein and Shayla Thiel-Stern you both provided valuable feedback on the earliest iterations of what developed into several chapters of the book.

Thank you to Henry Jenkins, Julian Sefton-Green, and Alan Albarran for reading drafts of the proposal and offering valuable advice when the manuscript was still in its infancy stage. To my colleagues at the University of North Texas, thank you Jordan Frith for keeping me sane over local libations and offering support along the way. I want to thank my chair, Eugene Martin, for supporting my research and providing time at the end for me to complete the manuscript.

To members of the CLRN team, thank you for allowing me to participate in your meetings and for your dedication to mentoring junior scholars. I especially want to thank Mimi Ito, Sonia Livingstone, Juliet Schor, and Kris Gutiérrez for feedback on early ideas for these chapters and for overall advice that shaped this project in many ways. Also a big shoutout to Amanda Wortman for supporting the network and being a great Twitter buddy.

The anonymous reviewers of the manuscript provided me with great advice and made the book much stronger than it otherwise would have been. I wish I could thank them in person for their kind support and careful critiques. They helped me develop as a writer, and I am appreciative of their time and suggestions. Susan Buckley, my editor at MIT, thank you for your enthusiasm for this project from the beginning and for helping me turn it into the book it is.

Lastly, thank you to my parents, Michael and Deb, for your unwavering support and confidence in all my dreams, and to my supportive family, including my sister Jen and my niece Brooklyn (who can always, without exception, make me smile). To Sharon, Ricky and Allison, and all seven of your amazing kids – thank you for the ongoing encouragement. And to my husband, Joshua, thanks for putting up with far too many all-nighters and stressed-out weekends and obsessive, rambling think-out-loud sessions. You are my perfect partner, even if you can't make me a salmon dinner. This is finally done, now let's hop on a plane and go celebrate.

This book is based on the Digital Edge research project, which was supported by the John D. and Catherine T. MacArthur Foundation as part of the Connected Learning Research Network, based at the University of California at Irvine. Any opinions, findings, conclusions, or recommendations expressed in the book are those of the author and do not necessarily reflect the views of the MacArthur Foundation or the University of California.

Introduction: A Generation at Risk?

No one expects a zero-risk childhood, yet society seems loath to specify a level of acceptable risk when it comes to children. One result is that media panics effectively construe all risk as unacceptable.

Sonia Livingstone (2009, p. 174)

I want to begin with three stories. The first is from an episode of the television crime drama *Law & Order: Special Victims Unit* (*SVU* for short). In an episode titled "Crush," a teenage girl, Kim, takes nude photos of herself with her cell phone. She intends to send them to her boyfriend Stephen, but sends them to her platonic friend Ethan by mistake. After accidentally sending the photos to Ethan, she then sends them to the boyfriend. Stephen snoops through her phone (something he frequently does) and finds the pictures that Kim accidentally sent to Ethan. Stephen assumes she is cheating on him—even after she explains it was a mistake—and proceeds to send the photos to the entire school; he uses a service to disguise his number so it appears that Kim is the one who distributed the photos. Everyone at school is relentlessly mocking and harassing Kim; she is so distraught that she accidentally trips and falls down the stairs at school and ends up in a coma. While she is in the hospital, it is revealed that someone has been physically abusing her for several months, but she refuses to disclose the identity of her abuser. She believes she is to blame for the incident: "This is all my fault, if I hadn't taken those pictures, none of this would be happening." After much reluctance—and after a judge convicts her of possessing and distributing child pornography—Kim admits that her boyfriend Stephen has been physically abusing her and that he beat her up after he found the nude photos on her phone.

Now let's consider the tragic true story of Megan Meier, a 13-year-old girl battling low self-esteem and depression. She successfully convinced her mother to allow her to have a MySpace account; her mother did so reluctantly and monitored Megan's activities; she even had the password to the account. In other words, Megan's parents did everything right—they were in communication with their daughter about her online practices and were actively monitoring her behaviors in order to protect her. In October 2006, Megan was contacted by 16-year-old "Josh Evans" via MySpace. Flattered by his attention, and attracted to the young admirer, Megan's mother agreed she could add Josh as a friend, and the two began corresponding via MySpace. After winning Megan's trust and affection, Josh turned on Megan and told her he no longer wanted to be her friend "because of the way she treats her friends." Josh and others began to post bulletins on MySpace calling Megan "fat" and a "slut." Upset, Megan called her mother to tell her what was happening. Her mother advised her to get off the computer, but Megan didn't comply. She then received a message in which Josh told her "the world would be a better place without you." Megan proceeded to hang herself in her bedroom closet and died in a hospital the next day.

Six weeks later, a neighbor informed the Meiers that "Josh Evans" was a fake persona created by Lori Drew, the mother of one of Megan's former friends who lived only four houses away from the Meiers. Drew had created the fake profile to monitor what Megan was saying about her own daughter (a former friend of Megan's). The Meiers were outraged that an adult had emotionally deceived, manipulated, and abused their daughter. Lori Drew knew Megan well, knew that she struggled with mental illness and was on medication for depression, and yet she still betrayed and taunted Megan, even going so far as to suggest that she kill herself. The FBI spent the next year investigating the Drew family without their knowledge, and not until November 10, 2007 did the story surface in various media outlets (Maag 2007; Pokin 2007).[1] The story generated national attention for months and was the impetus for many states to write new online harassment laws (Michels 2008).

Finally, let's take a brief look at the lives of two brothers, Marcus and Miguel,[2] whom I had the privilege of getting to know in 2012. The undocumented 14-year-old identical twins had emigrated from Mexico City to Texas with their mother when they were six years old; their father had moved to Texas three years earlier to establish connections and income before the rest of the family joined him. Marcus and Miguel were in their first year of high school at a large, ethnically diverse, low-income, low-performing public high school. At school they appeared quiet and reserved. They were polite and respectful, yet would struggle to make eye contact upon first meeting someone. They were still learning to negotiate the terrain of a large public high school as they worked to construct peer networks. The brothers lived with their parents and two younger brothers in a mobile home on the suburban fringe of town. They did not own mobile phones, but they used their Wi-Fi-enabled Nintendo DS creatively to maintain mobile contact with peers for free via Facebook messenger. The brothers shared an outdated computer that was kept in the family's living room.

Although their parents restricted their Internet use to a couple of hours a day, they spent much of their leisure time playing console-based and online video games. Their favorite game at the time that I met them was *Minecraft*.[3] Though they were reserved and shy at school, online they engaged actively and openly in robust social communities. Through computer games, the brothers had forged relationships and friendships with peers across the country. These relationships transcended the gaming spaces and had been carried into Facebook, YouTube, Skype, and online chats. YouTube provided a gaming-based community in which the brothers connected to other gamers and participated in an active networked audience. Although their passions for the game—as well as for peripheral aspects of the gaming community—were largely driven by social interests and the pleasure of connecting with peers in the spaces, their investment in the gaming community also allowed them to "geek out" (Ito et al. 2010).

What do these three stories have in common? Well, obviously they are all about youth and digital media technology. But beyond that, each of them reveals something about our collective understandings of risk—more specifically the relationships between risk and young people's use of media technology. The first two stories probably resonate more with your general association of youth and digital media risk: sexual exposure and bullying. In both the television episode and the cyberbullying incident, technology presented a seemingly clear and present danger to the young people, to the young girls specifically. *Law & Order: SVU* often creates narratives based on actual crimes, "Crush" being merely one of many, many, examples. The series is known for its sensational "ripped from the headlines" approach to re-telling true crime stories and scandals (Barnes 2014; Collins 2009). This trend is also popular in other US television crime dramas, such as *CSI* and *CSI: Cyber*. Lifetime original movies and other made-for-TV movies utilize a similar approach of re-telling fictional accounts of crimes based on true events (O'Rourke 2013). All these genres provide multiple examples, season after season, of teens' being harmed—even killed—as a result of their digital media practices. Research indicates that the "perceived realism" of for-profit entertainment narratives makes it difficult for audiences to differentiate fiction from truth (Collins 2009). The communication scholars

Jonathan Cohen and Gabriel Weimann argue that "the highly stylized, stereotyped, and repetitive images portrayed on television have been regarded as an important source of socialization and everyday information" (2000, p. 99). For that reason, some audience members are susceptible to believing that some televised crimes are more prevalent than they actually are.[4]

Outside of the crime genre, we frequently see similar story lines in popular media. Teens sexting or meeting strangers online has become a common and popular trope within narrative media. Megan Meier's story was even the inspiration for an episode of *SVU* called "Babes."[5] Undoubtedly her story is tragic; in the decade since her death we have witnessed countless stories of teens taking their own lives after being bullied, often online. Popular media and journalism are quick to feature sensational headlines that blame both youth and technology for such serious problems, without much consideration of the broader context. Headlines such as "Teenager commits suicide after 'sexting' nude photo to her boyfriend" (Hastings 2009) and "Nine teenage suicides in the last year were linked to cyberbullying on social network site Ask.fm" (Broderick 2013) are not hard to find in today's news and media culture. Within these narratives—both fictional and journalistic—technology is depicted as a risk, and parents are told that they must protect their vulnerable children from the intrinsic threats. Such stories capitalize on and exploit fears about the risks young people face when they are online. These kinds of tragic and fear-driven stories come to dominate our collective imaginations and shape our expectations of harm.

But how does the story of Marcus and Miguel fit with these other narratives? Certainly their story is about risk too, isn't it? Perhaps you're thinking about the risk of gaming addiction, a topic that gets attention in journalism and in popular media. Maybe you're thinking that the brothers are sacrificing too much sleep to play their games, or you're concerned that they are isolating themselves from peers or family. Or perhaps you're anxious about the kinds of strangers the two boys are meeting online. Do we know if they are being smart about hiding their identities and location? Or maybe you're worried that their video game time is interfering with school and their capacity to focus on homework and other academic obligations. And on the basis of the little you know about Marcus and Miguel, these are not entirely misdirected concerns.

However, these elements of risk—addiction, isolation, strangers, and distractions—are not the kinds of risk that actually worry me in this story. While all those concerns are valid to a limited degree, for Marcus and

Miguel the risks they took were not harmful. Rather, they were beneficial. Marcus and Miguel worked collaboratively on missions in their games, forged friendships, solved problems, attained cultural and social capital, developed digital literacies, produced shared knowledge, and constructed identities around their gaming accomplishments. In a lot of ways, their online identities and friendships served to supplement their limited offline experiences. Although they had friends at school, they struggled to find a niche. For that reason, their online personalities and communities could be interpreted as more authentic expressions of their identities, skillsets, and confidence. Through their involvement in online games and gaming communities, the twins were more socially connected and digitally knowledgeable than they would have been otherwise. Further, for two brothers without much disposable income or mobility options, online gaming was a lot safer than the kinds of social interests they could have been developing. They were not in gangs, and they were not taking drugs, drinking, or getting into trouble. They were safely and happily benefiting from an online world in which they felt accepted, connected, and accomplished. Clearly risk does not equate to the likelihood of harm, a point that will be expanded upon frequently in this book.

Nonetheless, there is a risk in their story that concerns me more than addiction, strangers, isolation, and distractions, and that is the risk of inequitable opportunities for participation. Notably, the brothers worked around technical barriers in ingenious and creative ways. Despite their ingenuity, they faced many technical and material obstacles that excluded them from participating more fully in the online worlds they loved. Financial constraints and obligations precluded access to up-to-date computers, higher Internet speeds, or mobile phones. School policies banned their favorite social media sites, video tutorials, and games. Familial obligations to take care of their younger brothers prevented them from benefiting from their peers' shared resources; circumstances necessitated that they spend most of their leisure time at home so their mother could attend English classes at the community center and their father could go to work. While there were many benefits to their gaming experiences and the risks they took, there were also significant limitations that kept them disconnected and prevented them from participating more fully. For example, Miguel learned a lot about *Minecraft* from watching amateur YouTube videos, but explained: "I only use [YouTube] to comment and subscribe and stuff. When I get a new computer, I want to make YouTube commentator videos about *Minecraft*." Although he spent much of his time immersed in the gaming community, his participation was peripheral (Lave and Wenger

1991). This form of peripheral participation also inhibited him from developing other forms of digital literacies that are cultivated via video production and distribution in networked communities such as YouTube. In other words, while there were many benefits to their participation, the brothers' participation was marginalized, and they did not have the opportunities for digital literacy development that their more connected peers had.

Expectations and Lived Experiences

As the story of Marcus and Miguel demonstrates, today's mediated society provides innovative opportunities for young people to participate in the creation of their own mediated cultures. Social and technological changes have given rise to new modes of socialization, production, and learning. As with previous technologies—such as the telegraph, film, television, and phones—we have seen a rise in optimistic discourses that promise technologies will make society more democratic, lessen social inequalities, and bring positive social changes (Baym 2010; Carey 1989; McChesney 2013; Peters 1999; Rainie and Wellman 2012). However, alongside these optimistic expectations are concerns about the risks and harms that new technologies bring to our attention. Those concerns also have a historical context in which new modes of communication technologies tend to lead to adult anxieties about how young people engage and participate (boyd 2014; Livingstone 2009; Marwick 2008; Springhall 1998). Computers, the Internet, mobile technologies, computer games, and social media are not exceptions; that is, they are simultaneously considered to be technologies of opportunity, as well as technologies of risk in the lives of young people; they evoke a lot of adult anxiety and attention.

The opening three examples in this introduction contribute to a discourse of fear and risk that is all too familiar by now. Such cautionary tales about predators, sexting, bullying, pornography, and suicide affect the ways we think about technology and youth. A focus on the negative and harmful ways teens use and are affected by technology has fueled a moral panic about technology. While such a panic cannot be solely blamed on media representations and descriptions of teens and technology, as a media scholar I am particularly interested in the role of media in shaping our understandings of cultural phenomena and populations. Media play an integral and inextricable role in shaping our understandings of risk— understandings that, in turn, shape our expectations of youth and technology. Thus, one of the central questions of this book is "How do expectations of youth, technology, and risk shape policies, practices, and lived experiences?" A second central question is "By focusing on the loudest and most visible risks, what are we overlooking in terms of risk and opportunity?" (In other words, "What else should we be worried about?")

I approach these questions from multiple levels in order to gain both a "big picture" understanding of risk and a localized and contextualized understanding of how expectations shape the everyday "lived experiences" of actual youth (Bloustein 2003). As I will explain further, I do this through an analysis of popular culture, journalism, and policies—all of which are spaces and institutions that symbiotically construct and reflect discourses of risk, and therefore have power to shape our expectations of youth and technology. I also aim to answer these questions through extensive ethnographic research with high school students in Texas. A majority of the students who were subjects of my research are marginalized because of income, ethnicity, and/or immigration status. Many of the teens mentioned in this book are involved in after-school digital media and film clubs, and that involvement provides insight into their digital media practices and values. Combining discursive analysis of popular culture, news media, and policy with the ethnographic data about teens' lived experiences allows me to analyze the real-life implications that risk discourses have on the lives of actual young people. I demonstrate that how we talk about risks—whose anxieties are given a voice, whose stories are told, whose stories are silenced—has the power to significantly shape our expectations and understanding of youth cultures. And, as will be argued, expectations shape experiences in competing and inequitable ways. We have an obligation to pay close attention to what and who is labeled a risk, and how risk is mobilized in the spaces that structure young people's everyday practices and opportunities.

In this book I am referring to risk—and, by extension, to risk discourse—from a social constructivist perspective that is focused less on objectively identifying the probability of harms and dangers than on understanding how society identifies, mediates, and constructs understandings of what is considered to be a risk.[6] As Lupton writes (1999, p. 29), "a risk, therefore, is not a static, objective phenomenon, but is constantly constructed and negotiated as part of the network of social interaction and the formation of meaning." Notions of what is considered a risk are socially embedded within systems of power and change over time and differ in different contexts. For example, what a teenager deems risky will probably differ from what an adult or a toddler deems risky, because perceptions of risk are contextually bound. The philosopher Francois Ewald explains that "anything can be a risk; it all depends on how one analyzes the danger, considers the event" (1991, p. 199). What a society deems risky is not neutral, but rather is constitutive of a society's morals and beliefs about objects, populations, and practices. Notably, as will be further discussed throughout the book, constructions of risk overwhelmingly rely on expert knowledges that have the power to identify and draw public attention to particular understandings and phenomena, often at the expense of alternative explanations and interpretations. According to Lupton (1999, p. 33), "distinguishing between 'real' risks (as measured and identified by 'experts') and 'false risks' (as perceived by members of the public) is irrelevant. ... Both lead to certain actions. It is the ways in which these understandings are constructed and acted upon that is considered important." While I acknowledge that objective harms related to young people's online interactions do of course exist, I want to point out that it is important to distinguish between harm and risk, which are often conflated yet are quite distinct. In late modernity, "risk has been co-opted as a term reserved for a negative or undesirable outcome, and thus is synonymous with the terms *danger* or *hazard*" (Fox 1999, p. 12). The conflation of risk and harm leads to a perception that all risks are negative and ought to be avoided, which obscures the benefits of taking risks. Equating risk with harm also disciplines us to practice risk-avoidance strategies at the expense of beneficial opportunities. Throughout the book I use the concept of risk less as a way to describe the probability of potential harm than as a social construct that is produced via various discourses of power (e.g. the government, policies, media, and experts). I do so in order to analyze their effects and actions.

My analysis of risk reveals how expectations about youth and technology can be categorized into *harm-driven expectations* and *opportunity-driven expectations*. (See figure I.1.) These categories (which are not mutually exclusive and are not polar opposites) provide a way to think about how primary expectations—whether articulated or latent—shape experiences, opportunities, and practices. Harm-driven expectations are revealed through policies, practices, and narratives that are based on fear or anxiety. They respond to a concern about—or rather an expectation of—potential hypothetical harms. Such expectations are often formed, and decisions are often made, even in the absence of sufficient evidence to demonstrate collective harm. The mere *threat* of individual harm—that is, the risk itself—serves as justification for fear-based policies, decisions, and practices. Harm-driven expectations rationalize restrictive policies, intuitions, and practices that try to control technology—and therefore young people's agency—within various spaces. Such policies, practices, and narratives often reify constructions of young people as passive victims and tend to focus too much on the

Figure I.1
Characteristics of harm-driven and opportunity-driven expectations.

technology itself—as the agent of change—rather than on the collective experiences of young people themselves. Harm-driven expectations enact control on the basis of perception of risk—as a danger that is typically identified by perceived experts—and therefore the perceptions have the cyclical nature of reinforcing and reifying expectations of harm.

Contrast expectations of harm with opportunity-driven expectations, which start with the assumption that digital media practices, policies, and narratives ought to be designed to maximize benefits and positive opportunities for youth. Rather than presuming all risks are negative and must be controlled, opportunity-driven expectations enable and trust young people to identify and manage risks responsibly. Based on evidence and lived experiences, opportunity-driven expectations allow us to design spaces, tell stories, and write policies that will facilitate positive outcomes for young people—not only as individuals, but also as a collective population. Rather than merely controlling technology, opportunity-driven expectations produce discourses that acknowledge the practices and the agency of young people as experts on their own experiences. Society tends to privilege harm-driven expectations and thus to overlook or even diminish the positive opportunities afforded by technology. Lastly, through a lens of expectations we also can examine the competing expectations of adults and youth as a framework for understanding how adults' expectations—often responding to fearful understandings of risk—overshadow the ways young people themselves make meaning out of their digitally mediated practices and how they mitigate risk in creative and agentive ways. We ought to create spaces in which the experiences of young people are valued and in which they are able to agentively contribute to or even challenge discourses of risk, technology, and teens.

I believe we have reasons to worry about young people's use of technology, but not for the prevailing and popular reasons that dominate news accounts and policies (porn, predators, bullying, addiction, and so on). For one thing, such concerns are overly individualistic in nature; that is, they are concerned about risk to an individual and thus responsibilize individuals to protect themselves from harm, or rather to actively practice risk-avoidance strategies (Burchell 1996; Foucault 1991; Hunt 2003; Hier 2008; O'Malley 1992). This narrative of individual responsibilization ignores the ways institutions, experts, and discourses structure choices (Dean 1997 1999; Hier 2008; Kelly 2000). On the contrary, what concerns me is not so much individual harm (important though it is) as collective harm and the shared responsibilization for not only protection but equality. I'm worried about an entire population growing up without the digital literacies that are needed to equip them with equitable opportunities for success. This is not an individualized responsibility; instead it ought to be of wide social concern, and therefore a collective responsibility. When only particular (privileged) populations have the opportunity to develop skills and literacies that will lead to opportunity, we are living in an unjust society. When risk reflects the privileged concerns of the privileged class, we are failing to defend the most vulnerable among us, who already suffer from disproportionate injustices.

What deeply concerns me is the extent to which narratives, policies, and practices having to do with digital media are used to exacerbate rather than alleviate inequities. I'm concerned about a generation growing up at a time when surveillance is a normative part of their everyday lives. I worry about the potential for exploitation and discrimination, which are unintended consequences of individuals' sharing their social lives online. I am troubled by online filters that purport to block objectionable material, yet normalize harmful advertisements that are aimed at capitalizing on young people's self-esteem. I am uncomfortable with policies that block opportunities for participation and access to information, rather than contribute to the development of digital literacy and the attainment of social capital. And I get anxious when I hear politicians, tech industry representatives, teachers, and young people repeat discourses that blame teens for their grievances without considering the broader context in which adult society has created unequal structures and barriers that limit their agency and their ability to safely participate in the creation of their own mediated cultures. I believe we can create a more equitable, healthy, and safe digital future, but it requires a holistic approach in which policy makers, educators, technology companies, researchers, and commercial institutions work together with young people to meet their needs and to understand their practices, rather than merely working on their behalf. As Sonia Livingstone writes (2009, p. 153), "though the arguments against engaging with the risk agenda seem compelling, engage with it we must if we wish to recognize children's own experiences and give them voice." This book is an effort to engage with the risk agenda in a positive and opportunity-enhancing way.

How then did we get here? Why are fears and anxieties seemingly increasing when research just doesn't justify it? Why are policies continually attempting to regulate young people's use of the Internet, rather than empower them to embrace new technologies in healthy and positive ways? Why do so many high schools insist upon monitoring and blocking students' access to educational resources in the name of safety and protection, rather than developing positive curricula that embrace new opportunities? Why is the mainstream news full of scary big-bad-world stories that depict the exceptional harms rather than the benefits of new technologies? All this stems in part from the creation of a moral panic that perpetuates fear, in part from the novelty of the technologies that lead to uncertainty, and in part from a generation gap that does not seek to understand young people's everyday practices. As will be further discussed, expectations of risk and harm can be explained via the disconnections between (a) young people's lived experiences and the sensational mediated narratives that influence fear-based policy and reproduce harm-driven expectations, (b) the value of young people's practices as compared to the value of adult practices, and (c) the myopic view on the novelty of technology and the greater context of social change. (See figure I.2.) Taking all of these elements into consideration, we have a society that focuses on particular fears and harms (predators, bullying, porn, safety, addiction, and so on) that are often reflective of privileged understandings of risk and potential harm to privileged young people. Worries about the threat of risk to *individual youth*, rather than concern about the opportunities for *vulnerable populations of youth*, are at the expense of a much-needed focus on the collective risks to society—risks that, as I argue throughout the book, demand and are worthy of immediate attention.

I also want to acknowledge the growing body of academic work that contextualizes risks and focuses on the opportunities of new media technologies. I do not want to suggest that scholars are overly focused on the negative aspects of digital media; I am greatly indebted to researchers who

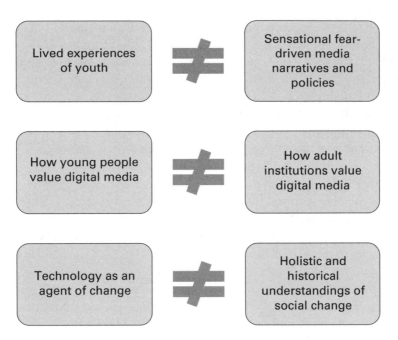

Figure I.2
Disconnections that contribute to harm-driven expectations.

continue to contextualize, theorize, and historicize the positive affordances of new media (Chau 2010; Ito et al. 2010; Jenkins 2006; Lange 2014; Rainie and Wellman 2012; Rheingold 2012; Scheidt 2006; Watkins 2009), and to work that contextualizes the risks and the opportunities associated with digital media (boyd 2014; Clark 2013; DiMaggio, Hargittai, Celeste, and Shafer 2004; Kalmus, Runnel, and Siibak 2009; Livingstone 2008, 2009; Livingstone and Sefton-Green 2016; Thiel-Stern 2014). In addition to contributing to this growing field, my research aims to make sense of the ways popular culture, policies, education, and industries continue to overly focus on, mobilize, and even capitalize upon perceptions of risks. While this book is written primarily for an academic audience, I also hope it will be read with interest and enthusiasm by a broader community, namely the adults and institutions who have the power to effectuate change in teens' (digital) lives: educators, policy makers, social workers, media industries, counselors, web and software developers, and parents.

It's All Connected: The Media Ecology Approach

As the media landscape becomes increasingly diversified, fragmented, and complex, so too should our methodologies for researching young people's media practices. Morley (2006) suggests that we move beyond medium-centric approaches to understanding youth and technologies (i.e., away from approaches that myopically focus on the effects of a technology in isolation from its broader context). Such a shift necessitates multi-method analyses that privilege individuals and populations—rather than media—as the primary lens of analysis. One such method that aims to be people-centric rather than technology-centric is the *media ecologies* approach to ethnographic research employed by Mizuko Ito and her colleagues (2010). In their ecological approach to home and media environments, Horst, Herr-Stephenson, and Robinson (2010, in the volume by Ito et al.) attempted to "emphasize the characteristics of an overall technical, social, cultural, and place-based system, in which the components are not decomposable or separable. The everyday practices of youth, existing structural conditions, infrastructures of place, and technologies are dynamically interrelated; the meanings, uses, functions, flows, and interconnections in young people's daily lives located in particular settings are also situated within young people's wider media ecologies" (p. 31). In other words, in order to understand the distinct and dynamic experiences of young people and their engagement with media, it is important to fully consider the context in which their interactions occur.

For example, rather than separating school life from social life from socioeconomic status, the media ecology approach acknowledges that they are always already related to one another—i.e., that society and media are mutually constituted and constitutive. The media ecology approach considers the co-constituted cultures of adults and youth, as well as the various institutions and geographies of young people (home, schools, work, online, etc.), in order to contextualize teens' media practices within a broader understanding of their everyday lives. In terms of learning ecologies, school, after-school clubs, peer cultures, and home are all different interacting nodes through which young people participate, engage, and learn. Likewise, these various nodes also present various opportunities for attainment of social and cultural capital, through which inequalities are often articulated and reinforced. This model has been expanded on to develop a model of learning and opportunity known as the *connected learning model* (Ito et al. 2013). The connected learning approach contends that sustained successful learning is best supported via the interconnectedness and support of students' peers, personal interests, and academic settings (as will be further examined in chapter 7). It is my goal to begin to delineate how risk is discursively constructed, managed, and negotiated within and between these nodes that constitute young people's learning and media ecologies.

As will be further discussed, understanding the driving motivations for and expectations of participation in digital media spaces provides insight into the educational value of young people's mediated practices and is of paramount importance in understanding how students learn and the changing role of schools. In *Hanging Out, Messing Around, and Geeking Out*, Ito and her colleagues argue that "the most engaged and active forms of learning with digital media happen in youth-driven settings that are focused on social communication and recreation" (2010, p. 12). Their research focuses on the different genres of participation in which youth engage with new media, and the practices which are rendered meaningful to youth themselves. They identify two primary genres of participation used to describe young people's learning and media engagement: *friendship-driven* and *interest-driven*. "Friendship-driven practices" refers to "those shared practices that grow out of friendships in given local social worlds" (p. 16) and includes the day-to-day interactions with friends and peers offline and in networked publics (e.g., Facebook and Twitter).

"Interest-driven practices," however, refers to interests and practices that "youth describe as the domain of the geeks, freaks, musicians, artists, and dorks—the kids who are identified as smart, different, or creative, who generally exist at the margins of teen social worlds" (Ito et al. 2010, p. 17). Teens certainly develop friendships through interest-driven participation; but whereas with friendship-driven practices the friendships come first, with interest-driven participation a recognition of mutual interests typically precedes the development of friendships. These genres can be contextualized within a broader notion of learning known as *situated learning*. Situated learning posits that learning is not so much an individualized and isolated process, but rather occurs as part of a shared cultural system and collective social action (Lave and Wenger 1991). Thus, in order to understand how and what students learn through their participation in digital media culture and creation, it is important to recognize the broader social setting and structures motivating participation and engagement. Ito et al.'s friendship-driven and interest-driven genres of participation provide a useful conceptual framework for approaching young people's expectations of digital media, as well as the motivations for participation, media production, and learning.

Not All Kinds of Participation Are Created Equal

It is also important is to recognize that not all media and learning ecologies are created equal. As was previously indicated, I am concerned about the inequitable opportunities for participation that have the potential to exacerbate social inequities. In the early days of the dissemination and adoption of the Internet, scholars were rightfully concerned about digital divides—that is, unequal access to technology. Early users of the Internet were primarily male, white, educated, urban, and middle-class (Perrin and Duggan 2015; Roberts et al. 1999). However, as technology and the Internet have become more affordable, and as a result of policies and institutions aimed at providing affordable and accessible technology to all populations (e.g., public libraries), the gap between those who do and do not have access to the Internet has closed considerably. By 2012, 95 percent of teens in the United States were online (Teens Fact Sheet 2012). The mobile phone, once considered a luxury of the middle and upper classes, has become an essential tool for closing digital divides. In 2015, 88 percent of US teens had access to a mobile phone, 73 percent had access to a smartphone, and 71 percent had an account on at least one social media platform (Lenhart 2015). The mobile phone—often less expensive than a home computer, and with pay-as-you-go plans that do not require monthly contracts or credit checks (both of which are barriers to access for low-income populations)—has become a valuable resource for low-income populations. In fact, 25 percent of teens report that their mobile phone is their primary means of Internet access, and teens in lower socioeconomic groups are more likely to rely on their mobile phone as a primary access point than are middle-class teens (Pew Research Center 2013). From a purely quantitative perspective of who has access and who doesn't, the digital divide appears to have been essentially eradicated in the United States.

However, scholars have productively expanded their focus beyond the binary perspective of access to consider the *quality* of access and modes of participation. Not all access is created equal, which is why we must continue to conduct empirical research into the distinct practices of youth on the margins of society—what S. Craig Watkins refers to as "the digital edge." According to Watkins (2012, p. 2), "investigations of the digital lives of black and Latino youth must focus less on the access gap and more on the 'participation gap.' Whereas the former defines the issues of technology and social inequality largely as a matter of access to computers and the Internet, the latter considers the different skills, competencies, knowledge, practices, and forms of capital that different populations bring to their engagement with networked media." Although digital media provide opportunities for youth to participate in networked publics and create, access, and share media relevant to their unique identities and cultures, we must consider who is afforded such opportunities. Just because teens have access to media does not mean they are all provided the same opportunities to fully participate in the creation and distribution of media content.

Research indicates that relying primarily on free access at a public library hinders one's ability to learn digital skills.[7] Likewise, accessing digital media via a mobile phone has many limitations, such as improperly formatted content that lags or cannot load[8] or large files and streaming services that require more bandwidth than the user can access. However, from the perspective of digital equity, we must also consider how a reliance on mobile devices hinders full participation in online communities and content creation. While mostly sufficient for consuming information, mobile media present many barriers to the creation of media content. I would face severe challenges in writing this book utilizing only my mobile phone or even a tablet. Similarly, video production and editing, remixing music, designing a website, and other creatively generative media practices are still best suited to desktop and laptop computers. Mobile apps such as Vine, Snapchat, Instagram, and Periscope are increasingly facilitating easier modes of content creation, yet still pose limitations in terms of length, editing functions, and collaboration.

Barriers that limit media production are typically referred to as indications of a participation gap or a lack of digital inclusion. Scholars have begun to pay greater attention to the ways online practices are differentiated even when access is considered equitable (Jenkins et al. 2009). Through extensive quantitative data, Hargittai and Walejko (2008, p. 252) found that creating and sharing creative content online was linked to socioeconomic status: "While it may be that digital media are levelling the playing field when it comes to exposure to content, engaging in creative pursuits remains unequally distributed by social background." They argue that understanding such differentiated uses is imperative for closing participation gaps, gaps that inhibit more equitable opportunities for upward mobility via the acquisition of social, cultural, and economic capital. This necessitates a deliberate effort to foster equitable digital literacies so that all populations can participate and benefit from mediated participatory cultures.[9] As Watkins (2012, p. 9) poignantly contends,

One of the most urgent challenges regarding technology, diversity, and equity is the need to expand digital literacy; that is, the development of young people's capacity not only to access and use digital media but to use digital media in ways that create more enhanced and more empowered expressions of learning, creative expression, and civic engagement. The emphasis on digital literacy shifts the focus from access to the skills and expertise that establish more robust and more meaningful learning outcomes. The divide that deserves increasing attention from educators, media researchers, and practitioners is the "digital literacy divide."

Through an analysis of risk discourse, I map out the ways historical fears related to teens and technology work alongside harm-driven expectations to hinder the creation of more equitable learning environments for youth on the digital edge (see chapters 5 and 7). Participation gaps and digital literacy divides reveal the extent to which young people's digital media opportunities are reflective of other inequalities (Jenkins 2006). I argue that risk discourse serves to limit opportunities for marginalized youth by hindering and controlling their learning ecologies. Young people's practices, identities, and values are further marginalized in the name of "protection," but in actuality policies and practices aimed at minimizing risk often have the unintended outcome of also expanding gaps in equity and opportunities for participation.

Methodologies and Approaches

This book benefits from many different methodologies and fields of research, including media studies, critical studies, sociology, history, law and policy, psychology, journalism, feminism, and education.[10] It largely draws from a media studies and critical cultural approach for discursively analyzing and deconstructing popular culture and media. Methods include the contextualization, historicization, and discursive analysis of popular culture texts, policies, and young people's own mediated practices and perspectives.

In order to better analyze and asses the ways in which harm-driven and opportunity-driven expectations and discourses of risk function in the everyday lives of young people, the book also relies on ethnographic research conducted with teens. The research includes ethnographic data collected as part of "The Digital Edge" research project led by S. Craig Watkins.[11] With a team of researchers, I spent almost nine months in after-school digital media and film clubs at Freeway High, a large public high school in central Texas. The project involved conducting weekly one-on-one semi-structured interviews with nineteen high school students from diverse ethnic and class backgrounds and with varied digital media interests and skills. Interviews were also conducted with several of their teachers at school. A minimum of one in-home interview was conducted with a parent or guardian of each participant (several participants did not live with a biological parent at the time of the study). The project also gathered observational data from attending classes, after-school clubs, football games, film screenings, and student assemblies. In addition to one-on-one interviews, the project conducted focus groups with several students, analyzed school and school district policies and curriculum requirements, and conducted textual analysis of students' media productions and online interactions.

I have made an effort to include young people's thoughts and words in the write up of this research. I incorporate many direct quotations from young people in order to convey their experiences and attitudes in their own language and to provide them with a voice in the analysis. I attempt to preserve the intent and integrity of their words and would like to call attention to the fact that their words were spoken in conversation, often in informal and relaxed environments. Although transcribed, the quotes are taken from oral conversations wherein participants used colloquial and conversational tones; their grammar and their slang should not be misattributed to a lack of written communication skills. I have changed the quotations only where it seemed necessary in order to clarify something (such as a reference to an earlier conversation) or to protect confidentiality and privacy.

The Site: Freeway High School

The school I will call by the pseudonym "Freeway High" is located off a highway in a mid-size Texas town. Access to the school is difficult, particularly for students without access to personal transportation. The school is ethnically diverse (the majority of the students are members of ethnic minorities), economically challenged (more than half of the students qualify for free lunches), and academically struggling (the majority of the students are seeking employment after graduation, rather than attending college). While at the school, I observed two after-school clubs on a regular basis: the Digital Media Club and the Cinematic Arts Project.

The after-school Digital Media Club was started as a joint venture between the students and the Tech Apps teacher, Mr. Lopez. The students met after school in a well-equipped computer lab to work on personal projects, collaborate with other students, or work on assignments for other classes or from the Tech Apps classes. Several of the students were interested in film production and used the time to work on scripts, shoot and edit footage, or work on musical scores. Other students were interested in photography and came to the club to learn how to edit photos or create online portfolios.

The Cinematic Arts Project was a film project in its second year at Freeway. As a club, the students wrote, shot, produced, edited, and directed a short narrative film, which they submitted to an international film festival. Individual students and groups of friends also worked on their personal projects as part of the film club. The club met several times a week for many hours at a time, as well as on weekends, in order to finish the films in time to submit to local and international festivals. The mentors' and the teachers' connections within the local film community enabled students to gain access to resources and expertise.

Defining Terms

Digital and Social Media

The terms *information communication technologies* (ICTs), *social media*, *digital media*, *media technology*, *Internet*, *new media*, *Web 2.0*, and *social network sites* are often loosely applied to encompass many different platforms, hardware, software, and applications. In discussing my research, I use the term *digital media* in its broadest and most inclusive senses, encompassing web-enabled or mobile-enabled games, applications, networks, software, platforms, devices, and communication. Though sometimes it is productive to separate content and platforms from the material devices and hardware, I use the term *digital media* broadly to encompass both content and technological devices. When a distinction is necessary, I am specific about which platform, service, or physical device I am referencing.

Social media is another encompassing term that is used as part of everyday vernacular. An oft-cited definition of social media comes from Kaplan and Haenlein 2010: "a group of Internet-based applications that build on the ideological and technological foundations of Web 2.0, and that allow the creation and exchange of user-generated content." This definition has been criticized for overemphasizing the affordances of Web 2.0 and ignoring the history of earlier participatory and user-generated spaces that existed before Web 2.0 (sometimes referred to as Web 1.0). Earlier participatory platforms such as chat rooms, bulletin boards, blogs, and instant messaging applications also facilitated interaction via the creation and sharing of user-generated content, but are often erased from the history of participatory media that supposedly began with the development of Web 2.0 (Hanna, Rohm, and Crittenden 2011; O'Reilly 2005).[12] Notably, many of these earlier participatory spaces privileged sociality above economic gain or commercial exploitation; *Web 2.0*, then, is typically a business term and marks a turning point in the commercial aspects of participatory media (Scholz 2008). Web 2.0 ushered in not only an era of enhanced sociality and user-generated participation, but also the capacity for commercial institutions to capitalize on users' participation within these spaces (Hanna, Rohm, and Crittenden 2011; van Dijck 2013) (a point I address in chapters 3 and 6).

Another oft-cited definition within scholarship is boyd and Ellison's (2007) approach to social network sites. They define online social network sites[13] as "web-based services that allow individuals to (1) construct a public or semi-public profile within a bounded system, (2) articulate a list of other users with whom they share a connection, and (3) view and traverse their list of connections and those made by others within the system" (p. 211). The 2007 definition is probably the most frequently cited definition at the time of writing, yet in 2013— recognizing the evolution of the technical affordances and social norms of these spaces—Ellison and boyd offered an updated definition that is more encompassing. Their updated definition of social network sites states that "a social network site is a networked communication platform in which participants 1) have uniquely identifiable profiles that consist of user-supplied content, content provided by other users, and and/or system-provided data; 2) can publicly articulate connections that can be viewed and traversed by others; and 3) can consume, produce, and/or interact with streams of user-generated content provided by their connections on the site" (Ellison and boyd 2013, p. 158). This definition focuses on the capacity of the site to facilitate public interactions via the visibility of the network and is thus quite useful, particularly in analyzing publics and privacy. It often is misused in scholarship as an all-encompassing definition for social media more broadly, but the original definition is limited to sites that function as social networks more specifically—it is not intended to be interchangeable with the term *social media*.

I use *social media* as a broader umbrella term that encompasses social network sites and other online participatory spaces that do not necessarily fit the limited definition of social network sites. For example, at the time of writing Snapchat does not provide a public articulation of users' connections or a personalized user profile; similarly, the neighborhood-based app and website Nextdoor[14] automatically connects residents of a neighborhood in a public space (similar to a bulletin board), but does not allow for public user-to-user connections. Neither site fits the definition of a social network site according to Ellison and boyd's description, yet each of them is considered to be part of social media as a broader classification. Daniel Miller's characterization of social media is useful for incorporating sites such as Snapchat:

Social media helps draw attention to the development of a series of practices of communication which lie between traditionally dyadic forms such as the phone call or indeed most webcam conversations, and on the other hand public broadcasting as in most traditional media. Social media could imply that the communication is social in the sense of going to a larger group, but social also in that it helps create and maintain relationships rather than the one-way communication of broadcast media. ... An orientation to the social as opposed to merely the personal seems to keep us close to the intuitive semantics of these words. (Miller 2013)

Similarly, I define *social media* in the broadest sense: as (1) participatory media spaces whether web platforms or mobile apps that (2) facilitate communication beyond the interpersonal (i.e., one-to-one), to include options for two-way communication of one-to-many and/or many-to-many, and (3) facilitate the creation and sharing of user-generated content in a semi-public or public space; this does not have to be exclusive; user-generated content can exist alongside the creation and sharing of commercial media that is generated by more traditional corporate and institutionalized organizations. This definition includes, but is not limited to, social network sites, and offers a broader inclusion of online participatory media spaces in the absence of user profiles and public connections. Throughout the book, wherever it is necessary and appropriate, I identify specific content platforms, websites, apps, and sites in order to clarify my references, descriptions, and arguments.

Literacies

Literacy is a theme that runs throughout the entire book and is discussed in detail in chapters 3–5. Although I make distinctions between different literacies, in all instances I use the term *literacies* to refer to different aspects of media literacy. Broadly speaking, media literacy has been defined as "the ability to access, analyze, evaluate, and communicate messages in a wide variety of forms" (Hobbs 1998, p. 16). Drawing from other media scholars, I also use the term to refer to the ability to produce media texts (Jenkins 2006; Buckingham 2003). In other words, media literacy is not just about critical consumption of media content; it also involves the capacity to produce mediated texts and to confidently and safely navigate mediated spaces.

Youth

Youth is a fluid social construction often used to describe a range of demographic categories. Because my research is conducted in a high school and the participants in this study are between the ages of 14 and 19, when I refer to youth I mean people of high school age, young people, and teens. I generally avoid describing participants as children or kids; however, I preserve the language of the scholarship I reference. At times I use the broader term *child* or *adolescent* when writing about discourses of childhood and youth, but I do not use either of those terms when directly referring to the participants in this study. I do, however, use *child* when discussing a familial context, such as when describing parental relationships. Regardless of age, parents' offspring tend to be referred to as children even into adulthood; thus I use *child* within the context of parental relationships. I use the term *minor* within a legal context to refer to citizens under the age of 18, whom the US government defines as minors.

Structure of the Book

Each chapter addresses different spaces, discourses, and institutions that shape expectations, mobilize narratives of risk, and regulate opportunities. The chapters are divided into two parts. Those in the first part primarily address how discourses of risk regulate and control technology; I include quotes from participants to support my analysis, but the overall focus is on how discourses are mobilized and enacted. The chapters in the second part focus on how harm-driven expectations affect the everyday lived practices of teens and focuses more overtly on *how* teens and schools negotiate policies, regulations, and understandings of risk, as well as the consequences of such practices. Each chapter addresses the dualistic relationship between particular harm-driven expectations and opportunities. Within each chapter, I contextualize how different aspects of society construct both technology and youth, attempt to regulate both youth and technology, and what the intended and unintended consequences are in terms of young people's experiences and opportunities. I also call for more productive, nuanced, and equitable approaches to regulating teens' digital media practices and spaces.

Chapters 1–4 all address the relationship between risk, teens, and regulation. Chapter 1 explores the relationship between technology and social change as a way to analyze moral panics; it also historicizes fears and anxieties related to youth and technology in order to provide context for understanding contemporary discourses of risk. Chapter 2 traces how moral panics and adult anxieties related to young people's online engagement shape public perceptions of risk, and how public concerns affect public policies. The policies largely focus on three risks: pornography, predators, and peers. Additionally, chapter 2 demonstrates the ways that federal, state, and local policies construct youth (and specifically girls) as passive subjects at risk rather than agents capable of managing online risks. In it I demonstrate how harm-driven expectations—largely perpetuated via fear-inducing news and popular media—lead to overly restrictive policies that limit young people's opportunities and fail to help young people safely navigate risk.

Chapters 3 and 4 continue to analyze regulations, but more specifically focus on the policies and curriculum at Freeway High. Chapter 3 analyzes the harm-driven expectations that are used to justify blocking students' access to digital content at school. The rules are aimed at minimizing the risks of (1) inappropriate online (sexual) content and (2) misinformation and information overload. I demonstrate how such restrictive policies miss an opportunity to help students develop critical digital literacies, as well as opportunities to think critically about the commercialization of the web and to participate in digital activism. Chapter 4 shifts the focus to the school's policies that prohibit students from using mobile devices at school. The policies derive from harm-driven expectations of distraction and stress. I demonstrate how competing discourses of (adult) control and (student) trust lead to frustrations and missed opportunities to help students develop healthy boundaries and social norms. Chapter 4 also examines students' expectations of boredom and considers how opportunity-driven expectations of mobile media can enhance learning rather than detract from it.

By extensively examining teens' lived practices, expectations, and experiences at school and online, the next three chapters shift the focus away from critiques of harm-driven expectations and instead draw attention to opportunity-driven expectations and the effects of regulations. Chapter 5 debunks the expectation that young people innately possess digital media skills and literacies. I go into greater detail about participation gaps and the literacies young people need in order to fully take part in networked publics. That chapter relies on students' experiences to understand the barriers that prevent some of them from sharing their creative media productions in online networked spaces. As will be argued, discourses of risk have taught young people to expect harm online; instead high schools ought to empower students to safely network online, create professional online identities, and share their work in peer-supported online networks. The chapter makes a case for helping students develop three specific digital literacies: nuanced understandings of intellectual property rights, social literacy, and network literacy.

Following up on the theme of sharing that was discussed in the previous chapter, in chapter 6 the locus of opportunity moves beyond the school setting to explore participants' own expectations of social and peer privacy and how they navigate the everyday risks of socializing via mobile and social media. This chapter considers how commercial platforms, largely regulated by the market, often undermine teens' own expectations of visibility, and thus exacerbate privacy risks. I also examine the challenges of negotiating multiple social contexts online and discuss participants' agentive strategies for maintaining social privacy.

Chapter 7 also draws from students' experiences in order to examine what connections are necessary for helping students achieve their goals. I highlight the stories of four students as a way of connecting risk and expectations to future opportunities. That chapter is situated within the connected learning model of education (Ito et al. 2013) and demonstrates how different nodes of students' learning ecologies—academic, peer, home, adults, interests, and extracurricular—support or hinder opportunities. It considers the broader context of students' online participation, goals, and expectations and how each can alleviate or contribute to inequalities.

In the conclusion, I revisit the role digital media can play in structuring opportunities for youth and articulate what I believe we should be worried about: inequities related to regulation, access, control, participation, visibility, and opportunity. With today's technologies, teens have the power to take an active role in helping to create and mold learning environments, their local cultures, and social norms. With the right tools and support, schools can equip and empower students to contribute to knowledge formation and discovery. It is my hope that this research identifies a need for schools, policy makers, and institutions to rethink their role in shaping teens' media and learning ecologies. I demonstrate that opportunity-driven expectations can guide and regulate young people in ways that balance protection and agency.

It is my intent that the nuanced complexity of the three stories at the beginning of the book will be made increasingly evident through a multifaceted examination of the relationship between youth, technology, and expectations of risk and opportunity. There is no monolithic narrative of youth and digital media because the relationships are inherently fraught with contradictions. Young people can simultaneously be agentive and victimized, educated and misinformed, risk takers and safe. Technology can be simultaneously beneficial and harmful, private and public, a threat and a tool of protection, an opportunity and a risk. It is crucial that we investigate how unequal expectations and discourses of risk shape experiences for the most vulnerable populations within society in an effort to both protect young people and create more equitable opportunities for them.

I   Risk

1 Historical Fears: Teens, Technology, and Anxiety

Risk anxiety, engendered by the desire to keep children safe, frequently has negative consequences for children themselves, serving potentially to curtail children's activities in ways which may restrict their autonomy and their opportunities to develop the necessary skills to cope with the world.

Stevi Jackson and Sue Scott (1999, p. 103)

Youth are now viewed as either consumers, on the one hand, or as troubling, reckless, and dangerous persons, on the other.

Henry A. Giroux (2009, p. 3)

When technologies are first developed and incorporated into society we begin anticipating their beneficial uses, but also speculating about the potential negative effects. Within the history of mass media, each new communication technology is typically praised for its potential democratic effects and ability to solve world problems, but also feared for how it will negatively disrupt social order.[1] When these two reactions run to the extreme they fall into camps that can be either described as utopic or dystopic rhetoric, ultimately the responses are two sides of the same coin: they are both unrealistic and ungrounded reactions to new technology. Both views assign too much agency to technology by assuming technology alone has an inherent ability to drive social change; such an approach views technology as having pre-determined and inevitable effects on society, whether positive or negative (Mackay and Gillespie 1992; Stallings 1990). Technology and media scholars refer to this approach that assigns agency to technology as *technological determinism*.

Instead of presuming that technology affects society in a unilateral and unavoidable manner, a more nuanced approach seeks to understand the symbiotic relationship between technology and social change; this approach is referred to as the *social shaping of technology*. This view acknowledges that technologies are designed by humans with certain intentions and purposes, but are also open to interpretive flexibility (i.e., technology can be used in unintentional ways) and have unintended and often unforeseeable consequences (Lievrouw 2006; Mackay and Gillespie 1992). Social shaping considers how the uses and effects of technology are contextually situated and are regulated in different ways, in different spaces, and by different social variables. In other words, it is not technology itself that determines uses, effects, and change, but rather the social shaping approach argues that individuals and collective society are the regulators of technology and can choose to design and use technology to drive either positive or negative social changes.

However, while individuals have the power to manage uses and effects, they do not do so wholly autonomously. Other social factors—as well as the affordances and constraints of the technology itself—mediate possibilities (Hutchby 2001; Lievrouw 2006). For example, a paperback novel enables me to easily highlight and write notes in the margins, but a digital book that connects to a larger database affords me the opportunity to also easily view the highlights and notes from other readers—something the paper-back version is unable to do. Yet on the other hand, I can easily lend the paperback version to my mother when I am finished with it, whereas the digital version is locked within a proprietary system that makes it much more difficult for me to share it with my mother who does not own the same digital reader as I do. This simple example illustrates the technical *affordances* and *constraints* of various media technologies and formats.

Beyond the technical affordances and limitations, we regulate the effects and uses of technology in other ways as well, such as copyright laws that prohibit the illegal copying and distribution of a paperback novel. While copy machines make such uses possible, laws prohibit the practice in order to try to control the undesirable effects that unrestricted copying would have on the marketplace. Social regulations are indicative of collective attempts to not only control media technology, but also to minimize or manage the perceived risks and harms associated with the use of technology. Individuals exercise agency over preferred uses of technology, but we do so within the constraints and structures of social regulations.

Regulating Technology, Shaping Practices

There is a long history of complex regulations intended to protect youth from perceived harms and risks. For example, many parents choose to monitor what television shows their children can watch or restrict the amount of time they are allowed to watch television. Additionally, industries self-regulate as evidenced by the rating system employed by the Motion Picture Association of America (MPAA), which is intended to prevent or discourage young people from viewing content that the industry has deemed inappropriate. Another example is the Comics Code Authority of the 1950s, wherein comic book publishers self-regulated content that society was likely to consider harmful or inappropriate for young people. At other times it is the government that regulates media technologies. Take, for example, the V-chip, which the US government required to be included in all television sets sold in the United States after 2000. At that time, the federal government also decreed that the industry should create a voluntary rating system that would allow parents to block content on the basis of ratings. The V-chip is an interesting example in which inappropriate content (the perceived risk) was regulated through a joint effort of the federal government, the television industry (the National Association of Broadcasters and the National Cable Television Association), and parents. In all of these examples the regulatory stakeholders—whether government, industry, or parents—have attempted to protect young people from potential risks associated with their media use.

Similarly, information communication technologies (ICTs) are also regulated in different spaces and by various stakeholders. Schools, governments, industries, parents, the market, and peers all shape the ways in which young people use ICTs to interact, communicate, and participate in their own media and learning ecologies. Though regulations are not always shaped by perceptions of risk, there is an undeniable relationship between discourses of risk and policy regulations (Castel 1991; Foucault 1991), which co-exist within a symbiotic relationship—that is, risk shapes policy formation, likewise policy shapes perceptions of risk.

The attorney, scholar, and political activist Lawrence Lessig (2006) demonstrates that there are four constraints that function as modalities of regulation: architecture (or "code" in digital spaces), the market, (social) norms, and law. He uses the example of smoking as a way to illustrate different modes of regulation. At times, laws regulate smoking, such as age restrictions or banning smoking in certain public spaces. Other times norms regulate smoking, such as the etiquette of deciding whether it is appropriate to smoke in someone else's car or home. The market also regulates individuals' access to cigarettes, for example, an increase in cigarette prices could determine how often an individual smokes. And lastly, the physical architecture of a cigarette regulates an individual's decision to smoke. For example if an individual has an adverse reaction to tobacco they are unlikely to smoke. While all of these modalities—law, norms, market, and architecture—regulate behavior in different spaces and at different times, one factor could present a greater regulatory constraint on behavior than another factor. It is also worth noting the extent to which each of these regulatory constraints is affected by the others. For example, changes to the constraint of law (such as banning smoking in restaurants) could also negatively affect society's attitude toward smokers (change to the constraint of norms). Or, for example, changes to the law could also affect the constraints of the market (such as laws raising tobacco sales tax). Though all these variables are always already interacting, at times certain constraints regulate more intently or transparently than others.

In a similar way, technology is also regulated through the modalities of law, norms, the market, and architecture. In the context of young people's lives, norms include peer and familial values, cultures, and expectations. Laws at all levels—federal, state, city, school policies, and familial rules—affect what young people can do with technology, when, where, and with whom. The architecture, or code, of digital media technologies, software, and platforms affect how technology is used, in what ways, and by whom. And not to be understated, the market heavily regulates teens' access to technology hardware, platforms, and software. Embedded within all of these regulatory nodes are discourses of risk that also shape individual access and collective participation. Likewise, these regulatory factors also affect risk by either increasing or reducing the probability of harm. In order to create more equitable opportunities for young people online, and in order to shift risk discourse away from harm-driven expectations to opportunity-driven expectations, we must take a holistic approach that considers the multiple nodes shaping teens' experiences and practices. Throughout the remaining chapters of this book, I focus on different and competing ways in which young people's encounters with technology and risk are mediated and negotiated via the law, norms, the market, and architecture.

From a social shaping perspective of technology, the effects of technology are rarely, if ever, wholly "good" or "bad." Likewise, in the context of risk, I argue the effects of regulation rarely, if ever, entirely reduce or exacerbate risk, but rather the effects of regulation always have the potential to simultaneously reduce and increase risk differently for different populations. For example, enabling GPS tracking on a teen's phone simultaneously provides parents' access to their child's whereabouts (potentially reducing the perception of risk), but also increases the likelihood of a stalker (perhaps an ex-boyfriend/girlfriend) locating the teen (potentially increasing risk and harm). As with most designs, technology can be simultaneously used in beneficial or harmful ways, and can produce both positive and negative effects.

What is of particular significance for the research in this book is to also understand the ways in which young people's practices in particular are strictly regulated. Unlike adults, who are permitted a great degree of autonomy over their use of technology, young people are not afforded such freedoms. Laws, social norms, policies, educational institutions, controlled and limited finances, parental authority, and familial responsibilities, all mean that young people's digital media practices are highly regimented. Young people are granted a significantly lesser degree of autonomy and choice over the ways they access and use media. Further, because teens' practices differ from adult practices, they tend to be misunderstood and invoke anxiety, and are thus highly scrutinized. Such scrutiny can lead to even greater surveillance, control, and regulation. It is within an approach that recognizes the highly regimented ways that adults regulate young people's practices that I consider how adult expectations of young people's practices—expectations that are often driven by fear and anxiety—differ from the ways young people themselves understand and value digital media.

Youth and Moral Panics: It's Not About the Technology

When technologies are embedded into our daily lives in deeply private and personal ways—such as technologies we bring into the home—we can anticipate initial anxiety about their purpose and roles. As a society, we are fearful of how they will disrupt our lives in potentially negative ways. Likewise, when media are utilized and valued by young people—a population often constructed as vulnerable—we can also anticipate their practices will be a source of widespread concern. For example, despite the fact that reported Internet crimes are declining, news reports and social fears about youth and the Internet seem to be increasing (Cassell and Cramer 2008; Finkelhor 2011). The reactions to young people's use of novel technology tend to be fearful and anxiety-driven, which can lead to moral panics.

Baker (2001) defines moral panics as "the efforts of a particular group to exert collective moral control over another group or person. They are characterized by the identification of a 'problem' perceived as a threat to a community or subset of a community's values or interests." Journalists, educational institutions, policy makers, and other experts have identified young people's online practices such as cyberbullying, porn, sexting, pedo-philes, privacy (or lack thereof), addiction, and distractions as problematic and threatening. Consequently, there is a lot of discord and uncertainty about what exactly should be done, how, and by whom, which contributes to a sense of panic.

Discussions of moral panic often begin with Stanley Cohen's influential 1972 book *Folk Devils and Moral Panics*, which focuses on the mods and rockers of the 1960s in the UK.[2] According to Cohen, panic arises when society's response to a perceived threat is disproportionate to realities or actual occurrences of threatening behaviors. News media, alongside expert opinions and institutions, became the vehicles for perpetuating negative narratives that rely on overblown or exaggerated data, stereotypical stock images, and sensational headlines. Through such strategies and represen-tations, repeated fallacies begin to function as a hegemonic truth (Hall et al. 1978). Society then responds with fear and a general sense that some-body should do something; within this approach I would add that harm-driven expectations lead to increased punitive policies, surveillance, and control.

Many scholars have elaborated upon and critiqued Cohen's original conceptualization of moral panics. For example, Stuart Hall (1978) and his colleagues at the Birmingham Centre for Contemporary Cultural Studies argue that media serve as primary means for creating moral panics, but only because they reflect pre-existing relations of hegemonic domination. In other words, moral panics become a vehicle for dominant ideology. Inte-gral to both Cohen's and Hall's conceptualization is the argument that media contribute to the creation of moral panics. However, reducing moral-panic conceptualizations to disproportionate reactions by media becomes problematic since measuring irrational fears and reactions is not a produc-tive methodology. That is, at what point do fears and responses transcend from reasonable observations and analysis to irrational reactions?

Cultural studies scholars such as Angela McRobbie, Stuart Hall, and Dick Hebdige have noted the ways in which panics are often gendered, classed, and racialized. The "folk devils" are often ethnic minorities, females, the poor, queer, and/or youth, in other words, populations whose practices and values often differ from mainstream white, middle-class, straight, cisgen-der, male, adult hegemonic society. Moral panics present youth as scape-goats for broader and more complicated economic, political, and social problems. For example, as will be further discussed in the next chapter, continually and aggressively constructing youth at risk within cyber preda-tor discourse subjects young people to surveillance and regulation. The discourse presents the at-risk youth as the social problem to be solved, rather than the perverse adult pedophile who is the actual threat and problem. Moral-panic discourses divert attention away from deviant adult behaviors—behaviors which are difficult to control—and instead exert control over the bodies and lives of young people.

Such panics about young people's media practices have a long history dating back to the introduction of the paperback novel, to comic books, radio, television, film, the landline telephone, beepers, and video games— all of which have invoked fear and concern about young people's uses and practices (Springhall 1998). The rise of digital and mobile media is once again drawing attention to—and causing panic about—the potential risks of young people's mediated practices. Research demonstrates that social anxieties concerning adolescents' behavior are strikingly similar throughout the nineteenth and twentieth centuries. Pearson (1983) notes that moral panics often involve a nostalgic look back at a "golden age" of social control in which discipline seemingly functioned as a deterrent for delinquent or risky behaviors; however this was simply not the case. In their discussion of Pearson (1983), McRobbie and Thorton (1995, pp. 561–562) note that across time "the same anxieties appear with startling regularity; these involve the immorality of young people, the absence of parental control, the problem of too much free time leading to crime, and the threat which deviant behavior poses to national identity and labour discipline." The focus of panic and the face of deviance have changed with time, yet the social anxieties and fears have tended to remain strikingly consistent. The dissemination and domestication of computers and the Internet have given rise to new channels for moral panics.

The Friend Factor
In her 1977 book *The Damned and the Beautiful*, Paula Fass examines the relationship between youth and social change in 1920s America and the ways young people were paradoxically perceived to be an optimistic guide for the future, as well as a threat to traditional values and ways of American life. She claims the emergence of a modern American youth culture instigated change, but likewise was a result of broader societal changes. The transformation resulted in adult anxieties and contributed to the perception of a growing generational gap. As related to current moral panics about youth, I want to demonstrate some of the similarities between moral panics about youth cultures of the 1920s and today—specifically the changing role of peer groups.

In the 1920s, schools in urban industrialized society began to play an increasingly important function in developing and shaping peer culture, one which challenged the traditional socialization role of the family. Schools provided homogenous age-segregated environments in which young people spent an increasing amount of their time. Youth began to develop their own language and slang, peer groups contributed to conspicuous patterns of behavior, youth developed their own communication networks, and increasingly managed an identity that was distinct from adult cultures. In fact, Fass writes (1977, p. 375), youth "knew that they lived in a changing world that demanded new understanding, new conventions, and constant readjustments. And they conceived of their behavior and attitudes as positive response to these conditions. ... Acutely aware of being observed and criticized, the young would often artfully accentuate certain qualities to which they knew adults would react." In other words, youth behaviors should be understood as deliberate responses to broader social changes (particularly economic changes and changes within the family structure), rather than solely the cause of social change. As youth cultures changed, there was an increasing generation gap between youth and adult expectations, values, and behaviors—gaps that triggered adult alarm. As peer cultures became a more influential socializing aspect in young people's lives, families and adults inevitably lost a degree of control.

This is similar to what we are experiencing with today's "digital generation."[3] Society and technology are simultaneously and symbiotically changing, and, much as in the 1920s, young people are at the forefront of these changes. Digital technologies afford youth increased opportunities to develop peer languages, cultures, and communication networks that are separate from adult cultures and norms. Some adults are slower to embrace new technologies, as evidenced by young people's earlier adoption of digital media, as well as the education system's reluctance to incorporate new media technologies into the classroom. For today's youth, new technologies are par for the course, yet they invoke anxiety from adults and institutions who do not always understand how young people are engaging with one another via media.

Technology does not cause these cultural and generational changes—young people created communicative networks and unique communities before technologies for doing so existed—but technology does facilitate and intensify young people's ability to stay connected with their peers. As the telephone, the Internet, and the mobile phone have entered the domestic space, they have further challenged boundaries between what is conceived of as public and private (boyd 2007, 2008; de Souza e Silva and Frith

2012). Digital media disrupt spatial and temporal boundaries and allow teens to be simultaneously positioned as members of peer communities, as well as members of the family within the same space. To a certain extent, modern youth have always occupied both public (i.e., peer) and private (i.e., familial) roles, but new technologies, such as mobile phones and the Internet, serve to further collapse these social roles even when young people are not physically in the presence of their peers or family members. This is a concept mobile media scholar Richard Ling (2010) refers to as *co-presence*. The landline phone certainly facilitates co-presence as well, yet the mobile phone intensifies and individualizes the experience. Text messaging plays a large role in this as it provides rapid communication that does not require the full attention of the sender or the receiver and is sent directly to an individual, rather than an entire household (i.e., mobile phones enable person-to-person communication rather than the place-to-place communication of the landline phone). Perhaps Livingstone (2009, p. 11) says it best: "the combination of young people, positioned betwixt and between public and private spheres, and the media, with their unique power to penetrate private spaces and to construct publics … is resulting in some ambiguous, exciting yet explosive renegotiations of self and other, private and public." This is easily observable as many young people socially navigate constant contact with peers and family members even in the absence of shared physical space. Instead, peers and family members may share a virtual space that renders the role of peers more visible to adults and family members—what boyd (2010) refers to as "collapsed contexts" (e.g., when a teen's friend shares their picture on a social media site that a parent also accesses).

Young people caused anxiety in the 1920s as a result of broader social changes that intensified the role of peers in teens' social lives. We see similar changes today as the role of peer cultures become increasingly integral to the daily rhythms of teens' lives. Ultimately, technology may render young people's social, sexual, and political behaviors more visible, but technology is not driving these behaviors, nor are they necessarily that different from previous generations' practices. However, moral-panic discourses about teens in the digital world would have us believe they are more sexual and deviant than earlier generations, hence harm-driven expectations that continually focus on regulating sexting, provocative selfies, porn, and predators. Yet such discourse ignores the social and sexual norms of contemporary peer cultures, often by literally denying youth a voice in their own stories (Mazzarella and Pecora 2007). "Every new generation," Fass writes (1977, p. 325), "seems to rediscover sex. When it is an individual adventure, it is amusing, but when it is a group experience, it looks alarming." Moral-panic discourses elevate youth peer practices to an alarming group experience so as to attempt to control them.

The Network Factor

Digital media afford young people unique opportunities to participate in media culture, which also has a longer history beyond the Internet. For example, fandom provides an avenue and outlet for youth to participate in mediated cultures via participation in fan communities, writing fan fiction, making art, and appropriating themes, narratives, and characters into their own identities and communities (Jenkins 1992). Amateur bands participate in musical culture via the practice and performance of music. Young women have a long history of being encouraged by adults to write as a way to engage with culture—for example, through the private (and often educational) practice of journaling (Begos 1987; Hunter 1992).

In the 1990s, middle-class girls and young women made their writing public and created a mediated community through zines (mini-magazines), which were part of a counterhegemonic do-it-yourself culture in which girls published and distributed their own zines. Girls often created zines as part of a musical fan culture, the female-centric punk culture known as Riot Grrrl being one of the best-known. These zines were often hand-written and hand-drawn, and often incorporated and responded to images from commercial media texts. Girls used zines as a discursive space to negotiate identities and represent themselves in ways that often challenged mainstream representations of girlhood (Kearney 2006). Unlike journaling, zines were voluntarily self-authored and operated outside of educational or authoritative spaces, in fact, in many ways zines challenged hegemonic and capitalistic society. They offered a mediated space for the formation of supportive girl communities through the negotiation of identities. As Mary Celeste Kearney writes in *Girls Make Media* (2006, p. 154), "though female identity is a dominant discursive framework within grrrl zines, many female youth who produce these texts reveal their savvy about zinemaking as a mechanism for experimentations with, rather than simply reflections and thus reproductions of, identity." Zine culture (and, later, girl-centric and feminist blogging culture) enabled young people to participate in the creation of their own public media cultures through textual practices, self-authorization, and mediated community formation.

The affordances of new media technologies contribute to what are referred to as *networked publics*. Although the term has evolved, it was first defined by Mizuko Ito to "reference a linked set of social, cultural, and technological developments that have accompanied the growing engagement with digitally networked media" (2008, p. 2). The ethnographer danah boyd expands upon this notion to pay more explicit attention to the role of "publics" in shaping identities, community, and our understandings of the world (2010, p. 39): "Networked publics are publics that are restructured by networked technologies. As such, they are simultaneously (1) the space constructed through networked technologies and (2) the imagined collective that emerges as a result of the intersection of people, technology, and practice. ... While networked publics share much in common with other types of publics, they ways in which technology structures them introduces distinct affordances that shape how people engage with these environments." As with previous generations, young people desire to shape their culture and participate in a public life. Yet, owing to limited life experiences, developmental stages, and institutions that attempt to restrict their access to public spaces and civic engagement, they are often silenced and marginalized within public discourse. Young people are talked *about*, yet rarely provided opportunities to speak for themselves or to be validated and heard by the adult public who are charged with making decisions on their behalf. Furthermore, young people are hanging out together more online precisely because physical spaces designated for young people are increasingly being diminished or heavily regulated and structured by adults (thus diminishing the peer-centric aspects of those spaces) (boyd 2014; Livingstone 2009). Digitally mediated networked publics provide an avenue through which youth can communicate and participate collectively as peers in spaces they define and design for themselves. As boyd also writes (2014, p. 14), "Because of their social position, what's novel for teens is not the technology but the public life that it enables. Teens are desperate to have access to and make sense of public life." Yet teens' foray into public life tends to illicit at best concern or dismissiveness from adults, and at worse restrictions, control, or exploitations.

As will be further discussed in chapter 2, harm-driven expectations lead to policies that attempt to regulate where and what teens can access online. Many high schools continue to ban the use of mobile devices and websites that provide access to a public sphere and avenues for civic engagement (see chapters 3 and 4). Media industries commoditize and naturalize surveillance in many different ways, for example, through behavioral tracking or GPS-enabled mobile devices that allow parents to monitor teens' geographical locations (Vickery 2014). Embedded within all of these adult reactions are concerns about risk and harm—concerns that are to a certain degree legitimate, but that also detract from the more positive and empowering ways teens participate in networked publics. Rather than demonizing or pathologizing teens' practices, or constructing all behaviors as risky, society ought to be paying careful attention to helping teens navigate new opportunities and experiences. Gabriel (2014, p. 109) points out that if we believe that young people's digital practices "constitute unacceptable behaviours because they threaten the well-being, reputations and futures of young people, then the discourses used to make sense of these practices can (and ought) to be subject to critical interrogation," which is precisely what the rest of this book aims to do.

Teens need guidance in negotiating changing notions of public and private. Digital technologies afford greater opportunities for public participation, challenge traditional notions of formal education, and offer new prospects for civic engagement. As Rainie and Wellman caution (2012, p. 271), "networked individuals need to develop nuanced understandings of what to make public, which publics to make information available to, and how to intermix technologies of privacy with those of public narrowcasting." Yet media industries often attempt to exploit young people's online engagement; identities and practices are simultaneously commercialized and constructed as commodities. "In a society in which politicians and the marketplace limit the roles available for youth to those of consumer, object, or billboard," Giroux explains (2009, p. 14), "it is not surprising that young people are so easily misrepresented." Instead of compassion, education, and a desire for democratic opportunities, it appears anxieties and harm-driven expectations are the predominant influences mediating the relationship between youth and a public sphere. It is imperative that we help teens navigate a changing mediated landscape alongside broader societal changes in ways that empower youth to fully participate in the creation of their own publics and cultures.

The Power of a Label: Youth at Risk

The categorization of youth is a fluid concept which changes throughout various historical and cultural moments. Current conceptualizations of young people fluctuate between "active, knowing, autonomous individuals, on the one hand, and as passive, innocent dependents on the other" (Scott, Jackson, and Backett-Milburn 1998, p. 689). Discursively childhood has been constructed as a period of vulnerability and innocence, and young people get constructed as either "at risk" or "as risk." Risk, as a sociocultural and socio-historical construct, serves to identify populations that are deemed to be at risk and serves to position them in need of institutional protection.

However, what is novel in terms of the youth-at-risk discourse is that in contemporary literature potentially *all* behaviors, practices, and groups of young people can be constructed in terms of risk (Tait 1995). Similarly, new media are almost always constructed as threatening and risky because they either facilitate new modes of interaction or provide access to potentially harmful content that is often difficult to regulate. We can see this throughout history and the ways moral panics circulated around the initial dissemination and adoption of media and technologies including comic books, film, television, and the landline telephone (Springhall 1998). The intersection of youth and contemporary media technology continues to be constructed as risky due to the potential for inappropriate interactions or exposure to potentially harmful content. As young people explore, create, and interact with new information technologies in ways which adults do not understand—or at times are not even aware—adults lose the ability to control, surveil, and monitor their activities. Anxiety stems from a loss of control as young people exert agency in new mediated environments. It is no surprise then that the Internet, social network sites, and cell phones become lightning rods for moral panics. Anxiety stems from the continued historical perception of youth as vulnerable, innocent, and in need of (adult) protection combined with perceptions that online spaces threaten young people's safety and well-being. Understandably, adults are anxious and want to protect young people by regulating and censoring their online practices. However, as will be further elucidated in the next chapter, it isn't necessary to establish the probability of harm in order to enact regulations intended to protect presumably innocent and vulnerable at-risk populations who occupy these online spaces.

Peter Kelly's work focuses on how youth transitions are being remade within networked and neoliberal societies; he has noted how youth and youthful identities are a source of institutional and state apprehension. "A major problem for young people today," he writes (2003, p. 166), "is that they increasingly cause adults anxiety," and contemporary society discursively constructs all youth (and by extension youth practices) as potentially risky. Batten and Russell claim that, as a result of the "social stresses and tensions" associated with adolescence, "all youths are in some sense at risk" (1995, p. 1), because adolescence is conceived as a period of risky transition. Elsewhere (2000, p. 465), Kelly argues that the construction of all youth as at risk is a "historically novel development in attempts to regulate youthful identities." The risk industry serves to identify populations deemed to be at risk, and therefore position subjects as-risk who pose a threat—be it social or economic—to society (Castel 1991; Lupton 1999; Foucault 1991).

Some youth populations are identified as particularly threatening to the social order; such subjects are explicitly labeled "at risk" by institutions such as schools, hospitals, social workers, and law enforcement. "The 'at-risk' label," Lupton writes (1999, p. 114), "tends either to position members of these social groups as particularly vulnerable, passive, powerless or weak, or as particularly dangerous to themselves or others ... [which positions] them in a network of surveillance, monitoring and intervention." Individuals are labeled "at risk" on the basis of characteristics that align them with an at-risk population, thus governmental intervention gets founded on calculable preventative strategies and techniques (rather than individual intercessions). "A risk," Castel writes (1991, p. 287), "does not arise from the presence of particular precise danger embodied in a concrete individual or group. It is the effect of a combination of abstract factors which render more or less probable the occurrence of undesirable modes of behavior." The at-risk subject is produced within discourses of youth and the label is used to justify monitoring, measuring, and regulating youth in what Lupton (1999) refers to as a "web of surveillance."

With this understanding of the power of the "at risk" label, it is no surprise that labeling students as "at risk" has become a common facet of everyday life within US academic institutions, which became commonplace in the late 1980s (Nardini and Antes 1991). Within an institutionalized education setting specifically, Finn and Rock (1997, p. 221) explain the "at risk" label as follows:

The concept of risk, drawn largely from the field of medicine, embodies the notion that exposure to particular conditions, or risk factors, increases the likelihood that an individual will experience certain adverse consequences. In terms of academic outcomes, well-established risk factors include group status characteristics associated with academic difficulty or dropping out of school, for example, being a minority student attending an inner-city school, or coming from a low-income home or a home where English is not the primary language. ... All too often, these risk factors are accompanied by a set of risk behaviors, which, manifested by individual students, create impediments to learning, such as skipping school or skipping classes, not attending to the teacher, or not completing required class work or homework.

Schools define as "at risk" students who are deemed to be at considerable risk of failing to make a successful transition into adulthood. By focusing on adulthood, discourses of youth invoke a narrative of future-selves, as

Kelly (2001) argues, the construction of youth is largely organized around "becoming" (e.g., an adult, citizen, independent, responsible, autonomous). The future-oriented narratives are internalized by youth as they actively construct narratives of their future identities, expectations, and lives (Livingstone and Sefton-Green 2016). Youthful at-risk behaviors threaten preferable hypothetical futures (for youth and the state) which therefore serve to justify institutional interventions, monitoring, and surveillance. Risk works to responsibilize both youth and the family, and I would add the school. Public schools, as extensions of the state, tend to use the "at risk" label to foreground the economic concerns at-risk youth pose to the state.

It can also be argued that the "at risk" label is a strategy of inclusion and exclusion, of imposing control and order among populations perceived of as a risk (Bauman 1991). More precisely, Jeannie Oakes' (2005) research focuses on the ways in which American schools track students' academic performance in order to sort them into different groups: namely high-achieving and low-achieving, which have significant implications for students' achievement, engagement, and future success. Oakes found that low-income, Latino, and African-American students (all of whom are often labeled as "at risk") are disproportionately enrolled in low-track classes and are more likely to take vocational courses than are white or middle-class students, who are more likely to be encouraged to apply to college. Oakes argues that low-track and high-track classes offer different opportunities to learn and provide different kinds of knowledge (high-track being the advantageous track). By separating students on the basis of differences, tracking actually exacerbates the inequities between students. "It is through tracking," Oakes writes (ibid., p. 112), "that these educational differences are most blatantly carried out." In other words, tracking not only reinforces but exacerbates racial inequalities. I return to the effects of tracking and vocational curriculum in chapter 7 as a way to understand the relationship between digital media, opportunity, expectations, and risk for students in this study.

Notably, Kitty te Riele (2006) argues the "at risk" label problematically draws attention to what is wrong with individuals, rather than what may be wrong with schooling (systemic problems). "In order to redirect attention from deficiencies in students (and their families) to critical reflection on the processes of schooling," she proposes "replacing the concept of youth 'at risk' with that of 'marginalized students.'" " Use of this term," she continues, "easily leads to the question: marginalized by who or what? This is logically answered by considering aspects of society and schooling.

Marginalized students are not identified through their personal characteristics, but through their *relationship* with (mainstream) schooling. In other words, marginalized students are those who are not served well by senior secondary schooling." The students discussed in the present book are marginalized within the school, within their local community, within their mediated practices, and within society at large. In accordance with te Riele, I also use the term *marginalized youth* or *marginalized students* in lieu of describing the students themselves as "at risk." (I use the expression "at risk" only when referring to how the school has labeled students.) This also transfers the focus of risk and harm-driven expectations away from the individual and instead more appropriately frames risk and harm as a collective and institutional concern.

It is here that I would like to bring discourses of risk and youth into conversations with digital media production. As will be examined later in the present book (specifically in chapters 3–5), fostering digital literacies and enabling youth to create and produce media can serve as opportunities for equity and risk reduction. The lives and stories of the marginalized students in this book make evident that digital media production has the potential to function as "technologies of intervention" (Foucault 1991) insofar as students harness opportunities afforded by digital media. The affordances of the informal learning space, and the opportunities presented by digital media production, allow marginalized youth opportunities for empowerment and facilitate alternative aspirations and identities beyond the marginalized subject position. This compliments the work of other media scholars who have also demonstrated the ways in which media production positions young people as creative cultural entrepreneurs (Kearney 2006; McRobbie 1990; Rose 1994). I want to avoid excessively celebratory and technologically deterministic discourses that posit that digital media alone can solve all problems and create a more equitable society. As will be demonstrated, discourses of risk mediate opportunities, and at times they counter equitable intentions and practices. What is needed is a more opportunity-driven approach to learning and guidance that moves beyond harm-driven expectations of risk and instead acknowledges that the relationship between risk, digital media, youth, and opportunity is contradictory, messy, and diverse. The following chapter examines the ways harm-driven expectations shape policies that inhibit young people's autonomy, choices, and opportunities.

2 Policies of Panic: Porn, Predators, and Peers

Something about the combination of sex and computers, however, seems to make otherwise worldly-wise adults a little crazy.
Philip Elmer-Dewitt, *Time*, July 3, 1995

[The girls] just fell into this category where they victimized themselves.
Major Donald Lowe, investigator in the Louisa County High Instagram sexting scandal, November 2014 (source: Rosin 2014)

The rise over concerns about young people's use of digital media has led to public pressure for "somebody to do something." Often that "somebody" comes in the form of formal governmental interventions, such as policies and public campaigns aimed at controlling risks. As will be demonstrated, regulating technology and young people's use of technology is not as straightforward as it may at first appear. Even when there is consensus over what constitutes harm such as online predators (who universally threaten normative understandings of young people's innocence and are thus a seemingly easy example of something that young people need to be protected from), the mechanisms through which we protect young people are inextricably linked to other competing values that make regulation difficult. For example, regulations that deny minors access to computers or websites must be balanced with rights of privacy and freedom of speech. For that reason, regulation is fundamentally complicated and often controversial. Through an analysis of various attempts at regulating young people's use of digital media in the United States, we are able to more fully investigate expectations of both youth and technology and examine how constructions of risk are mobilized. Even when harm is universally agreed upon (e.g., when there is agreement that online predators are dangerous), the ways in which we attempt to intervene are value-laden and make visible our assumptions and expectations of young people and risk.

Discourses of risk, youth, and technology are so deeply embedded within our collective imagination that it can be difficult to unpack the assumptions and expectations that produce such concerns. Because discourses are often visible in their effects but often are invisible in their constructions, it is imperative to examine moral-panic discourses alongside their effects. Risks are often so taken for granted that it can be difficult to understand how they are constructed, enacted, and mobilized throughout culture, history, and society. "Moral panics," Lumby and Funnell write (2011, p. 280), "constitute an intense site of debate about ideas that are grounded in belief systems and that are connected to embodied and visceral ways of knowing and to ideological systems of meaning." Federal and state intervention strategies, in the form of policies, offer a visible response to moral panics that allow us to examine how constructions of risk and expectations of youth and technology are articulated, enacted, and legislated.

The goal of this chapter is not to offer a comprehensive and exhaustive account of all attempted and actualized policies aimed at regulating young people's use of technology. Nor is it to deeply analyze the moral panics and actualized risks about young people's media use, as there already exists great empirical research about risk, youth, and media.[1] As was noted in the introduction, this book aims to shift our focus away from the loud prominent risks dominating media attention; however, such a move must to be contextualized within the broader mediascape of dominant panics and concerns, which is what this chapter aims to do. Rather than chronicling all the panics in detail, the goal here is to use government-sanctioned policies as an entry point for examining how risk and anxiety are mobilized in society and, accordingly, how they shape expectations of youth and technology.

In her justification for studying sexting discourse through an analysis of policies, Amy Adele Hasinoff explains (2015, pp. 166–167).: "Law and policy texts position themselves as authorized by the institution of democracy. While political rhetoric usually advocates a position, it is designed to and often claims that it represents public interest and opinions even while attempting to persuade. Policy makers routinely rely on anecdotes and statistics to make their arguments, but there are no norms or standards that prevent gathering evidence from dubious sources." Relying on unsubstantiated claims and statistics are common characteristics of many of the policies I address, which demonstrates how data are sometimes used to represent "public interest" even when the studies are not sound. Policies are certainly not the only area we could consider in order to investigate how discursive constructions of risk are mobilized, but they do offer a productive site of analysis because they are highly controversial. The controversy aims to appeal to mainstream public assumptions about youth and tend to generate a lot of media and public attention. State-sanctioned regulations require policy makers, advocates, and opponents to articulate their competing viewpoints, which are fruitful sites of analysis. Further, if passed, policies have a measurable and visible impact on the day-to-day lives of youth. In sum, policies are an appropriate space of risk discourse analysis because they reflect and inform expectations of youth and technology.

Since the 1990s there have been three substantial waves that reflect policies of panic regarding young people and digital media technologies. I refer to them as *the porn panic, the predator panic,* and *peer fear.* The three waves are not mutually exclusive and at times overlap; each offers a categorical organization for examining how media and lawmakers respond to the perceived risks associated with adolescents' online practices. The porn panic refers to the fear that young people will be inadvertently "bombarded" with perverse pornographic content online, and more broadly a fear about minors' access to inappropriate sexual content in general. The predator panic is similar in that the fear centers on concerns about sex(uality), specifically inappropriate contact between minors and adults who are "lurking online" for young unsuspecting victims. Peer fear complicates discourses of youth and risk by focusing on harm associated with inappropriate behaviors among and between peers (rather than adults and adult content). Specifically I examine the peer fears about cyberbullying and sexting, which are distinct but which overlap in some instances. With peer fear, youth become a complicated site of discursive tension because there are no clear victims or perpetrators—an individual can simultaneously be both—and thus young people themselves are concurrently considered to be at risk and at fault.

Policies aimed at protecting young people's digital media use and practices reflect harm-driven expectations and privileged perspectives of risk and harm. They construct young people in paternalistic and narrow ways that do not account for young people's agency, discretion, consent, and contextualized practices and desires, but rather rely on overly restrictive and protectionist policies and constructions of minors as vulnerable. Despite the fact that many of the studies and texts which contributed to the panics have since been debunked, the threat of risk continues to discursively construct the Internet as a dangerous space for young people. From Foucault's perspective,[2] research that identifies a population (in this case minors) as being "at risk" renders the population governable. The label "at risk" is used to justify control and intervention, often in the form of policies. The act of naming a population as being at risk and constructing the Internet as risky shapes discourse and expectations, which in turn implicates practice. In other words, if the Internet is constructed as a dangerous space, then young people are positioned at risk, which positions policy as a necessary intervention. This is not to deny the existence of potential harms associated with young people's online practices; however, it is to say that policies are constructed on the premise that risks should be entirely avoided. Foucault argues:

Truth isn't outside power. ... It is produced only by virtue of multiple forms of constraint. And it induces regular effects of power. Each society has its regime of truth, its "generalized politics" of truth; that is, the types of discourse which it accepts and makes function as truth, the mechanisms and instances which enable one to distinguish true and false statements, the means by which each is sanctioned ... the status of those who are charged with saying what counts as true. (1980, p. 131)

Within policies of panic, the accepted "truth" is that the Internet is inherently dangerous for youth and that safety must be upheld above all other values. Young people—and by extension their families—are tasked with the burden of enacting risk-avoidance strategies.

Policy interventions attempt to reduce the risks young people may encounter online, but they also aim to reduce adult anxiety. Jackson and Scott (1999, p. 86) assert that "risk anxiety helps construct childhood and maintain its boundaries." In part this is because anxiety results from the continual historical perception of young people as innocent and in need of (adult) protection (Kincaid 1992). Scott, Jackson and Backett-Milburn (2003, p. 700) write that "the social world of children is divided into safe and dangerous places which has consequences for children's use of space, where they are allowed to go and the places they themselves feel safe in, frightened, or excited by." Harm-driven expectations continually construct the Internet as a dangerous space and effectively construe all risk as harmful. Rather than enabling young people and empowering adults to help youth navigate risks, they attempt to prevent risky encounters and behaviors altogether—often with unequal consequences for different youth populations. Further, policies contribute to monolithic constructions of minors that fail to account for developmental, cultural, and emotional differentiations. In the remainder of the chapter, through an analysis of a six federal policies and a few state policies, I examine the harm-driven expectations and consequences of privileged constructions of risk and youth.

Regulation Is Tricky

There are various ways in which we as a society aim to regulate young people's use of digital media. Some parents actively monitor how much screen time their children can have every day; other parents choose to put filters on the home router that block objectionable material; still others deny their children access to computers without direct parental supervision, or may require their children to earn screen time through good grades, chores, and other behaviors. In all these examples, parents are relying on different modes of regulation as a way to monitor their children's behaviors and practices directly and indirectly. As was noted in the introduction, Lessig (2006, p. 124) categorizes the four constraints that function as modalities of regulation as: architecture (or "code" in digital spaces), the market, norms, and law: "The constraints are distinct, yet they are plainly interdependent. Each can support or oppose the others. … Norms constrain through the stigma that a community imposes; markets constrain through the price that they exact; architectures constrain through the physical burdens they impose, and law constrains through the punishment it threatens." All these variables—law, norms, market, and architecture—regulate behavior in different spaces and at different times, but one factor could present a greater regulatory constraint on a behavior than another factor. Take smoking as an example again. Minors' ability to smoke is most strictly enforced via laws, whereas adults' smoking practices may be more notably regulated via social norms (e.g., whether or not their friends smoke) or concerns about their health. All these variables are always already interacting, and at times certain constraints regulate more directly, intently, or transparently than others.

Because it is inherently difficult to directly regulate young people—due to parental autonomy over raising their children, as well as the difficulties in regulating private businesses such as Internet service providers—public spaces become a way to indirectly regulate media and technology. Public schools and libraries are central spaces for risk interventions and regulations. In the United States there is a long history of the federal government's mandating specific protections and educational initiatives to protect minors from real and imagined harms, including the sales and availability of tobacco and alcohol products, exposure to and the effects of advertising, data collection, obesity, and exposure to sexual and violent content. In view of this history, it is no surprise that the government would intervene in managing young people's digital media practices as a way to protect minors from potential harms. In other words, the fact that the government

is regulating practices is of little interest in and of itself. What is worth considering is how risks are produced in the first place. Understanding how risks are constructed allows us to interpret regulations from a value-laden perspective, rather than as a neutral intervening strategy of protection.

The Porn Panic

One of the earliest and still ongoing concerns about young people's online experiences focuses on access to pornography and sexually explicit content. Obviously there are potentially negative and detrimental consequences of exposing young people to graphic sexual content before they are emotionally mature enough to process and understand what they are experiencing. The harmful effects of pornography are inconclusive (Bryant 2010; Owens et al. 2012; President's Commission on Obscenity and Pornography 1970), yet society's continued focus on protecting young people from presumably harmful pornographic material reveals the normative expectations of childhood innocence. Harm-driven expectations clearly propel regulatory conversations related to pornography and sexual content.

Although it may seem simple enough to pass regulations that decrease the likelihood of young people coming into contact with online pornography, the ins and outs of such regulations are much more complicated. For one thing, filters that block all sexually explicit material infringe upon adults' rights to freedom of speech and autonomy of choice, and lead to complicated debates about censorship and morality (Godwin 2003; President's Commission ... 1970). Second, while most would agree that young people of a certain age should be barred from exposure to pornographic images (i.e., expectations that porn harms innocence), there is little consensus as to what that "certain age" should be. As will be demonstrated, conversations about porn and sexual content (including information about sexuality and sexual health) rely on constructions of childhood as a naturally (i.e., biologically) innocent developmental stage (Gabriel 2013) and presume that all exposure to sexual content will threaten innocence and result in harm. Third, what actually constitutes porn is elusive. "Definitions of 'pornography,'" Attwood writes (2002, pp. 94–95), "produce rather than discover porn texts and, in fact, often reveal less about those texts than they do about fears of their audiences' susceptibility to be aroused, corrupted or depraved." Attwood argues that the indistinct definition of porn—which has been applied to Pompeian frescoes, to Shakespeare texts, and to a variety of erotic media (Kendrick 1987)—leads to confusion and regulatory

challenges. Many policies that aim to regulate or prohibit access to sexual content fail to acknowledge young people's deliberate and healthy desire for information, education, and understandings of their own emerging sexuality. Even if we as a society can come to an agreement about how to define porn and agree that is a threat to young people, the regulations are controversial and problematic when we try to put boundaries around rights of access.

In the sections that follow, I analyze three federal policies aimed at regulating pornography, but more broadly at sexual content writ large: the Communications Decency Act (1996), the Child Online Protection Act (1998), and the Children's Internet Protection Act (2000). Like other media scholars (Mazzarella and Pecora 2007; Thiel-Stern 2014), I do not analyze the policies in isolation; I also take into account how journalism and media construct youth sexuality. Mediated discourses are important to consider because they have the power to name—and thus produce—risks; they work alongside policy to shape public opinions and expectations about youth and technology.

The Communications Decency Act

In 1996, Congress passed the Communications Decency Act (CDA), which was an attempt to regulate sexually explicit material; the most controversial and relevant section addressed indecency on the Internet. At that time, the Federal Communication Commission (FCC) already regulated indecent content on television and radio, but the Internet had not previously been affected by indecency policies in the United States. After the National Science Foundation Act opened up the Internet for commercial use in 1992, there was rising concern about the accessibility of inappropriate material, namely pornography. Arguably, the anxiety about the availability of sexual content was widespread, but, as will be demonstrated, minors became the locus of concern because they were easier to regulate and control than legal consenting adults. In order to understand the challenges of regulating sexual content, it is important to distinguish between obscenity and indecency from a legal perspective. Whereas obscenity[3] is not granted protections of free speech under the First Amendment, indecent and erotic material is more subjective and open to interpretation. Historically, indecent speech has received First Amendment protection in the United States. Pornographic material includes both obscene and indecent content, thus making regulation difficult since the US government cannot ban or censor non-obscene material.[4]

In an attempt to regulate pornography, CDA criminalized the transmission of "obscene or inappropriate" material to anyone under the age of 18. Because a sender cannot know who might have access to information posted online, CDA essentially limited adults' access to sexual content and criminalized indecent speech, thus limiting adults' First Amendment rights to freedom of speech. CDA, also referred to as "The Great Cyberporn Panic of 1995" (Godwin 2003), was overturned almost immediately after opponents argued that it would have chilling effects on adults' right to free speech. It was also argued that CDA infringed upon parental autonomy because it denied parents the right to decide what material was acceptable for their children (ibid.). Also contributing to the overturning of CDA was the fact that the language intended to protect young people from indecency was deemed too broad (Quittner 1996).

Though CDA was overturned, I want to back up and consider the context in which pornography and sexual content was being addressed in order to understand how media, journalism, and politics worked together to produce expectations of harm and to mobilize risk. When CDA was being debated in Congress, mainstream news media were also discussing the risk of pornography and inappropriate online material available to minors. In a 1996 paper presented at a conference of the Librarians Association of the University of California, Santa Barbara, Dorothy Mullin (1996) chronicled the "porn panic" of the early 1990s. She found that journalists and popular news sources reported the ease with which young people could access pornography and sexual content on the Internet. Politicians and journalists drew analogies such as "the internet's red light district" (ibid.) and confidently proclaimed the prevalence, pervasiveness, and perverseness of minors' access to pornography on the Internet.

One of the most memorable and influential accounts that fueled the porn panic was a 1995 issue of *Time* that featured a cover photo of a traumatized boy (white, approximately 10 years old) looking at a computer screen with a look of horror and fear on his face. The headline "Cyberporn" spanned the cover, followed by "Exclusive: A new study shows how pervasive and wild it really is. Can we protect our kids—and free speech?" (Elmer-DeWitt 1995). The *Time* article made the public aware of the *risk* of access to pornography, although it did not actually demonstrate the *harm* of inadvertent access. Risk and harm were conflated as a way to construct technology as threatening and therefore in need of government regulation, essentially mobilizing a discourse of the Internet as risk throughout society.

The *Time* article relied on a study known as the Rimm Study (Rimm 1995), which incorrectly claimed that 83.5 percent of the content of Usenet (a popular bulletin-board system at the time)[5] contained pornographic images and obscene content. Although the claims have been debunked, the inaccurate statistics have nonetheless worked to effectively construct the Internet as a scary and dangerous space for youth. The fallacious study produced harm-driven expectations that continue to be used as the justification of regulations more than two decades later. The study was conducted by a Carnegie Mellon University undergraduate engineering student named Marty Rimm. An article titled "Marketing Pornography on the Information Superhighway" was published in the *Georgetown Law Review*, a non-peer-reviewed law journal. Since its publication the study has been accused of being misleading at best and has been completely discredited by other researchers as outright unsupported and inaccurate (Cohen and Solomon 1995; Godwin 1998; Hoffman and Novak 1995; Marwick 2008; Post 1995; Rheingold 1995).[6] Nonetheless, the debunked statistics from the Rimm Study were repeatedly reported and used to justify CDA regulations and restrictions intended to protect young people.

Drawing from the ways media are implicated in inciting fear and panic, scholars (Godwin 1998; Mullin 1996) largely blamed the porn panic on the rhetoric that was used in the *Time* article. The article was presented with the following headline and tagline:

ONLINE EROTICA: ON A SCREEN NEAR YOU

IT'S POPULAR, PERVASIVE AND SURPRISINGLY PERVERSE, ACCORDING TO THE FIRST SURVEY OF ONLINE EROTICA. AND THERE'S NO EASY WAY TO STAMP IT OUT

After an eight-sentence introduction about how easy it is to access pornography and erotica *offline*, the article's author, Philip Elmer-Dewitt, turned his attention to online erotica. His language both incited and indicated fear: "[S]uddenly the press is on alert, parents and teachers are up in arms, and lawmakers in Washington are rushing to ban the smut from cyberspace with new legislation—sometimes with little regard to either its effectiveness or its constitutionality." His evidence of this claim? The now-debunked Rimm report, which was to be released later that week. The article contained a bullet-point list describing the findings of the study, which included information about: the pervasiveness of perverse content, details about how men are the dominant consumers, claims that online pornography is a worldwide phenomenon, and a discussion of how much money is made from the sales of these images. Elmer-Dewitt concluded that "the appearance of material like this on a public network accessible to men, women and children around the world raises issues too important to ignore" (p. 40). Right above this statement he explained that access to pornographic bulletin-board systems cost, on average, $10–$30 a month and required a credit card. On those grounds it is reasonable to assume that a majority of consumers were not children but rather consenting legal adults, but nonetheless children were lumped in as consumers. The article went on to discuss the benefits and negative consequences of the Internet: "This is the flip side of Vice President Al Gore's vision of an information superhighway linking every school and library in the land. When the kids are plugged in, will they be exposed to the seamiest sides of human sexuality? Will they fall prey to child molesters hanging out in electronic chat rooms?" (p. 40). Although the Rimm Study was about sexually explicit content (and more so scanned images of already existing pornography), the article lumped predators in with porn, thus further inciting fear and precipitating the need for government regulation.

In making an effort to quell fears, Elmer-Dewitt addressed the difficulties minors faced in accidentally accessing pornography:

According to at least one of those experts—16-year-old David Slifka of Manhattan—the danger of being bombarded with unwanted pictures is greatly exaggerated. "If you don't want them you won't get them" says the veteran Internet surfer. Private adult BBSs require proof of age (usually a driver's license) and are off-limits to minors, and kids have to master some fairly daunting computer science before they can turn so-called binary files on the Usenet into high-resolution color pictures. "The chances of randomly coming across them are unbelievably slim," says Slifka.

Here we have a potential adolescent victim explaining that the odds of a minor's chances of inadvertently accessing porn were "unbelievably slim." What Slifka implied, of course, was that if minors were jumping through hoops and acquiring technical skills and currency to access pornographic content on Usenet, it was deliberate. The panic construed all exposure to porn as harmful and ignored that it can also be intentional, and not necessarily harmful. Although the *Time* article criticized the Rimm Study (particularly for the fact that the data were taken from self-selected users interested in erotica), presented other similar studies that revealed less shocking findings, addressed the complications of regulating the Internet, and quoted experts and politicians on both sides of the debate, it nonetheless contributed to the rising panic about minors' access to porn online. Toward the end of the article, Elmer-Dewitt mused "How the Carnegie Mellon report will affect the delicate political balance on the cyberporn debate is anybody's guess." What unfolded was a continued reliance on the study as evidence of risk and harm.

Despite the limitations of the study, Senator Chuck Grassley (R-Iowa) entered the study into the *Congressional Record* when he relied on the data and rhetoric as the basis for his Protection of Children from Computer Pornography Act of 1995. Senators James Exon (D-Nebraska) and Slade Gordon (R-Washington) used data from the study when they co-sponsored the CDA bill. The misleading, fear-mongering, and discredited study fueled a porn panic that was taken up by the media and by politicians.[7] Fiction was functioning as truth (Walkerdine 1997) in that fallacious studies were used by authority figures and experts to justify policies. Although CDA was overturned, the expected and perceived threat of pornography has continued to shape policies and practices more than twenty years later. On the twentieth anniversary of the publication of the *Time* article, Elmer-Dewitt wrote an article for *Fortune* explaining the fallout and how the article shaped his career and fueled a panic. He even disclosed that a *Time* researcher assigned to his story remembers the study as "one of the more shameful, fear-mongering and unscientific efforts that we [*Time*] ever gave attention to" (Elmer-DeWitt 2015).

The combination of the Rimm Study, the *Time* article, and the article's use as fodder for politicians and "expert" opinion allows us to trace how harm-driven expectations produced a discourse of fear and risk that fueled a moral panic and increased calls for restrictive regulations. Congress' attempt to regulate the Internet was an example of collective harm management overriding self-responsibilization—particularly because government regulation was not the only mode of protection at this time, as is addressed in the following section.

The Child Online Protection Act

Congress tried again in 1998 to draft a policy that would protect minors from inappropriate material online (again, primarily pornography). The Child Online Protection Act (COPA) was a watered-down version of CDA. Unlike CDA, COPA only attempted to restrict commercial communication and only affected Internet service providers (ISPs) in the United States. Rather than criminalizing the transmission of sexual content to minors, the Act attempted to regulate the private sector by requiring ISPs to restrict minors from accessing sites that contained materials deemed "harmful to minors." COPA defined "harmful to minors" in a much broader sense than obscenity, but also included material that "appealed to prurient interests" as deemed by "contemporary community standards" (Child Online

Protection Act, 1998, section 231). This included all sexual acts and human nudity, including all images of female breasts but not male nipples, which reveals the sexist double standard that renders the female body as categorically and inherently sexual, and thereby explicit.[8] Most detrimentally, such a broad definition also blocked minors' access to educational information, including health and sexual information online, even though access to sexual health education is a valuable part of adolescents' developing sexual identities.

In contrast, an opportunity-driven approach would recognize that increased access to sexual health information is a risk, but is also an opportunity to promote healthy and safe sexual exploration and development. As will be further addressed in the next chapter, offline sex-education material may be available to some youth, but the Internet provides an accessible way for minors to seek out information *in private*. This is particularly beneficial for young people whose questions, desires, and sexual orientation may not align with parental and cultural expectations. In addition to educational resources, the Internet also provides a supportive space and community for gay, lesbian, transgender, queer, and questioning youth to explore their sexuality and sexual identities (Gray 2009; Kanuga and Rosenfield 2004; Vickery 2010). Yet COPA framed youth sexuality as inherently harmful and attempted to deny minors access to sexual content.

Interestingly, although COPA insisted upon stricter regulations of private businesses, the congressional findings also recognized that the industry was already attempting to provide parents with ways to protect their children. In other words, the controversy had less to do with whether or not we restricted young people's access to sexually explicit (and educational) content than with who should be responsible for such regulations, and how. There were other modalities of regulation in place that balanced risk and opportunities, including the market, norms, and technological solutions. The congressional findings included the following statement: "To date, while the industry has developed innovative [technological] ways to help parents and educators restrict material that is harmful to minors through parental control protections and self-regulation, such efforts have not provided a national solution to the problem of minors accessing harmful material on the World Wide Web" (congressional findings, COPA, 1998, section 1402). The report acknowledged technological advances that enabled parents to protect their children, yet the problem was explicitly constructed as a national problem that required a national (read: government) form of regulation. Such language is indicative of the ways in which risk discourse contributed to a panic that deemed parents' and educators' self-regulatory behaviors insufficient means of intervention and protection. With COPA we see how moralization discourse called for government intervention and constructed sexual content not as a risk, but as a harm (despite the fact significant harm had not been clearly demonstrated). This is an example of the way harm-driven expectations work to push collective harm management to the frontline of public discourse, rather than self-responsibilization (Hunt 2003; Hier 2008) and education.

COPA was eventually deemed unconstitutional for infringing on the protected speech of adults. It was also criticized for its broad language, which made it difficult to define or enforce. Lowell A. Reed, a US District Court judge, struck down the bill for violating the First and Fifth Amendments and interestingly added "perhaps we do the minors of this country harm if First Amendment protections, which they will with age inherit fully, are chipped away in the name of their protection" (Urbina 2007). Youth in the United States are often denied legal rights they later attain as adults. Often the more productive approaches—stemming from opportunity-driven expectations—are parental regulation, education, and professional guidance that help youth safely (and eventually autonomously) navigate or avoid risks, rather than harm-driven expectations that deny minors legal rights.

Additionally, Judge Reed's remarks highlight the continued discursive binary of child/adult, which ignores the complexity of "youth" that is neither fully child nor legally adult. Youth occupies a transitional period from childhood to adulthood and highlights the limits of the discursive boundary (Gabriel 2013). At the age of 18 young people are automatically granted the rights of adults. But, as Judge Reed hinted, perhaps young people ought to gradually attain rights and responsibilities—to legally "come of age." Such an approach would recognize youth as a transitional period between childhood and adulthood, rather than an absolute either/or existence. For that reason, regulation could protect the most susceptible and vulnerable populations (e.g., young children) while granting older youth responsibility and rights.

Looking Beyond the Law

There have been attempts to account for complexity within our legal understandings of protection, risk, and harm; however, the logistics of passing such nuanced regulations are complicated. When Congress initially passed COPA, it also created an eighteen-member committee whose purpose was to "identify methods to reduce minors' access to harmful material on the internet" (Goldstein 2002, p. 1190). After two years of evaluation the panel recommended that libraries promote public awareness of technological tools available to protect adolescents, that schools and libraries adopt acceptable use policies, and that policies should focus on the design and adoption of curriculum and education intended to protect adolescents. Remarkably absent from the committee's recommendations was any mention of requiring filtering software in libraries; instead the focus was on education and self-regulation. One member of the committee—Jerry Berman of the Center for Democracy and Technology (a free speech advocacy group)—wrote the following: "Acknowledging the unique, global character of the Internet, the commission concludes that new laws would not only be constitutionally dubious, they would not effectively limit children's access to inappropriate materials. The Commission instead finds that empowering families to guide their children's Internet use is the only feasible way to protect children online while preserving First Amendment values" (Statement of COPA commissioner Berman, 2002). This approach would have allowed for other modes of regulation (e.g., norms, the market), rather than legal restrictions, to offer protection.[9] Additionally, the approach allowed for a more continuum-based construction of youth and empowered adults to implement discretion in protecting young people.

The members of the congressional panel were not the only authorities to suggest less restrictive technological regulations; other experts also suggested less restrictive means of regulation. For example, in the mid 1990s the World Wide Web Consortium (W3C) suggested a model of industry self-regulation similar to the self-regulation implemented by the Motion Picture Association of America (MPAA) and the National Association of Broadcasters.[10] The W3C recommended that a voluntary rating system that would enable parents to block certain content be embedded within the HTML protocol. The Internet Engineering Task Force was also working on embedding a ratings system into web addresses (Abernathy 1995). This would have allowed the industry to empower parents, schools, and libraries to filter content on the basis of self-regulation and localized community standards rather than overarching government intervention. It also would have also enabled schools to implement filtering systems that would account for increasing maturity and responsibility. Elementary schools could block out material deemed inappropriate for young children; high schools could choose to allow more mature content, such as sex-education material or nude art. However, when Congress once again attempted to regulate indecency, this time via the 2000 Children's Internet Protection Act (CIPA), paternalistic restrictive regulation continued to take precedence over education and parental guidance.

The Children's Internet Protection Act

After CDA and COPA were struck down as unconstitutional, Congress tried yet again to restrict minors' online engagement via law and technical restrictions. In 2000, Congress passed the Children's Internet Protection Act (CIPA). After many challenges in court, CIPA was upheld as constitutional by the US Supreme Court in 2003. It is still in effect at the time of writing. Unlike CDA and COPA (which attempted to directly regulate access to inappropriate material), CIPA relied on existing economic regulations and government-funded institutions as a way to indirectly regulate content. Under the universal service doctrine of the 1934 Telecommunications Act (revised in 1996), many schools and libraries receive federal subsidies for telecommunication services (e.g., telephones, computer equipment, and Internet service); these services are colloquially referred to as E-rate discounts or E-rate schools.

Unlike earlier attempts at regulation, CIPA did not criminalize indecent material writ large, nor did it require schools or libraries to block access to inappropriate content; instead it required recipients of E-rate funding to utilize technical filters to block access to inappropriate material on all computers accessible to minors. Specifically, CIPA required all K–12 public schools and public libraries that receive E-rate funding to enable technology that blocks access to obscenity, child pornography, or content harmful to minors. CIPA also required E-rate recipients to adopt and enforce a policy to monitor and surveil the online activities of minors (FCC Guide to CIPA, 2000). Blocking access to obscenity and child pornography is rather straightforward and mostly uncontroversial, as obscenity is not granted First Amendment protections and child pornography is illegal. "Content harmful to minors," on the other hand, is a much broader, more subjective, and more controversial stipulation that opens up a multitude of interpretations as to what constitutes harm. As has already been noted, risk and harm are often conflated within discourses of risk, and CIPA's language allowed for the censorship of all content that presented even the *threat* of harm.

The E-rate program is an example of how governments indirectly regulate practices. With CIPA, the constraint of the market is used to indirectly fulfill legal objectives that had otherwise been ruled unconstitutional. As a similar example, Lessig (2006) recounts how the Reagan administration required doctors in federally funded clinics to advise patients against abortion as an appropriate method of family planning. This was not necessarily the medical opinion of the doctor, but rather government regulation intended to indirectly reduce abortion rates. Through indirect regulation, the government "gets the benefit of what would clearly be illegal and controversial regulation without even having to admit any regulations exist" (ibid., p. 135). Lessig asserts that indirect regulation is not necessary problematic, but he argues transparency of regulation is of the utmost importance in a democratic society. Similarly, by making technical filters a requirement for E-rate funding recipients, CIPA did not directly regulate access to indecent content online; rather, it relied on pre-existing market constraints. Many of the more than 100,000 schools and libraries that serve low-income populations have little choice but to accept E-rate funding, and therefore they must also comply with the restrictions of CIPA (Patton 2014; Long-term strategic vision ... 2009). The very population CIPA was intended to protect—adolescents—is the one disadvantaged by restrictive policies that block access and opportunities for learning. Harm-driven expectations continue to dominate our perceptions of risk, and thus outweigh the potential benefits of a less restrictively filtered Internet. As is further discussed in the next chapter, the unintentional and trickledown effects of CIPA exacerbate rather than alleviate risks when enacted in high schools serving low-income and marginalized populations.

It is important to note that often it is adult institutions that benefit from a moral-panic discourse of youth at risk. The risk discourse positions young people as the scapegoats for broader social, economic, and political problems. Insisting upon boundaries between adulthood and adolescence "enables adults and their institutions to blame youth for a variety of problems created by those very same adults and adult institutions" (Mazzarella 2003, p. 238). I argue that constructing the minor at risk within the cyberporn discourse subjects them to surveillance and regulation and presents the "at-risk" adolescent as the social problem, when in fact the actual problem is morally conservative America's desire to contain the "deviant" desires of adults who access porn online. Moral-panic discourses divert attention away from (socially constructed) deviant adult behaviors— behaviors that are difficult to control—and instead exert control over the boundaries of childhood. Cloaked as policies purely intended to protect young people from pornography, CDA and COPA infringed upon adults' right to freedom of speech and can be interpreted as attempts to regulate the sexual morality of American citizens. This echoes Stuart Hall's (1978) assertion that moral panics serve as vehicles for disseminating dominant ideology—in this case America's continual struggle over sexual morality as represented through debates about pornography.

The Predator Panic

Concerns about porn have not been completely quelled, but around 2005 risk anxieties were displaced by louder concerns regarding online predators—largely as a result of evolving technologies and changes in how young people engaged with the Internet around that time. The introduction and adoption of social network sites such as MySpace in 2003 and Facebook in 2004 precipitated a shift in how young people engaged and communicated online. The popularity of social network sites allowed teens to create profiles to stay in touch with friends, form communities, and virtually "hang out" online in ways strikingly similar to the ways teens hang out in physical spaces such as malls and parks (boyd 2007; Livingstone 2008). As social network sites such as Facebook and MySpace became increasingly popular, so too did concerns about young people's interactions with strangers. The "stranger danger" fears have a much longer history in the public imagination. First incited via public-service media campaigns in the 1970s and the 1980s, they continued to gain public attention as cyber chat rooms gained popularity in the mid 1990s; they have only intensified as teens make themselves more visible and accessible via online social network sites. As in the porn panic, misleading statistics linking social network sites to unwanted sexual solicitation proliferated fears about online child predation.

Quantitative data demonstrate that, although online social network sites pose some risks, the risk of sexual solicitation is extremely low (Finkelhor 2013; Hinduja and Patchin 2008; Rosen 2006). Nonetheless, fears about "stranger danger" are on the rise (Keohane 2010; Skenazy 2009), but research tells us that there has never been a safer time to be a child in America (Ingraham 2015). News reports and crime dramas often espouse the risk of child abduction and harm at the hands of a stranger, yet the most likely place for a child to exploited, molested, and assaulted is in the home and by someone the child knows, not by a stranger (Finkelhor 2011, 2013). According to the Bureau of Justice Statistics, the rate of missing-person reports for children has fallen more than 40 percent since 1997 (Cooper and Smith 2011). Both state and national trends consistently report a decline in the number of crimes committed against children (Finkelhor 2013). David Finkelhor, director of the Crimes Against Children Research Center, points out that only 0.01 percent of all missing children in the US are taken by strangers or slight acquaintances; that means the overwhelming majority of child predators are friends of the child or family (ibid.). Lenore Skenazy (2009), in her book *Free-Range Kids*, points out the irony of driving children to school or the bus stop to be safe rather than allowing them to walk: children are 40 times more likely to be killed in a car accident than to be abducted on the streets. Nevertheless, fears about strangers far outweigh fears about riding in a car (which is constructed as a quotidian experience). Skenazy also purports that statistically it would take 750,000 years to guarantee that a child left alone in public would be abducted by a stranger (Friedersdorf 2014). The point of these statistics is that there is an inherent risk in everything a child does, including riding in a car, walking alone in public, and creating a profile on a social network site. But there is also the risk that a child may be harmed by falling down stairs (a leading cause of death; see Iyamba 2012) or by choking on his or her lunch (another leading cause of death; see Nationwide Children's Hospital, 2010) or may die as a result of a freak heater malfunction (Blackburn 2016), but we understandably do not discourage or outlaw young people from using stairs, eating, or staying warm. Statistics are a way to identify and quantify harm and can also be used to incite fear.

There is little evidence to support "stranger danger" rhetoric, yet it has worked to effectively construct the home as the locus of control and safety for young people and contributed to a construction of the (online) public as a dangerous place. Media have played a pivotal role in shaping these perspectives. Benjamin Radford (2006) goes so far as to blame the online predator panic directly on media sensationalism. In particular he notes that the popular NBC Dateline series *To Catch a Predator*[11] played a significant role in fueling a panic. He accuses the show of being misleading because it incorporated completely inaccurate or even made-up facts. The show used adults as decoys pretending to be underage children. After conversing online in increasingly sexually explicit and graphic ways, the predator would agree to meet the "child." When he arrived, the host, Chris Hansen, would ask the predator "to take a seat"; he would then reveal that the conversations had been staged. The show concluded with the predators' guilty, shocked, and shamed reactions to getting caught. *To Catch a Predator* made it seem as though lewd men were lurking around every virtual corner just waiting to victimize a child at any moment. The perverseness of their online conversations were often highlighted, which included unnecessary graphic and sensationalized details of sexual acts.

To Catch a Predator is important to consider because, by definition, moral panics must be publicly accessible (Marwick 2008). Additionally, according to Cohen (1972), moral panics rely on "ready-made stock images" (p. 57) and serve as "dominant vehicles for diffusion" (p. 63). The series relied on the conception of the stereotypically innocent and naive child and the inherently vile and perverse predator—it went to great length to include the perverse and graphic ways predators conversed with their potential targets, which understandably contributed to and incited fear in parents. The media scholar Alice Marwick (2008) chronicles the 2006 cyberpredator panic, what she refers to as a technopanic; the panic was concerned about sexual predators on the most popular social network site at the time, MySpace. She asserts that technopanics have three defining characteristics: "First, they focus on new media forms, which currently take the form of computer–mediated technologies. Second, technopanics generally pathologize young people's use of this [*sic*] media, like hacking, file-sharing, or playing violent video games. Third, this cultural anxiety manifests itself in an attempt to modify or regulate young people's behavior, either by controlling young people or the creators or producers of media products." Similar to the porn panic, popular discourse constructed MySpace (and teen-populated social network sites and chat rooms writ large) as a space for pedophiles to prey upon children who were discursively constructed as innocent, vulnerable, and lacking maturity or agency to protect themselves.

Child predation is a legitimate concern and one that we as a society ought to actively take steps to minimize and prevent. However, the predator panic of the mid 2000s falsely blamed technology for increasing the risk of predation when no such data existed to support the claim. In fact, Finkelhor (2013) points out that the *decline* in crimes against children can actually be partially attributed to an *increase* in available technology.[12] This is in stark contrast to rhetoric that blames technology for the imagined increase in crimes committed by strangers. The focus on strangers as suspect reflects a privileged understanding of risk and sexual harm. Middle-class parents are increasingly restricting the public spaces they allow their unaccompanied children to occupy (boyd 2014; Livingstone 2008; Skenazy 2009), which in itself is a privileged choice. Working-class and poor children often do not have the same options for supervision as children from middle-class homes. Because of financial instability and precarious living situations, working-class children are more likely to spend time alone after school, to care for younger siblings, to be in the care of someone other than a parent, to rely on access to public transportation, bikes, and walking as a means of getting home from school or to and from work, and so forth. Thus, while all children are at risk of sexual predation from family members and acquaintances, working-class children are more likely to spend time unaccompanied in public (Dodson et al. 2012; Lareau 2003).

The Internet has become the new public and has given rise to growing middle-class concerns about child predators. At the beginning of the predator panic, middle-class youth were more likely to be using social network sites—or at least have reliable and frequent access to the sites—than were working-class and poor youth (Lenhart, Madden, and Hitlin 2005). This distinction reflects the classed nature of what garners public attention and what gets constructed as risky. More than ten years later, teens' participation on social network sites has become commonplace, yet fears about online sexual predators are still frequent and visible. While working on this book one afternoon, I happened to read a story on the website of WFAA, the local Dallas ABC affiliate, about predators' using games to lure children. In the story (Eiserer 2015), a 10-year-old white girl was sent an inappropriate message while playing a game on her phone. "It was frighteningly simple," the opening line read, "for 10-year-old Olivia to accidentally connect with a child sex predator through a game." In response to the incident, the girl's mother replied: "We don't let our kids walk anywhere. We don't let them go out by themselves. If they're outside riding bikes, somebody's out there with them. That's who we are. We know bad things can happen." Such rhetoric is consistent with middle-class fears of the public and reflect the options middle-class parents have in supervising their children—options not always available to working-class families. Hence the privileged way the problem is framed. The mother's comment "That's who we are" points out how she believes she is doing "everything right," she is not a "bad" parent, and her child does not fit the description of a child at risk. Yet even within this middle-class home children are at risk. Markedly, Olivia immediately told her parents about the incident, the user was blocked, and no real harm was encountered; nonetheless, the risk itself reasonably incites fear even in the absence of harm.

Online "stranger danger" incidents are significantly rare and stand out as exceptional, yet stories such as these continue to make the news and provide narrative fodder for crime dramas precisely because they are about "good" children with "good" parents. They disrupt our understanding of who is at risk. The story of the abused runaway from a broken home is far less likely to attract media attention compared to an attack on a child we collectively perceive as privileged—and thereby innocent and entitled to protection. Research consistently demonstrates that marginalized youth—youth of color, from poor homes, with unstable family lives, and some others—are not granted the same presumptions of and entitlement to innocence as are white, middle-class youth from "good" homes. Marginalized young people are constructed as "deviant," and their stories of risk and harm are much less likely to make the news (unless they are in trouble with the law) and remain largely absent from our collective imaginations (Giroux 2009; Hasinoff 2015; HoSang 2006; Rios 2006). Stories of privileged youth, such as the WFAA one (and so many like it), are disproportionately more likely to catch the attention of the media than are the more frequent scenarios of sexual abuse to which runaways, homeless youth, and other marginalized young people are subjected (Fernandes-Alcantara 2013).

My point isn't that we shouldn't be concerned about child predation (we should), but that we ought to consider the root of the problem, understand who is at risk, and approach the problem from a less myopic view than one that narrows in on the "cyber" or "online" nature of the crimes. What we see, though, are policies that aim to regulate and restrict how young people use social media—platforms that are integral to their ability to communicate with peers, construct identities, seek out information, engage civically, and form supportive communities—rather than controlling adult predators who are the actual problem. In the sections that follow I examine the Deleting Online Predators Act and the Protecting Children in the 21st Century Act in order to explore the production and mobilization of predator risk discourse.

The Deleting Online Predators Act

It is important to note that the Children's Internet Protection Act did not require schools to block access to social network sites, but that many schools have chosen to block students' access to all social media. The 2006 Deleting Online Predators Act (DOPA), which was passed by the House of Representatives by a vote of 410–15 but was not voted on by the Senate, would have required schools receiving E-rate funding to block access to all social network sites and chat rooms. Social network sites were broadly defined as commercial sites that "(i) allow users to create web pages or profiles that provide information about themselves and are available to other users; and (ii) offer a mechanism for communication with other users, such as a forum, chat room, email, or instant messenger" (section 3, Deleting Online Predators Act). DOPA contributed to the acceptance of the Internet as a dangerous space in particularly gendered ways by relying on a media discourse that constructed girls as especially vulnerable and at risk of predation. Although the bill was overwhelmingly passed by the House, opponents were worried that it would be overly restrictive and that it would block access to potentially educational or useful websites, such as Amazon, blogs, and wikis, that might fall under the bill's overly broad definition of social network sites.

DOPA eventually failed, but a decade later its legacy still shapes policies and practices in many schools. Despite little to no evidence to suggest that social network sites pose an increased threat to the well-being of students, many schools (including Freeway High, as will be discussed in chapters 3–5) continue to block students' access to social network sites. The Internet certainly presents risks for young people (and adults); however, as has already been noted, there is little evidence to suggest that young people are at greater risk online than they are elsewhere (e.g., at home, at school, or on a playground). The Crimes Against Children Research Center reports that since the rapid adoption of the Internet "sex crimes overall and against adolescents have dropped dramatically in the US" (Finkelhor 2011, p. 5) and that overall crimes against and by youth have been declining since the adoption of the Internet.[13] Nonetheless, harm-driven expectations have led to a perception that the Internet poses a greater threat to young people than it actually does (Holloway and Valentine 2003; Olfman 2008; Livingstone 2009; Finkelhor 2011)—a perception that was fueled by cyberporn and cyberpredator panics and validated by the introduction of policies such as those specified by DOPA.

The Protecting Children in the 21st Century Act

After dying in Congress, DOPA was reintroduced in 2007 as the Protecting Children in the 21st Century Act (part of the broader Broadband Data Improvement Act). Rather than completely banning social network sites, the 2007 version required E-rate funded schools to "protect against access to a commercial social networking website or chat room unless used for an educational purpose with adult supervision" (Protecting Children in the 21st Century Act, section 203, ii).[14] Requiring direct adult supervision of all social media practices puts an undue and unreasonable burden on teachers. In practice, most schools probably would have chosen to deny access altogether, rather than actively monitor and be held liable for students' social media practices.

However, in 2011, as the bill was being debated in court, Congress began to acknowledge the educational value and potential of social media. In a positive move, the Protecting Children Act amended CIPA and issued a statement that by the 2012 fiscal year schools' Internet safety policies must include provisions for educating students about appropriate online behaviors and interactions on social network sites. Instead of banning social media altogether, the FCC publicly noted that "social networking websites have the potential to support student learning" (Donlin 2011). The Protecting Children Act was not necessarily reflective of a decreased concern about risk, but rather can be viewed as an appropriate response to an increased concern about cyberbullying (ibid.) (or more accurately, relational aggression among peers, which is the focus of the next section). Additionally, the FCC concluded that, although individual pages on Facebook or MySpace might pose a risk to minors, those sites are not in and of themselves "harmful to minors." As a result, they did not fall into a category of websites that must be blocked.

This is a positive step for schools, teens, and educators who have long acknowledged the educational potential of social network sites, as will be more fully explored in the second half of the book. Stephanie Winfrey, senior compliance specialist at Funds For Learning, a leading E-rate compliance services firm, applauded the adoption of the additional guidelines, adding that the changes should help to "foster a generation of responsible Internet users" (FCC releases Order … 2011). This is perhaps the first time we see evidence to suggest that students' positive online experiences can influence policies aimed at reducing risk. CDA, COPA, CIPA, and DOPA were all shaped by harm-driven expectations that consistently constructed the Internet as a harmful space and youth as passive subjects. However, the Protecting Children Act implemented opportunity-driven expectations by taking into consideration the positive values of social media. The act appropriately enabled schools to play an active role in helping youth navigate social media and positioned educators and students as experts of their own experiences. Empowering educators is a notable shift in risk discourse because it breaks away from sensational and exceptional narratives of harm, and instead takes a more nuanced approach that aims to balance risk with opportunity, instead of just trying to eliminate risk altogether. Conversely, E-rate funded schools now face the challenge of remaining compliant with CIPA while also deciding whether and how to incorporate social media into their classrooms. Many schools still choose to block social media, but at least it is at the discretion of the school rather than a federal mandate. This enables schools to exercise discretion, curriculum, scaffolding, and policies that fit the localized needs, values, and practices of their communities.

Peer Fear: Cyberbullying and Sexting

Back in 2008, I wrote about the suicide of 13-year-old Megan Meier, who had hanged herself after being bullied via her MySpace account (Vickery 2008). Little did I know, at that time, that the case would become a locus for all sorts of cyberbullying concerns, attention, and legislation. In the decade since her death there have been far too many other similar stories in which teens, many of whom face mental health challenges, have taken their own lives after experiencing bullying, rejection, and aggression from peers. I want to revisit Megan's story not only for the media attention it garnered and the legal questions it posed, but also because her story complicates constructions of the child/adult binary and serves as an appropriate introduction to what I call peer fear. *Peer fear* refers to the fear and anxiety about the ways young people communicate and interact *with one another* via digital and mobile media; it shifts the focus away from strangers and instead onto the interpersonal relationships between young people. As an example, I specifically consider the panics and legislation that have circulated around two headline-grabbing concerns: cyberbullying and sexting.

Cyberbullying Becomes a National Concern

To begin, let's take a deeper look at the coverage of Megan Meier's story. The words "cyberbully" and "bully" were notably absent from either the local coverage of the story (which received frequent coverage for years on STLto-day.com, the website of the *St. Louis Post-Dispatch*), as well as from national coverage. Megan's suicide became the locus of media and legal attention for what we now refer to as cyberbullying,[15] Yet at the time the media were not yet identifying or naming the problem as cyberbullying. The act of labeling something, of categorizing it—be it an object, a population, or a phenomenon—gives it credibility and power.[16] Language both creates and alters perceptions of the world and is constituted by, and constitutive of, power, values, and ideologies. "By naming something," Armstrong and Fontaine write (1989, pp. 7–8), "one actively carves out a space for it to occupy, a space defined by what one values in the phenomenon and by how it appears to be like or unlike other parts of one's world view." Cyberbullying intentionally draws attention to the presumably unique aspect of the online environment, the "cyber element" of bullying. Identifying cyberbullying as a phenomenon works to incite fear and panic. Labeling cyberbullying as a unique and unprecedented problem produces harm-driven expectations by identifying it as something distinctive, harmful, and worthy of attention. Nonetheless, at the time of Megan's death the term was not being invoked in a story such as hers, a story that today would undoubtedly garner a cyberbullying headline.

The year 2007 appears to have been the "tipping point" (Gladwell 2000) at which cyberbullying garnered national concern. The term was taken up in various spaces within popular culture, media, and research. A public-service campaign to end cyberbullying was launched by the Advertising

Council (in partnership with the National Crime Prevention Council, US Department of Justice, and Crime Prevention Coalition of America). The Ad Council released an anti-bullying video as part of an ongoing educational campaign. In June, the Pew Internet and American Life Project released its first report that included data about cyberbullying and online harassment of youth (Lenhart 2007). Harris Interactive, a market-research firm that tracks popular trends and releases the results of polls, published an entire newsletter about youth and cyberbullying: *Trends and Tudes*, written by Chris Moessner, the Research Director for Youth and Education (Moessner 2007). That same year, the Centers for Disease Control and Prevention described cyberbullying as an "emerging public health problem" (David-Ferdon and Hertz 2007; Hertz and David-Ferdon 2008).

There has been much research and funding directed toward "solving" cyberbullying as a social and legal problem, but it has proved particularly challenging to legally regulate for many reasons. First, regulation of inter-personal communication often infringes upon freedom of speech. Second, peer relationships transcend the liminal boundary of when schools can regulate off-campus behaviors. Third, it can be difficult to demonstrate when cyberbullying constitutes harm or presents a credible threat rather than playful teasing. Fourth, online speech is often anonymous, pseudony-mous, and/or collaborative, and thus it is difficult to identify wrongdoers. Despite the practical and legal challenges to regulation, there is a general consensus that someone ought to do something about cyberbullying. The cry intensifies every time there is another teen suicide that is allegedly the result of peer aggression, harassment, and bullying. "Cyberbullying," the legal scholar Alison King writes (2010, p. 848), "is already too grave a problem to be ignored, and it is quickly escalating with the proliferation of Internet use and the popularity of social-networking sites." Such a state-ment reveals the taken-for-granted-ness that the problem must be addressed and regulated. King goes on to declare that "the time has come for legisla-tive action" (p. 849). However, as she and other legal scholars and school administrators are well aware, the logistics of regulation are challenging. Further, it is unclear whose responsibility it is to regulate cyberbullying. Should it be the responsibility of schools, the federal government, parents, or the social media industry and its platforms?

State Laws Address Cyberbullying

To date, there are no federal anti-bullying laws. However, in April 2015, Montana became the fiftieth and final state to sign an anti-bullying bill into state law (Baumann 2015)[17]; the anti-bullying laws of all but eight of the states address cyberbullying directly. The majority of state laws address bullying at the (public) school level by describing at a minimum what (public) school district policies must address regarding bullying. The laws vary greatly, but have some similar components. Most provide a definition of bullying, but the definitions vary greatly. According to a report prepared by the US Department of Education (Stuart-Cassel, Bell, and Spring 2011, p. 25), "some state laws focus on specific actions (e.g., physical, verbal, or written), some focus on the intent or motivation of the aggressor, others focus on the degree and nature of harms that are inflicted on the victim, and many address multiple factors." Notably, such definitions are not consistent with research-based definitions of bullying, which focus on a "repeated pattern of aggressive behavior that involves an imbalance of power and that purposefully inflicts harm on the bullying victim" (ibid., p. 1). Many of the laws conflate "bullying" and "harassment," which, although similar, have different legal definitions: "Harassment is distinguishable from more general forms of bullying in that it must be motivated by characteristics of the targeted victim. It is generally viewed as a subset of more broadly defined bullying behavior. Harassment also violates federal civil rights laws as a form of unlawful discrimination" (ibid., p. 17).

Not surprisingly, there is much disagreement about whether schools can regulate student speech, particularly when it occurs off campus. Regulating student speech both on and off campus has some legal precedents,[18] but still poses challenges to students' First Amendment rights (King 2010).

Only two states (Massachusetts and Rhode Island) specify that disciplinary action must be balanced with education about appropriate behavior (Sacco et al. 2012). The state laws are overwhelmingly trending toward a legal approach that aims to punish and criminalize bullying (cyber or otherwise) rather than to address the larger social context and implications of bullying. This is consistent with the increased criminalization of youth practices and behaviors (Giroux 2009). The Department of Education reports:

Recent state legislation and policy addressing school bullying has emphasized an expanded role for law enforcement and the criminal justice system in managing bullying on school campuses. Though historically, authority over youth bullying has fallen almost exclusively under the purview of school systems, legislation governing the consequences for bullying behavior reflects a recent trend toward treating the most serious forms of bullying as criminal conduct that should be handled through the criminal justice system. ... An increasing number of states also have introduced bullying provisions into their criminal and juvenile justice codes. (Stuart-Cassel, Bell, and Spring 2011, pp. 19–20)

Similarly, the Megan Meier Cyberbullying Prevention Act (2009) took a punitive and criminalizing approach to addressing cyberbullying. In 2009, Representative Linda Sanchez (D-California) brought the legislation before the US House of Representatives, but it was not enacted. Both Democratic and Republican representatives feared the bill was too broad and would have chilling effects on free speech. The bill proposed that violations be prosecuted as a felony rather than a misdemeanor.[19] Representative Louie Gohmert (R-Texas) said the legislation "appeared to be another chapter of over-criminalization [of minors]" (Kravets 2009).

The majority of state provisions, as well as the Megan Meier bill, rely heavily on punishing bullying only after it has occurred and are unlikely to deter a would-be bully from harassing someone. We have seen that when young people are framed as social problems, they become subjects of control, surveillance, and criminalization. The focus of many of these policies is on the perpetrator, rather than the target or even the social conditions leading to bullying. Many state and school policies ignore the reality that numerous perpetrators are also victims, and thus our understanding of victim/offender is complicatedly disrupted. Within the legal framework, blame is bounced around from youth to technology to parents and to schools. This is evident when schools deny students access to sites such as MySpace, Facebook, Instagram, and YouTube, and also when parents sue school districts for failing to appropriately prevent cyberbullying incidents.[20]

Other legal scholars have proposed amending the Communications Decency Act in order to hold ISPs and website administrators (collectively referred to as Online Service Providers or OSPs) responsible for facilitating bullying via their services and platforms. King (2010) suggests creating a notification system in which OSPs would be required to remove defamatory content. The process King proposes would function similarly to the "safe harbor" provision of the Digital Millennium Copyright Act (DMCA), which holds service providers liable for material that infringes upon copyright law only if they are made aware of the material. King argues that OSPs need "a legal incentive to combat cyberbullying that occurs by means of their services." Since the publication of King's article, we have seen many social media platforms implement anti-harassment policies (as part of their Community Standards and Terms of Service agreements) and enable users to report violations of the harassment policies (Rubin, Sawyer, and Taye 2015). It is up to the discretion of platforms as to whether or not they will remove the content or ban the user, but there are nonetheless mechanisms in place for reporting inappropriate content and users in cases of harassment and bullies. Such forms of regulation are not the results of legal liability so much as they are industry self-regulation driven by economic incentives. If users regularly have negative encounters on a particular platform, or if enough parents and adults hear about negative encounters, users are likely to leave that particular site altogether, which in turn has a negative economic impact on the site. As van Dijck (2013) argues, social media platforms have an economic incentive to enhance (safe) sociality. Social media platforms' anti-harassment policies are an example of how social norms and the market often work together to incentivize industry self-regulation as opposed to heavy-handed legal action from the state.

This brings me to my final point about the legal regulation of cyberbullying, which is that the criminalization of youth behavior addresses the symptoms, but not the causes, of bullying. Rarely do the policies address mental health and the social conditions of the school climate that perpetuate power imbalances, social hierarchies, intolerance, and bullying in the first place. One policy that stands out as an exception is the 2009 Student Internet Safety Bill.[21] The bill, proposed by Representative Adam Putnam (R-Florida), would have allowed school districts to use federal funds to "educate their students about appropriate online behavior, including interacting with individuals on social networking Web sites and in chat rooms. They could also use the funds to protect students against online predators, cyberbullying, or unwanted exposure to inappropriate materials, or promote involvement by parents in the use of the Internet by their children" (source: Representative Cathy McMorris Rodgers' testimony before the House of Representatives, retrieved from *Congressional Record* for June 15, 2009). The proposed bill took an educational approach and offered funding for education. One criticism of many state bullying laws is that they require schools to create policies and curriculum, but do little in the way of funding research, policies, and curriculum (Sacco et al. 2012). The burden rests on already strained school districts to fund such policies. Unfortunately, the Student Internet Safety Bill died in the Senate (after it was passed unanimously by the House).

Problematically absent from most discussions of cyberbullying are larger discourses of social hierarchies, mental health, race, gender, class, and sexuality. Discourses organize the social world in such a way as to make certain aspects of problems seem relevant: our focus is frequently on what is happening, who it is happening to, and how we can punish it, but rarely are we overtly addressing *why* it is happening in the first place. or why some targets of bullying are less equipped to cope or seek help. Over the past eight years, conversations about cyberbullying have productively moved away from overly blaming technology (although technology remains heavily regulated and banned in many schools). Technology exacerbates the problem and presents new challenges, but we have come to a better understanding of the ways cyberbullying is merely an old problem with a new and more persistent, instantaneous, and intensified face. What is seldom discussed within conversations about regulation is the overt prevalence of homophobic, sexist, and ableist nature of bullying that is so common among reported cyberbullying incidences. We know that young LGBTQ people are significantly more likely to be bullied and harassed than their heterosexual and cisgender peers and are four times as likely to commit suicide (Bullying and LGBT Youth 2009), yet these variations are not often accounted for in news reports addressing bullying. In fact, Hasinoff (2015, p. 8) points out that media repeatedly overlook stories involving people of color and queer youth when they are victims of crime, instead such mainstream discourses focus on "the benevolent but misplaced desire to protect the supposedly inherent sexual innocence of white middle-class girls."

The larger questions of diversity and tolerance (or lack thereof) remain unaddressed in far too much of the cyberbullying discourse. Perhaps one reason is that addressing the *why* of bullying draws attention away from the controllable behaviors of young people and shifts attention toward an adult society that teaches and socializes young people to be racist, homophobic, sexist, and ableist in the first place. Additionally, cyberbullying is largely constructed as an individualized problem (often constructed as an individual pathology), rather than as symptomatic of larger social, cultural, and collective issues that extend beyond individuals. Cyberbullying is constructed as a problem of the young (never mind that Megan Meier's bully was an adult); however, a 2014 Pew study found that 40 percent of adult Internet users have experienced some form of online harassment (Duggan 2014). The problem is significantly greater for women, who disproportionately experience gender-based online harassment (Chemaly 2014; Duggan 2014), which is becoming an "established norm" (Hunt 2016). These numbers are strikingly similar to the numbers of young people who report being bullied online. Notably, Pew used the word "harassment" in its survey of adults. Although Pew may have done so because of the legal definition of harassment, it also highlights the juvenile connotations of the word "bully," a word that further signifies a "youth" problem.

As long as cyberbullying remains an individualized "youth problem," it can be subjected to collective control and management, and young people can be simultaneously blamed and protected within legal discourse. But the moment the problem becomes a larger societal problem, the blame must be (at least partially) placed on adults' racist, sexist, ableist, and homophobic attitudes—attitudes that cannot be controlled through criminalization. Young people have become scapegoats onto whom larger social anxieties are displaced and whose behaviors society places under control and surveillance. Cyberbullying discourses distract us from larger racist, sexist, and homophobic discourses that cannot be so easily disciplined and reify harm-driven expectations of youth and technology.

The Problem with Sexting

Sexting—broadly defined as digitally producing, distributing, and/or consuming sexually suggestive, nude, or explicit images of oneself or one's peers—is an appropriate conclusion to a discussion of panics and policies.[22] Not only is sexting the subject of the most recent panic to gain national attention, but it combines all three aforementioned anxieties: it incites fears of pornography (particularly of underage female teens), of predators (who coerce young people to engage in activities to produce images), and of bullying (in which peers distribute images without permission in order to shame or harass an individual). As with the previously discussed panics, there are valid risks and legitimate harms that can accompany sexting. There are incidences in which young people are coerced into producing sexual images against their will and are blackmailed, harassed, or abused. These instances are never justifiable and often constitute physical, emotional, and/or sexual abuse as defined by the law and breach psychological and emotional understandings of autonomy. However, the purpose of this section is to consider the practices of older teens who willingly produce and share sexually suggestive and explicit images with a (would-be) romantic partner. The former examples are inexcusable and often criminal, but the latter warrant a deeper understanding of youth agency, sexuality, privacy, and consent.

As with the Communications Decency Act, the porn panic, the Deleting Online Predators Act, and the predator panic, we are again witnessing data being used as scare tactics. Depending where you look, there are numbers reporting that 20 percent of teens have sent or received a sext (Knorr 2010). However, other studies have found a mere 7 percent of teens have sent or received a sexually explicit photo and only 1 percent of those potentially violated child pornography laws (Mitchell, Finkelhor, Jones, and Wolak 2012). These numbers are a far cry from the "sexting ring scandals" the media present as commonplace and that have contributed to a moral panic (Bryner 2012; Fields 2014; Rosin 2014; Searcey 2009). Contrary to the picture the media present, the majority of teens are not producing and sharing random sexual images, but are doing so in the context of trusting relationships (Hasinoff 2015; Mitchell, Finkelhor, Jones, and Wolak 2012). The discrepancy between reality and panic is attributable in part to vague definitions of what constitutes sexting, discrepancies between adult and teen norms, and teens' reluctance to disclose private sexual practices with adult researchers.

In the second of the epigraphs at the beginning of this chapter, Major Donald Lowe, the investigator of the Louisa County sexting scandal,[23] describes teen girls as culprits who had "victimized themselves" via sexting. The public distribution (via Instagram) of sexts from teens at the school caught national attention with the headline "Police bust Virginia sexting ring involving more than 100 teens" (Fields 2014). The headline presented the story as though the teens had been involved in some sort of organized crime ring. The girls were shamed through public reactions, including online comments that included gendered epithets such as "slut," "ho," and "tramp." Other reactions called for legal prosecution; it was suggested that the teens should be charged with the production, possession, and distribution of child pornography. The quotation from Major Lowe draws attention to our need to rethink discourses of youth when laws that are intended to protect minors are also used to prosecute and harm them. With sexting there is not always a clear victim or offender, and in many cases the "victims" may not identify as such if their practices were consensual and deliberate and when the images were not circulated outside of the intended context.

Laws pertaining to child pornography are intended to protect young people from sexual exploitation. However, as we have seen with many media stories about sexting —and as teens themselves report—sexting can be a part of a consensual and deliberate sexual practice among peers. It is a way for some teens to explore their sexuality, arouse interest and desire, flirt, and express intimacy (Hasinoff 2015). It is inherently problematic that most states acknowledge older teens' right to make decisions about engaging in sexual activities[24] and yet simultaneously condemn youth for recording those very same sexual practices they legally engage in. Certainly it can be a challenge to legally specify intent (Sacco 2012), but laws that automatically criminalize teen sexting are derived from harm-driven expectations that are based on the assumption that sexting innately and inevitably results in harm. Criminalizing sexting can actually do more harm than good. Instead of protecting young people, which is the goal and purpose of the law, criminalization labels a minor as a sex offender. I agree with

Hasinoff's argument that "ensuring that adolescents have the right to sext is the most effective way to protect them from these kinds of unfair prosecutions" (2012, p. 161). The legal right to sext within consensual relationships and within particular circumstances grants teens protection from unnecessary criminalization.

I struggle with restrictive and all-encompassing policies that monolithically construct all minors, from toddlers to high school students, as a singular legal category that ignores developmental, emotional, and cultural differentiations. Policies that aim to restrict minors' digital access (whether to pornography or to sexting) in the name of preventing harm have to rely on a stereotypical image of the innocent "child"—an image we can normatively agree deserves protection. However, such an image erases the agentive and coming-of-age teenager from our collective understanding of minors. Harm-driven expectations problematically conflate the legal status of a minor with the fluid cultural and discursive constructions of "child," "youth," and "adult." Consequently, such a monolithic approach falsely constructs a uniform understanding of "risk and harm" and "child and youth." Conflated discursive constructions are produced by and reflective of harm-driven expectations of technology and rely on a reification of (white middle-class) youth as inherently innocent.

With sexting, a minor as both a victim and an offender disrupts our discursive understandings of youth because young people's exploration of sexuality cannot be encapsulated by a child/adult or innocent/knowledge binary. Fleur Gabriel (2013, p. 105) writes: "Popular discourses on sexualisation, however, rely more on traditional and Romantic assumptions about childhood and youth in responding to sexualisation debates, seeing them as naturally innocent and therefore rightly lacking sexual knowledge." Policies that label all sexting practices as deviant, harmful, and pornographic leave no space for the deliberate and consensual ways young people explore their sexuality as part of a healthy developmental process. Gabriel (ibid., p. 106) argues that coming-of-age narratives are problematic discursive constructions of youth because they rely on false binaries between innocence/knowledge and child/adult: "Young people are called to 'come of age,' yet I argue that this concept of youth is grounded in a contradictory logic that produces conflicting aims: a desire to preserve the innocence of youth and a simultaneous expectation that they 'grow up.'" If childhood is about the preservation of innocence (or lack of knowledge and experience), then any exposure to knowledge—or in this case, expression of sexuality that transcends legal definitions of minors—is considered an assault on said innocence. Youth is a transition from childhood to adulthood, and that transition involves a loss of innocence. As a society we normatively agree that children need to "grow up," yet there is much debate, anxiety, and concern about how and when it is appropriate for youth to "grow up." "The discourse of 'coming of age,'" Gabriel further explains (p. 110), "describes something that is supposed to happen given the values and structures of modern society, but which at the same time is *prevented* from happening by those very structures." Growing up inevitably leads to a loss of innocence, or rather the acquisition of knowledge and experience, including explorations of one's own sexuality. This framing de-sensationalizes sexting and instead considers it as an optional aspect of healthy sexual exploration.

Debates that regulate or prohibit all sexting practices are similar to Judge Lowell Reed's remarks about pornography—should we outright deny young people rights they later inherit as adults? There are major distinctions between (a) adults coercing young people into sexual activities or adults consuming images of minors outside of a context in which the image was intended to be shared and (b) young people willingly producing and sharing images with peers, particularly within the context of a romantic relationship. Hasinoff (2015, p. 140) argues that "erasing consent is particularly problematic when legal and school officials completely ignore malicious behavior and choose to instead punish everyone involved [in sexting] equally." She argues, and I concur, that we must move toward an explicit model of consent for everyone, and that "scholars, policymakers, technology developers, and users alike should adopt an explicit consent standard for the production, distribution, or possession of private media and information [including sexting]" (ibid., p. 139). This model also deviates from harm-driven expectations by considering the intent, consent, and agency of teens' practices, rather than presuming an inevitable outcome of harm.

Peer Culture and Social Norms

As with cyberbullying, what we need is an evolution of norms. Laws are important and have a role in shaping practices, but they are insufficient in and of themselves. An analogy to drunk driving is appropriate. We certainly need laws that regulate drunk driving; however, by nature such laws can only ever be reactive—that is, they punish only after a person drives drunk. Social norms play an important proactive preventative role in changing attitudes about drunk driving. Two successful campaigns have transformed cultural attitudes about driving drunk: the 1988 "Designate a driver" campaign (Harvard Alcohol Project 1988) and the Ad Council's 1983 "Friends don't let friends drive drunk" campaign (Drunk Driving Prevention 1983). The former offers something proactive for people to do; it shifts from a restrictive approach (i.e., don't drive drunk) to an affirmative tactic (i.e., designate someone to drive). The latter encourages a culture of peer accountability that extends beyond the realm of the law to encourage an attitude change about the acceptability of drunk driving. The message "Friends don't let friends drive drunk" was frequently incorporated into popular television shows such as *Cheers*, *L.A. Law*, and *The Cosby Show* (Winsten 2010). Incorporating the messages into pop culture is a powerful strategy for changing norms and attitudes. These examples did not rely on scare tactics related to drunk driving (graphic images, harrowing statistics, and so on), but rather shaped new norms about drinking responsibly. Both campaigns have been considered successful in changing cultural attitudes about inebriated driving in the United States and have contributed to a decline in alcohol-related accidents (Harvard Alcohol Project 1988; Winsten 2010). Both rely on social norms, rather than the law, as a mode of regulation. Similarly, we should think about how schools, parents, media, and young people can work together to shift cultural norms and attitudes about sexting, privacy, and consent. And importantly, these strategies must move past archaic gendered stereotypes that shame teenage girls for their sexuality and instead contextualize sexting within larger understandings and norms of consent, agency, privacy, and sexual education.

Conclusion: Implications of Fear-Based Regulation

This chapter has demonstrated how discourses of risk—often fueled by fallacious and exaggerated data—work alongside harm-driven expectations to incite anxiety and justify control. No matter how misleading or overblown the claims about porn, predators, cyberbullying, and sexting are, harm-driven expectations have power. As Stuart Hall aptly articulates (1997, p. 49), "Knowledge linked to power, not only assumes the authority of 'the truth' but has the power to *make itself true*. All knowledge, once applied in the real world, has real effects, and in that sense at least, 'becomes true.' Knowledge, once used to regulate the conduct of others, entails constraint, regulation and the disciplining of practices." It does not matter if there is conclusive evidence proving the Internet presents an increased risk of harm, because the notion of adolescents at risk and the construction of the Internet as a dangerous space have already been "made true" via discourses of "knowledge." Moral panics are vehicles for harm-driven expectations and work to produce and mobilize particular discourses of risk and to distract from other risks, harms, and concerns.

This chapter has demonstrated at least some of the implications of constructing the Internet as dangerous and youth at risk—constructions that are used to justify policies of panic. These overly restrictive policies are derived from expectations of harm and ignore the positive opportunities associated with learning to navigate risks. Through an analysis of policies aimed at regulating young people's online participation over the past twenty years, I have argued that risk discourse protects against some risks at the expense of other competing values and opportunities, privileges particular youth populations, and fails to prepare youth to safely navigate risk and positive opportunities.

The reliance on statistics and "expert" opinions brings certain risks to the forefront of public attention and functions as truth, even when the information is misleading or inaccurate. In and of itself this is not particularly harmful; however, a focus on sensationalized harms diverts attention, research, and resources away from more serious threats to the safety and well-being of youth. Research consistently demonstrates that we cannot blame the Internet for most of the crimes committed against youth, and there is even evidence to suggest that technology makes young people safer. Yet harm-driven expectations provide justification for restrictive policies that exert control and surveillance over young people's practices, speech, and movements, all the while ignoring broader contextual variables that lead to harm. Discourses of risk—even in the absence of demonstrable harm—are used to sublimate other rights, including freedom of speech, access to educational content, and a recognition and validation of young people's emerging sexuality, autonomy, and agency. The old adage "safety first" is circulated as a normative value that is never supposed to be questioned. Safety is important, but notions of risk must always be questioned. We must never fail to recognize that risks do not objectively exist "out there," but are always socially produced through mechanisms of identification, categorization, and propagation by institutions of power. We ought to strive for policies that minimize harms *and* protect young people's legal rights, values, and agency.

A second takeaway from this chapter is that policies of panic that ban technology are unlikely to actually protect youth from harm; instead their function is to reify boundaries between child and adult as a way to protect perceptions of childhood innocence. As was noted, conversations that demand public attention are often dictated by the concerns of the privileged. The law professor Mary Anne Franks (2015) rightfully points out that recent concerns about online privacy draw attention to the fact that the poor, people of color, and criminals have historically been subjected to privacy violations daily, and that violations of their privacy have been largely ignored.[25] Franks argues that if we as a society really cared about privacy violations—as we claim to every time we feel a social media platform has invaded our privacy—then we would have had these conversations about privacy much sooner. She makes a convincing case that members of the privileged middle-class and predominantly white society do not actually care about privacy as a universally protected right until our *own* comforts are invaded. In a similar way, panics and restrictive policies about pornography, sexually explicit content, bullying, and sexting also reflect a privileged understanding of risk and are most concerned with protecting privileged populations. Particular marginalized youth populations have always been at risk of violence, sexual exploitation, and predation, yet their stories garner little attention from media or policy, and they struggle to receive the resources they need to alleviate these risks. This same population faces additional risks of hunger, poverty, and incarceration, but their stories—and the proposed solutions—go largely ignored. When their stories are told, it is often through a lens that constructs the victims themselves as a social problem, rather than the systematic injustices or perpetrator. Thus we come to expect that such youth must be controlled, surveilled, and contained rather than protected.

The panics discussed in this chapter demonstrate that risks become visible only when they threaten otherwise protected and privileged young people, who do not fit the stereotypical image of "at-risk" populations. When privileged young people are perceived to be threated, their stories gain attention and concern. This is evident when parents and teachers speak to what a "good kid" a victim or an offender is, or how they are "surprised this could happen to their child" (Thiel-Stern 2014). News coverage emphasized how Megan Meier's parents did "everything right." Such rhetoric is largely absent when "at-risk" youth are subjected to harm; instead they are likely to be blamed or held responsible for any harm they encounter. The policies that have been explored in this chapter demonstrate how online risk and harm have been shaped by middle-class understandings of protection and innocence and how technology and youth become discursive sites for governmental intervention and control.

Both of these implications—drawing attention to sensationalized harms and protecting childhood innocence—lead to the third takeaway from this chapter's harm-driven policy analysis: the failure to equip young people with the resources and education to safely navigate risk. There is inherent risk in everything we do. Banning social media will not eliminate the risk of exposure to unwanted pornography, sexual predation, or peer aggression. If our goal is to eliminate risk, we will fail every single time. And even if we could craft a policy that eliminated all these risks by denying young people access to particular content or websites, young people would still lose these regulatory and restrictive protections when they turn 18 and gain the constitutional rights of adults. And how then could we expect them to be prepared for the inevitable risks they will eventually face? Youth is a time of learning and preparing for adulthood, and that means helping young people identify and navigate risks, not avoid them.

As an alternative approach, opportunity-driven expectations recognize our responsibility as a society to help young people identify and assess risk. Regulations that move beyond minimizing risk to balance and expand opportunities will help young people make decisions about which risks are potentially beneficial and worthwhile and which decisions are not. As will be discussed in the following chapters, an educational approach recognizes and values young people's desires and experiences by building trusting relationships with adults who, rather than look over their shoulder, "have their back" (to paraphrase from Jenkins 2007). This approach validates the experiences and expertise of educators and school districts to discern the appropriate measure of guidance for their students. Opportunity-driven expectations do not construct a monolithic view of youth, but instead account for variations within different communities, developmental stages, and experiences. Opportunity-driven expectations balance risk by crafting regulations that simultaneously expand opportunities for positive experiences and minimize exposure to harm. Safety should not be polarized as the opposite of risk; rather, a discourse of safety must strive to separate risk from harm and to help young people learn to navigate positive and negative opportunities by respecting their experiences, their values, and their rights.

The rest of the book examines how discursive understandings of risk and harm-driven expectations shape local policies and practices. These prevailing fears—porn, predators, and peer interactions—dominate public imagination, conversation, resources, and policies. However, what effect does this narrative have on the lived experiences of actual young people? Such a question is particularly challenging to answer when we remember that many policies are predicated on insubstantial claims and assumptions of harm in the first place. Equally as important, what are the other risks and harms that are subsumed by these visible and attention-demanding discourses? To answer these questions, I explore the unintentional consequences of the Children's Internet Protection Act at Freeway High in order to examine how the policy actually exacerbates some risks. I then address the second question: What else might we be concerned with—that is, what risks are rendered invisible as a result of these media-fueled panics? It is far more attention-grabbing to discuss and worry about porn, predators, bullies, and sexting than it is to concern ourselves with the intensification of social inequities. But we must address those inequities if we want to create a safe and equitable digital world for all young people—a world in which risks are minimized regardless of privilege and opportunities are maximized across all populations.

3 Access Denied: Information, Knowledge, and Literacy

It's weird what sites are blocked and which aren't when I think about. ... They have this whole list of sites that you can't go to. If you try to go to them it says "Access denied." Even when they're useful sites, like tutorials and things you look up for school or need for a project, nope.

Anna (18 years old, Mexican-American)

Schools undoubtedly have an obligation and responsibility to protect students and ensure safe learning environments. In compliance with the Children's Internet Protection Act (see chapter 2), Freeway High enables a firewall that heavily regulates students' (and most of the time teachers') access to online content. The firewall blocks access to websites deemed inappropriate or harmful. This includes sexually explicit content (porn, nudity, and so on), but also educational sexual resources (e.g., resources related to contraception and to sexually transmitted infections). Additionally, the firewall blocks both students' and teachers' access to all online videos. Sites such as YouTube are blocked entirely, whereas CNN and local news broadcast stations are accessible, but the embedded videos are blocked. The school also blocks students' access to Facebook, Instagram, Twitter, and other social media platforms. Images on sites are blocked if the filter deems them inappropriate; this includes all nudity even artistic renderings of the human body (e.g., Michelangelo's *David*) and human anatomy, even in the context of sex education (with the exception of some pre-approved sites). Other sites are blocked on the basis of violence or derogatory language. All these sites are blocked in compliance with federal laws based on the premise that they reduce exposure to risky or harmful material, but are actually executed at the discretion of commercial firewall services. Filters reveal expectations of risk, and thus I want to step back and analyze the embedded assumptions about what kinds of content are deemed harmful and what kinds of content are not.

The central debate over technology use at Freeway High is, on the surface, about access—who can access technology when, where, why, how, and for what purposes. On the one hand, the policies appear to be restrictive and to stem from harm-driven expectations; on the other hand, the school's curriculum stems from opportunity-driven expectations that enhance learning. The students of Freeway High are largely from low-income families, and the school is dependent upon E-rate discounts for telecommunication services; this means it is required to enable firewalls that block students from accessing information deemed inappropriate. Consequently, the effects of federal policies, such as the Children's Internet Protection Act, play a role in shaping harm-driven expectations and enacting risk-minimizing practices. Filters, in addition to bans on mobile devices (see chapter 4), work in tandem to construct technology as a risk or threat that must be regulated and controlled. However, alongside prohibitive policies, the school also provides students with opportunities to attain and enhance their technology skills. Freeway High provides several computer labs with up-to-date equipment and software, offers several technology courses, and financially supports after-school digital media clubs (see chapters 5 and 7). Thus, at the other end of the spectrum, we see opportunity-driven expectations via practices that support—and even celebrate—technology as a creative and vocational opportunity for students. In view of the contradictory messages "technology is harmful" and "technology is an opportunity," it is understandable that students are frustrated by the policies and practices that regulate access to and use of technology at school.

In this chapter I map out the ways harm-driven expectations about media and technology shape the policies, discourses, and contours of everyday practices at Freeway High. I also analyze the school's approach to incorporating media literacy as part of the formal curriculum (as opposed to the informal learning that occurs in the after-school spaces, which is the focus of chapters 5 and 7). I argue that the school should expand its definition of digital literacy beyond skills—and beyond basic understandings of information literacy—to also incorporate and value *critical digital literacy*. Harm-driven expectations approach technology as something that must be controlled and contained. As I will demonstrate, the school focuses on helping students avoid risk, rather than helping them to manage it. What is particularly significant here is not just the import of managing risk but also the missed opportunities to develop nuanced critical digital literacies. Rather than overly worrying about the risks that technology poses, educational institutions should worry about how to also effectively and equitably equip students to manage risks and capitalize on the opportunities of digital media and technology. Likewise, schools must consider how technology can mitigate other risks. This necessitates a shift in what we expect from students and schools—a move away from expectations of harm and misuse toward expectations of responsibility, value, and learning.

Threats of Sexual Risk

It is a normative modern value in the United States to protect young people from premature exposure to sexual content and information (Heins 2001). Within collective popular imagination, young people are discursively constructed as being sexually innocent and pure, and so exposure to sexual content—or even acknowledging young people's potential sexuality—is often deemed inappropriate and damaging (Heins 2001; Odem 1995). From such a perspective, filtering access to sexual information on the Internet is an appropriate strategy for protecting and reifying young people's perceived sexual innocence. However, this rhetoric is complicated when students begin to develop their own sexuality and sexual identities. By high school, the majority of students have begun to explore and negotiate their own sexuality—including their desires, identities, values, and practices. What are the consequences of denying pubescent adolescents access to sexual information online? Yes, schools have a responsibility to protect students, but at the same time they also have an obligation to teach students about sexual health and consensual practices. Harm-driven expectations construct protection *from* sexuality as a normative value that trumps students' acknowledgment of their own sexualities and their *right* to access educational sexual resources. Risk discourse presumes that access to sexual information is a threat and is therefore harmful, when in actuality access to sexual education is a form of protection that empowers young people to make healthy and safe decisions.

The state of Texas implements an abstinence-only approach to sex education—an approach that has been highly criticized by parents, students, physicians, and federal lawmakers (Bridges 2008; Kohler, Manhart, and Laggerty 2008; Trenholm et al. 2007). It has been criticized on moral and ethical grounds, and also because of its continued ineffectiveness (ibid.). According to the Centers for Disease Control and Prevention, 52 percent of Texas high school students are sexually active, versus 47 percent nationally. Consequently, abstinence-only education seems to do little to deter Texas high school students from engaging in sexual activities

(HIV, other STD, and pregnancy prevention education … 2012). What is troubling is not necessarily that teens are sexually active, but rather the risky behaviors associated with their sexual practices. Texas ranks third in the nation in rate of teen pregnancy[1] and has the nation's highest teen birth rate[2] (Bridges 2008). Further, Texas has the third highest number of people living with HIV, and young people accounted for 20 percent of new HIV cases in Texas in 2006 (ibid.). Additionally, young people in Texas—especially young women—are at a high risk for contracting sexually trans-mitted infections, the majority of all chlamydia and gonorrhea infections affect young women (Texas HIV/STD surveillance report, 2014). There are many more harrowing statistics about the sexual risks Texas teens face. The point here is that many teens in Texas are not practicing safe sex. In view of the lack of education in public schools this should not be too surprising, but it should be alarming.

Teen sex is a complicated issue, and many factors such as economics, education, geography, religious affiliations, and ethnicity affect access to sexual health resources, yet we must also take into consideration the lack of comprehensive sex-education courses in public schools in Texas. By law, Texas sex-education courses may not include information about contracep-tives or condoms, and must teach that sex outside of marriage is shameful and financially, physically, and psychologically harmful (Culp-Ressler 2013). This approach has not been supported by research or science and fails to educate and empower young people to make safe sexual decisions. Further, it promotes a heteronormative understanding of sexuality that completely overlooks the sexual desires, identities, and practices of queer youth. Texas is one of seven states that prohibit positive portrayals of homosexuality in schools (Ford 2014). The state-mandated educational materials go so far as to state that homosexuality is "not an acceptable life-style and is a criminal offense" (Texas Health and Safety Code). In practice such language is rarely used; however, it is indicative of the overall approach to controlling teens' access to comprehensive knowledge and education regarding sex and sexuality.

If teens are not receiving medically effective and scientifically accurate information about sexual health at school, where then do they turn for information? Research indicates that almost 80 percent of US teens report talking to a parent about at least one aspect of sexual education, including how to say No (Martinez, Abma, and Casey 2010). Research also reveals that these conversations do not necessarily include accurate information about contraception and safe sexual practices (Eisenberg et al. 2004). Teens also report that peers and the media are popular sources of sexual information (Brown, Steele, and Walsh-Childers 2011). Data indicate that teens frequently turn to the media, including advertisements, television, magazines, and the Internet, for information about birth control and protection against infection. Not surprisingly, the Internet has become a more frequent source of information for young people regarding sexual health; 89 percent of young people cited the Internet as a top source of sexual health information in 2011 (Boyar, Levine, and Zensisus 2011). By contrast, only 20 percent of respondents in a different study cited formal education in schools as a primary source of sexual health information (Brown 2008).

Balancing Protection and Access

What does all of this have to do with Internet filters at Freeway High? What these numbers—and far too many other statistics like them—demonstrate is that many teens are sexually active in high school, yet they are at risk of unwanted pregnancies and infections due at least in part to a lack of education and safety strategies. What is actually risky in these scenarios is unsafe teen sexual practices, *not* access to sexual health information. The presumed risk of accessing unwanted or harmful sexual content online often goes unchallenged outside of debates about First Amendment rights. Since the passage of CIPA, it has become largely acceptable to deny students access to sexual content on school computers. We should challenge the normative assumption that access to sexual content is inherently harmful. What we ought to be discussing are ways schools can intervene and promote safer sexual practices.

The school's firewall does not block all sexual health information (some sites—such as the Center for Disease Control and WebMD—are allowed), but plenty of other sites are blocked because of explicit sexual content. This is particularly true of user-generated message boards and other peer-based sites where students search for sexual information that transcends basic health questions. Because many students at Freeway High come from low-income households and face precarious living situations, they do not have consistent high-quality access to the Internet outside of school; a significant portion of the student body relies on the school's free Wi-Fi and public computers for access to the Internet. If school is the primary source of Internet access and schools block access to sex-ed content, then some students face significant challenges in accessing information and support regarding questions of sexual identity and health.

It should go without saying that there is inappropriate sexual information online; however, search engines have their own filters that can be activated to block the explicit sexual content without filtering sexual content to the same restrictive degree as the school's firewall. It is possible that a student would deliberately seek out obscene content at school, but it is also reasonable that the majority of students seeking information would be driven by healthy sexual curiosity and a need for information. District-approved sites such as WebMD and the site of the Centers for Disease Control provide medically accurate and important information about sexual health but do not include information about social norms of sexuality or offer a generationally specific understanding of emerging sexuality. Teens often seek answers about sexual desires and norms in private (Kanuga and Rosenfeld 2004), and could feasibly access such information on a school computer after school (in semi-private) if the filters did not block access to these kinds of websites. In her ethnographic research about queer youth in rural America, Mary Gray (2009) found that queer teens turned to the Internet to not only seek out health information but also to express and learn about their sexual desires and queer identities. These kinds of information seeking practices connected queer teens to supportive online communities that were often not available in their offline lives. The kinds of information, questions, and communities that teens seek extend beyond health information, but also include learning about and participating in a shared discourse of generationally specific sexual identification, practices, language, values, and norms.

Rather than banning sexual content at school, administrators could establish a set of rules and address violations—such as accessing pornography—on a case-by-case basis. For example, according to the education scholar Mark Prensky (2008, p. 44), schools "can address the 'inappropriate use' issue, particularly in the higher grades, with one simple rule: If something comes on the screen that a student knows shouldn't be there, he or she has two seconds to shut off the computer—or lose all privileges." This rule shifts harm-driven expectations away from outright control and instead places responsibly on the student to make smart decisions and earn privileges through a dialog of trust. This approach echoes Jada's (16 years old, black) own frustrations with and understanding of the filter rules at school:

Q: Do you find the school blocks things that would be helpful?

Jada: Sometimes, yes. It's frustrating.

Q: Things that aren't distracting or bad, but just things you need to look up are blocked?

Jada: Yeah. It upsets me a lot.

Q: Why does it upset you?

Jada: I think we're just older—it's one thing for middle school to block stuff, but we're in high school. You're still going to have people who try to look up stuff that's inappropriate, but we're older. Just punish that one person's privileges.

Obscene material could continue to be blocked, while other sexual content could be allowed. If a student violates rules by intentionally accessing obscene material, they could be disciplined, just as they would be for breaking other school rules. This approach protects opportunities for teens to seek out sexual information and acknowledges and safeguards their highly contested First Amendment rights. The court has acknowledged that "minors are entitled to a significant measure of First Amendment protection" and that the "state may not prohibit a minor's right to speech based alone upon a belief that the content is unsuitable (McLaughlin 2012, p. 337). Yet CIPA regulations and the implementation of commercial firewalls bar students from accessing sexual content on school computers or networks that they legally should have the right to access. The filtering of content is predicated on the assumption that sexual content does not merely pose a risk, but is inherently harmful. When I asked students in personal interviews if they would ask a teacher to unblock an informative website that was filtered for sexual reasons, the answer was an unsurprising and resounding No, citing embarrassment as the primary reason. Students' rights to speech are often undermined in the name of protection, yet students are disempowered from claiming stake to these basic rights.

Providing teens with a space in which to learn about their sexual preferences, identities, and practices can help mitigate the risks associated with sexual behaviors. There is no research indicating that mere *access* to sexual content increases risk or harm to teens at school, yet there is ample research indicating that lack of education increases sexual risk and harm (McGrath 2004). We need a discursive turn away from protecting youth from sex. Instead we must embrace a discourse that empowers youth to manage risk via greater access to information and education. Access to accurate online sexual content in and of itself is not necessarily harmful, but ignorance about one's own sexual health and desires is.

Information Overload

The web provides young people with unprecedented access to a seemingly endless amount of information and students need help navigating the

overwhelming amount of information they can access. With peer file sharing, user-generated forums, live up-to-date streaming of information in the
form of videos, Twitter feeds, blogs, and professionally produced news and
op-eds, the web allows students to seek and find answers to a multitude of
questions. In fact, it is downright impossible to even attempt to keep up
with all of the information constantly being added to the web—nor would
it be beneficial. As of 2015, YouTube reported that users uploaded 400 hours
of content to the site per minute (Robertson 2015)! As of 2013, there were
41,000 Facebook posts added per second and 3,600 photos added to Instagram in that same amount of time (Woollason 2013). Per minute there were
20,000 Tumblr photos posted, 278,000 tweets sent, and an astonishing 571
new websites created (ibid.). That is a lot of information, more than we can
possibly find, read, and absorb.

Experts argue that so much information can be both a positive and a
negative thing. On the one hand, some critics are concerned about the
harms of what has been dubbed "information overload" (Bawden and
Robinson 2009; Freedland 2013; Hemp 2009; Himma 2007). Some experts
worry about the potential risks or harms of being exposed to too much
information in an "always on" world. If you do a quick Internet search for
"information overload" you will find a seemingly unending stream of articles warning adults about the "real danger for children [who] feel like they
are drowning in this torrent of information" (Taylor 2012). On the other
end of the spectrum, you'll find claims that young people are "immune to
information overload" and that "younger people just don't feel as weighed
down by their digital-centric lives [as adults]" (Murphy 2010). What we are
experiencing is a debate about and an expansion of our conception of
what constitutes information. In today's networked society, information
includes traditional conceptions of knowledge and opinions that are generated by reliable expert sources. But today's media ecology also includes
user-generated content, social media streams, and up-to-date news about
what our peers are doing across multiple platforms at any given moment.
In the past, this form of mediated information about peers primarily
resided within the realm of social information which was accessed via
interpersonal communication, such as making a phone call or writing a
letter. But today, factual news and information coexist alongside streams
of social information in a way that some experts fear we might not be
equipped to handle unless we intentionally develop digital literacies that
help us make sense of new modes of information (Rheingold 2012).

The media scholars Jenkins, Ito, and boyd remind us that a shift in the
concept and amount of information is not unprecedented; previous

generations also experienced a radical shift in access to and production of technology, media, social lives, and information:

There's a dangerous tendency to talk about these experiences of media change and information overload as if this had never happened before. We might productively go and look at the turn of the twentieth century, when an explosion of mass media was impacting American life, urban areas were experiencing the introduction of electric lights, signs and billboards cluttered the landscape for the first time. ... Progressive-era writers described people as overwhelmed by information, unable to keep pace with the changes. There were so many signs and so much noise and so much to take in. People talked about sensory overload. (2016, p. 100)

Yet as individuals, and as a society, we have survived. We have developed techniques, norms, and strategies that allow us to navigate new environments in collectively beneficial ways. This has not come without growing pains, without loss, or with equal consequences for all populations, but we have adapted and even thrived amid great change. Even those who argue that too much information can have negative influences probably would agree that, on the whole, more access to more information is positive progress—we just have to learn how to manage it. This is where school plays a significant role in the lives of students today.

Educators have a responsibility to help young people develop healthy boundaries and critical digital literacy. Yet research indicates that pressure to "teach to the examination" prevents some teachers from incorporating digital and information literacy into the classroom. Teachers are pressured to pass along information (so students can pass state-mandated standardized tests), rather than help students solve problems and seek out information on their own (Julien and Barker 2009). At Freeway High, digital literacy was primarily compartmentalized as a component of courses that explicitly taught technology skills. However, from a research and problem-solving approach to learning, critical digital literacy skills can be incorporated into virtually any subject or classroom. Incorporating digital literacy in the classroom necessitates a move away from harm-driven expectations that perpetuate a discourse of control (and thus purport to minimize risk) and toward an attitude that embraces student-driven learning in a networked society.

Traditional learning has focused on passing along information from teacher to student or pointing students toward books and classroom resources. However, a critical digital literacy approach encourages and empowers students to seek out information in the classroom in a similar way that they do outside of school: by asking peers for help or using search engines or video tutorials to solve problems and find answers (Ito et al.

2010; Tapscott 1998). There is a risk that a student could stumble upon misinformation or even inappropriate information, but helping students navigate these risks ought to be of the utmost importance in contemporary classrooms. If teachers and schools do not actively guide students' online information seeking practices, they are left to do so informally without assistance or nuanced strategies. Pedagogically, this requires educators and students alike to resist the urge to conflate knowledge acquisition with information management. In a digital information age, it is equally imperative to not only acquire knowledge, but also to be able to "construct new knowledge through a critical thinking process" (Zheng 2006, p. 55), which is an essential component of critical digital literacy. Rather than just teaching students *about* media, students benefit by learning *about*, *with*, and *via* media in real-world circumstances. Learning with media requires us to help students think critically about media in a holistic approach and to critically question aspects of media such as, production, audience, commercialization, power, representation, and the values embedded within the everyday webpages and search results that they encounter. In the following sections, I analyze the resources and approaches at Freeway High in order to understand their strategies for managing information risks and benefits. As part of the analysis, I highlight the differences between students' perspectives and practices and those of the school.

Misinformation

By now it should be common knowledge that you cannot trust or believe everything you read online. We know that the web is littered with a plethora of misleading and inaccurate information. Some of it, classified as disinformation, is intentionally designed to deceive and mislead, such as hoaxes. One such example of disinformation is the white supremacist website MartinLutherKing.org, which is deliberately constructed to appear as a legitimate educational site about Martin Luther King Jr. but which intentionally propagates racist lies and conspiracy theories. Founded in 1999 by a former Ku Klux Klan leader, it is operated by a white supremacist organization whose intent is to deliberately spread disinformation and lies. Although full of despicable information, it has provided some students and teachers with a useful lesson in the importance of media and information literacy (Thomson 2011).

Misinformation, on the other hand, differs from intentional deception, and is typically classified as unintentionally false or inaccurate information that spreads via unsubstantiated rumors, urban legends, and myths (Stahl 2006). Misinformation abounds online, but technology cannot be blamed. Instead, I attribute the root causes for why misinformation spreads to at least three things: bias, incorrect inferential reasoning, and a commercial marketplace of information. First, biases lead to the spread of misinformation because people want to avoid cognitive dissonance—the mental stress or discomfort of experiencing contradictory ideas, behaviors, and attitudes (Festinger 1957). We like to encounter information that supports our preconceived notions and ideologies, even if it is not entirely true (Killoran 2012; Sunstein 2009, 2014). When we come upon information online that supports our beliefs, we are susceptible to sharing it even without checking its validity if it supports our perspectives.[3] Second, incorrect inferential reasoning is what happens when people construct a "reality from the messages to which they are exposed by making inferences about what they do not know based on extrapolations from what they see or hear," which results in a belief of incorrect information (this differs from mere ignorance in which people simply do not know something) (Hofstetter et al. 1999, p. 353). This contributes to the spread of misinformation when people come to fallacious conclusions based on lack of evidence. Third, a commercial marketplace of information describes the news cycle that pressures news organizations to compete with one another to be the first to present new information; this can negatively affect professional fact-checking processes and lead to the spread of misinformation (Saxena 2004). These three explanations account for at least some of the ways in which both professional journalists and citizens contribute to the spread of misinformation.

It is easy to blame social media for perpetuating misinformation because the platforms connect us to large networks that allow us to quickly access and disseminate information almost instantaneously.[4] However, the spread of disinformation and misinformation is certainly not unique to the digital age, and for that reason it is important that we not take a technologically deterministic approach that falsely blames the Internet for the proliferation of misinformation. Preachers, town criers, newspapers, radio broadcasts, and television reports misreported and propagated the spread of false information long before the development of the web. This becomes clear in the midst of a crisis, when there is a high demand for information, even at the expense of fact checking and vetting. For an example we can turn to the televised news coverage that followed the 1995 bombing of the Alfred P. Murrah Federal Building in Oklahoma City. Initially it was falsely reported by local media outlets—and later picked up by national media—that the bomber was a Muslim (Stammer and Hall 1995). Later we would learn that was patently false (probably explained by the priming of racist attitudes, incorrect inferential reasoning, and commercial pressure to be the first to break the news). We now know the bombing was an act of domestic terrorism committed by two US citizens: Timothy McVeigh, an army veteran with alleged connections to white supremacist groups (German 2005; Solomon 2003), and Terry Nichols, an anti-government extremist. Yet the assertion that the bombing had been committed by a Muslim spread quickly—via television news outlets, newspapers, and every-day rumors—and was not easy to retract, even before the days of social media (or even widespread access to the Internet).

Two decades later, we have witnessed a multitude of misinformation that has spread via social network sites, message boards, and even via online professional journalism. There are those who will try to maliciously spread disinformation in the form of conspiracies and rumors to propagate their own biases and interests (as MartinLutherKing.org has done), but we know that even well-intentioned individuals and groups sometimes circulate mis-information. For example, after the 2013 Boston Marathon bombing the online community Reddit accidentally identified an innocent man as the bomber.[5] His name was then picked up and circulated within traditional and professional media outlets. Even many technologically savvy individu-als with well-developed media and information literacy initially believed the false reports—Pete Williams at NBC, Ross Newman at Digg, Dylan Byers at Politico, and Brian Ries at *Newsweek* all circulated the misinformation (Lee 2013; Madrigal 2013). Given the fast-paced, high-demand nature of information—particularly at times of crises—we must develop nuanced strategies for fine tuning literacy skills. This is true of both youth and adults, but schools have a unique opportunity to help young people formally learn practical critical media literacies. Critical media literacy is feasible only if schools actively embrace and validate the tools and platforms that teens use to seek and share news and information.

Critical Digital Literacy

Scholars from various fields recognize that young people (and adults) must develop new literacies to navigate multimediated environments, not just the Internet but also television, film, advertising, and computers. These literacies tout many different yet similar labels, such as "information literacy" (Bruce 1997; Bawden 2008), "media literacy" (Livingstone 2004; Buckingham 2003; Aufderheide 1997; Jenkins et al. 2009), "new media literacy" (Livingstone 2004, Gilmor 2008), "computer literacy" (Goodson and Mangan 1996), "technical literacy" (Fueyo 1988), and "cyberliteracy"

(Gurak 2001). Here I pay particular attention to students' information-seeking behaviors—as well as their evaluation of and participation in consuming and generating information—in order to examine the literacies necessary for critical engagement. I avoid the term "information literacy," which has been criticized for being overly functional in its conceptualization (Buckingham 2003). Likewise, many conceptualizations of Internet literacy tend to focus on functionality (that is, the ability to seek out, access, and evaluate information), but without a more critical consideration of production and power. The British education scholar David Buckingham writes:

Most discussions of Internet literacy remain at the level of assessing the reliability or validity of online *information*—and therefore tend to neglect some of the broader cultural uses of the Internet (not least by young people). To a large extent, the concern here is with promoting more efficient uses of the medium—for example, via the development of advanced search skills (or so-called 'power searching') that will make it easier to locate relevant resources amid the proliferation of online material. This ability to access or locate information is undoubtedly important; yet the skills children need in relation to digital media go well beyond this. (2007, p. 47)

In accordance with Livingstone, Couvering, and Thumim (2005), Buckingham highlights how typical approaches to information literacy—which largely focus on teaching individuals how to discern factual and accurate information—is a functional approach that neglects larger issues of power and ideology. Such critical questions extend beyond "Is this information correct?" to include questions such as "Who benefits from the spread of this information?" and "What are the underlying assumptions of this text?"

Bettina Fabos (2004, p. 95) connects critical media literacy with digital literacy when she writes that students need to understand "how political, economic, and social context shapes all texts, how all texts can be adapted for different social purposes, and how no text is neutral or necessarily of 'higher quality' than another." Critical media literacy also considers issues of power; however, Fabos' contribution draws attention to the ways the information literacy approach often privileges "authoritative" and "accurate" information from professional sources by marginalizing the value of amateur texts. She argues that, rather than seeking an objective "truth," all texts ought to be considered within different contexts and recognized as serving different purposes. A networked society that promotes amateur voices is not entirely unprecedented—amateur and citizen media pre-date the Internet by more than 100 years (Burns 2008; Smith 1944)—but the Internet nonetheless provides students greater access to amateur voices, including their own peers. Digital media texts require a more nuanced approach to determining the value of information that moves beyond dichotomous understandings of what is or is not reliable.

Taking these various perspectives into consideration, I utilize the term *critical digital literacy* in order to refer to the amalgamation of both Buckingham's and Fabos' concept of digital and media literacy. Buckingham's approach, in particular, encompasses and combines aspects of information literacy, digital literacy, and critical media literacy: "Approaching digital media through media education is about much more than simply 'accessing' these media, or using them as tools for learning: on the contrary, it means developing a much broader *critical understanding*, which addresses the textual characteristics of media alongside their social, economic and cultural implications" (2007, p. 48). In the following sections, I analyze Freeway High's approach to online information, risk, and opportunity by examining the school's policies, technology strategies, and resources. To emphasize missed opportunities for developing critical digital literacy, I also highlight the discrepancies between school practices and students' expectations.

Searching for Meaning

Freeway High is part of the Central School District (CSD), which sets guidelines and policies for curriculum development, technology plans, and learning objectives for the entire school district.[6] One of the CSD's Technology Planning objectives is to ensure that all students have the opportunity to participate in technology for "collaboration, communication, critical thinking, and innovation." One strategy for achieving this goal is to subscribe to multiple online databases (EBSCO, Gale, Questia, Facts on File, Encyclopaedia Britannica, etc.) that support information acquisition and instruction in libraries, classrooms, and labs. In itself this is not problematic; arguably the more resources to which students have access, the better. Online databases are valuable resources in students' learning ecologies. From a basic information perspective, databases provide students with access to reliable information and expert opinions on a given topic. However, static databases—no matter how frequently updated—cannot compete with up-to-date information found online. Students mocked the library online resources. As Jada (16 years old, black) said, "Seriously, nobody uses them." In a separate interview, Gabriela (16 years old, Mexican-American) commented: "They have, like, three suggestions on them.

It's not usually what you're looking for, or it's outdated. I don't think anyone actually uses them."

There was a substantial disparity between what the school was investing in and promoting and the ways students sought out information on their own outside of school. When asked how they typically looked up information, it was not surprising that students relied on free online sources such as Google, Wikipedia, and YouTube. Despite students' dismissive attitudes about library resources, these resources serve a purpose and offer a valuable starting point for research. However, databases are clearly limited from the perspective of critical digital literacy: pre-approved and authoritatively validated databases do not allow students an opportunity to critically evaluate the broader context of information production, consumption, and dissemination. School-sanctioned databases privilege authoritative sources and expert opinions at the expense of amateur knowledge and peer perspectives.

Students consistently reported that teachers and librarians at the school actively encouraged them to use library resources rather than general online sources such as Google, YouTube, and Wikipedia. In part, this was because sites such as YouTube were banned at school. Although other sources (e.g., search engines) were filtered, they were not banned outright. Schools are doing students a disservice when they fail to make easily accessible and free resources available to students. Although the CSD's Technology Planning policy stated that teachers should be equipped with "up-to-date technology and online skills" (which teachers were expected to incorporate into student curriculum), in practice participants were navigating the Internet without much classroom guidance or teacher support.

Valuing district-approved sources over students' preferred modes of learning is a form of control that works contrary to what research tells us about how today's students learn and make meaning out of their own online searches. Studies consistently demonstrate that learning is enhanced when students are allowed to experiment with their own procedures for solving problems, seeking out information, and when they are encouraged to pursue personal interests in their own ways (Ito et al. 2010; Parker 2010; Schofield and Davidson 2002). Horst, Herr-Stephenson, and Robinson explain:

Looking around online and searching is an important first step to gathering information about a new and unfamiliar area. ... Online sites, forums, and search engines augment existing information resources by lowering the barriers to looking around in ways that do not require specialized knowledge to begin. Looking around online and fortuitous searching can be a self-directed activity that provides young people with a sense of agency, often exhibited in a discourse that they are 'self-taught' as a result of engaging in these strategies. The autonomy to pursue topics of personal interest through random searching and messing around generally assists and encourages young people to take greater ownership of their learning process. (2010, p. 57)

The district's policies and teachers' practices, which aimed to direct and control students' information-seeking practices, were antithetical to the ways research tells us students prefer—and expect—to learn. Controlling access to information denies students a sense of agency over their own quests for knowledge, and instead reinforces adult-centric ways of being taught. The mechanisms controlling students' practices are reflective of harm-driven expectations that are intended to minimize risks that students may encounter when searching online on their own. Yet autonomous searching leads to greater opportunities for self-guided learning, as well as opportunities for the development of critical digital literacy.

Students noted that teachers did not necessarily discourage the use of search engines, but few recalled teachers actively encouraging online searches for information related to homework and school projects.[7] Notably absent from the CSD's Technology Planning policies was *any* mention of the value of incorporating online resources into students' information-seeking practices. The primary focus was on the school-approved databases as the privileged sites of information seeking. The education professor Jessica K. Parker points out that discussions of online sources and school resources should not be presented as either-or questions; rather, "teachers should concern themselves with the *quality* of sources. ... We can now be critical of all sources and determine which sources will help us find answers to a specific inquiry" (2010, p. 76). Additionally, the hyperlinked structure of the Internet connects information within a broader context that can lead to unintentional yet beneficial discoveries that static resources cannot provide.

Students at Freeway were asked how they determined if search results were accurate. Some said that they compared answers between sites— in other words, if the same answer appeared elsewhere, they assumed it was accurate and reliable, a strategy journalists refer to as "triangulating." This was not necessarily a bad strategy; however, few participants said they paid much or any attention to the source, URL, author, date, or publication type (e.g., they did not distinguish between user forums such as Yahoo message boards and actual published articles). The web also validates and provides access to amateur voices alongside professional and learning how to interpret these distinct perspectives is an important skill students need to learn within a participatory media culture. Jasmine (16 years old; multiracial[8]) said "You can just tell if a site looks right or not." Javier (18 years old, Mexican immigrant) agreed: "You have to use common sense [when determining if a source is accurate]." These are not misinformed strategies—common sense and triangulating information can be effective approaches to validating information online (what Rheingold refers to as "crap detection"). However, there were missed opportunities for developing deeper critical digital media literacy that extend beyond deciphering validity and accuracy.

Google has become easier and easier to use, and search results are increasingly more reliable, but discerning valuable information is not an innate skill. Contrary to the "digital native" discourse, which presumes that young people naturally know how to use digital media tools, research indicates that young people often lack critical thinking and literacy skills necessary to mindfully navigate the web (Oblinger and Oblinger 2005); instead such skills must be intentionally and actively honed through experience and teaching (Ito et al. 2010; Lange 2014; Rheingold 2012). For example, while discussing Google with student participants, few acknowledged that they utilized advanced search features, such as placing phrases in quotation marks or using a dash to filter out results they did not want.[9] Most recognized and acknowledged that not everything online was valid and accurate, but they struggled to articulate their own strategies for finding, evaluating, and deciphering information. Critical digital literacy is where formal education can intervene, because teachers have a valuable opportunity to guide learning and foster critical digital literacy in meaningful ways.

Wikipedia: Analyzing Knowledge Production

Wikipedia is a free collaborative user-generated online database that virtually anyone can have access to and contribute to. Its name derives from the Hawaiian word "wiki" (which means "quick') and the Greek suffix "pedia" (which is related to learning, as in "encyclopedia"). Wikipedia's very name implicates its value as a source for quick learning. The entries are created and edited by users all around the world. Wikipedia's collaborative nature makes it a contentious site of debate in the classroom, and understandably educators are concerned that students may over-rely on it as a source of information without questioning the implications of how the knowledge was produced. Wikipedia provides opportunities to explore the construction of knowledge in ways that traditional sources do not. Parker argues (2010, p. 68) that this is precisely the educational value of Wikipedia: "not only does it bring to our attention the construction of media ... but also our ability to change it." At Freeway, though, Wikipedia was rarely incorporated into the classroom in pedagogically beneficial ways.

Most students at Freeway used Wikipedia for looking up personal interests, but few admitted to using it for school work. This can partially be attributed to the fact that several participants noted that teachers outright discouraged the use of Wikipedia for school. Only a few participants reported engaging with Wikipedia in more advanced ways, such as clicking on embedded links, checking cited sources, or viewing the editing history. The "History" and "Discussion" tabs on each Wikipedia entry provide students with access to how and why information is generated on the entry's main page. Unlike other online sources or school databases, Wikipedia allows students access to the "backstage" production of knowledge. According to boyd (2007b), "The key value of Wikipedia is its transparency. You can understand how a page is constructed, who is invested, what their other investments are. You can see when people disagree about content and how, in the discussion, the disagreement was resolved." Parker (2010) suggests that teachers can lead classroom exercises that help students explore the discussion and history tabs on Wikipedia entries in order to discuss and analyze the construction of knowledge. Discussing the construction of information leads to deeper understandings about power and representation, which are key facets of critical digital literacy. Largely absent from any of the interviews I conducted with teachers or students was a focus on encouraging students to contribute to Wikipedia. The value of the participatory web lies in students' ability to not only consume information, but to also contribute to knowledge production. Diving deeper into the back pages of Wikipedia also provides an opportunity for students to correct or add their own knowledge to a topic or debate.

There were some students at Freeway High—among them Sergio (18 years old, Mexican-American)—who viewed Wikipedia as a resource rather than an authoritative text. Sergio explained: "Sometimes people say don't use Wikipedia because it's not always accurate, but I'm not using it for accuracy. I'm using it more as a guide to compare one thing to another to see if they're the same—similar—and that way I'll understand. Wikipedia's more like enlightenment, a little part of the subject, but then I'll do more research." Sergio constructed a learning ecology that tapped into the benefits of Wikipedia and simultaneously acknowledged its limitations. Other students avoided Wikipedia altogether (at least for formal educational purposes) because they were concerned it might not provide accurate information. Here we see evidence of harm-driven expectations actively shaping and limiting students' learning ecologies, instead of helping them navigate the site with confidence and critical awareness.

Avoiding Wikipedia simply because it might be wrong reflects Fabos' (2004) argument that digital media require us to approach texts beyond a framework of "accurate" and "inaccurate," but that we must aim to understand the broader context in which the information is embedded and accessed. Critical digital literacy involves considering what purposes a text serves, as well as the ability to interpret its mode of production. Sergio's use of Wikipedia as a starting point for further research demonstrated his ability to critically engage with Wikipedia in a productive way. But by not incorporating Wikipedia into the classroom, teachers missed a valuable opportunity to dissect and analyze various modes of knowledge production, collaboration, and collective intelligence. Wikipedia is a space that invites ontological questions: How do we know what we know? How do we prove it? Whose voices are validated and allowed in different discourses of knowledge production? But rather than using Wikipedia as a site for critical digital media lessons, teachers frequently reified harm-driven expectations and dismissed it as unreliable, and therefore as inherently lacking value. Of course, Wikipedia does include some misinformation—but this is all the more reason why students ought to learn strategies and skills for finding and interpreting information online.

Wikipedia is only one example of the ways in which literacy needs to move beyond questions of reliability to also include questions of power, production, and ideology. Such skills should not only be taught in artificial simulations—that is, through pre-fabricated lesson plans—but should also be incorporated into real-time classroom situations that inevitably arise as students seek out information in formal learning environments. Of course these modes of learning would be more easily facilitated if students were encouraged to use their own mobile devices during class (see chapter 4) and if online searches were not strictly limited by CIPA filters. Many teachers encouraged students to rely on resources officially approved by the school district, rather than working *with* them to teach real-world critical digital literacy that bridges formal and informal modes of learning.

The Commercialized Web: Analyzing Motivations

To bring literacy discussions into conversation with discourses of risk, it is important to consider not only what material was blocked by school filters but also what content was *not* blocked by filters. Julie Frechette encourages us to think about cyber-safety and critical digital literacy within a broader context of critical media education. She argues that cyber-safety discourses exploit vulnerable parents and educators:

The discourse of cyber-safety and cyber-censorship manufactures consent through a hegemonic force that overlooks the invasion of online advertising or marketing strategies targeted at children. ... I contend that the mainstream articulation of cyber-paranoia attempts to reach the consent of parents and educators by asking them to see *some* internet content as value-laden (i.e. nudity, sexuality, trigger words, or adult content) while disguising the interests and authority of profitable commercial and computer industries (in the form of advertising, marketing, tracking, and filters). (2006, pp. 149–150)

If we were to truly block out all potentially harmful information, then filters would also block advertisements aimed at exploiting teens' insecurities (e.g., diet ads, beauty products, etc.), such advertisements are intent on capitalizing on students' insecurities. The classroom should be a space that is free from the exploitation of teens' online practices and potentially low self-esteem. Additionally, if we were to truly try to protect against harm then filters would prohibit websites from collecting data about students; data that is sold and traded as a way to profit from students' online activities at school.[10] Harm-driven expectations position some content—namely sexual content or misinformation—as inherently risky, but distracts us from considering the motivations of commercial software, databases, and advertising that are also potentially harmful to youth. This kind of information is not blocked via commercially profitable filters. It is technologically possible for filters to block online advertising and data collection, but both practices are presented as value-neutral or as unavoidable aspects of the web. Failure to block advertisements and data tracking highlights the importance of questioning how risks are socially constructed and emphasizes the power of harm-driven expectations to neutralize or sublimate other problems.

One way teachers could incorporate questions of power into critical digital literacy lesson plans is to have students look up the same information on Google and then compare it to the school's library resources and discuss what the differences are—and, importantly, *why* information is different. This could involve not only discussing information accuracy and the value of amateur perspectives, but would also consider elements of design, ownership, motivations, advertisements, and the values or connotations therein. Additionally, all students could look up the same information online using the same search engine; due to personalized algorithms students would inevitably get different search results. Comparing students' differing search results and advertisements is an opportunity to discuss echo chambers, personal biases, and to make visible the power of algorithms to influence access to information. Understandably teachers, librarians, and students were often critical of CIPA filters that blocked access to valuable and educational content (which I also argue limits critical media literacies), but Frechette's point cannot be understated: filters are not only significant because of what they block, but also because of what they present as innocuous (e.g., commercial interests). So long as filters are left to third-party or profit-making companies "then educators, librarians, and parents need to ensure that they serve the public interests, rather than private commercial interest" (Frechette 2006, p. 170). I would add that, so long as filters are produced by profit-making companies, schools should strive to play an active role in empowering students to understand the full context and motivations of the information they encounter online. Schools have a responsibility to equip students to challenge hegemonic ideologies that overlook the proliferation of consumer culture online and in schools. Risk discourses and policies that focus on predators, pornography, and inappropriate (sexual) content serve to silence other value-laden concerns such as advertising, data collection personalized search results, and exploitation. By failing to acknowledge and validate students' preferred information-seeking behaviors, such as Google and YouTube, schools miss out on important everyday opportunities to incorporate critical digital literacy skills into the classroom.

Crisis News and Activism: Navigating an "Always On" Participatory Culture

Another way schools could actively help students develop critical digital literacy would be for teachers and students to consume and evaluate news information together in real time. During the time of the study, Trayvon Martin—an unarmed black teenager in Florida—was shot and killed by a neighborhood watchman named George Zimmerman. This story made headlines across the nation and particularly resonated with some of the students at Freeway High, a significant portion of whose students were black. Some students were upset or scared in the wake of the incident, and their anger and frustration were exacerbated when Zimmerman was not arrested or charged with a crime. The lack of justice propelled Martin's killing to national news as (black) activists across the country called for justice. Once the story was in the national spotlight, media outlets insinuated and perpetuated the idea that Trayvon looked suspicious because he was wearing a dark hoodie (Graeff, Stempeck, and Zuckerman 2014). Schools and protesters across the nation appropriated the hoodie as a sign of solidarity for Trayvon and as a call for justice (Weeks 2012). Along with other schools across the nation, students at Freeway High staged a "hoodie day" in memory of Trayvon Martin. For several weeks, some students at Freeway discussed the developing details of the incident and the lack of justice. When they were asked where they received information about the situation, the most frequent answers referred to some combination of parents, peers, and social media.

Some students reported discussing the situation in class; however, none of them reported using the Internet or social media in class to seek out more information about the case or protests. Cassandra (18 years old, biracial) explained: "[Martin's death] was big at school. Like, we had a hoodie day at our school for him. Like, we talk about it in our classes. And a lot of the kids are getting involved in the conversation, 'cause I guess, I mean, everybody knows about it." After Zimmerman was not initially arrested, Martin's family created a Change.org petition to urge law enforcement to seek justice for Trayvon; the petition became the fastest-growing campaign in the site's history (Ehrlich 2013). Many of the students at Freeway, along with most of the nation, learned about Martin's initially silenced murder via social media. (His death gained national attention after Martin's family and attorneys created the petition and tried to fight for justice. See Graeff, Stempeck, and Zuckerman 2014.) Beyond the details of the murder, Martin's death sparked a broader conversation about racial tensions, injustices, and biases in US culture and news. Rather than merely learning where and how to access accurate information, students were turning to social media to make sense of what was happening on a larger cultural scale of racial politics in the United States. Cassandra recounted a conversation from one of her classes:

Somebody would say, like, "If that was black man that shot a black man, it wouldn't be on the news." If it was a white man who shot a white man, it wouldn't be on the news. But it was a white man who shot a black kid, so that's why it's so big and a topic and stuff. ... Like, I can see what they mean when it's a different situation to the news than a white man shooting a white man or a black man shooting a black man. 'Cause black people are stereotyped as gangsters and, like, ghetto. And he had his hood on and it was the nighttime. ... There's still people that are racists, and there's still people that might not be racists but, like, they stereotype races, which is still kind of racist because not all races are that stereotype that people think they are or whatever.

Cassandra struggled to articulate her thoughts about the incident as she attempted to understand how media perpetuate particular racial stereotypes. She rightfully points out that traditional print and television news have a long history of propagating stereotypes and promoting racial biases (Dixon and Maddox 2005; Mastro 2009; Oliver 2003; Peffley, Shields, and Williams 1996). These biases and prejudices are further complicated on participatory platforms such as Twitter, where everyday citizens can voice opinions and provide context alongside journalists, politicians, celebrities, and activists. Social media, and specifically Twitter, became a popular space for people to articulate and express the injustices and biases of Trayvon's murder (Jurkowitz and Vogt 2013). Some have gone so far as to argue that Trayvon's death sparked a new generation of (black) activism (Smith 2014), which has largely used social media such as Twitter and Tumblr as a way to organize and share their views.

The school had a unique opportunity to not only help students evaluate the accuracy of online information (albeit important), but to also help them navigate a multitude of mediated ideologies, perspectives, and emotions that eventually became the foundation of the #BlackLivesMatter movement. As part of helping students navigate the emotions and information, they also could have helped students learn how to contribute their voices and perspectives in safe and valuable ways. During the time of this study history was being made, in large part as a result of the murder of an unarmed black teenager—something that influenced the teens at Freeway. They were seeking guidance—and the school provided spaces for dialog— but they did not help students navigate the plethora of information they were encountering online. There was a unique opportunity to help students not only decipher between accurate information and misinformation, but also to understand how social media contributes to larger conversations and activist movements. There was a missed opportunity to help student students view themselves as agents of change, to help them learn how they could actively participate in the dialog, and how to get involved in an emerging movement that resonated with their lives.[11] In other words, an opportunity to expand critical digital literacy beyond consumption, to active online civic participation.

The purpose of this example is to illustrate the ways particular modes of literacy are inhibited by harm-driven expectations of control (and policies of panic), which in turn hinder students' abilities to fully engage with digital media tools and resources in a participatory culture. As Watkins poignantly states (2012, p. 9), "one of the most urgent challenges regarding technology, diversity, and equity is the need to expand digital literacy; that is, the development of young people's capacity not only to access and use digital media but to use digital media in ways that create more enhanced and more empowered expressions of learning, creative expression, and civic engagement." I too see critical digital literacy as more than just access and skillsets, but as a way to close equity gaps and empower students to civically engage online and in their local spheres of influence. Critical digital literacy exceeds beyond the limits of critical consumption, but also enables, encourages, and empowers young people to actively participate in the creation of knowledge and information—to be part of their own mediated cultures and publics. In this way, I also echo Kellner's (1998, pp. 103–104) conceptualization of critical pedagogy:

Media literacy involves teaching the skills that will empower citizens and students to become sensitive to the politics of representations ... and the need to cultivate a wide range of types of critical literacies to deal with the exigencies of the cultural and technological revolution in which we are currently involved, ranging from computer literacy to multimedia literacy to new forms of cultural literacy. Such concerns are part of a critical pedagogy that summons educators, students, and citizens to rethink established curricula and teaching strategies to meet the challenge of empowering individuals to participate democratically in our increasingly multicultural and technological society.

The social-justice reaction to Trayvon Martin's death provided an opportunity for the school to focus on the potential of social media to facilitate literacy development and student activism. Instead the example highlights the ways in which policies that block social media actually limited the role of teachers to empower students to participate in an increasingly mediated society.

Conclusion: Access Is a Right

It is problematic that students have received mixed messages regarding the school's view of digital media: on the one hand they were told that mastering technology and online tools could provide a pathway to future success (see chapter 7), and on the other they were told they were not trustworthy enough to fully engage with digital media and online resources. Prensky (2008, p. 43) argues that schools are overly focused on teaching the past—and by extension, skills and literacies from the past—rather than on preparing students for future careers, intellect, and knowledge: "[If schools were future-oriented] students would be learning and practicing such future-oriented skills as collaborating around the world electronically and learning to work and create in distributed teams." Such collaborative, global, and future-oriented skills are exactly what some of the technology teachers were trying to do (as will be discussed in chapter 7), but policies that restricted access often prohibited teachers from fully incorporating critical digital literacies into the classroom.

What is important here is to connect how historical fears and policies of panic mobilize harm-driven expectations that effectively limit the incorporation of critical digital literacy in the classroom. Policies that restricted access to online content—from objectionable material to social media—prevented students from practicing the kinds of critical literacies and skills they need as active citizens and will need in their future careers. Some students, but by no means all students at Freeway High were adept at working around access restrictions (see chapter 4). Students who broke the rules to bypass filters risked getting into trouble and students who did not or could not work around restrictions were barred from accessing potentially valuable content. It is also important to remember that restrictive policies do not affect all students equally, but students with limited online access outside of school were further marginalized as a result of blocked content. Students who relied on school as their primary point of access were barred from opportunities to develop and practice the essential skills they needed to participate as 21st-century learners. School ought to be an equalizer for students and provide access and opportunities not afforded in the home (thus alleviating families of the burden of providing equitable resources), yet restrictive policies have the potential to exacerbate (digital) inequities by denying economically disadvantaged students access to tools and resources they need.

This chapter has also demonstrated that controlling access to objectionable content is always a socially constructed and value-laden choice. Blocking access to sexually explicit content or controlling access to authoritative and verified information may have reduced some risks, but they also exacerbated other risks—such as missed opportunities to participate in the creation of collective knowledge and online activism. If we look for ways that the Internet can be harmful, we will find them. Yet policies of panic frame information as something that students must be protected from, rather than as part of a networked culture in which students can also actively participate. The construction of content as something students passively consume is archaic and out of date with the affordances of digital media and participatory culture. Rheingold (2013, p. 218) explains that "a participatory culture in which most of the population see themselves as creators as well as consumers of culture is far more likely to generate freedom and wealth for more people than one in which a small portion of the population produces culture that the majority passively consume." It is important to remember that Wikipedia is not just for static information consumption, but is a way for students to contribute to and analyze the construction of knowledge. Twitter and social media are spaces for critical public activism, open dialog, and the privileging of amateur voices alongside expert opinions. Policies must expand beyond one-way understandings of information and instead embrace the participatory nature of knowledge and students' contributions.

Finally, and equally important, harm-driven expectations that aim to avoid risk fail to help young people identify and manage risks on their own. Outside of the authoritarian school environment, many students have access to and come across potentially inappropriate content on a regular basis. Schools should equip students with the literacies necessary to intentionally and safely navigate risky online spaces. Mr. Lopez, a teacher whose views stood out in stark contrast to the official school policies explained: "I just think we need to have more balance [in our approach] so we can truly empower students to learn how to think. I think there's so much information out there now because of the Internet, you really have to teach people how to think and how to utilize that information to solve our world's problems." Schools must help build trust and dialog between students and adults so they will feel comfortable seeking guidance. We cannot create a risk-free environment—at school or elsewhere. Instead we must empower young people to understand how to manage the risks they will inevitably encounter. To do this we must stop conflating risk and harm. That students may encounter inappropriate content does not necessarily mean they will be harmed by it. We must acknowledge teens' emerging sexualities and equip them to search for resources and information, rather than shame them for it. And we must validate students' civic identities in ways that empower them to participate in online spaces not as passive recipients but as active citizens who can confidently navigate networked publics. Blocking access to valuable and educational content does not insulate students from the potential harms they may encounter online, but it could lead to greater inequities and missed opportunities. We must approach online content with expectations of opportunity, rather than fear and control. Equitable access is not just a goal, but a right.

4   Negotiating Control: Distractions, Stress, and Boredom

I would change the electronic rule at Freeway High, because it just limits the students to be free. They're just sort of like a prison. ... Like in prison, you're locked in the room for a long time, and then they give you breaks sometimes and they feed you. School and prison both feed you. School and prison both keep you in a room for a certain amount of time. Then there's times where they take you outside, so gym and the prison field would be a similar thing. It's just a way students compare the two. They compare school to a prison because they just lock you down and take away certain rights.

Sergio (18 years old, Mexican-American)

Walk through the halls of Freeway High on a typical school day and you will quickly notice mixed messages regarding media and technology. Friends meet up at their lockers in between classes to pass off an iPod Touch. Students walk by wearing hoodies to conceal earbuds. Girls gather around a phone to laugh at a friend's video before heading off to their next class. Teens shoot off quick text messages to their parents to coordinate after school plans. And adult administrators stroll down the hall wrapping up a conversation on their mobile phones. Enter one of the two well-equipped computer labs and you will find students listening to music, watching videos, editing photos, reading news, writing papers, updating their Facebook profiles and checking their grades.

All of this is taking place amid multiple signs declaring the school a "No Personal Electronic Device (PED) zone." Like many other high schools in the United States, Freeway has a "can't be seen or heard" policy regarding personal technology. There are signs posted in the front office, in classrooms, and in the hallways to remind students not to use their mobile devices at school. Yet when one speaks with students and teachers it is immediately clear that the rules are ambiguous and negotiable. Ask just about any student about the technology policy, and you're likely to hear a long-winded, frustrated rant about the rules. Or perhaps you'll pick up on a general sense of exhaustion, as students are tired of the daily negotiations related to their use of technology. As you can also imagine, many teachers share the same frustrations and tire of the constant battles about phones, MP3 players, and tablets.

Through an analysis of legal literature, as well as personal experiences in schools across the US, Cramer and Hayes (2010, p. 43) have found that schools' acceptable use policies for mobile devices "are often more 'unacceptable-use' policies, which focus on how students shouldn't use mobile phones and the consequences for breaking the rules." In other words, rather than incorporating mobile technologies into learning environments and teaching students how to responsibly use mobile devices, school policies focus on banning and limiting students' and teachers' use of personal electronics in the classroom. The Video Game Production teacher at Freeway, Mr. Warren, expressed frustration with the restrictive policy: "We say no to the iPad, then we see the admin coming into the room with their iPads and telling the students, 'No iPads.' You can't say no to the future tool of learning that is shared by other students. So, I'd rather have a policy that is about 'Here's how we teach responsible usage.'"

Mr. Warren's remarks iterate the need to shift focus away from "unacceptable use" policies to a policy of "acceptable use." Further, as Mr. Warren also alludes, research consistently demonstrates that teens increasingly use mobile media outside of school, thus media ought to be incorporated as a tool of learning. Cramer and Hayes (2010, p. 43) contend that "the next step toward truly connected youth is bridging the gap between in-school and out-of-school technology use, both in policy and practice." As will be demonstrated, "unacceptable use"—or rather harm-driven expectations— describes the practices and policies regulating mobile devices at Freeway High.

The ambiguity around technology led to frustrations from students, but on a deeper level it reflected a more general uncertainty about the school's overall value of technology for learning. For example, Sergio noted that the school "is really anti-technology, but then it supports the technology program that it has, so it's just anti-technology toward the students using it in the hallways and in class, unless the classroom involves that." His statement acknowledges the abstruseness of the school's relationship with technology and the growing disparity between how students prefer to learn and how schools perceive learning. He goes on to say "I would change the electronic rule [at school] because it just limits the students to be free." By and large, all of the participants stated that they were frustrated by the restrictive rules. The general attitude was that they felt the school should allow students more freedom and responsibility with technology because it would help maintain their interest and aid in school work. These attitudes also reflect contemporary research that demonstrates the ways mobile media can enhance learning (Ito et al. 2010; Katz 2006; Kolb 2008).

Students and teachers were also frustrated by the fluid and negotiable nature of the rules. When asked if there was a punishment for bypassing filters or using a phone, many students alluded to the fact that the rules were flexible; they were dependent upon students' relationships with their teachers. Gabriela (16 years old, Mexican-American) explained what happened when teachers noticed students bypassing filters: "It depends on what teacher that you have. If you're a student and you do your work, some teachers just don't care. Because they know that you're going to get your work done anyway. It really depends." The fluidity and subjectivity of the rules led to exasperations from students who did not get away with breaking the rules. Selena (17 years old, Mexican-American) explained: "I used to get in fights and stuff, so, like, the teachers, they just have it out for me. Too many. They just expect me to be bad, right? So, like, if a girl they like, she break the rules, they just be, like, whatever. But me, they kick me off the computer or outta class, 'cause, like, they think I must be doin' something bad. I'm not. I'm like them, I'm just looking things up for school and stuff." Anna (18 years old, Mexican-American) reiterated Selena's point when she explained: "You know, for the most part, teachers don't really mind, especially if you're, like, not a troublemaker. If you're a good student, then they're not going to bother you about it." Anna's and Selena's explanations highlight the extent to which the rules are mediated by students' behaviors. Rather than being a transparent policy that would give all students opportunities to earn particular privileges, participants agreed that each teacher had different rules for different students. The rules were opaque and subjective, and even the "good" students agreed that the inconsistent enforcement was unfair. Students expect transparency and objective policies that provide all students with opportunities to earn privileges, rather than rules that are murky, negotiable, and subjective. Without equal opportunities to earn technology privileges, it is not surprising that students responded to restrictive rules by covertly breaking them or by learning how to negotiate rules with particular teachers.

In this chapter, I consider how adults and students value technology and media in different and sometimes competing ways. Beyond struggles over access and rules, there are deeper and significant concerns about students' rights and expectations. Rules matter, of course; however, at the heart of students' frustrations is a struggle for validation and respect. This chapter compares and contrasts the attitudes and expectations of adults in the school with those of the students in order to demonstrate a discursive tension over expectations and values. As I will demonstrate, the discursive tension between adults' struggle for control and students' struggle for rights can help us better understand the role of technology at school.

Adults' Expectations: A Discourse of Control

Policies regulating the use of mobile media are often constructed as a way to protect schools from legal liability associated with predators, sexting, bullying, and pornography (Cramer and Hayes 2010). As early as the 1980s, schools in the US began banning pagers because they feared they would be used to traffic drugs—fears that were fallaciously fueled by media panics (Sims 1988; Trump 1995, 2009). Similarly, in accordance with the official policy, students at Freeway High were told to leave all personal technology devices in their lockers, pockets, or purses during school. Rightly concerned that devices left in their lockers would be stolen, most students carried small devices with them. Because laptops were difficult to carry all day, and because lockers were not secure, many participants chose not to bring laptops to school. If a student was seen using a mobile device, or if one made a noise during class, it was up to the teacher's discretion to administer a warning or to confiscate the device; in the latter case, a parent would sometimes be asked to come to the school and retrieve the device.[1]

In addition to liability, schools are also concerned about other risks. Two reasons frequently cited as justifications for banning mobile devices at school include reducing the risk of *distraction* and reducing risk of increased *stress* that can be a result of constant mobile phone usage (the latter is often lumped together within a rhetoric of media addiction, but as will be explained, I purposefully avoid the term). Certainly distraction and increased stress are legitimate concerns related to the use of mobile media at school. I want to review some of the research that supports banning mobile media on both of these two premises, and also consider alternate explanations and approaches that demonstrate that these concerns do not wholly justify banning the use of mobile media in schools. I will also incorporate the perspectives of participants at Freeway High in order to contextualize and examine the array of opinions and approaches.

Controlling Mobile Media

When asked why her school enforced a restrictive policy regarding mobile media, Anna speculated the rules were there to "keep people on task":

Try and keep them working on school work so everyone can pass, the district looks good, they get paychecks, everyone gets paid. Because if you're sitting there on You-Tube all day you might not be learning anything at all. ... Then at the same time it sounds like they're going too far with [the rules] in general. I don't know. It's one of those situations where you're not really sure why the rule's there, but at the same time if it wasn't there it might be worse. At least it stops some people who don't know what the proxy is or something from getting on [to blocked sites]. Then again, who's to stop them from just sitting there not doing anything in general? It's not like they need their phone to not pay attention.

Anna's statement echoes other participants who also expressed ambiguity toward the technology rules. Most students understood, to a certain extent, that the rules were designed to keep students "on task"; however, virtually all participants felt the rules went too far. Some felt they limited creativity; others adamantly believed they were more productive when they could listen to music, look up tutorials and information online, or read and take notes on their mobile devices. For example, Cassandra (18 years old, bira-cial[2]) got frustrated that teachers did not allow her to use her phone in class: "I like using the notepad on my phone [to take notes], but I can't because of my teachers. And sometimes we have to turn in our notes or we're allowed to use our notes on tests, but I can't have my phone out during a test looking at my notes." Other participants also commented that they preferred to take notes on a mobile device because it was faster and more convenient, and because they always had the device with them. These practices were discouraged or banned because of the threat of distraction.

Such policies are not new. By the late 1990s, most schools banned or strictly regulated mobile devices in order to minimize classroom disruptions, as was advised by the consulting firm National School Safety and Security Services (Cell phones and text messaging in schools, n.d.).[3] Likewise, teachers at Freeway cited concern about the possibility of distraction that personal technology posed. Mobile phones undoubtedly have the potential to disrupt formal learning environments by distracting teachers and students. Indeed, I witnessed plenty of instances in which students at Freeway were distracted by their mobile devices during class. However, I also witnessed plenty of instances in which a student was distracted by other students, by a stuck zipper on a jacket, by an air vent blowing cold air on his or her papers, and by emotional distractions related to such matters as the instability of the student's home life, a lack of lunch money, or the struggle of the student's mother to find a job. In other words, with or without a mobile device, students get distracted at school.

While I will argue that banning mobile media misses valuable opportunities for developing literacies, there are those on the other side of the debate who argue that mobile devices have no place in formal education at any level, including college (Felipe 2015). There are some compelling arguments for completely banning mobile devices, and they are worth consideration.

For example, a recent study in the UK found that test scores improved by 6.4 percent after a school banned mobile phones, and that low-performing students were the ones most likely to see improvements in their test scores (Beland and Murphy 2015). The underlying assumption of that study is that mobile phones pose a distraction that inhibits learning. The logic supposes that when the phones are removed, distractions are minimized and attention increases, leading to improved test scores. This argument and data led Beland and Murphy to conclude that "schools could significantly reduce the education achievement gap by prohibiting mobile phone use in schools" (ibid., p. 3). From a particular angle, this makes a lot of sense, which is likely to be the reason why, in the first six months after the study was published, it gained a lot of national and international attention in news and education circles.[4] But it should be noted that, though the sample was large, the results must be interpreted within a particular context: 16-year-old students, at 91 schools in four cities in England, who were taking rigorous qualification exams in 2013. We must exercise caution before assuming the findings are representative of other populations or that the results can be directly applied to a US context.

The data of Beland and Murphy are persuasive, and perhaps their study makes a case for banning mobile phones *in particular contexts*—for example, during preparation for high-stake exams, such as the state-mandated standardized tests that students in the US must pass. However, the Beland and Murphy study does not assess the relationship between mobile phones and overall academic success or career preparation. I am cautious of conclusions that claim test scores alone will "close education gaps." Equating gaps in test scores to overall educational achievement gaps presents a narrow focus of academic success and heavy-handedly blames technology as a root cause of educational inequality. Yet in the United States, and more specifically in Texas, standardized test scores have been heavily criticized for not accurately reflecting and predicting trends in academic success (Sacks 1999; Weiss 2012). In his 1999 book *Standardized Minds*, the educator Peter Sacks writes:

Evidence strongly suggests that standardized testing flies in the face of recent advances in our understanding of how people learn to think and reason. Repeatedly in the research over the past few years, especially in the grade school arena (K–12), one finds evidence that traditional tests reinforce passive, rote learning of facts and formulas, quite contrary to the active, critical thinking skills many educators now believe schools should be encouraging. ... At the K–12 level, teachers often don't believe that tests accurately measure their students' abilities, and do believe that widespread practice of 'teaching to the test' *renders tests scores virtually meaningless.* (p. 9, emphasis added)

Rather than educating students as critical thinkers and productive citizens, the primary purpose of standardized achievement tests is to allow school boards and funding agencies to rate the effectiveness of teachers, schools, and school districts (Popham 1999; Weiss 2012). A ban on mobile phones might close the gap in test scores, but that does not mean that a ban better prepares students for academic success after graduation, nor does it indicate better preparation for the workforce. On the contrary, as I explore in the following sections, learning how to manage the use of mobile devices is a necessary and valuable digital literacy that schools ought to help students develop. The emphasis on test scores alone overlooks other educational, creative, and empowering benefits of responsibly incorporating mobile media into the classroom—benefits such as facilitating collaborative distance learning (Ally 2009), enhancing engagement via interactivity (Huizenga et al. 2009), and bridging gaps between formal education and out-of-school learning (Ito et al. 2010).

Another recent study, conducted in 2016 at the US Military Academy at West Point, made similar claims that support banning mobile devices at school. The faculty members who conducted the study found that removing tablets and laptops from an introductory economics course led to an improvement in students' grades, especially among males and students with high grade-point averages (Carter, Greenberg, and Walker 2016). The researchers compared the final exam grades of students who were allowed to use laptops and tablets against those of students who were not allowed to use them and found that those who did not use such devices in class scored higher than those who did. These results seem compelling. The experiment clearly demonstrates a negative correlation between in-class technology use and exam scores. But Carter et al. (ibid., p. 28) are hesitant to offer conclusive explanations for the results: "We ... cannot test whether the laptop or tablet leads to worse note taking, whether the increased availability of distractions for computer users (email, Facebook, Twitter, news, other classes, etc.) leads to lower grades or whether professors teach differently when students are on their computers." Inserting technology into a classroom is likely to disrupt traditional modes of learning and engagement, and I would never suggest it does not present a distraction. However, in order to take advantage of the availability of technology in the classroom, education must change its approach to learning and evaluation. In other words, the dyadic one-way transmission of information from professor to student may not be best suited to teaching with and through technology. A collaborative, peer-driven, problem-solving approach to learning may be better for integrating technology in the classroom. In this model the teacher is not the expert at the front of the room merely imparting information for students to jot down; instead, the teacher charges students with the task of creatively solving problems and seeking out answers collaboratively. Similarly, exams that ask students to regurgitate information they have heard and transcribed in class may be best accomplished in the absence of technology.

My point is that we cannot insert technology into a classroom, continue to teach as we always have, rely on traditional assessment tools, and then draw the conclusion that technology is detrimental to learning. By analogy, if we wanted to measure whether or not technology made people more social, we should not measure only the amount of face-to-face communication. If we did that, we might erroneously come to the conclusion that technology leads to less sociality. Yet if we expanded our definition of sociality to also measure and account for mediated conversations via phone calls, text messaging, emails, social media, etc., we would find that technology affords greater communicative contact and can enhance personal communication and sociality (Baym 2010). Or, if we wanted to measure how yoga affects health and we measured only weight loss, we might wrongly conclude that yoga does not significantly lead to improved health. But if we were to also measure increased strength, flexibility, balance, and stress levels, we would draw very different conclusions about the relationship between yoga and health (Heid 2014). The studies cited above rely on limited variables and measurements that support their findings but overlook other tools of assessment and effects. Technology affords different modes of engagement, collaboration, and learning and necessitates a transformation in how we teach and how we evaluate learning outcomes. Studies of the standardized tests used in the UK and of the classroom trials at West Point merely demonstrate that technology does not enhance traditional models of learning and knowledge dissemination when we measure outcomes as we measured them in the past; they fallaciously rely on traditional assessments to evaluate new engagements. They fail to consider how technology can be positively incorporated into new approaches to pedagogy and new teaching styles, as well as the need to develop new tools for assessment.

I do not discount the findings of the aforementioned studies, which provide evidence that technology can be detrimental to traditional educational settings. But I believe that we should expand our approach to understanding and evaluating the affordances and limitations of technology as a tool for enhanced learning. Decisions about technology need not be all-or-nothing decisions. In particular learning contexts—such as lectures and one-way transfers of information—perhaps it is best to prohibit technology. But in other contexts, such as group work, project-based learning, and problem solving, technology may enhance rather than detract from students' engagement and learning. Technology affords different modes of classroom engagement, teaching, and learning that resonate with how today's students learn informally outside the classroom. Unfortunately, the results of studies such as those mentioned above often are egregiously over-generalized and incorrectly used to justify bans on technology in the classroom.

Controlling Distractions

Technology, as a tool for enhancing learning, challenges the normative assumption that distractions are inherently risky or harmful. If we take a step back we can see that to justify completely banning mobile devices on the premise that it reduces distractions is overly simplistic and problematic. First, it presumes that an ideal "distraction-free learning environment" is possible, beneficial, and necessary. Students have always found ways to deliberately and intentionally distract themselves during class, for example, by doodling, writing and passing notes to friends, reading a magazine tucked away in their school book, making to-do lists, daydreaming, staring out the window, or working on assignments or personal interests that are not related to course material. In other words, we know the mobile technology did not create the temptation of distractions in the classroom; however, it can of course exacerbate temptations and distractions. Obviously teachers ought to strive to reduce distractions, however, to ban mobile media simply because it poses a distraction is fallacious. By that logic, teachers also ought to ban pens and paper, which have the potential to distract students as well. Students can and do use pens to draw, write notes to their friends, work on other homework assignments, and so forth and so forth. Of course, the idea of banning pens seems ludicrous and would never hold up—nor should it—for the simple fact that students need pens and paper to aid in learning. In the same way that the pen and paper has the potential to be a distraction, we also recognize its inherent value as an appropriate tool in the classroom. Why then should mobile devices be banned simply because they pose a potential threat or distraction in the classroom? We must expand the conversation beyond harm-driven expectations of mobile media to also consider their potential as tools and resources in the classroom.

Another problem with the assumption that banning mobile media is productive—or rather that distractions are harmful—is that it overlooks the reality that outside of school young people must constantly negotiate norms and rules for when and where they should use mobile devices. Managing distractions is not unique to the school environment. In the workplace, adults must learn how to simultaneously use technology as a tool for productivity, while also minimizing the temptation to use technology as a distraction. In preparation for adulthood and the workplace, schools ought to help students create boundaries, develop and enforce norms, and manage the distractions that mobile devices present. Within this vein of thinking, it is important to point out that not all teachers agree with the restrictive policies. Mr. Warren was increasingly frustrated with the ban on personal devices: "Now, when we have our students go on field trips to the real world and go to see companies, they see the people with the cell phones out on the tables. Do they see them being used irresponsibly? No. Not really. They aren't tempted. They know how to use technology responsibly." His comment highlights the ways in which the distractibility argument has constructed technology as a distraction for young people when actually it has the potential to be a distraction for anyone, including adults. Like adults, students must learn how to manage distractions. Mr. Warren may have overstated the claim that adults are not tempted by distractions, but his observation is accurate insofar as adults in the workplace learn how to manage distractions. In the same way, schools can and should teach students how to manage and resist distractions. Learning responsible and acceptable use of technology, and learning to resist temptations, is a valuable skill for young people while they are in school; it also prepares them for their roles and responsibilities as adults in the workforce.

Outside of school, young people's use of technology is not strictly managed; they must learn to use technology responsibly, and that includes resisting temptations of distractibility. According to Howard Rheingold (2012), learning to manage our attention is a valuable literacy that takes deliberate practice. Rheingold's argument draws from research that goes so far as to maintain that some distractions, rather than being harmful, are necessary and beneficial for survival. For example, it would be dangerous to be so focused on an important task that one wouldn't be aware of the smell of smoke in the next room. No matter how focused or important a task, we need to be distracted at times—for instance, to alert us that there is a fire. This is an extreme example, of course, but the point is that not all distractions are negative, risky, or harmful. From an evolutionary perspective, humans have learned how to block out or pay attention to distractions that are beneficial for survival.

In his book *Net Smart*, Rheingold expertly and simply puts forth the idea that attention skills are a digital literacy that must be intentionally and deliberately developed (2012, pp. 42–43): "The executive control we all exercise when we maintain focus on a task becomes useful when we move from understanding attention to controlling it. ... Gaining control of your attention while you are online requires, first of all, intention. When you formulate a goal, you need to *intend* to achieve it. Goals and intentions enable your executive control to attune to the part of your information environment that matters most, and tune out what is irrelevant, at least for the purpose of your goal." Avoiding a technologically deterministic approach, Rheingold recognizes that fine tuning of attention skills dates back as far as humankind, but also recognizes that the development and domestication of technology necessitates the evolution of new skills and literacies.

The incessant buzzing of a mobile phone in our pocket, or the constant bleep of an email notification in our browser, or the flashing notification of a new tweet is potentially distracting, even to the point that it could have negative effects on productivity. For that reason, the removal of such distractions can be used to explain the test results of Beland and Murphy's UK school test scores study or Carter, Greenberg, and Walker's economics classroom trials. But compulsory authoritative approaches to regulating media—and therefore distractions—miss the point. Students do not need distraction-free environments, but rather, *they must learn how to develop appropriate and effective attention literacies* so that they can learn how to responsibly manage distractions *on their own*, outside of authoritative control. Schools have the opportunity to help students develop and shape the norms necessary for appropriately managing mobile media use in a beneficial manner. Helping students manage distractions can only be accomplished through the incorporation of mobile devices at school, rather than a punitive ban on personal technology. Banning mobile devices in order to create "distraction-free" learning at school constructs a superficial environment that ignores the reality that young people, just like adults, must learn to negotiate the distractions posed by mobile media.

Further, the discourse around distraction, media, and youth tends to assume that young people themselves are unaware of distractions. The discourse often positions youth as passive dupes who are unable to manage distractions, who are oblivious to the risks of distraction, or who can only manage distraction through authoritative control. These assumptions and constructions of youth and technology are evident of the harm-driven expectations that are common in policies of panic (see chapter 2). This rhetoric is also seen in headlines such as NBC's "Students can't resist distraction for two minutes … and neither can you" (Sullivan 2013) and this *Slate* headline: "You'll Never Learn! Students can't resist multitasking, and it's impairing their memory" (Paul 2013). Such assumptions fail to recognize young people's own agency with regard to both unintentional and intentional distraction. Amina (17 years old, East African) articulates her own understanding of deliberate distraction.

Q: Okay. So, another thing that we've heard is that technology is a big distraction. What do you think about that?

Amina: Oh, yeah. We all know it. We all know it. We all talk about how we have a paper to do, but "Look at me. I'm on Facebook." Or we'll talk about homework that's not going to get done. Yeah. We always talk about Facebook and Twitter. We know it's a distraction.

Q: Okay. You and your friends talk about all that stuff a lot?

Amina: Everyone talks about it. We all know it's a distraction. I feel like a lot of other people are always talking about how our phones and computers are a distraction without us being aware of it. But that's not true. We're aware that it's a distraction. You only do what you want to do and that will be your distraction. I feel like Twitter and Facebook are only a distraction because we want to be on Twitter and Facebook. Playing basketball could be a distraction if all you want to do is play basketball. Video games are a distraction if all you want to do is play video games. Anything can be a distraction.

Q: So, that's interesting. Are you saying that adults oftentimes say that?

Amina: Just the idea of when the teacher's talking about "Oh, you're always on your phone. It distracts you. You never get your work done." It's not because oh no, we're doomed for life. What are we going to do? It's because we want to be on our phones. If we don't want to be on our phones it won't be a distraction. Sooner or later it will get old and it won't be a distraction anymore. That's probably going to be when we get older or when we go to college or however we get over it.

Amina's interview reveals the extent to which students are acutely aware of distractions, but she transfers the debate to a framework of *choice*, rather than passivity or victimhood. Teachers—and adult society more broadly— can benefit from listening to Amina and other teens when they discuss distractions and media. Teens don't need adults to eradicate distractions— an impossible goal anyway—but rather, they need help making smart and responsible decisions. Amina assumes as she gets older she will be less distracted my media. However, Rheingold's (2012) research demonstrates that adults also need help developing and employing attention literacy strategies that minimize distractions. Setting healthy and productive boundaries is not simply a youth problem, but schools can help young people manage distractions.

In her research focusing on teens' social uses of mobile media, Nicola Green (2003) argues that we ought to shift our focus away from the differences between teen and adult uses of mobile media. She contends that by focusing on differences between teen and adult use of technology that we erroneously construct teens as a uniform category and ignore the differences within teen populations. I would add that identifying particular practices as teen practices ignores the similarities between teen and adult media use as well. The ways teens use mobile media are not inherently in opposition to the ways adults use mobile media—yes, sometimes as a distraction, but also as a way to enhance a learning environment. But additionally, constructing problems as "youth" problems, opens doors for surveillance and policy intervention not typically applicable to adults (Shade 2011). Distractions from mobile devices are not a youth problem, but rather we should extend our focus to "attention literacy" as a skill that both young people and adults must develop and practice. School environments could incorporate mobile media as a way to scaffold students as they learn to manage distractibility in school and beyond. There must to be a balance between completely restricting mobile media and forgoing any level of control. This harkens back to Cramer and Hayes (2010) point from the beginning of the chapter, electronic device policies should expand beyond "unacceptable use" and instead focus on "acceptable use."

Such strategies could include writing down goals, focusing on tasks for set periods of time, allowing students opportunities to multitask or take media breaks, determining what kinds of classroom activities are conducive to technology use, and helping students evaluate what is working and what isn't. In other words, it's about helping students "be mindful" (to use Rheingold's language) about their practices. Teachers could help students reflect on what aids and detracts from productivity, media being merely one variable in the equation. A larger reflective approach would help students identify when, where, and how they are most productive. For example, what time of day they are most alert, how much sleep they need to focus, if noisy or quiet spaces are better, if they need to work alone or with a friend, and so forth. This extends attention literacy beyond an overly technologically determinist focus on media in order to situate technology as part of a broader understanding of attention and distraction.

We can also look to the affordances of technology to help manage distractions. While most mobile phone apps default to push notifications, these can be turned off. Facebook provides a way to unsubscribe from notifications both in a browser and on a phone, a strategy that can be beneficial when certain updates are not relevant or are a distraction. Gmail has a "do not disturb" feature that essentially blocks your access to your email for a specified period of time and does not alert you to new messages. A student recently alerted me to a new app, called Pocket Points,[5] that allows students to earn points for keeping their phones locked during class; the points can be redeemed for discounted food on and around campus. Both Android and Apple mobile devices have a customizable "do not disturb" feature that you can schedule to prevent notifications during certain times of day, such as bedtime or during class. The notifications are still visible, but they do not actively alert you of incoming information (both allow exceptions for your favorite people, or if someone calls multiple times in a short period, as would be done in an emergency). Although these strategies and techniques are easy to implement, they are not widely publicized within the interfaces or platforms, and thus schools could help students learn about these features and encourage using them in particular contexts. This would help them agentively manage distractions in productive and intentional ways.

As a reminder, I am specifically addressing a high school context; a scaffolding approach would be necessary to prepare students for this mode of trust and responsibility. For example, in elementary school personal devices may best be banned, but students could be given opportunities to earn privileges (or lose privileges) as they get older. By high school, the focus would expand beyond mere trust and responsible use, but include specific strategies for fine-tuning and developing attention literacy strategies. This shifts focus from mobile media as a risk that must be controlled to expectations of opportunities for enhanced learning. It also turns attention away from expectations of misuse, and instead empowers and respects students to develop necessary and beneficial attention literacies that they will undoubtedly need to learn as students at school, but also as adults at work, and responsible citizens in society. Distraction is a risk, but failing to help teens manage distractions autonomously is an even bigger risk.

Controlling Stress

Another argument for banning mobile devices in the classroom is that they increase stress and anxiety for young people (Billieuz et al. 2007; Brosseau 2013; Takao, Takahashi, and Kitamura 2009; Vitelli 2013). As happens with almost all media technologies when they are new, adults are concerned about the negative effects a technology will have on the emotional, psychological, social, and physical well-being of young people. Headlines and news stories are full of anxiety-inducing expectations of harm that highlight the inherent risk of young people's media engagement and practices. When considering the emotional and psychological anxiety associated with constant mobile media interaction, the concerns are often related to social pressures to always be connected to peers, to family members, and to what is happening online. Culture has created a new word—FOMO (Fear of Missing Out)[6]—to describe the anxiety young people experience in an information-saturated world. Social media are often blamed for contributing to a "desire to stay continually connected with what others are doing" (Przbylski et al. 2013, p. 1841). Like other harm-driven expectations and phenomena, FOMO is an adult-generated explanation of what young people might be experiencing (Schreckinger 2014). The communication scholar Joseph Reagle (2015) provides an historical analysis of how anxiety related to "missing out" is actually "a continuation of century-old issues" dating back to the printing press and the telegraph. The desires to see and be seen did not arrive with social media, but are grounded in broader social issues Reagle refers to as "conspicuous sociality." Some young people do experience feelings of addiction and anxiety in relation to their phones or their online social lives. However, we must recognize this is a small percentage of the population and that media cannot be solely blamed for feelings of anxiety or isolation, which are typically indicative of other mental health, social, developmental, or environmental issues.

Within popular media and academia, mobile phone use has been dubiously linked to sleep loss (Phillips 2011), social isolation (Carral 2015; Turkle 2011), anxiety (Brosseau 2013), and narcissism (Firestone 2013). The psychologist Suzanne Phillips (2011) wrote an article for Psych Central titled "Teens sleeping with cell phones is a clear and present danger." In it, she presents evidence that "texting as an addiction jeopardizes sleep, cognitive functioning and real relating—making dependence on it greater and greater." She describes how cell phone use can foster feelings of obligation and even equates the brain's response to the pleasure of texting with that of heroin. Despite the pathological and alarming evidence presented in Phillips' article, she concludes by urging parents to "plan with their teens to [help] relive the 'on call' demands [of staying connected]" and makes the point that self-regulation is better than policing teens' mobile media use. There is a history of associating new behaviors or intense interests (obsessions) as pathological instead of habitual or intentional; this is particularly the case when describing the practices and interests of women and young people (boyd 2014; Giroux 2009; Ringrose 2006). Failing to recognize the motivations and intent behind young people's use of technology, "many adults project their priorities onto teens and pathologize their children's interactions with technology" (boyd 2014, p. 83). The pathologizing discourse problematically positions teens as lacking agency and is driven by expectations of harm.

Concerns about the psychological and social effects of new technology are far from unique or new. Let's take a brief look back at a few relevant examples. According to Socrates, writing was going to disrupt people's memories, which of course it did (Baym 2010). Yet it would be hard to argue that the cost–benefit tradeoff of oral culture and writing culture was not worth it. Before mass media, news was heard in the town square or from the pulpit. With the development of newspapers, there were concerns that mass print would socially isolate us and reduce spirituality (Eisenstein 1983). In 1936, the magazine *Gramophone* reported that because of the radio children had "developed the habit of dividing attention between the humdrum preparation of the school assignments and the compelling excitement of the loudspeaker" (Bell 2010). Again, this might be true—radio stories probably did distract (entertain) children—but were the benefits of radio as a communication technology not worth the tradeoff? Fears about social isolation, distraction, and anxiety are not new. New technologies can be disruptive, but as a society we develop techniques for maximizing the benefits and learn how to minimize the potential risks and harms.

Perhaps the most appropriate comparison, however, is between the discourse on television in the early 1960s and the discourse on mobile phones today. In the early 1960s, television had been a common facet of American life for only about ten years (similar to the timeline of the smartphone today). Similar to today's debate about the risks and benefits of mobile media, experts in the 1960s were debating the risks and benefits of television viewing both at home and in schools. There were concerns that television would distract young people, make them aggressive, and negatively influence their academic performance; there was also worry that the "fantasy world" of television would render school too boring (Schramm, Lyle, and Parker 1961). There were debates about television's ability to stimulate or inhibit intellectual and creative activity and people were concerned that television would negatively affect family life, routines, and sociality (Spigel 1992). In a way, those concerns were valid. Research indicates that there are risks associated with too much television viewing, such as negative effects on physical health (Faith et al. 2001)[7] and the perpetuation of harmful stereotypes (Bissler and Conners 2012; McGhee and Frueh 1980; Ward 2015). But with time the overall anxiety about television has diminished as we have come to recognize that parents, schools, and children can exercise agency over the amount of television they watch, as well as the quality of content they view.

On the other hand, we have also learned that television can be educational and can have positive effects both in and out of the classroom (Anderson 1998). Television viewing has also been found to facilitate language acquisition (Fisch 2004) and contribute to cognitive development (Fisch 2004; Lesser 1974). And far from being antisocial, television as popular culture can bring people together by providing common topics of conversation—a phenomenon often referred to as the "water-cooler effect" (Anderson 2006). Likewise, despite fears of social isolation, television viewing can be inherently social, as is the case with live sporting events and award shows that encourage group watching (e.g., at sports bars and watch parties) and facilitate bonding via collective fandoms and identities (Earnheardt and Haridakis 2008). Many of these studies and concerns related to the early days of television-as-risk discourse are strikingly similar to the questions we are debating and researching about mobile media today, including questions of addiction, social isolation, and physical and mental health.

In 1961, the mass-media scholars Wilbur Schramm, Jack Lyle, and Edward Parker productively posed the question "Are schools doing everything possible to connect television to the intellectual growth of children?" (p. 184). Rather than suggesting that television should be viewed only outside of school or encouraging unregulated access to television at school, Schramm, Lyle, and Parker made this poignant and balanced suggestion:

Schools can be of enormous help, it seems to us. … *Anything to which children devote one-sixth of their waking hours has obvious importance for schools.* If children are helped to know good books from poor ones, good music from poor music, good art from bad art, there is no reason why they should not be *helped to develop some standards* for television. How to read the newspaper (borrowing Edgar Dale's title) is a subject treated increasingly in school; 'how to view television' is just as important. Furthermore, television is a real resource for examples, assignments, and what the teachers call 'enrichment.' It seems to us all to the good to bring television into *the real-life process of learning, to break down the barrier* between passive fantasy experience and active use. (pp. 184–185, emphasis added)

The similarities between the cultural anxieties about television in the 1960s and the concerns we are facing today with mobile media allow us to look back and learn a few lessons from history. As with television (in the past and today), students spend a lot of time with mobile media; thus it is hard to argue that schools do not have a responsibility to help students manage media. In the 1960s, the average American child spent approximately one-sixth of his or her waking hours "using" television (Schramm, Lyle, and Parker 1961). Depending on where you look, screen time accounts for an estimated average of 7½ to 9 hours a day for the average American teen (Ahuja 2013; Common Sense Census 2015; Kaiser Family Foundation 2010). Similarly, the Pew Research Center found that 24 percent of American teens are online "almost constantly" and more than half go online several times a day (Lenhart 2015); these numbers are not dissimilar from statistics about adults, who also spend, on average, between 8 and 11 hours a day with media (Karaian 2015; Turrill 2014). Since teens spend at least as much time with media as they spend sleeping, in school, or with their parents, it is important that we consider what role media ought to play at school. According to the cultural anthropologist Michael Wesch (2009), "we [teachers] use social media in the classroom not because our students use it, but because we are afraid that social media might be using them— they are using social media blindly, without recognition of the new challenges and opportunities in might create."

I can entertain the argument that school ought to be one place in which teens are able to get away from the distractions and pressures to engage with mobile and social media, perhaps school should offer a reprieve from the pressures of media. Yet when students were asked if their phones caused them stress, the most frequent response was "Like when it doesn't work?" For students in this study, stress was related to technical limitations of their phones, especially for students with outdated phones. It was only when we explicitly asked about social pressures of always being connected, that students would think to tell those stories. None of the participants felt their phone or the constant availability was a negative thing or expressed much stress or anxiety about it. For the most part, the consensus was that if you could not reply or talk, you should at least send a short text saying that you'll get back to the person later. This practice was an acceptable and agreed-upon social norm that students utilized with peers and with their parents. They did not say that this caused them stress; they simply considered it socially polite. Other students said that their phones could be annoying, but overall they felt they were managing mobile communication without much difficulty. Jada (16 years old, black) explained:

Jada: Yes, my phone does get annoying at times. Because it's, like, rude not to answer, and people will get the hint that you're not answering purposely.

Q: Really, so are you expected to answer when your friends text you or call? Do you feel a pressure to respond?

Jada: Maybe sometimes, because maybe one of my friends they had the comment "Gah, what's the point of having a phone [if you don't answer]?" And I'm the wrong person to do that, I call back and stuff, so don't do that. Just on my own time. Am I pressured? I don't think so, but I know just to get [it] outta the way, just to get it [it] outta the way, yes, I'll respond. I don't know if you would call that pressure or not.

Q: Just to expect it.

Jada: Yes, because sometimes it's irritating and I'm doing something, [and they will ask] "Oh, can I have this?" It just messes up my whole aura. When somebody calls, you think they're going to call about something important, you answer and it's something stupid. A question, you just don't want to do but you don't want to sound rude. But I don't really care sometimes because I won't answer if I don't want to. And I know it's seen as rude and they know that too, but, like, stop calling all the time.

Q: So is it perceived rude to ignore people's calls?

Jada: Some people would consider it rude, but it's just if you keep calling to ask favors and stuff, you'll burn me out. Because I like doing it on my own terms, Hey, I'll do it for you, when it's mutual. But when it's too much, I can't work well with that.

Jada's explanation points to the context of the call, specifically if someone continues to call instead of recognizing that she is deliberately not answering. She also gets frustrated when people ask favors of her that she does not want to do (a topic that came up several times in other contexts). However, she also noted this is a more frequent occurrence at home in the evenings or on the weekends, and not at school, since her friends are also at school and unavailable during that time. We must interpret Jada's comments in the context of her current subject position, one that may not articulate the pressures associated with constant contact, but we also must validate her own explanations of her experiences. Adults can help young people balance pressures and reflect on feelings of anxiety.

There is evidence to suggest that the constant availability and contact that mobile phones afford can cause young people stress or anxiety, but for the most part students in this book noted that was not often the case at school. In fact, "parents" was one of the most common answers about who they texted from school. Students frequently texted their parents to arrange transportation, sibling care, or to let them know about changes in after school plans. In the context of school, students expressed more frustration that mobile media were banned than about stress or pressure to always be connected. The common theme was that students wished their teachers would more actively incorporate media into education and the rhythm of the school day by allowing them opportunities to use their phones in productive ways (as will be further discussed later in this chapter.

Setting Healthy Boundaries

Concerns about anxiety in an "always on" world are valid to a certain extent and within particular contexts, but we should scrutinize a language of addiction that pathologizes young people's practices and experiences. For one thing, pathologizing language exoticizes young people's practices, which contributes to harm-driven expectations that neglect to take into consideration agency, motivations, and actual experiences. Yet, pathological language seeps into popular discourse on a regular basis. For example, "Screen addiction is taking a toll on children," a 2015 post by Jane Brody on the *New York Times'* Well blog, describes children as "heavy users of electronics" and refers to texting as "the next national epidemic." Dramatized language is far too common within discourse about young people's media practices. "The language of addiction," boyd writes (2014, p. 78), "sensationalizes teens' engagement with technology and suggests that mere participation leads to pathology." This approach presumes that what young people are experiencing is an "illness" that needs to be "remedied" (Reagle 2015). The media scholar John Jones (2015) is critical of language that perpetuates fear and harm around media, both within popular culture and scholarship. In a response to a *Washington Post* op-ed piece written by a teacher who regretted incorporating the iPad into her classroom (Hall 2015), Jones wrote:

The intellectual support for this movement [banning media at school] has recently been provided by the questionable research of MIT professor Sherry Turkle, who provides concerning anecdotes that support the fears of anyone who has begun to suspect that our screens are having noxious effects on the human need to [fill in the blank]. ... The basic problem with research like Turkle's is that it magnifies anecdotes from this time of social upheaval of media creation and consumption into universal truths about technology, and it is not yet clear how our technology is actually changing us. Put differently, the unique social impact(s) of these technologies is hard to parse because they are not yet held in check by cultural expectations.

His opinion, like those of many other media scholars (Jenkins, Ito, and boyd 2016), iterates a point I made earlier in this section: When media are initially adapted into society, they are disruptive, but over time society develops cultural norms that help manage disruptions, maximize benefits, and minimize harms. It is risky to respond to new disruptive technologies before we have had a chance to develop cultural expectations and social norms that will regulate practices in more responsible ways. Lessig (2006) reminds us that there are many modes of regulation other than laws and rules. Technology can and should be regulated via agreed-upon social norms that establish etiquette and boundaries. This necessitates patience, time, and a trust that collective norms will balance the risks and opportunities of mobile media practices.[8]

Instead of overly focusing on the risk of addiction, we should focus on expectations of healthy boundaries. S. Craig Watkins argues that digital media have become such necessary and integral aspects of our daily lives that we incorporate technology—and check our phones—out of habit, more so than out of a compulsive harmful behavior. "Addiction," he writes (2009, p. 134), implies something altogether different [than a digital life-style] and far more serious—a mental disorder that makes self-destructive behavior nearly impossible to stop." Although addiction may accurately describe a small percentage of the population, such a rhetoric implies that young people lack agency or ability to change their behaviors, or to form healthier habits. More so, it feeds into harm-driven expectations that are used to exercise control over the already surveilled and controlled lives of young people. According to boyd (2014, p. 96), "as teens seek out new spaces where they have agency, adults invent new blockades to restrict the power of the young. The rhetoric of addiction is one example, a cultural device used to undermine teens' efforts to reclaim a space. Restrictive adults act on their anxiety as well as their desire to protect young people, but in doing so, they perpetuate myths that produce the fears that prompt adults to place restrictions on teens in the first place." This is evident in school policies that aim to overly regulate and restrict students' access to mobile and social media at school. Banning mobile media aims to create a superficial environment of control and misses a powerful opportunity to help young people manage risk—including stress and pressure to always be connected—and instead attempts to eliminate the temptation and challenges altogether.

I propose that we approach feelings of stress and anxiety as indicative of a need to help young people manage their time, their social lives, and their media practices. In other words, as is true of non-mediated aspects of their lives, students need help identifying and maintaining healthy boundaries. This is true emotionally, socially, and physically in many areas of life—for example, developing healthy friendships, having a healthy physical lifestyle, and managing one's time. Young people (and adults too) need guidance in the use of media. Schools offer a unique opportunity, or perhaps even have a responsibility and an obligation, to help students negotiate healthy boundaries by supporting the development and practice of new habits.

Students' Expectations: Discourses of Trust and Negotiation

As is often the case in highly regimented spaces, students at Freeway High found ways to circumvent policies. The majority of participants did not passively accept the regulations and restrictions enacted via institutional policies, but rather they played active roles in subverting restrictive constraints. Michel de Certeau (1984) would describe these instances as tactical practices that allowed students to subvert the rules from within without transforming the strategic structures of the classroom. Some students actively sought ways to undermine barriers and filters; others relied on peer networks to help them bypass restrictions; others did not demonstrate a desire to bypass barriers. This section highlights some of the ways students resisted institutional constraints and barriers that attempted to limit their access to and their use of mobile and digital media.

Instead of framing students' actions as merely mischievous or devious, I draw from work by Morgan O'Brien (2009), who considers how students enact their own agency even within highly regulated educational environments. O'Brien demonstrates "how young people's use of the mobile phone represents the adoption of particular 'tactics' to assert their agency within the 'strategic' context of a specific power structure, in this case, school"

(p. 30). As other studies have also found (Green 2003; Ito 2005; Taylor 2005), students at Freeway High have developed ways to covertly use mobile and social media during school hours—for example, by texting under their desks, hiding earbuds under hoods, by using proxy servers to bypass technical filters, and by negotiating leniency with particular teachers. Alex Taylor describes these acts as "locally assembled resistance against an established set of social structures or 'rules'" (2005, p. 163). Drawing from de Certeau's concept of resistive tactics, O'Brien argues that disciplined subjects subvert power with whatever possibilities at hand, but he is careful to point out that tactics only allow subjects to "escape without leaving the dominant order" (2009, p. 34). In other words, students work within institutional discipline without completely overruling it. It is also worth noting that students' resistive tactics reflected both the aforementioned interest-driven and friendship-driven practices (Ito et al. 2010).[9] O'Brien's framework is useful for discussing other modes of student resistance with relation to media use, such as bypassing institutional barriers that restrict access to content at school. Although teens' tactics may seem inconsequential, these practices, O'Brien writes (2009, p. 38), "are a part of the way through which everyday life is rendered livable for young people." It is in this vein that I consider the resistive tactics participants exercised in order to cope with constraints of control that the school aimed to enact.

Participants had many motivations for breaking the rules—motivations which are significant because they make visible students' broader expectations about school, technology, and formal education. By examining students' motivations for breaking the rules about media, we can see how students expect to be able to stay in contact with peers (and family members), expect to have access to content they deem valuable, and expect that school will be boring. All three motivations for negotiating in-school media use—sociality, access, and alleviating boredom—provide insight into students' values and expectations of school and learning.

Negotiating Sociality

Social interaction may not be a primary function of school, especially from an adult and institutional perspective, but schools are an integral part of the socialization of teens (Catalano et al. 2004; Giroux and Penna 1979). From an adult perspective, sociality may seem superfluous to or a distraction from the primary goals of formal education. However, school is a place where students learn how to develop healthy relationships, acquire social capital, and prepare to participate in social and political spheres. As with most aspects of life, peers help render the monotony and obligations of school more pleasurable. Having a strong social support network of adults and peers has been linked to reduced stress (Cobb 1976), higher academic achievement (Catalano et al. 2004), and higher graduation rates (Lee and Burkam 2003). Sociality should not be dismissed as secondary to institutional goals of education; rather, students' social life at school plays an important role in achieving the broader goals of education. It is not surprising that students frequently break the media rules and risk punishment in order to stay in contact with peers (and family members) during school hours. Ultimately this struggle is between what school values (a controlled learning environment) and what is of value to a student (social life, the support of peers, and the student's place within the social hierarchy of the school).

The tension between control and trust is related to the previous discussion of helping students manage healthy boundaries in an "always on" connected world. Students' social expectations also reveal the extent to which the boundaries between formal and informal learning are blurred, as are the boundaries between mediated and non-mediated interactions. As will be discussed, teens use media at school to socialize. At times the motivation is primarily friendship-driven; at other times, what at first appears social is actually motivated by interest-driven learning incentives. A consideration of the different social motivations and genres of participation sheds light on students' expectations of media use and their negotiations of school rules.

Let's consider two 14-year-old participants in the study; the identical twins Marcus and Miguel (undocumented Mexican immigrants). Certainly Marcus and Miguel should not have been messaging their friends during class time, which would obviously distract them from lesson plans and the teacher. However, between classes, at lunch, and during free periods, Marcus and Miguel reached out to their online friends, just as other students met up at lockers to chat or walked together to their next class. The brothers had friends at school, but at times they valued the online friendships they had forged via video games even more than the face-to-face relationships with peers at school. This is consistent with recent research out of Murdoch University that found online friendships and face-to-face friends to be "equally as potent" in providing emotional support to teens. There was little evidence in this preliminary study to suggest young people identified a difference between online and physical friendships when describing feelings of connectedness (Gartry 2016). For Marcus and Miguel, using mobile media at school was a way to stay digitally connected in a physical space in which they often felt alienated or disconnected from the social world of their peers. Allowing them to stay connected during appropriate times, and with appropriate boundaries, would create a space in which school rules would be more in line with students' values and expectations. Mobile media allow students a way to maintain contact with their peers even within the regimented space of the schools, which hinders certain modes of sociality. These friendship-driven practices revealed the ways teens' use of mobile media at school fits into their everyday expectations and social practices.

Because filters on the school's browser blocked access to social media, some participants downloaded a different browser onto their mobile devices. The alternate browser allowed them to bypass the school's filters and to connect to peers via social media. This tactic was particularly important for students with restrictive phone plans that limited the number of text messages they could send over mobile networks. Students with limited data plans relied on apps such as Facebook to send messages to their friends for free over Wi-Fi. Amina explained:

Some people don't get text messages — I know some people who get stuff on Facebook faster than they get text message stuff so and, like, sometimes I'll be, like, "Where is this person?" and I'll go on their Facebook and be, like, "Where are you?" I'll be in school at lunch or something and someone will talk about someone I'll be, like, "Who's that person?" And they'll be, like, "Look it up. You know who it is." I'll look them up on Facebook. Honestly, Facebook is the new yearbook—you go and you find people through Facebook—that's how I've got to know a lot of people in school—I'm still kind of new here [so it helps].

Amina's point is that Facebook and other social media sites provide an alternate and more efficient way to contact peers with limited mobile data plans. Several students showed me how to work around school filters that blocked social media sites; they could access Facebook and YouTube from school using Opera and other browsers on their mobile phones and iPods (the school's Wi-Fi filters were set to only block sites in certain browsers).

Jasmine (16 years old, multiracial) showed me an app on her iPod Touch that looked like Facebook but was an alternative app that was used to access Facebook and was not blocked at school. Interestingly, she had not installed the app on her iPod; her friend Bianca (16 years old, Mexican-American) had installed it. Jasmine did not check Facebook on a regular basis throughout the day, so it didn't bother her that she couldn't access it from school. However, Bianca borrowed Jasmine's iPod Touch often, since she had a limited text message plan, and she downloaded the app to communicate with friends. Peers often relied on each other via economies of sharing to learn how to bypass filters and as a way to resist institutional limitations. Notably, students did not necessarily have to possess the technical prowess to bypass restrictions, instead they drew from resources available within their respective peer networks. Regardless of your view of rule-breaking, teens demonstrated great levels of ingenuity and resourcefulness in their attempts to work around school restrictions and stay connected with peers.

Since Bianca did not have a mobile data plan or home Internet service, free Wi-Fi was her sole point of access to the web. She relied on the school's Wi-Fi not only for educational resources but also for maintaining her social life online. Blocking students' access to social network sites might make sense within a framework of educational expectations (i.e., to minimize distractions); however, for low-income disconnected students this restriction was a further disadvantage. Research consistently demonstrates the importance for teens to maintain online identities and connections via social media platforms (boyd 2014; Watkins 2009), yet not all teens have equal access. As will be discussed in the next chapter, school could play a significant role in helping alleviate inequalities for marginalized teens by providing a way for them to create online identities and connections. Privileging adult expectations of educational value at the expense of teens' expectations of sociality created rifts between administrators and students. But more importantly, the school's policy had the unintended consequence of further marginalizing disadvantaged teens by hindering their already limited opportunities for participation in networked publics.

Coping with Restrictions

Students deliberately bypassed the school's filters when they felt they had a right to access information. Here I am not merely focusing on social media as I did in the previous section, but rather I consider how students worked around barriers in order to access content they deemed educational and valuable. For this kind of material, the struggle was much more about a balance between control and trust. Time and again, students expressed frustrations that the school did not trust their discretion. Students believed they should have a right to access content they deemed valuable to their learning environments. This struggle revealed the extent to which students and adults valued different information and modes of learning.

Several participants were experts at finding proxy servers that enabled them to bypass the school's Internet filter. Others, who didn't know how to find a proxy, relied on friends to show them how to bypass filters. Michael (18 years old, black) explained his frustrations:

Oh God. The school's Wi-Fi is so restricted, it's like, you can't go to YouTube, you can't go to Facebook, you can't go to most of the site that you would use that aren't even bad. I'm not saying that you can only go to Google, and all that, but there's some sites you can go to, and some sites that you can't, that you need, it's just annoying. …That's what's stupid. That's why people use proxies, which is a way to get into the websites without being noticed by the school WI-FI.

Antonio (17 years old, Mexican-American) and Sergio (18 years old, Mexican-American) were close friends who were adept at finding proxies. They discussed their success with an element of pride; they knew they were skirting the system, and they enjoyed being able to deliberately bypass filters. They both mentioned that their primary motivation for bypassing the filters was to gain access to information that was interesting and useful. "It's not bad or anything, like, I should have a right to access something that is for a project or whatever," said Antonio, countering a discourse of control with his own expectations of rights.

Some students even belonged to a Google Group called "Free Proxy A Day" as a way to stay one step ahead of the institutional restrictions that blocked access to websites. Despite their best efforts, though, the school eventually discovered each new proxy and blocked it. Antonio and Sergio enjoyed finding new proxies so they could gain access to online tutorials, videos, and other blocked content. Both students said that their preferred mode of learning was to watch online tutorials, which demonstrated techniques for software they were learning.

Sergio: That's another thing I didn't like about Freeway's computers. Like, a lot of the tutorials seemed really cool when I got the visual preview of it, but when I tried to open it, it would be blocked, because apparently it had some unknown content that the school didn't want. And sometimes I would try to download images from file-sharing sites, and they wouldn't let me, and I really needed those images to compose an art piece.

Q: Huh? Yeah, that's kind of a bummer, right?

Sergio: Yeah. Like, YouTube is blocked, here, and at home YouTube is one of my main sources for tutorials, because then I get a spoken kind of tutorial rather than just going back and reading it. … Someone would just be speaking on what I need to do, and that way it would be more efficient.

Because videos were blocked at school, Sergio had to find ways around the filters. His resistive tactics were interest-driven, in that he was motivated to bypass filters in order to access content which he believed expanded his learning ecology. Sergio's comments highlight the extent to which both his preferred mode of learning and his out-of-school mode of learning (video tutorials), were incompatible with the school's preferred method of teaching: reading. Of course reading is a valuable tool for learning and has a place in the classroom. However, when students are learning to produce and edit videos, it stands to reason they should be able to learn via the very medium they are using to create. We can all agree that it would be difficult to teach someone how to read by using only audio content—learning how to read necessitates visual content. In the same way, video production is arguably best learned via video tutorials. Again, students receive mixed messages about media: on the one hand, videos are valuable enough that students learn video production; on the other hand, students are told that videos are not considered a valuable learning choice in the classroom. Often Sergio and Antonio wanted to access a video for the purpose of on-the-spot troubleshooting rather than in response to techniques they had already learned in class. They were experimenting with new editing techniques, and they wanted to learn more about them by viewing video examples. The school's policy of blocking videos and YouTube tutorials was a disservice to students striving to learn the art and skill of video production.

Other students, such as Javier (18 years old, Mexican immigrant), found proxy servers more trouble than he thought they were worth. When I asked if he used them, he responded "No, it's too much work. You go to one and then the next week it's blocked so you try another, and then you ask someone, and that one is blocked too. Or it's just too slow. It's too much, I just quit trying." Interestingly, like Sergio and Antonio, Javier also told me that the sites he was trying to access were usually tutorials, or sites that contained images and music he wanted to use in his films—not social network or video sites. But Javier stopped attempting to resist the school's institutional constraints. This reminds us that we should be careful not to assume that all students want to bypass such constraints.

The well-intentioned policy of blocking inappropriate content had the unintended consequence of exacerbating inequalities for disadvantaged students. Some students were able to access blocked content via their data-enabled mobile devices or via the Internet at home, but these options were not available to all students. Selena, for example, did not have any Internet access at home, and her pay-as-you-go phone plan was limited and at times completely unavailable to her for financial reasons. School was her primary point of access to the Internet. Her interests included photography and writing creative fiction and screenplays. Although at home she had an outdated computer that she could use to write, the lack of Internet access prevented her from sharing her stories online. Additionally, her biggest source of inspiration for her photos was Tumblr, a site that wasn't available to her at home or at school. As will be further discussed in chapters 5 and 7, Selena's practices were restricted by school policies that barred access to valuable resources and content that would have expanded her personal and educational interests. Restrictive policies that block access to content not only miss opportunities to help students navigate online risks; equally as significant, they reflect a privileged understanding of access that presumes students can access resources outside of school. Rather than being an equalizer, schools intensify inequalities by creating barriers that hinder opportunities for already marginalized students.

Alleviating Boredom

A frequent response to why participants used media at school was that they were bored. As many students explained, it was a way to "kill time" in class. When asked if they used social media during class, the frequent answer was "Only if I'm bored." "When I'm bored," Gabriela said. "I try my hardest to get on Twitter from school." When asked if she used social media at school or while doing homework, Amina quickly said "No" but then continued as follows: "Well, yeah, when I'm in school and I'm bored." This was a common theme: social and mobile media were ways to alleviate boredom at school. Perhaps not surprisingly, "boring" was a word many participants used frequently to describe school. When Antonio was asked if school was interesting, he responded "For the most part no." This was disappointingly a common response from many participants regardless of academic achievement and aspirations (i.e., this answer was consistent between high-achieving and low-achieving students).

Regardless of our opinions about media use at school, we should be concerned that students "compare school to a prison," as Sergio said. (See the epigraph at the beginning of this chapter.) Comparing school to prison alludes to the control and boredom that students associate with—or rather expect—from school. It is also indicative of the "school-to-prison pipeline," a term that "refers to the policies and practices that push our nation's schoolchildren, especially our most at-risk children out of classrooms and into the juvenile and criminal justice systems" (Locating the School-to-Prison Pipeline, p. 1). The prison comparison can also be interpreted within a larger framework that criminalizes the practices of the young. There has been an increase in the policing of school hallways and harsh disciplinary policies that criminalize students instead of practicing the use of restorative justice (González 2012). "It has been consistently documented that punitive school discipline policies not only deprive students of educational opportunities, but fail to make schools safer places ... and [increase] the likelihood of future disciplinary problems, and ultimately increasing contact with the juvenile justice system" (ibid., pp. 282–283). Understanding the school-to-prison pipeline adds to a more troubling interpretation of Sergio's comparison of school to prison. Punitive tactics and restrictive practices lead to student disengagement and can have the unfortunate effect of increasing dropout rates, or even incarceration rates.

Boredom is a symptom of disengagement, and nearly all of the students in the current study used digital media to cope with boredom. "Young people's use of the mobile phone in school," O'Brien explains (2009, p. 34), "is indicative of the way in which they subvert the explicit order of the classroom and redirect their attention away from the specific content of the topic in progress." Trivial as it may at first seem, the rhetoric of boredom actually highlights larger discourses and expectations about technology and learning that merit further exploration. On the surface, boredom may seem inconsequential—just as students have always been distracted in class, students have always found aspects of school boring (Azzam 2007; Nett, Goetz, and Daniels 2010; Prensky 2008; Yazzie-Mintz 2007). Being bored is something young people must learn to cope with, both in school and out of school. Just about any parent can recall the irritation of hearing a son or a daughter whine about being bored. Parents strive to teach their children that boredom is to be expected and that life isn't always fun. As an inevitable aspect of life, young people must learn to cope with boredom. Parenting magazines and blogs offer a lot of advice about how to address young people's boredom, and an entire genre of Pinterest boards is dedicated to the topic.[10] It might seem easy to write off complaints of boredom as juvenile or to dismiss them under the assumption that boredom is just part of life. But boredom plays a significant role in students' lives at school, and that should be taken into consideration. Boredom is the number one reason students give for dropping out of high school (Azzam 2007; Vogel-Walcutt et al. 2012). There are other factors that may actually play more significant roles, such as financial constraints, instability at home, pregnancy, or delinquency, but when the perception is that boredom is to blame we ought to take a closer look at its relationship to expectations about school and learning.

Let's consider some more research about the relationship between boredom and academic achievement. When asked to choose three words to describe their typical feelings about school, more than half of American teenagers chose "bored," according to a Gallup poll; more than 40 percent also chose "tired" (Lyons 2004). These words may not be surprising, but they should be concerning—school may not always be exciting, but there is no reason why learning should be boring. In a survey of more than 81,000 students in 110 high schools in the United States, Ethan Yazzie-Mintz (2007, p. 5) found that nearly 75 percent of students characterized school as boring because "material wasn't interesting." Another 39 percent explained they were bored in class because "material wasn't relevant to me," and 32 percent reported that they were bored because "work wasn't challenging enough" (ibid.). Research indicates that boredom, attitudes about learning, and school performance go hand in hand. The journalist Amanda Ripley spent time at high schools investigating and examining the day-to-day lives of American teens. What immediately struck her when she went back into a high school for the first time as an adult was the high degree of boredom. "It's important, I think, to remember this boredom. Otherwise, adults can build fictional schools in their heads, places where time behaves normally, where one can go to the bathroom without asking permission. Then they can obsess over things that matter only in these make-believe schools, not in real students' real lives. … Boredom, it turns out, is toxic. It is related to depression, poor grades, substance abuse, hopelessness, and loneliness" (Ripley 2013).

Ripley found that students turned to social media as a way to cope with boredom. She found it particularly revealing that students took "selfies" in which they strove to express boredom through expressions and posture. She was also impressed by the creativity that some students employed to make their tweets, vines, and Instagram posts about boredom anything but boring. Like the students Ripley observed, some of the students discussed in the present book turned to social media to alleviate boredom, sometimes scrolling through other people's posts, sometimes messaging friends, and sometimes talking about boredom. As an example from the current study, Gabriela used Twitter as an outlet for emotions and thoughts in the moment. Scrolling through her Twitter feed turned up her weekly updates about feeling "bored enough to die" at school.

Burkus (2014), Gasper and Middlewood (2007), and Mann and Cadman (2014) have argued that boredom can foster creativity. However, their research describes specific contexts (mostly experimental settings) and often describes tedious tasks (e.g., stacking cups or reading a phone book) that fail to mirror the highly regimented and controlled spaces of high school. Boredom isn't merely the absence of stimulation; it is an unpleasant state that prompts a person to want to escape and disengage. It is often cited as "a motivational barrier" that can be "a detriment to academic learning" (Pekrun et al. 2002, cited in Vogel-Walcutt et al. 2012). Different individuals assess boredom differently, but it is often induced by tasks that are perceived of as pointless and repetitive and tasks over which people have little control (Vogel-Walcutt et al. 2012). When considering research that suggests boredom can be a positive motivation, we must also consider how individuals respond to boredom. In a German study of 976 teenagers, Nett, Goetz, and Daniels (2010) found that students who evaded boredom—that is, who distracted themselves to alleviate boredom—did worse in school and experienced more boredom than students who reappraised the situation, coped with boredom by trying to find the value in what they were doing, and attempted to talk themselves out of boredom. The findings of Nett et al. suggested that reappraising was a more productive coping strategy than evasion. However, at school many students reach for technology or other distractions as a way to evade boredom, rather than search for more productive or creative ways to cope.

On the other end of the boredom spectrum, educational environments that deliberately construct engaging conditions that alleviate boredom have "the potential to be of considerable value to educators and may ultimately improve student performance (Belton and Priyadharshini 2007, cited in Vogel-Walcutt 2012). Engagement (i.e., the lack of boredom) is best achieved in challenging and motivating environments that facilitate autonomy (Belton and Priyadharshini 2007). Unfortunately, many participants in our study described school in ways that were antithetical to engagement and learning. Participants often felt that they had little control over their physical environment or their academic pursuits (i.e., that they lacked autonomy). Others expressed frustration that school hindered opportunities for them to pursue their own creative interests. Far too often students reported that they did not understand the larger purpose of what they were learning and that they considered the methods of teaching boring or outdated. For example, some expressed frustration that they could not choose what literature to read, or that they were not allowed to listen to music to help them concentrate when working on assignments by themselves in class. Other students complained that teachers relied too heavily on boring PowerPoint presentations and wished that more teachers would incorporate media and interactivity into the classrooms. When asked what would make school more engaging, Antonio replied:

Maybe if they had better lessons, because most teachers, they do the old stuff. They stand in front of a board, they'll say it many times. People won't get it. Maybe if they had a video to go with that, it would be better, because I know I learn better if I see a video or something. In my astronomy class, my teacher shows us a lot of videos, and I actually learn like that—projects that let you be creative and do stuff. Or where you move around, because if you're standing still in one class for a long time, you get bored of that and you stop learning. Moving around gets blood flowing to your head and everywhere ... and the brain starts working more, so I think moving around would be good.

In saying this, Antonio echoed many other participants who were frustrated that school did not allow them to be more active or to incorporate their interests into assignments. In a different interview, Antonio expressed irritation that his English teacher would not let him write a book report in the form of a script. "She says she wants me to write. But a script is writing! And it's what I like, it's more creative, you know?" Antonio's interests in screenwriting exemplified an opportunity to connect his personal interest with formal education, but in this particular instance his teacher would not allow him to do a more creative writing project instead of a more traditional book report. As will be discussed in the concluding section of this chapter, students consistently described projects as their favorite mode of learning because projects allowed them to bring in their own interests, express creativity, and often allowed them to incorporate media into the projects.

Antonio felt passionate enough about the technology rules at school that he chose those rules as the topic for a required paper in his English class. In that paper he raised many of the points that I have addressed in this chapter. He explained his viewpoint in the following interview:

Antonio: One of my teachers, every time you walk into the class, she'll tell you to get your headphones out, put your cell phones up, put everything and all your electronics up, and it gets really annoying because she says it every day. After a while it's just, like, "Why? People are going to have them and have them out. What's the point of enforcing this?" I think electronics can help a lot—that's why I wrote the thesis paper on it.

Q: You wrote a thesis paper?

Antonio: Yes. On personal electronic devices in school.

Q: Do you mind telling me about it?

Antonio: I basically just searched up online why do they ban electronics in school? I mean—most schools have all these resources—electronic, they buy laptops, they buy computers, but they stop it at cell phones and iPods. But why if they're free and they already come with the student—they don't have to pay for anything. ... They're just being weirdos and not letting us use them because they think it's going to distract us. And I know it distracts some people, but for me, I can actually get my work done and not get distracted and then just plug in my iPod after I'm done. Or if the class is loud and you're trying to concentrate on something, why not put your head-phones in? I know for me, it makes it way easier if I have headphones in and I'm trying to read a book and the class is loud—it's just easier.

Q: What do you think is easier?

Antonio: It helps me drown out—for me, the music is helping me concentrate and—I put this in my thesis paper—there is proven fact that music helps you study and learn, so if it helps you study and learn, why not have it in schools? It just bugs me that they're not allowing it. We're in a new age—it's the 21st century. People are buying technology every single day no matter what the price is—they're very useful. You can write notes on them or keep an agenda—that's basically what I wrote in my thesis paper.

Q: You are writing an argument in favor of more technology in school?

Antonio: Yes. In favor.

Antonio's comments highlight a larger problem with the school environment: it's distracting. Many participants complained about the lack of discipline in class, for example, that students talked too much during class and made it hard to concentrate. As Antonio put it, "If the class is loud and you're trying to concentrate on something, why not put in your head-phones." Far from being a technology problem, this reveals a larger concern about lack of control in classrooms. For students such as Antonio, music was not a distraction; it was a way to cope with an already disruptive environment—a way to bolster his ability to be productive, not detract from it.

Media technology has the potential to make the classroom a more engaging and interactive space that can enhance learning. Yet instead of finding ways to bring interactivity and media into the classroom, the majority of teachers banned it. Without opportunities to use media in responsible ways that enhanced learning, students relied on media as a way to alleviate boredom. Creating barriers that prevented students from incorporating their personal interests into the curriculum is another way in which formal learning environments are at odds with the ways young people expect to learn. Rather than harnessing the educational potential of mobile media or validating the educational ways teens were already using mobile media, banning mobile media sent the message that mobile media were essentially risky and therefore dismissible in the formal learning environment. In fact, however, research has demonstrated that mobile media can enhance learning, particularly for disengaged teens (Ison, Hayes, Robinson, and Jamieson 2004). "Modern mobile phones," Brian Ferry contends (2009, p. 47), "can be used to help learners access web-based content, remix it, share it, collaborate with others, and create media-rich deliverables for the classroom teacher as well as a global audience." How the students mentioned in this book view media—as entertainment, as a distraction, as a tool for socializing, as a way to learn autonomously, and as a resource—differs greatly from how many teachers and adults view media—as merely a distraction and a threat to learning.

Conclusion: What Can We Gain If We Lose Control?

In his statement comparing school to prison, Sergio invokes a discourse of rights with relation to technology. Right or wrong, students feel entitled to media and technology at school. Despite the rules, they expect the right to be autonomous learners (at least in some contexts) and they expect access to the social aspects mobile technology facilitates—aspects that can bolster learning. Teachers, on the other hand, largely expect media to be a distraction, to be a risk, and to disrupt the learning environment. And they aren't wrong; it can be all of those things. Where then is the middle ground? Are students using their phones in disruptive and distracting ways simply because those are the only means of use they are afforded? If they were expected to use media responsibly—if they were entrusted with the privilege of media, rather than having it punitively banned—would their expectations and practices change? How would a policy of "acceptable use," rather than "unacceptable use," shift students' and teachers' frustrations, expectations, and trust? I do not deny that there are potentially harmful psychological, social, and physical risks associated with misuse of mobile media. But policies making the use of such media unacceptable—policies that reflect harm-driven expectations—fail to take into account what is lost when we ban media at school: opportunities to develop literacies, as well as more equitable opportunities and access for disadvantaged students.

There are nominal benefits to controlling mobile media at school, and certainly rules help minimize some risks. Yet I worry about students' ability to navigate risks if schools and teachers do not play an active and intentional role in shaping mobile media norms, boundaries, and practices. Risk is inevitable, yet we must help young people manage risk. Aiming to eradicate risk but doing it ineffectively leaves students navigating precarious terrains of the mediated world without guidance or adult advocates. Instead of myopically focusing on potential harms, we should expand our focus to balance the beneficial opportunities that accompany risk.

To bring this chapter into conversation with chapter 3, my final point is that formal education has a unique opportunity to help students identify,

assess, and negotiate risks via the intentional development of digital literacies. But also, and of the utmost importance, media and mobile technologies provide a unique opportunity to bridge students' interests and modes
of learning with formal learning in ways that can counter boredom, fatigue,
and risky behaviors. Schools and technology can function in complimen-
tary spaces that work together to create more equitable opportunities for
marginalized and disadvantaged learners. This can only come about when
schools abandon a discourse and practice of authoritarian control and
punitive reactions, and instead invoke expectations of trust.

I think we should interrogate and update the same question that
Schramm, Lyle, and Parker posed more than fifty years ago about television, but in today's world the question becomes "Are schools doing
everything possible to connect mobile media to the intellectual growth
of students?" This question will be addressed in part II the book. The
goal of part I has been to analyze how harm-driven expectations of risk
affect policies at the national and state levels, and how and to what effect
those policies are implemented at Freeway High. I have established that
historical fears produce discourses of risk that lead to policies of panic.
These restrictive policies inequitably and unproductively regulate students'
autonomy, ingenuity, and access. The policies are well-intentioned and
may minimize some harm, but they also exacerbate other overlooked risks
and are rarely balanced with opportunity-driven expectations. My aim is to
more closely consider how expectations affect student experiences at school
and online. In the following chapters I aim to answer the question "What
are the implications of risk discourses in the everyday lives of teens at
school and online?" I answer this by connecting and focusing on different
aspects of teens' lives, including the influence and intersection of peers,
school, and home life. The analysis builds upon the connected learning
model that will be more fully explained and explored later in the book.

II   Experiences

5   Networked Sharing: Participation, Copyright, and Values

A lot of what's on YouTube is amateur; I don't want to be seen as that so I wait until I think my film is ready. I want to build a professional portfolio.

Javier (18 years old, immigrant from Mexico)

"Do you ever share your films on YouTube," I asked an 18-year-old senior named Javier one afternoon after school. Javier had written and produced several short films, some as part of the Cinematic Arts Project, and others with his older sister (an alumna of Freeway High currently attending in film school in Mexico). Javier spent his evenings watching foreign films on YouTube because he enjoyed learning different cinematography techniques. He was technologically savvy, took pride in his films, and valued feedback and collaborative learning. He was passionate about pursuing a career in filmmaking and was planning to apply to film school in Mexico after graduation. I was surprised when he told me "No, I don't ever post what I have created." This was not how I had expected this mature and confident aspiring filmmaker to respond.

As it turns out, Javier's response was part of a broader trend among the young media makers I got to know at Freeway High. Time and time again, students who were heavily invested in online participatory cultures (e.g., Tumblr, Flickr, YouTube, Vimeo) revealed that, although they enjoyed consuming amateur and professional media online, and although they were actively producing creative media content, they were not sharing their creations online. This surprised me for several reasons. First, many of these students were accustomed to sharing their creative media content formally in technology classes and informally with peers in after-school clubs. Second, many students actively sought feedback and support from peers and teachers, and they had expressed a preference for informal, peer, and collaborative learning styles. They spent a lot of time watching and commenting on amateur films, and they relied on tutorials, music, and images that they could access within online amateur communities. Many of the students I met expressed explicit interest in pursuing careers in film, photography, music, or video game production. They worked to actively construct entrepreneurial identities and aimed to transcend the role of media in their lives from mere hobby to a pathway to a future career (see chapter 7). I had mistakenly anticipated that such students would be actively consuming, producing, *and sharing* their creative media in the spaces in which they appeared so heavily invested. The scholarship I was familiar with about young media makers and participatory cultures indicated a trend or an expectation that young people wanted to share their projects online. But for the most part, that was not the case with the teens I got to know at Freeway High. This is in direct contrast to narratives of young people that expect them to innately possess both the desire and capacity to network and share their creative media content online (Bennett, Maton, and Kervin 2008; Prensky 2001 2005; Tapscott 1998).

Why were these technologically savvy, ambitious, creative, and (somewhat) digitally connected teens consuming and producing media, but not actively sharing and networking online? And is it important? Was it merely a matter of individual personality? If so, was it sheer coincidence that this was common among the working-class, minority, and marginalized teens in the study? Was it that they simply lacked motivation to participate in that way, or was there something else embedded within their practices that inhibited these young media makers from more fully participating in the online worlds they enjoyed inhabiting? By "practices" I do not simply mean what teens are doing; I also mean the context that renders participation meaningful (Wenger and Lave 1991). "Practices," Harlan, Bruce, and Lupton argue (2012, p. 570), "are more than the visible enacted actions; they include the values, unarticulated roles, sensitivities, and worldview of the context [of the action]." Questions of how, who, when, and where young people participate are pivotal to understanding how class, identity, literacies, and institutional and adult support structure the practices of young people. If we believe that digital technologies and participatory cultures have the potential to leverage more equitable opportunities for youth, then we must pay serious attention to why some teens publicly share and network online and why others do not.

Schools such as Freeway High provide significant opportunities for young people to explore and expand their creative identities and skills by producing media. Yet, as I will explain, technical skills and competencies are a necessary, yet not wholly sufficient aspect of becoming digitally literate participants in today's networked publics. I am certainly not the first or the only researcher to make this argument (I will explore this momentarily); however, what I want to explore here are the barriers that inhibit some young people from developing the literacies and confidence necessary to meaningfully and fully participate in the creation of their own mediated spaces. In more positive terms, what are the necessary conditions that facilitate the development of participatory literacies? In this context, I am specifically addressing teens who are actively *creating* media—thus participating in their own mediated cultures—yet are not going a step further to *share* their own practices in networked publics.

I want to back up and contextualize my analysis within a broader literature related to digital literacies and participatory cultures. I will situate this particular population within a larger discourse of young people as media makers, a discourse that is seemingly at odds with, and yet wholly situated within discourses of visibility and risk. And I provide more context about the structure of the after-school media clubs. With these contexts established, I analyze the ways in which several creative media makers at Freeway High navigated opportunities and barriers to participating online. Their stories highlight the structural, cultural, and personal conditions that inhibit or facilitate networking and sharing in online creative environments.

Participatory Cultures

Be it a professional-looking short film on YouTube, a silly meme on Facebook, or a funny remix or political mashup on Tumblr, we know that teens are actively creating and sharing creative media across many different online platforms. Data from the Pew Research Center reveal that the percentage of teens uploading their own content online has continued to go grow; as of 2012, 30 percent of older teen Internet users had recorded and uploaded a video online, up from 14 percent in 2006. Further, it was found that frequent social media users were more likely to record and share videos as in comparison with teens who were not active on social network sites (Lenhart 2012). Some teens are creating wholly original media in the form of music, films, and photography, while others participate in a practice known as *remix*. Remix uses existing content and then adds to, mixes, or otherwise alters the text, sound, or images to create a new iteration of the original creation, often with a different meaning, message, or purpose. Technological advances and evolving cultural practices have lowered the barriers for participation in a mediated culture. In the academic literature, the current media environment is often referred to as "participatory culture" or a "remix culture" (Jenkins et al. 2009).

Lessig (2008) makes the case that through most of history people lived in a "read/write" culture. Individuals and collective societies actively participated in "reading" and "writing" cultural artifacts and practices. Think about telling stories around a campfire, singing popular songs together, dancing the waltz or the macarena, or playing musical instruments together in one's own home or church—in all of these examples, cultures relied on well-known tropes, folktales, and melodies that they themselves may not have created, but they incorporated into their own practices and imbued with localized meaning. Society was both "reading" (i.e., consuming) popular culture (which is always localized within particular places and time) and simultaneously "writing" (i.e., producing) culture by actively participating in story-telling, singing, dancing, and music-making.

With cultural and technological developments from the nineteenth to the twentieth century, society began to increasingly shift from a primarily read/write culture to what Lessig refers to as a read-only culture. The majority of individuals began to spend their time consuming media and popular culture, but they were not as likely to actively produce their own media or culture. This is not to suggest that only professionals and corporations were creating content; however, there was a significant shift in who had access to the capital, skills, and prowess to produce content. This is due in part to technological changes in media production—clearly it costs a lot of money and requires a lot of skill to create a film or a television show. Additionally, media ownership was increasingly consolidated and corporatized, thus limiting the public's access to community stations, amateur presses, and distribution outlets. This shift coincides with the birth of what we typically think of as "mass media." As a society people consumed much more media content than they created; they "read" culture and media, but were less likely or less encouraged to "write" or create cultural artifacts and media. We were not passive recipients, yet we were not invited to participate in the creation of mediated culture.

With the development of the Internet and the World Wide Web, affordable personal computers, and high-speed Internet access, the media landscape evolved in notable ways—both technologically and culturally. Lessig contends that the Internet provides the opportunity for a potential revitalization of a read/write culture—one in which the majority of citizens can again consume and create (read/write) a mediated culture. The barriers to participation—that is, the requirements for material and capital resources and skills and competencies—have been lowered significantly.

Additionally, the Internet provides an outlet for amateurs to distribute their media, and also opens up spaces for consumers to "speak back" to media culture (e.g., reviewing films, commenting on a news article, or posting a video response to someone else's video).

In a similar vein, other scholars refer to the present media landscape as part of a "participatory culture." The media scholar Henry Jenkins has written extensively about participatory cultures, though he is cautious not to attribute the cultural shift entirely to changes in technology. He points out that even within "read only" cultures people still found ways to participate in popular and mediated culture—for example, "Trekkies" organized conventions for *Star Trek* fans to come together and participate in mediated fan cultures (Jenkins 1992). Invested fans of a particular show, band, film, book, or genre have always found ways to connect and participate in ways that transcended merely consuming a media text. Jenkins is also acutely aware of the ways in which the Internet, affordable personal computers, and mobile technologies democratize the ability of fans and citizens to participate in the creation of media culture. According to Jenkins et al. (2009, p. xi), participatory culture is defined as "a culture with relatively low barriers to artistic expression and civic engagement, strong support for creating and sharing one's own creations, and some type of informal mentorship whereby what is known by the most experienced is passed along to novices. A participatory culture is also one in which members believe their contributions matter, and feel some degree of social connection with one another (at the least they care what other people think about what they have created)." With Sam Ford and Joshua Green, Henry Jenkins also discusses how commercial corporate media are responding to new modes of consumption, distribution, and creation; they correctly point out that participatory cultures do not exist outside of or necessarily in conflict with corporatized conglomerate media structures, but rather they function alongside and within more traditional models of media production and distribution. (Jenkins, Ford, and Green 2013).[1]

What is exciting about online participatory cultures is the potential to democratize media production and distribution. In a corporatized commercial media culture, the very few create and disseminate media for the very many to consume for a price (i.e., production is nearly always driven by profit). However, online participatory culture opens up opportunities for amateurs and those without millions of dollars, a film degree, or Hollywood connections to create their own media content and to disseminate it to potentially large audiences. As a society we have increasing opportunities to hear, see, and amplify the voices and bodies of those who are marginalized and silenced within a commercial model of media production (i.e., populations not easily capitalized upon in a corporate media system).

We have made some advances, yet research reveals that commercial media are still predominantly produced by, and representative of, white men. For example, women make up 51 percent of the US population, but hold less than 7 percent of all TV and radio station licenses. People of color make up more than 36 percent of the US population, but hold just over 7 percent of radio licenses and a shocking 3 percent of TV licenses (Diversity in Media Ownership 2015). Only 23 percent of US films feature a female protagonist, and only 31 percent of speaking roles are for women. (Puchko 2014). Women represent less than 20 percent of Hollywood producers, editors, writers, and cinematographers, and numbers are even more dismal for women of color. The dominant white male problem is evident from writing, directing, camera and set work, to on-screen representation (Hollywood Diversity Report 2014). A particularly poignant Tumblr page created by the writer and performer Dylan Marron called "Every Single Word Spoken" highlights the problematic representation of minorities in feature films by cutting them down to only the lines spoken by a person of color. Entire feature-length films are reduced to minutes, or even seconds. For example, *E.T.* is reduced to nine seconds and *Jaws* to seven, and the entire *Harry Potter* film series only includes 5 minutes and 40 seconds of talk time for people of color in all 1,027 minutes of film (Marron 2015).

The reasons for the lack of diversity in media production and representation are historically embedded within systems of discrimination, nepotism, and xenophobia; solutions are complex and will take time. A democratized participatory media culture has the potential to disrupt a media model that privileges the interests, voices, bodies, and experiences of white, straight, male culture. Changes in technology have led to increased opportunities for people of color, women, young people, immigrants, queer, disabled, and other historically marginalized populations to create and distribute their own stories. Struggles for more equitable media production, representation, and circulation have long been the focus and advocacy of media scholars invested in social justice, and participatory culture reignites such debates. Jenkins, Ford, and Green, writing about participatory culture, contend:

If we see participatory culture, though, as a vital step toward the realization of a century-long struggle for grassroots communities to gain greater control over the means of cultural production and circulation—if we see participation as the work of publics and not simply of markets and audiences—then opportunities to expand participation are struggles we must actively embrace through our work, whether through efforts to lower economic and technical obstacles or to expand access to media literacies. ... [Research suggests] our public sphere has been enriched through the diversification of who has the means to create and share culture. (2013, p. 193)

It is easy to be optimistic and hopeful about the potential of participatory culture to revolutionize the limited commercialized media markets, especially when we consider the growing numbers of young people creating and circulating grassroots and user-generated media. However, disrupting the status quo of a hegemonic corporatized media culture is much more complicated than merely providing alternative options for media production, we must also equalize opportunities and access to the literacies that often preclude the most marginalized from equally participating.

Unequal Participation

Not all media ecologies are created equal; within participatory culture there are divides and gaps in access and participation. As was noted in the introduction, early scholarship on the "digital divide" focused on the "haves" and the "have nots"—that is, who did and did not have access to computers and the Internet. Over the past two decades within the United States the digital divide has been significantly reduced across income, education, gender, geography, and ethnic divides. This is due in part to government initiatives which have provided subsidies for libraries and public schools to acquire computers, Internet access, and other digital technologies. Additionally, the lowered cost of personal computers, and more specifically mobile technologies, have enabled low-income individuals and households access to the Internet. For youth of color and youth in low income households, mobile technologies are more likely to be the primary access point to the Internet (Smith 2015). Mobile phones are less expensive than personal computers and pay-as-you-go plans do not require credit checks or contracts that bar some from attaining home Internet. Mobile phones alleviate gaps in access and are increasingly providing greater opportunities for media creation (e.g., Vine, Instagram, Snapchat), but they nonetheless are limited in terms of software and ability to create and edit professional content (e.g., it is still much easier to type a long term paper on a laptop than a mobile device). Watkins poignantly asks us to consider the limitations:

While mobile phones can be a tool for creativity, learning, and civic engagement, credible concerns have been raised that teens who are restricted to mobile phones for home Internet use may also be restricted to media ecologies and social networks that rarely, if ever, afford access to these kinds of experiences. Although only a small percentage of young people are using mobile devices as a powerful learning tool today, the percentage is growing. The issue is not whether rich and meaningful mobile learning ecologies will develop. ... Rather, the real question is, will these mobile learning ecologies be distributed in ways that close or maintain America's learning divide? (2012, p. 7)

Closing gaps in access is an important step in creating a more equitable society, but it would be fallacious to assume that access alone can eradicate inequalities. The assumption that technology in and of itself will eliminate inequalities relies on a technologically deterministic perspective—one that assumes the mere availability to technology will solve problems. This access-only perspective ignores the literacies, incentives, and systems of support that are necessary to effectively and meaningfully use technology. A myopic focus on access also overlooks the cultural values embedded within practices; access alone does not mean everyone will use technology in democratic, empowering, and educational ways. As the access divide has become less substantial, scholars have correctly shifted focus from access divides to "participation divides" (Hargittai and Walejko 2008) or the "participation gap" (Jenkins et al. 2009; Watkins 2012). A lens of participation requires us to consider how different populations use digital media technologies in different and unequal ways, and to what effect. Participatory culture necessitates the development of particular competencies and literacies in order to engage and participate in an online culture.

Literacy and Sharing

Scholarship has continued to consider why some populations or individuals are less likely to participate in socially networked online cultures in ways that are both individualistically and collectively beneficial. The answers lead to further questions of what it means to be literate in a digital society. For the sake of my research, the literacy approach is particularly useful because it clearly ties into Lessig's conceptualization of a read/write society; just as we simultaneously teach young children to read and write (i.e., we do not ask them to master reading before putting a pencil in their hand), we have an obligation to teach young people to both read and write in a (digital) media ecology. Society has a responsibility to invest in the advancement of digitally literate citizens.

Jenkins et al. (2009) have been influential in helping map out the challenges of a participatory culture in terms of the necessary digital literacies that online participatory culture requires. They identify eleven literacies that young people need to meaningfully and fully take part in a participatory culture: play, performance, simulation, appropriation, multitasking, distributed cognition, collective intelligence, judgment, transmedia navigation, networking, and negotiation. They demonstrate how these literacies move beyond mere skills, and they demonstrate rather persuasively that in the 21st century "new media literacies should be seen as social skills, as ways of interacting within a larger community, and not simply as individualized skills to be used for personal expression" (ibid., p. 32). Sociality and collaboration are embedded in each of the literacies Jenkins et al. set forth. Literacies are more than just access and skillsets; they are a way to close equity gaps and empower students to more fully participate in the formation of their learning and media ecologies, which is why this chapter addresses the question of why some students participate by sharing their creative content and why others do not. We must remember that participation is more complicated than individual motivation and choice, but rather it is indicative of structural and organizational differences.

We must interrogate the systems that produce and reproduce curricula, educational discourses, and norms. Digital and network literacies are an important aspect of participatory culture, but unfortunately schools are often barred from playing a more direct role in shaping students' online participation because of historically rooted understandings of risk anxiety and the harm-driven regulations that were addressed in the first half of this book.

Beneficial Visibility

Young people's online participation must be contextualized within discourses of visibility. As will be discussed further in the next chapter, discourses of visibility are often couched in expectations of harm. Risk discourse leads to concerns about the extent to which young people's voices, bodies, and experiences are made visible online. There are of course risks associated with increased visibility, such as bullying, predators, the creation of sexually explicit images, and so forth (as addressed in chapter 2). However, if we shift our expectations away from risk and instead consider opportunities, we find many beneficial, educational, and empowering aspects of intentional online visibility. A consideration of visibility as part of participatory culture requires a move away from expectations of harm, and instead implores us to consider the opportunities of deliberate visibility within networked publics.

Part of the value of participatory cultures lies in the potential for marginalized populations to produce and share creative media that privileges their unique experiences, identities, and communities. Yet, in a society that consistently and persuasively constructs the visibility of young people as a risk, we risk further rendering invisible the lived experiences of the very populations we ought to strive to empower via online participatory media. The effects of silence and invisibility are consequential on both individual and collective levels of society and deserve our critical attention. We need to consider how deliberate visibility can benefit teens on the margins of society, how we can support the pursuit of more equitable opportunities, and the expansion of social networks via intentional public participation.

There is a growing body of research that demonstrates the benefits of intentional and deliberate visibility. The key words are *intentional* and *deliberate*. Here I am not talking about the ways platforms and peer networks render private interactions public (as I will in chapter 6); rather, I am talking about the ways teens intentionally and deliberately make their identities, networks, and creative media content visible via participation in networked publics. It is not uncommon for some young people to share their own media content with the explicit goal of receiving feedback and to experience the benefits of finding an appropriate audience for their creativity. Lange and Ito (2010, p. 280) claim that communication and feedback in online communities "is one of the primary mechanisms through which creators improve their craft after entry into a creative practice." This feedback loop allows young artists and media makers to connect their practices with other like-minded individuals and find collaborative peer support.

Patricia Lange (2014) explores how young people use YouTube to construct what she calls "technical identities" as an avenue for developing productive digital literacies. She demonstrates that identity development is not only about the media production, but is also about their participation in online communities. In an examination of girls who express "geek" identities via the creation of YouTube videos, Lange (2014, p. 95) explains that

Girls perform being a geek not only through the media they create but through interactive and participatory practices such as joining a popular site early, crafting one's channel page to showcase technical ability, exercising command over interactive aspects of online spaces, espousing techno-cultural values such as being self-taught, and displaying self-perceptions of technical identities in words and images. Each performance is a proposal of identity expression that may be ratified or challenged by viewers, commenters, and other video makers.

Girls participated in visible online communities as part of their public identity construction. While their experiences were by no means always positive, they participated in ways that were beneficial to the construction of their identities and also developed valuable technical and social literacies. Further, Lange and Ito claim, "the ability of digital networked media to create new publics and audiences for amateur work is one of the most transformative dimensions of contemporary new media" (2010, p. 284).

The benefits of online sharing and participation have been well documented through studies such as those reported in Lange 2014, Jenkins 2006, Burgess and Green 2009, and Ito et al. 2010. As Lange writes (2014, p. 9), "[On YouTube] kids are exhibiting an awareness that they must have the skills to use new technical tools in order to self-actualize and achieve visible personhood among heterogeneous, networked publics." Scholars espouse the benefits of participating in networked publics which include fostering and leveraging civic identities (Bennett, Freelon, and Wells 2011; Raynes-Goldie and Walker 2008), collaborative peer learning (Ito et al. 2010), networking with others who share a common interest (Burgess and Green 2009), spaces for creative production (Lange 2014; Light, Griffiths, and Lincoln 2012), and the acquisition of cultural capital (Brader and Luke 2013). And participatory amateur culture and commercialized corporate culture are increasingly functioning alongside one another, insofar as amateur creators can capitalize on their participation as part of a hybrid participatory and commercial system (Burgess and Green 2009; Jenkins, Ford, and Green 2013). One example is YouTube Partners, which pays amateurs to incorporate advertising into their videos. The potential benefits of uploading creative media to YouTube are personal, educational, and economic.

In all the examples cited above, young people are actively learning, creating, and investing time in spaces that are structured around their vested interest in a particular form of media and popular culture. They are not merely creating media; they are doing so in collaborative, supportive, and visible spaces. Creating media and playing with popular texts have value in and of itself, but there is additional value in learning how to publicly participate in creative online spaces such as YouTube, Flickr, and Tumblr. Analyses of these modes of participation often include a description of the literacies young people develop through such practices. Yet there tends to be less focus on the literacies and dispositions that are necessary for participation in the first place. Notably, all of the aforementioned scholars pay attention to the discrepancies of participation and are concerned with unequal modes of engagement and the inequity of opportunity (i.e., the participation gap). What I am exploring is not a departure from earlier research, but rather echoes the concerns of other media scholars. However, I expand the lens of analysis from what students learn via participation in an online media culture, to a more explicit exploration of the literacies (or lack thereof) and dispositions that preclude some young people from participating in meaningful and visible ways.

An important caveat: I want to be cautious not to imply that all young people and all media makers must visibly share their creative productions online, nor do I want to reify a hierarchy of participation. Online participation is sometimes visually represented as a pyramid of different levels of engagement. At the bottom are the lurkers or observers who are constructed as passive consumers of information. In the middle are the collaborators, those who share, critique, and curate information. At the top are media creators, who are viewed as the most valuable participants (Horowitz 2006). This hierarchical model leads to statements that suggest that majority of the web is comprised of lurkers and only a small percentage of people are active creators (Khuffash 2014). There are several problems with this model. First, Ito et al. (2010) specifically describe "genres of participation" as a way to draw attention to individuals' *practices* rather than categories of people. A genres approach acknowledges that participation varies across different platforms and that at different times individuals move in and out of these different forms of engagement. It also takes into consideration the motivations for practices, including peripheral participation. Someone may actively contribute to Wikipedia during a presidential-election year, and then stop after the election. Likewise, someone may leave a lot of comments on a private Facebook account, but not do so on a publicly accessible Instagram account. These two simple examples highlight how practices fluctuate. Accounting for differentiations of practices disrupts the static hierarchal categorizations and instead emphasizes the "ecology of interactions between different participants" (Jenkins, Ford, and Green 2013,

p. 157). Additionally, Jenkins, Ford, and Green challenge the normative assumption that lurking is passive or inconsequential:

A "lurker" provides value to people sharing commentary or producing multimedia content by expanding the audience and potentially motivating their work, while critics and curators generate value for those who are creating material and perhaps for one another. … Research suggests that people initially learn through "lurking" or observing the margins, certain basic activities may represent stepping-stones toward greater engagement, and that key individuals help motivate others' advancement. (ibid., pp. 157–158)

Here Jenkins et al. draw from Lave and Wenger's (1991) influential argument that "legitimate peripheral participation" is a significant aspect of learning, questioning, and self-reflectivity. Peripheral forms of participation provide newcomers with an opportunity to familiarize themselves with the social norms of a particular space. Rheingold (2012) reasons that one crucial aspect of digital literacy is "netiquette"—that is, learning how to pay attention to and understand the norms of online communities. This involves lurking (observing) in order to get a better sense of how a particular online community interacts. Rheingold advises that newcomers jump in when they are able to add value; this benefits the community and the reputation of the newcomer.

This chapter is based on a normative evidenced-based assumption that intentional and visible participation in online communities is valuable, and in it I make a case that young people miss out on opportunities when they do not share their media creations in safe networked publics. Yet I am specifically addressing this question within the context of creative media makers who have expressed a desire to pursue a career in the creative media industries. I do not want to dismiss the ways teens participate peripherally, but during my time at Freeway High I was struck by students' reluctance to share their own creative media content. The question of why thousands of young people choose to perform and express identities online in visible ways while other students—with similar creative interest-driven mediated passions—choose not to do so warrants further investigation. As this chapter demonstrates, the answers are complex, and there probably are many factors that influence decisions and practices; however, I focus on the barriers that hinder the development of literacies. Young people must develop the appropriate digital literacies to safely navigate online networks and positively join online participatory media cultures. Furthermore, schools have unique opportunities and an obligation to help young people navigate networks and online participatory spaces. Yet, as was addressed in chapters 1 and 2, historical fears and harm-driven policies that reinforced expectations of risk limited Freeway High from playing a more active role in the development of students' digital literacies. The remainder of this chapter explores the contours of the participation gap in order to understand the barriers that prevent some students from sharing their creative media projects in socially networked publics and the conditions that would enable them to do so.

Barriers to Sharing Creative Media in Networked Publics

Some students at the school shared their projects online, and some even hosted their own YouTube and Vimeo channels, yet most of the club participants had never thought about sharing their creative content or were afraid to share it online. Explanations varied, but there was a common theme running throughout many of the reasons: that of fear and disempowerment. More specifically, the three barriers that predominantly inhibited students from sharing their creative media in socially networked publics can be summed up as fear that their content or ideas would be stolen, fear of unwanted criticism or fear that their production was not professional enough to share, and lack of time and payoff. The three barriers are reflective of harm-driven expectations and fears that overlook the benefits of taking risks. Their concerns were legitimate and valid, yet all three fears can be countered with the development of more nuanced digital literacies— literacies that empower young people to exercise agency while safely navigating safe learning communities.

"What if someone steals it?"

Selena—an artist, a writer, and a musician—kept several notepads full of her sketches and writings, and enjoyed playing the keyboard at home. She also enjoyed hanging out with friends in the Digital Media Club after school, because her family did not have access to the Internet at home. She had a pay-as-you go mobile plan that was not a reliable source of Internet access. Her favorite websites were Tumblr and DeviantArt[2]; she spent hours perusing those sites to find inspiration for her own art. Through participation in the club, she had recently started playing with Photoshop as a way to edit her photos and "make them weird"—something she had seen on Tumblr and had discovered she really liked. Despite the fact that she took a lot of pride in her art, which she often shared with me during our meetings, she had never shared anything on Tumblr or DeviantArt. When I asked her why she had not done so, she explained that she was afraid that people would steal her creations and claim them as their own.

Gabriela expressed her creativity in many ways, including writing, photography, and graphic design. She spent hours every week finding inspiration for her photography online. Tumblr was her favorite site because she liked the way people edited and "played with" images. She also liked browsing Flickr and Google Images for ideas and inspiration. She kept a collection of digital photos in a folder on her personal laptop, which her parents had bought her to aid in homework and school projects. At the time of the study, Gabriela was learning how to use the new camera that her photographer uncle had given her as a birthday present. In her Tech Apps course at Freeway High, she was learning how to use Photoshop to edit and manipulate her photos. Occasionally she printed out some of her favorite shots and added them to the collection on the wall beside her bed. Gabriela was an active and regular Facebook user, and from time to time she created photo albums of her projects on Facebook. However, she kept these private and used them more as a personal archive and repository for her photos than as a way to share her photos with peers or family members. Every now and then Gabriela shared them with a few close friends or her uncle, but expressed an overall desire to primarily keep them private.

Q: Would you ever share your photos or anything like that?

Gabriela: No.

Q: No. How come?

Gabriela: No. Not anything. That's just weird.

Q: Even your artistic photos?

Gabriela: Yeah. Even those. Because I know a lot of people on Tumblr, they copy a photo then they claim it's theirs. So I'm always worried about that.

Not only was Gabriela afraid of someone stealing her photos, she also expressed a belief that sharing her photos was "just weird," a point to which I will return.

As a final example, I return to Javier, whom you were introduced to at the beginning of this chapter. Javier was an inspiring filmmaker who admitted to staying up much too late watching foreign films on YouTube and Vimeo. He enjoyed watching amateur films because he felt they introduced him to unique cinematography techniques and because they were also low-budget, as his own projects were. However, like Selena and

Gabriela, Javier had never put his films on YouTube or Vimeo, despite the fact that he valued those sites as spaces for learning and sharing.

Javier: I don't put [my films] on YouTube.

Q: How come?

Javier: I don't know. I mean, it's not that I don't like it but I haven't tried to put them—I don't know. It's not, like, something that I really want to do to put my videos on YouTube. Now it's so easy to steal ideas, so that's why I haven't put them.

Q: Do you worry about someone stealing an idea from YouTube?

Javier: Yeah … [that someone could] take them, make them yours … . Yeah, I don't want people to—because it's really easy to steal ideas.

Similar fears that someone might steal their ideas were articulated by many other students.

Pointedly, public conversations about young people and copyright tend to focus on issues of piracy—that is, fears and concerns that young people are stealing copyrighted materials. The common assumption is that young people are the people most likely to steal someone's content or ideas. Cautionary tales of teens' stealing content or ideas seem to have abated in recent years (in part because affordable and accessible copyright-friendly online models such as iTunes, Pandora, and Spotify have become popular), but there nonetheless remains a lot of concern about how teens' media practices might infringe upon copyright laws. Readers may remember that the Record Industry Association of America (RIAA) sued children as young as 12 for downloading music on the now-defunct Napster (Borland 2003). Headline-grabbing cases understandably incited fear in parents and schools. Such examples dominated copyright conversations for most of the early 2000s, and were problematic for many reasons, not least of which because they limited their portrayal of young people as that of mere consumers, rather than as producers of media. In an increasingly corporatized and commercial media culture, copyright conversations are dominated by the perspectives of businesses and adults rather than those of young people, who have their own unique concerns about intellectual property.

At a more local level for students, copyright often revolves around a discussion of plagiarism. Teachers are increasingly and justifiably concerned about students' buying term papers off the Internet and submitting them as their own work.

In both of these cases, copyright discourse tends to overly focus on what is prohibited and punitive, rather than on what is acceptable and permissible. Piracy and plagiarism are legitimate concerns from business and educational perspectives, but what young people themselves are actually concerned about is theft of *their own* ideas. The harm-driven expectations of teens as deviants have dominated copyright conversations and neglected to account for teens as media producers. Harm-driven expectations means that many teens miss out on the benefits associated with sharing their own creative media projects online.

Understanding Copyright and Intellectual Property

I will be the first to admit that young people's concerns that someone might steal their original media content are valid. In today's digital culture it is all too easy to download or share something and claim it as your own. Furthermore, for students at a school such as Freeway High, theft is a daily threat and reality. Students frequently explained they would like to bring their laptop or tablet to school, but they didn't because they feared it would be stolen. Gabriela explained why she left her laptop at home this way: "The lockers aren't reliable, and then, just, I don't know, I don't trust people with it. I don't want it to go missing." Sergio even believed that the likelihood of theft might have been one of the reasons the school had banned personal technologies in the classroom: "They [school administrators] don't want people using their electronic devices at school because they don't want to deal with the problem of it getting stolen." Throughout my year at Freeway, I heard an abundant number of personal stories involving theft at school— from mobile phones to car break-ins on school property—theft, or at least the threat of theft, was an unfortunate reality for Freeway High students. Thus, concerns about theft of intellectual property must be contextualized within a larger context of risk: for these students, theft probably was more common than it might have been at more privileged or private schools and in more privileged populations.

Lawrence Lessig is particularly interested in helping young people—and society at large—learn how, when, and where it is appropriate to incorporate copyrighted content into derivative content. In a popular 2007 TED talk, he proclaimed: "We need to recognize you can't kill the instinct the technology produces. We can only criminalize it. We can't stop our kids from using it. We can only drive it underground. We can't make our kids passive again. We can only make them, quote, 'pirates.' And is that good? ... In a democracy, we ought to be able to do better." This is why Lessig is a strong advocate for the legal doctrine known as *fair use*, which dictates that under certain circumstances it is acceptable and legal for consumers to use copyrighted material in their own media creations. The copyright doctrine of fair use is complicated, but essentially it grants citizens permission to use limited portions of copyrighted works to teach, critique, parody, inform, or to remix it in order to create derivative works.

Mr. Lopez, the Tech Apps teacher and media club sponsor at Freeway High, was also an advocate for the incorporation of fair use as a way to enable students to create and remix media. He included lessons about intellectual property and copyright into his curriculum for the Tech Apps courses and was well aware that an understanding of and respect for copyright laws is an important aspect of digital literacy. The laws and boundaries of copyright are evolving and tenuous, which present many challenges in the classroom. Nonetheless, Mr. Lopez was an advocate of fair use protections and encouraged his students to remix content as part of their own projects. Additionally, he taught his students about Creative Commons, which was developed by Lessig as an alternative to traditionally restrictive copyright laws. Sometimes referred to as copyleft, Creative Commons licenses were developed as a different and flexible way to protect and share intellectual property. With Creative Commons licenses copyright holders retain some rights, but can also grant permission for others to use, share, copy, and create derivative works without obtaining additional permission from the artist or copyright holder. A copyright holder can choose between different degrees of restriction based on profit, how the content is used, who is using it (i.e., amateur or professional) and so forth. In other words, Creative Commons licenses aim to reinstate a balance between the artists' rights to profit from and/or protect their intellectual property and consumers' rights and desires to play with, appropriate, remix, and use existing media texts for fun, critique, or profit.

In addition to allowing anyone to generate a free Creative Commons license to protect their intellectual property, the website also serves as a depository for thousands of Creative Commons licensed work. The value is that media makers and artists can browse the site for music, images, and video clips that they can incorporate into their own productions and mediated texts. Users can rest assured that their use of work licensed under Creative Commons is legally protected so long as they abide by the terms set forth by the respective licenses. Mr. Lopez was a fan of Creative Commons and encouraged his students to take advantage of the repertoire of Creative Commons licensed work:

I teach kids about Creative Commons and about copyright and sharing, being able now to share. There's this one website now that has good pictures. I like using that website because you can pretty much find the Creative Common picture and find the ones that will allow you to use it without having to go request permission. The cool thing is finding the pictures. We do video, finding the raw footage that will look good in a video. The site will pull up, but you can't see any of the pictures because Freeway High is blocking the pictures.

Blocking sites that provided access to Creative Commons works had the unfortunate effect of inadvertently encouraging students to rely on copyrighted materials that weren't blocked by the school's filters.

As was discussed in the previous two chapters, students and teachers repeatedly complained about instances in which legitimate and educational material was blocked by the school's filters. In this particular case, Mr. Lopez's focus was on the ways the school restricted access to fair use material that would be valuable to the filmmakers in his class who needed music, images, and footage. However, what we need to also consider is how blocking the site disempowered students from creating their *own* Creative Commons licenses—that is, from safely and legally protecting and sharing their own creative media content.

This is yet another example of the ways understandings of risk undercut opportunities for students to exert agency over their own mediated practices. Instead of recognizing and validating students as producers, copyright curriculum reified a corporate risk discourse that positioned students as consumers. Understandings of intellectual property and respecting copyright laws are essential aspects of becoming digitally literate; however, it is imperative we go a step further and also enable young people to confidently protect their own creative content. Being digitally literate doesn't mean only understanding how to respect copyright laws (i.e., be a good consumer citizen); it is also about empowering students as creators so they feel comfortable sharing and fully participating in online communities. Many of the students I spoke with had heard of Creative Commons (mostly from Mr. Lopez) but were not aware that they could use the Creative Commons site to generate their own licenses to protect their own creative content.

An opportunity-driven approach would not be based on prohibitions and fear. Instead, expectations of opportunity consider young people as both consumers *and producers*, by teaching them to respect copyright laws and also to empower them to protect their own intellectual property. At Freeway High, harm-driven expectations abounded. Students were afraid of theft, and the school filtered the Internet to prevent access to inappropriate content. In both cases, students missed out on valuable opportunities to build their online presence, to network with other young media makers, and to fully participate in the online communities they valued. Likewise, because uploading content to public sites was not incorporated as part of the curriculum, teachers were disempowered from helping students in their classroom to protect their own content after it had been shared online.

"I'm not good enough yet": Professional Aspirations

There are two other overlapping, yet distinct, fears that students frequently expressed as a reason for not sharing their own media content online: fear of unwanted criticism and fear that their content was not good enough/ professional enough to share. Significantly, the young people I spoke with were not reacting to earlier negative experiences online, but rather were preemptively choosing not to participate because of expectations of potential harm. Students presumed that the potentially negative consequences and outcomes would outweigh the potential benefits and payoffs. Risks were myopically approached as harmful and therefore as to be avoided; students rarely considered the benefits of taking risks in online participatory spaces.

I met Sergio my first day at Freeway High. Mr. Lopez called on him and his close friend Antonio to show our group around the Digital Media Club and to introduce us to other members. Sergio was a polite young man who was eager to tell us about his positive experiences in the club and about the projects he and his friends were working on together. Over the course of the year, I saw Sergio regularly; he spent many hours in the club almost every day after school. He consistently stayed as late as the teachers would let him, even missing the last bus of the day and would walk home after the club was closed for the evening. Sergio was an active member and leader of the Cinematic Arts Project and was respected by his teachers and peers alike. He took a lot of pride in his films, as well as school. He frequently volunteered to help out with various projects and volunteered at a media camp for children over the summer. He actively sought out advice from his teachers and mentors in the Cinematic Arts Club and valued their input and feedback. In other words, in most respects Sergio was comfortable with critique, feedback, and sharing his media and perspectives. But, as has been noted, he was uncomfortable about sharing his films online.

Sergio: I haven't posted any of my videos because I'm not ready for the feedback from other people, so that's kind of one thing that's stopping me, criticism of other people.

Q: Oh, really?

Sergio: I'm not ready to accept it.

Q: Why?

Sergio: I don't like it, because I've seen how people can be on the Internet. They can be really mean, do really mean put-downs. I haven't really found a site yet that's supportive.

Because Sergio had shared his films with peers, with mentors, with teachers, with members of the local film community, and with researchers, it was evident that his concerns had more to do with the unique nature of online sharing than with a broader concern about sharing his films in general. Reflecting on the young participants in their study, Lange and Ito write: "Young people struggle over their sense of confidence and safety about sharing their work to wider audiences. As creators get more confident and involved in their work, however, they generally will seek out audiences, and the online environment provides a vehicle for publishing and circulation of their work" (2010, p. 280). Perhaps Sergio's desire to share was satisfied by sharing his media projects with mentors and peers at school, and thus he was not motivated to share his films with an online audience. However, because his attitude was similar to those of many other teens I got to know in the club, I tend to think it was more complicated than that.

If one had asked practically any student in the clubs whom he or she turned to for help with a film project, Javier's name probably would have come up. Javier was viewed as a leader within the clubs. Many of the students in the study were Mexican-American, but many had never been to Mexico, or had moved when they were quite young. But Javier had moved from Mexico to the US at the age of 14, and had an older sister who was currently in film school there; this gave him access to perspectives and worldviews different from those of many of his peers. Javier's mother was a musician and had a few connections in the artistic and creative world, although more so in Mexico than in the US. Unlike some parents I spoke with who were wary of or concerned about their child's participation in the creative arts and media (see chapter 7), Javier's parents actively supported his goals and creative aspirations. He was a mature student with lofty goals and never hesitated to share his perspectives and creative insight with you. In fact, the first time I met Javier, he began explaining his views on immigration and world politics; he was a confident idealist with a passion for storytelling and helping others.

Given Javier's self-assurance, professional aspirations, peer respectability, and technical prowess, I was again surprised to hear that Javier did not share his films online. This was even true of films which he would proudly share with me, his peers, and mentors. His latest film project was a silent, artistic, and reflective short about a mime who watched people as a way to experience and mimic the array of human emotions, from joy to sorrow and everything in between. When I asked why he didn't share his films online, he replied: "A lot of what's on YouTube is amateur; I don't want to be seen as that so I wait until I think my film is ready. I want to build a professional portfolio." Javier had received validation for his films—including acceptance to film festivals. His concern had more to do with his *online* reputation rather than a broader concern that his films were not ready to be viewed.

Amateur vs. Professional Video Sharing

From reports of recent research about young people and YouTube, one might get the impression that the so-called digital generation are all interested in sharing their videos online. And certainly some students in this study did upload videos to YouTube and other video sharing sites. For example, Jada (16 years old, black) had shared a user-generated video on YouTube even though she did not self-report to have much interest in media production. She had enrolled in the Tech Apps course to fulfill an elective requirement, but she spent her after-school hours practicing dance moves with the drill team. She was a stylish girl interested in and always ready to discuss the latest fashion trends. Although she didn't find the time to watch a lot of television, her favorite shows were on entertainment channels such as E! and BET.[3] She explained she enjoyed these shows more for the fashion inspiration than for the celebrity gossip. She also liked to get online just to peruse fashion blogs and websites. Her grandmother was teaching her how to sew so she could start making her own accessories and outfits. Jada was also a member of the Business Club, which provided a space for her to explore her interest in the business side of the fashion industry.

Jada had access to a shared Internet-enabled family computer (which was set up in the breakfast nook of the kitchen), to her own tablet, and to a data-connected smartphone (both of which her parents helped her purchase). She articulated that her phone was highly important to her, yet she regularly expressed a dismissive attitude toward technology and media production, claiming that it "wasn't her thing" and that she found computers complicated and "not that interesting." Jada was not a member of the Digital Media Club or of the Cinematic Arts Project, in comparison with students who were in the after-school media clubs, Jada could be described as a more casual user of technology. Her practices were primarily friendship-driven; her motivation for using media technology was as a way to stay in touch with her friends. This differs from the more invested practices of her peers in the Digital Media Club whose motivations were driven by an interest in media production. For that reason, it was surprising to me that Jada told me she had uploaded video content to YouTube when her more technologically savvy peers Javier, Selena, and Gabriela had not.

One afternoon, as Jada and I were casually discussing how her weekend had gone, she showed me a video that she and some friends had recorded at her house; in it they were trying to choreograph a dance to a new Drake song.[4] The video was similar to many user-generated amateur videos on YouTube: technologically it was simplistic and novice, the lighting was not clear, the camera movement was shaky, and it had not been edited in any way. In the video we see Jada and three other high school girls dancing and laughing as they try to learn the dance. The video ends with the girls playfully teasing one another and laughing at their own mistakes. In comparison with the sophisticated and technologically advanced videos that I was accustomed to seeing from students in the Cinematic Arts Project, this one stood out as markedly amateur and playful. Yet one of Jada's friends had shared it on her YouTube account (with the consent of the friends). Meanwhile, the aspiring filmmakers I knew had consistently chosen not to share their videos online. What was the difference? Why had Jada—a self-described novice with little vested interest in media production—uploaded a video to YouTube, while other more digitally literate young people interested in media production had not?

To help answer this question, it is useful to consider other similar research about young media makers. In her extensive ethnographic research about YouTube, Lange (2014) explored the identities, dispositions, social contexts, and literacies that structure young people's video production, consumption, and distribution practices via YouTube. In one of Lange's studies, all but one of the 40 participants had shared a video online, either on YouTube or on his or her own blog or website. Lange's study gives valuable insight into the collaborative and social process of learning, creating, and play, yet of course there is an inherent sample bias in studying young people who have already shared user-generated content online. Although we have a lot to learn from such young people, the work has the unintended consequence of further perpetuating the false assumption that today's "digital generation" are all actively participating in online communities. Lange is aware of the differentiated practices and avoids a monolithic argument; she certainly does not ignore or overlook social, economic, and cultural barriers to participation. Nonetheless, such work is valuable, yet unintentionally continues to contribute to an expectation that young people who share videos are the norm. Yet, we also must interrogate the barriers that prohibit some young people from participating fully in an online video sharing culture—particularly, when those who are not participating are the ones who might have the most to gain from participation.

Many of the videos Lange analyzed were similar to the casual dance video that Jada created with her friends. Lange refers to such videos as "personally expressive media," which is a broad definition used to describe a variety of youth-produced media that "enables a creator to communicate aspects of the self" (2014, p. 16). Beneficially, Lange distinguishes among novice, amateur, and pre-professional video makers. (Pre-professional video makers express concern about the technical aspects of their productions in relation to their own technical identities.) Not all of the students who participated in the after-school clubs had aspirations of working in the film industry, but many of them explicitly expressed such interests and goals. In Lange's terminology, they could be considered pre-professional media producers. These technical identities were explicitly articulated by the teens when describing their own interest and investment in the Cinematic Arts Project. This was also revealed in the amount of time students invested in the technical aspects of their films, which were primarily extracurricular, and not part of their formal education or grades. Students reluctantly—or even proudly—admitted to falling behind on their school work because they opted to devote their time to their film and media projects instead of their required (and graded) school work.

At first glance, it may appear that students involved in the after-school clubs were merely reluctant to share their creative media content because they were still constructing technical identities—identities they viewed as entrepreneurial and pre-professional. However, they often shared their projects with peers, with teachers, with parents, with potential adult supporters of the club, and even at local film festivals. The reluctance to share was intricately linked to the online environment. To the students, there was a difference between sharing their films in professional offline spaces and amateur online spaces that they had not reconciled; by constructing their identities as pre-professional, they were missing opportunities to construct professional online identities and networks.

Social Literacy and Resiliency

Fear of critique (e.g., mean and unwarranted comments) and fear that one's creative media projects aren't "good enough" are different, but they also overlap in that they both have to do with confidence. Many students who appeared confident in and proud of their skills and creativity feared how others would respond to their creative media content online. This may have been an individual issue of confidence, but given the prevalence of such attitudes among members of the club I tend to think it was something else. The sociologist Annette Lareau (2003) might argue that the reluctance could be linked to participants' classed subject positions. Lareau has found that young people from middle-class families tend to demonstrate more efficacious beliefs about their own school performance compared to students from working-class homes, and that students' perceptions and attitudes about their accomplishments are affected by their social class and their home structures. Perhaps the working-class, immigrant, and marginalized statuses of Sergio, Javier, Selena, and their peers has negatively influenced their individualized and collective senses of efficacy and confidence.

However, another productive approach is to additionally question whose dispositions, interests, voices, and "ways of being" are validated in society. That approach shifts the focus away from individuals and toward the cultural power structures within society. Here it is useful to turn to Sims' (2014) research on "differentiating practices" as a way to understand young people's mediated participation and production. In his ethnographic research with middle school students in a media-oriented school, Sims found that "the relative leveling of access and skills exhibited in the classroom did not mitigate differentiated use in situations where students had more control over how they spent their time. In students' more voluntary or 'interest-driven' activities … many historical structures of privilege returned to the fore." "It is clear," Sims asserted (2014, pp. 673–674), "that providing access and skills does not, in and of itself, lead to the media production activities that many digital inequality scholars endorse." Sims' findings differ in some details from the findings presented in this book, but his overall conclusion is similar to the experiences of students such as Sergio and Javier in this study. Because school did not encourage or facilitate sharing creative media content online, but rather the focus was almost solely on production, many students did not choose to participate in these ways.

What the "differentiating practices" approach allows us to do is ask, rather than how and why students "use" digital media differently, *what uses* and *which users* are validated and supported within these systems of practice—in this case, school and online communities. This requires us to consider participation as part of a broader social practice and structure, something that is not wholly individualistic or a singular choice. Rather,

participation in social practices often positions selves in relation to others. ... Through negotiations over participation, persons are identified and make their identities in part to say who they are and in part to say who they are not. (Sims 2014, p. 675, citing Holland, Lachiotte, Skinner, and Cain 1998)

In this way I find Sims' approach particularly applicable in helping unpack the reasons technologically skilled, creative, and otherwise confident students were afraid to participate in their online environments.

Networked publics and social media have positively disrupted traditional corporate media models by providing spaces for diverse representation, greater incorporation and visibility of marginalized voices, the validation of amateur works, and the emerging hybrid media markets.[5] Yet society still privileges the perspectives of white, straight, powerful, able-bodied, male adults. The commercial media that many of the students in this study valued, critiqued, emulated, and learned from, rarely depicted their values, bodies, lives, and class positions as (poor) young people of color. Further, when media do portray such identities and bodies, it is rarely in a positive and empowering (or realistic) manner (Gerbner and Gross 1976; Gray 1995; hooks 1992; Negra and Asava 2013). With this in mind, I cannot help but think that students' fear of critique was more acutely a fear of being further dismissed, further silenced, and further marginalized within a media culture dominated by white adults.

This fear can be further combined with what media scholars refer to as the "burden of representation" (Malik 2002; Mercer 1990), which describes the ways non-dominant individuals (who are marginalized on the basis of gender, race, ability, age, class, geography, religion, sexuality, or some intersection of any of these identities) carry the burden of positively representing their entire race, gender, religion, and so on. This is particularly true of young people, who "have had to carry a peculiar burden of representation; everything they do, say, think or feel, is scrutinized by an army of professional commentators for signs the times" (Cohen and Ainley 2000,

p. 89). One need only look at all the racist jokes about President Obama that imply that black men "make bad presidents" when the mistakes of the other 42 US presidents have never been blamed on the fact that they were either white or male. In this visible example, President Obama is evaluated not as a president, but as a *black* president, and is assumed to be representative of all future black leaders. This is the detrimental and racist burden of limited representation. In a culture that continually marginalizes, devalues, dismisses, and even demonizes youth (Gabriel 2013; Giroux 2009; Kelly 2003)—and more specifically, poor young people and young people of color, who rarely get media attention for reasons other than drugs, gangs, welfare, and criminality (Bullock, Wyche, and Williams 2002; Gilens 1996; Giroux 1996)—we must interpret students' fears in a more holistic context of generalized fear about how society perceives their identities, bodies, and voices. Just as students' fear that their ideas might be stolen online is part of a larger reality of theft at school, their fear of criticism and of not being "good enough" must be accounted for as part of a broader internalized fear that has historically and continually dismissed and misrepresented their identities and voices.

In terms of interventions, the school and the after-school media clubs are certainly validating students' perspectives and projects. This is demonstrated by the confidence with which students shared their projects with each other, mentors, teachers, and even me as a researcher. However, the disparity is between what they do and share in the club and what they choose to do and share online outside of school. What students needed help negotiating was the difference between constructive *critiques* and unproductive *criticisms*. Critiques offer suggestions for how to improve their ideas and content, whereas criticisms have little value in the learning process and can be dismissed. Fostering resiliency is a challenging but necessary part of growing up. Teens are understandably concerned about mean and hateful comments online. However, if sharing media online is part of the project's goals and curriculum—and an equalizing aspect of participatory culture—then at least when they are at school students have adults ready and willing to help them navigate the negative terrain of the comment section (rather than being left to deal with it on their own in out-of-school settings). Teens need adults to help them process, negotiate, and cope with the inevitable negative online experience, as well as teach them ways to block and report such incidents when necessary. We cannot deny the risks of sharing media content online, but students need encouragement to take risks that can also lead to beneficial outcomes. Once again historical fears and the conflation of risk and harm has led to limited expectations that fail to balance the opportunities of risky practices (such as visibly sharing creative work in networked publics) with potential threats.

We should help young people learn to appreciate and value their current subject positions, skills, and the learning process, alongside their pre-professional aspirations. It is valuable for schools to help students create professional online portfolios, but it is also essential that students do not only view their creative projects as pre-professional. It is important for young people to appreciate who they are and not just who they hope to become. Youth, as a social construct, is often built around discourses of becoming rather than being. To a certain extent students in our study had internalized these future-oriented narratives, perhaps to the detriment of valuing their current youthful amateur identities. This is also revealed by the students' own reliance on the word "work" as a way to refer to their projects and creative media content. The word "work" reflects and is embedded within market-driven discourses that value their creativity in terms of labor, capital, and the professionalization of their practices.[6]

It is not productive for students to compare themselves to professionals or to consider all of their films as part of their future professional work-oriented portfolio. There is value in sharing work in progress or amateur, playful, and self-expressive projects. Personally expressive and amateur media can help students learn how to network and share in a more relaxed and informal setting and can be beneficial outside of a market-driven understanding of value (in the same way that creative writing is a valuable practice outside of professional writing goals or rewards). The Cinematic Arts Project facilitated a safe environment for teens to take risks and fail, and to learn from those experiences. Certainly the consequences of failing online can be potentially detrimental, but they do not have to be. The social literacies that participatory cultures and networked publics require can only be learned through experimental trial and error, by reaching out, leaving comments, posting your own creative content, and so forth. Mistakes will be made, but typically they are not detrimental. Waiting until one's project is polished and professional may seem a good strategy, but by avoiding risks of negative online experiences teens instead run the risk of never learning other valuable digital literacies: networking and collaboration.

"It's just not my thing"

The third common reason why participants did not share their work had to do with the often unacknowledged amount of labor involved in maintaining an online presence and identity.[7] When we talk about young people who actively and routinely upload original creative content, respond to feedback, attract and retain followers, and sustain personal learning networks, we tend to overlook the amount of time and labor such participation requires. I want to emphasize again that I do not think we should automatically expect young people to invest in crafting visible identities within networked publics—and the fact that some teens chose not to disrupts otherwise homogenizing expectations of young people's digital practices. However, it is important that teens who are invested in crafting pre-professional technical identities learn how to benefit from intentional visibility.

One barrier that precluded some students from participating in networked publics as much as they would have liked was that they had other obligations. Many students either maintained part-time jobs as a way to contribute to household expenses; many others were expected to help care for younger siblings or cousins living at home. Several of the teens in the after-school media clubs lived with single parents, lived in multi-generation households, or had parents who worked at night, and the responsibility of caring for younger children at home was often displaced onto them. These competing responsibilities even interfered with regular school attendance, and prohibited some students from being able to attend meetings of after-school clubs as frequently as they would have liked. It is not surprising that some teens, already strapped for time, saw participation in networked publics and online participatory cultures as burdensome or too much work. Antonio was an active and regular member of the Cinematic Arts Project and hung out in the club many nights a week. Unlike some of his peers, Antonio had experimented with sharing creative photos as part of an online portfolio. His photos could be described as artistic, and he took pride and pleasure in photography. One reason he was reluctant to share them online—and later removed the photos—had to do with the quality of the images. He had taken the photos with an outdated phone, and he felt they weren't professional enough to share online. A member of our research team suggested that, instead of sharing his photos in a professional portfolio, Antonio could share them on Tumblr, which encourages an edgy and low-quality aesthetic. In an interview, Antonio struggled to articulate why he didn't want to share his photos, but eventually recognized that it had to do with the labor and time required to maintain a blog on Tumblr:

Q: Oh, you tried posting photos on Tumblr?

Antonio: I tried it, and then, I couldn't keep up with it, it was just … I didn't have any followers, or anything else, so I just, like, "No, not going to post a picture, that's too much for me."

Q: What? Why?

Antonio: I don't really know why. Even on Instagram, if I post something, I have my Instagram connected to Tumblr, and Twitter. All you have to do is create a little border on the photo, but no, I can't do it … . It's just not me. I don't like doing it for some reason.

As the interview continued, Antonio said he had tried following a few photography blogs on Tumblr, but he did not have the time to keep up with them. When asked if he had ever left comments or engaged with anyone on Tumblr, he said he hadn't. In response to the question "Why?" he replied "I don't know. On any of my social medias, I don't even comment, because I'm barely on them anyway, so any time I do, it's just usually [private] messaging [to friends]." Although he expressed interest in online communities, it was hard for Antonio to invest the time required to find followers to build a network and community; thus he got frustrated and decided not to participate on Tumblr.

During the interview, Antonio appeared to be surprised by his own answers. He struggled to find an explanation for his lack of participation. He settled for "It's just not me," which can be interpreted within many different explanations that are similar to other teens in the media clubs, such as Gabriela's comment that sharing her photography online was "just weird." Antonio did not have consistent quality access to the Internet and relied on school and the club as his primary means for getting online and creating media. The time in the club was primarily devoted to working on projects (i.e., producing and editing media), rather than maintaining personal profiles on social network sites. Additionally, although no one in his family had gone to college (his mother quit school around the fourth grade to take care of her family after her own mother passed away and his father dropped out around the seventh grade to get a job), his parents encouraged him to try to go to college. His parents cared about his grades and required him to pass all his classes in order to participate in after-school activities. Antonio's older sister had planned to go to college, but never did. His parents had aspirations that Antonio might be the first to continue his education and get a middle-class job (his father worked construction and his mother was a janitor). In addition to the media club, Antonio was also an active member of the art club and was a skilled artist. He spent a lot of time on homework, and what free time he had left was devoted to media and creative projects. When we think about the time constraints many working-class young people face, combined with limited access to social media, it begins to make a bit more sense that they are not as likely to be active participants in networked publics. Working-class students, who were strapped for time, did not expect the benefits of intentional online visibility to outweigh the sacrifices required by their other commitments.

Network Literacy

That Antonio had no followers on Tumblr is understandable. If you have recently created a new social media account or can think back to when you first signed up for a new social network site, you might recall the initial learning curve and difficulty in finding appropriate and valuable audiences and networks. It takes time and work to cultivate what Rheingold (2012) calls a "personal learning network." A personal learning network is comprised of valuable followers and connections who learn together by providing feedback, support, and interactions between novices and experts alike. Rheingold (2012, p. 122) sees this as an important part of literacy: "Making connections is a learnable skill that is amply rewarded by networked publics." Learning how to engage within networked publics as part of a participatory culture is a literacy that must be learned and constantly practiced. If you were to analyze the profile and network of an active vlogger on YouTube, or a well-connected Tumblr blogger, or a Twitter user with many followers and interactions, you would notice that the individuals exhibit a fine-tuned understanding and execution of network literacy.

Rheingold's (2012) approach to literacy—what he refers to as being "net smart"—is particularly productive because of its strong emphasis on the social aspects of digital literacy. He goes so far as to claim that the very value and power of participatory media are due to the active participation of so many people, and he makes a strong case that we need to learn how to tap into networks for the purposes of collective intelligence, collaborative action, and the formation of valuable communities. In accordance with other media literacy scholars (Gutierrez, Morales, and Martinez 2009; Ito et al. 2010), Rheingold demonstrates how these skills are not merely individualized, but are inherently social and must be learned in concert with others online. Connecting literacies back to equity, he asserts that "Net smarts are not just vital to getting ahead; you need this knowledge to keep from falling behind" (2012, p. 25). Participatory cultures necessitate the development of literacies that are intimately entwined with social skills that must be learned in practice by interacting with others.

Like other social skills, network literacies are always evolving, in flux, and open to interpretation; they are localized and contextualized in ways that must be experienced, learned, and re-learned. Miles (2007, p. 30) describes the social value of developing network literacy as "linking to what other people have written and inviting comments from others, it means understanding a kind of writing that is a social, collaborative process rather than an act of an individual in solitary. It means learning how to write with an awareness that anyone may read it: your mother, a future employer or the person whose work you're writing about." Miles' definition provides an explanation as to why an underdeveloped understanding of networks precluded some students (e.g., Antonio) from participating in online communities. The public aspects of online participation make participation in networked publics challenging, but also make it beneficial. Rheingold (2012) offers a poignant summation: "In the world of digitally networked publics, online participation—if you know how to do it—can translate into real power."

At Freeway High, students' lack of participation in online spaces limited their capacity to fully participate as peers and to join in the collaborative spaces afforded via networked publics. Javier, Sergio, Antonio, and Gabriela viewed media production not just as a mere hobby, but as a pathway to college and/or a career (see chapter 7); thus, it was important that they also develop a capacity to network online. Yet developing the literacies necessary to participate extend beyond professional goals. As Lee Rainie writes (2010, p. 3), "participation itself in the online world creates a distinct sense of belonging and empowerment in users." Schools should play a more active role in helping young people—particularly those from historically marginalized and disempowered populations—develop the confidence and skills necessary to participate online. In theory, formal education provides opportunities for upward mobility and should contribute to the eradication of inequities; however, in practice this does not always play out. When the opportunities for marginalized and disadvantaged students are already limited outside of school, the impact of social disadvantages at school are amplified. As Jenkins, Ford, and Green argue (2013, p. 194) , "Insofar as participation within networked publics becomes a source of discursive and persuasive power—and insofar as the capacities to meaningfully participate online are linked to educational and economic opportunities—then the struggle over the right to participation is linked to core issues of social justice and equality." The risk of invisibility—that is, the lack of visible and intentional online participation—has detrimental effects on the equity of opportunities and demands critical attention from educators, policy makers, and scholars.

Schools such as Freeway High would be better equipped to invest in the development of students' network literacy practices if they did not block students' and teachers' access to online social network sites such as Facebook, Tumblr, and YouTube. At Freeway, fear-driven understandings of risk blocked opportunities for students and teachers to work together to responsibly manage online reputations, build professional portfolios, acquire social and economic capital, and to network with other amateur and professional media makers. To be clear, some students were doing this, but typically they were students who had higher-quality Internet/computer access at home and more unstructured free time to spend online. This just further iterates the ways media ecologies are not created equal. Instead, restrictive harm-driven policies limited students' ability to develop the skills and competencies required to build social networks and acquire social capital.

The school could have facilitated network literacy through the creation of a class blog, Tumblr, website, YouTube channel, or portfolio that could have allowed students to network and share their projects collaboratively—with a collective class identity—rather than as individuals. Teachers would have been able to monitor the site and to help students navigate the risks. An additional benefit to collectively maintained online identities would have been dividing up the labor and the time necessary for maintaining students' profiles, finding and responding to an audience, and engaging with the larger community. In other words, the cost (time, labor, skills) and benefits would have been simultaneously divided and amplified.

Conclusion: Conditions for Networked Participation

Networking and sharing online are digital literacies that highlight the extent to which learning is not an individualized process that transpires in isolation but rather is always embedded within particular cultural systems and relationships. "The most important outcome of these debates," Burgess and Green write (2009, p. 72), "should be to understand that new media literacy is not a property of individuals—something a given human agent either possesses or lacks—but a system that both enables and shapes participation ... . The questions of how this system is shaped and who has access to it represent the key political questions of new media literacy." I hope this chapter has highlighted the potential benefits as well as the limitations of informal learning environments to alleviate participation gaps.

To address the question posed at the beginning of the chapter concerning the necessary conditions that facilitate the development of participatory literacies: It is clear that students need adult guidance in learning how to fully participate online. They also need educational structures that explicitly dedicate time to crafting online identities that will help them find spaces that are supportive of their amateur works. Adult validation and the support of appropriate literacies can empower young people to confidently navigate networked publics in safe ways. This requires both adults and students to intentionally value amateur identities and the risks inherent in the learning process. It also means that digital media education, whether informal or part of curriculum, needs to invest time to explicitly help students safely network and share their own media content online. These steps will equip students with the literacies, time, and dispositions necessary for meaningful and safe online visibility.

In addition, it is crucial that we counter negative harm-driven expectations of visibility with positive opportunity-driven expectations. Conversations of visibility have to expand beyond privacy and protection, to include perspectives that will help young people think intentionally about the benefits of deliberate visibility. The students mentioned in this chapter revealed the extent to which they expected harm as a result of sharing their creative media projects online. Few had actually experienced harm, but the risk and expectation of harm precluded some from even trying to learn how to network and share their creative media in networked publics. We must balance fearful and negative discourses of visibility with beneficial understandings of intentional visibility. Schools need to play a more active role in empowering marginalized young people to embrace the benefits of intentionally crafting positive online identities and networks.

Society should worry about the risk of *invisibility* rather than only the potential harms of visibility. Invisibility has consequences on two levels. On an individual level, young people who are trying to forge pathways to creative careers miss out on opportunities to forge professional online identities and to tap into beneficial online networks. On a collective level, when working-class youth and youth of color remain invisible, we all miss out on seeing their stories, experiences, and creativity. Both of these consequence carry with them the risk of reproducing a status quo of inequity.

Digital literacies are not a luxury, but are a fundamental component of 21st-century education and participation, and I worry about structures that inhibit young people's capacity to participate in networked publics. Young people today have a unique opportunity to represent themselves in ways that are counter to the often negative mediated representations of youth. Schools can and should take more active approaches to facilitating and supporting the development of networked literacies so that marginalized students can safely participate and share in online participatory spaces. Educational approaches to digital literacy must balance harm-driven expectations with the opportunities afforded young people in today's digital world.

6 Visible Privacy: Norms, Preferences, and Strategies

Everyone keeps their Tumblr private, usually because they post, like, actually what they're going through or what they feel. Nobody really wants the people from our school to know, because then that's how rumors start. That's how things get out of hand, so I think that's why we keep it really private.

Gabriela (16 years old, Mexican-American)

Remember when MySpace was the most popular social network site? Teens spent countless hours communicating with friends, decorating their profile pages, listening to music, taking quizzes, and hanging out on the site. A few years later we saw a migration away from MySpace and onto Facebook (boyd 2011; Watkins 2009). Out with the old,, "crowded," hyper-personal, and even "creepy" and "trashy" nature of MySpace, they said! Bring on the "clean," "educated," and "mature" nature of Facebook (Watkins 2009). This migration—perhaps an even exodus, as boyd (2011) called it—gained momentum around 2008. MySpace still existed, but its popularity had dwindled; now Facebook was where it was at. A few years later, we begin to see a move away from Facebook toward Tumblr, Instagram, and Snapchat. It is estimated that 3 million teens left Facebook between 2011 and 2014, when there was a 25 percent decline in Facebook among members of the 13–17-year-old demographic group (Saul 2014). What accounts for these changes in young peoples' preferences? Why does one site lose its appeal? Is this merely an example of teens' flighty preferences changing constantly to keep up with trends, or is there something else going on? More importantly, what do these changes reveal about young people's negotiations of visibility and expectations of privacy?

If we look at the migration from MySpace to Facebook, we see that this decision was not necessarily about the technical affordances of the spaces. In fact, Facebook afforded fewer customizable options than MySpace and imposed greater limitations on what teens could do on the site. MySpace had a similar feel to its predecessor, the blog. Like blogs, MySpace allowed and encouraged young people to personalize their pages with unique images, songs, videos, and other media. Alternatively, Facebook imposed a static format that offered few customizable options; for the most part, everyone's pages looked the same. For that reason, the move probably was not a result of an upgraded interface or options; it probably can be better accounted for by looking at the networks of users.

Young people (like adults) are drawn to social media platforms not because of what they necessarily allow users to do, but rather because of whom they can connect with via the platforms. The simple explanation is that teens abandoned MySpace for Facebook because that's where their friends were going. A deeper analysis reveals that perceptions of the two sites (more specifically, perceptions of who was using the two sites) were embedded in broader understandings of racial and ethnic identities. The exclusive nature of Facebook served to keep certain "undesirable" people out of the network. Watkins (2009) compares Facebook to a gated neighborhood that only the "right" people can enter. In the early days of Facebook, setting up an account required a college email address, which created a sense of exclusivity. In contrast to MySpace, most Facebook users were white and/or middle-class. Watkins notes that the ethnically diverse demographic of users on MySpace contributed to its perception as "crowded," "trashy," "creepy," and "uneducated" (ibid.). Watkins recognized that young people were using such language less to describe the site itself than to describe the perception of the kinds of people who were likely to still use the site—minority, non-college-educated, and/or low-income individuals. The site became a stand-in for describing and delineating ethnic identities. As boyd (2011) puts it, MySpace had become a "digital ghetto."

It has been more than six years since these observations were first noted and since then we have seen yet another change in the popularity of social media. To a certain degree, the move away from Facebook probably can be attributed to the number of adults now on Facebook. In 2014, Facebook saw an increase of more than 80 percent in the number of users 55 and older and an increase of 41 percent in users between 35 and 54 (Saul 2014). What was once considered a province of young people has become a common area for people of all ages.

In the physical world, teens desire spaces of their own. Historically, such spaces have included soda shops, drive-in theaters, arcades, and shopping malls. The Internet has become a popular "hangout" for youth precisely because physical spaces designated for young people have been diminishing (boyd 2014). As more and more teachers, parents, and authority figures began using Facebook, teens understandably sought out spaces away from the adults in their lives. If we look to the popular sites that have begun to replace (or at least supplement) Facebook—apps such as Instagram, Tumblr, Vine, and Snapchat—we note the use of photos and images has taken on increasing priority. Young people once wanted to move away from the cluttered pages of MySpace, but it appears the appeal of images and multimedia platforms is winning out over the static and still primarily text-based format of Facebook.

The changes in networks and the user interfaces are limited explanations for why teens are abandoning Facebook, but there is more to consider. Yes, teens are seeking their own spaces where they can converse with friends away from the watchful eye of parents and authority figures. However, I am also hearing that young people expect greater control over their networks, their identities, and ultimately their visibility. As 18-year-old Cindy (Asian-American) explained to me over breakfast one morning, "Facebook just doesn't give you a sense of control. They're always changing things. I don't know, I just feel it's easier to use Tumblr the way I want … and I don't know, it's more of our space, you know?" Her comment alludes to the ways Facebook has continued to expand its reach to many other areas of the web by serving as a portal to other sites. Owing to changes in the interface and the algorithms, more and more information and more and more interactions are publicized within and beyond the site itself. And the archival nature of the site records past relationships, interactions, and expressions, often in acutely visible ways. In and of themselves these are not inherently bad or misguided moves on Facebook's part. From an economic perspective Facebook's increasing visibility strategies may be a successful business decision, but from an identity and privacy perspective, they are adversarial to teens' preferential interactions, experiences, and expectations of visibility.

"Just don't post it": The Problem with Individualizing Privacy

Google's CEO, Eric Schmidt, explained his approach to privacy during an interview with Maria Bartiromo of CNBC: "If you have something that you don't want anyone to know, maybe you shouldn't be doing it" (Google CEO on Privacy 2010). This presumption that privacy is primarily about hiding "bad" information is also echoed by the advice adults give teens when discussing online privacy. Young people often are told not to do the "bad" thing in the first place, and they most definitely should not post anything online that they wouldn't want everyone to see. Research repeatedly and consistently demonstrates that young people care about their privacy (boyd 2014; Livingstone 2008; Madden et al. 2013); nonetheless there is an assumption that they reveal too much information about themselves online—information that "horrifies their elders" (Henley 2013). The practice of sharing information that adults do not understand gets misinterpreted as a disregard for privacy. Sharing information about oneself and one's peers often gets constructed in pathologizing or demeaning ways. For example, taking "selfies" (photos of oneself) is often described as narcissistic and self-centered behavior (Giroux 2015; Gregoire 2015) and is sometimes even linked to addiction, body dysphoria, or mental illness. The psychiatrist David Veal has been quoted as saying "Two out of three of all patients who come to see me with body dysmorphic disorder since the rise of camera phones have a compulsion to repeatedly take and post selfies on social media sites" (Keating 2014). This rhetoric is reflective of the harm-driven expectations of risk that we have seen throughout this book. These risk-driven narratives emerge frequently in medical, social, legal, and educational debates. The persistence of pathologizing and demonizing young people's social media practices makes it far easier to blame young people themselves instead of holding society responsible for violating their expectations.

For example, administrators at a Georgia high school wanted to teach students about the risks of sharing information about oneself online. To demonstrate their point, they gave a presentation to parents and students during which they displayed a photo that the administrators perceived as over-sexualized of a student, Chelsey Chaney, wearing a bikini. The photo was presented as an example of what kind of photos young people should not share online. It had been taken while the young woman was vacationing with her family; she had then posted it to her Facebook account, which was visible only to friends and friends of friends. By using the photo and the young woman's full name, the school—though aiming to teach about privacy—had violated her expectations of privacy by quite literally using the photo as an example of what not to do on social media. (Here I do not mean that the girl should not have shared a photo of herself in a bikini, but rather that the school should not have used the image as an example at a school assembly.) Chelsey Chaney sued the school for breaching those expectations. She explained: "I understand people are going to look at it, that I put it out there, but for a school administrator to target me as an example of a bad child?" (Judge tosses part of lawsuit … 2013). Her point is valid: it's one thing to re-share the photo to make a point, but it's another to shame a high school student in front of the entire school (teachers, students, and parents included). An attorney representing the school responded that he "finds it perplexing that someone is suing for millions for a picture she herself posted on the internet" (Rudra 2013).[1] What the lawyer and school failed to understand was the context in which the student shared the photo (a photo that was arguably not inappropriate): it was shared on Facebook for her friends and family members to see, it was not intended to be shown to the entire student body and their parents within a context that was intended to shame the student. The gendered nature of shame also needs to be emphasized. It is not inappropriate for a teen girl to be in a bikini on the beach with her family. It isn't likely that the school would have used a photo of a teen boy in his swimsuit on the beach to illustrate the point. The shaming and harm-driven rhetoric that aims to regulate teens' practices are often gendered and reify expectations that teen girls (and their adult-perceived sexuality) are inherently inappropriate and at risk online (see chapter 2).

Throughout the entire incident, the school held Chelsey Chaney responsible and blamed her for having posted a "sexy" picture of herself online. From the school's perspective, the expectation was that once the photo has been shared in *any* context, it was justifiable for others to re-share it in any other context. In attempting to teach students about the value of privacy, the school actually perpetuated the dangerous ways in which students (or anyone) should not act. As one social media theorist explained, "So obsessed with young women's sexuality, the school becomes preoccupied on the women in the photos, echoing that now familiar refrain that shames and blames the victims of privacy violations instead of focusing on the violators" (Jurgenson 2013). The adult expectation was that sharing anything online—in any context—negates an individual's right and expectation to privacy. In a talk to tech industry professionals, danah boyd (2007) drew an important distinction between public and publicity, arguing that just because something is publically accessible does not mean it is intended to be *publicized*: "Publicizing their material without their knowledge is a way of taking control away from them." Although boyd was talking about technical affordances of the platforms that publicize users' content (a point I will return to later in this chapter), the statement is applicable to other situations, particularly when adults re-appropriate young people's content in a different context. This is but one example of the ways in which popular discourses of risk and expectations of privacy falsely assume that privacy is an individualized norm and practice. Focusing solely on the individual dismisses and ignores the collective and contextual role that peers, adults, institutions, and networks play in shaping the contours and expectations of privacy.

Although young people do have a responsibility to manage what they choose to share online, including with whom and where they share information, they cannot control what platforms, institutions, and peers intentionally and inadvertently reveal about their identities and relationships. Discourses of visibility need to take into account how the disclosure of particular identities opens up some teens to greater risk for discrimination and judgment. Arguably, privacy expectations must expand beyond individual strategies for hiding "bad" information about oneself, but must also consider how collective peer contexts and various stakeholders are also responsible for respecting teens' privacy, norms, expectations, and online practices. What the participants in this book express is that they seek opportunities for networked online identity explorations and interpersonal relationships that are contextually situated (rather than the converged and public identity of Facebook) and they expect networks and adults to acknowledge and respect their practices and norms. As a strategy for maintaining privacy, they employ differentiated practices that allow them to use different media for different aspects of their lives and with different people. In doing so, their conceptions and expectations of privacy tend to differ from how parents, teachers, the law, and social media sites understand privacy. Analyzing what sites and apps participants are using and for what purposes provides productive entry into considering and analyzing young people's expectations of identity, privacy, and visibility; their expectations and practices highlight the need to approach privacy from a collective—rather than an individualized—perspective.

Doing Identity

From a discursive perspective, youth is often constructed as a transitional period of "becoming"—a period in which young people explore and experiment with different modes of expression and identification (Gabriel 2013). "Identity," David Buckingham explains (2008, p. 8), "is something we *do*, rather than simply something we *are*." Judith Butler (1990) explains that identity is something that is performed; such a perspective comes from an understanding that identity is not fixed, but rather is fluid. In other words, identity is never accomplished, but rather is constantly evolving and is constantly negotiated throughout a lifetime. Such a perspective understands that identity is contextually situated—individuals do not possess one true identity, but rather different identities are articulated and performed in different contexts. For example, a young girl constructs and performs the identity of "daughter" at home with her parents and constructs and performs the identity of "student" at school and that of "friend" with her peers. The girl is not any more authentic nor fake by articulating or performing any one of these identities at any given time, but rather each are authentic manifestations of her identity as they are experienced and expressed in particular moments, contexts, and roles.[2] We must also keep in mind that, far from being an individual choice, young people's understanding of their identities is largely constructed from the social and cultural cues in their environment, as well as from their embodied sense of self.

Since the 1990s, teens have used the Internet as a tool for exploring interests, experimenting with identity, and fostering a sense of community. Early Internet research is often critiqued for constructing a false dichotomy between offline identities as opposed to online identities. There was an inherent assumption that what happened online was somehow less authentic or real than what happened offline (Hine 2000; Walker 2000). Even today the language of "real life" is used to indicate something that happens in the physical world as opposed to the virtual world; but both are "real" in their articulation and effects. Over time, we have come to understand that the Internet provides a means through which we can express ourselves and communicate with others; thus the interactions are no less real or meaningful just because they are mediated. As Butler's theory of identity explains, if identity is constantly performed, rather than a fixed component of who we are, then both offline performances and online performances become equally significant and authentic. The platform or social context through which identity is performed does not discredit the performative expression of self. Even fantastical or fabricated instances of identity performance still reveal insight into how an individual desires to be perceived.

Take for example, 18-year-old Regina, whom I met via her blog in 2007. She attended an all-girls school and fell in love with her best friend, a young woman whom she referred to simply as "A." Because her mother and her friends disapproved of her lesbian relationship, Regina had to keep her relationship with A secret. Regina started a blog so that she could have a place to discuss her own sexual identity (which she admitted was still very confusing to her). Regina found a supportive community of girls online. Her dedicated readers left comments and offered her advice about how to handle her situation at home and at school. They would also suggest other blogs written by people who were in similar situations, thus she connected to a much larger community of lesbian and questioning girls her own age. Here, within the confines of the online world, Regina found both an outlet for sexual expression and identity negotiation, as well as a supportive community that was not available to her in the offline world. The support she found online influenced her offline life, just as her offline life was the impetus for starting a blog in the first place. Regina went to great lengths to keep her blog a secret from her friends and family members (and even her girlfriend)—she used a pseudonym and an alternative email address, she did not publicize the blog, nor did she let her family know she had a blog, and she did not use the blog to communicate with friends from her offline life. Though the blog was publicly accessible, it functioned as a secret and private space for Regina and was an authentic aspect of her life.

As Regina's example demonstrates, understandings of private and public are contextual—though she chose not disclose her sexuality in her embodied interactions with friends and family members, on the Internet she could be public about her relationship and her emerging sexuality. Revealing her sexuality online does not preclude Regina from desiring to keep her emerging sexuality private at home and at school. In other words, her having come out in one context does not mean that Regina should have no expectations of privacy in other contexts of her life. Additionally, what Regina's story highlights is the extent to which using digital media as spaces for expressing one's identity inevitably leads to questions of privacy. We know that sharing private and sensitive information about ourselves is essential to building healthy relationships, and we all choose to disclose particular aspects of our identities on a daily basis, sometimes willingly and sometimes less intentionally. However, we also understand and assess the risks and benefits of such disclosures and make decisions based on the context of the interactions and relationships. For Regina, the benefits of coming out on her blog—and the community the blog provided her—outweighed the potential privacy risks, but did not negate her expectation of privacy in other spaces.

As we discuss privacy we must keep in mind that identity and privacy are intricately linked. We willingly and unintentionally give up private information continually, but as we assess expectations of privacy we must always take into consideration the context in which information was disclosed, by whom, and for what purpose. Additionally, privacy is more complicated than merely being "not public"; rather, privacy—both online and offline— is a matter of degree, context, visibility, and control (boyd 2014). Privacy is not a simple binary of "private" and "not private," although laws, policies, and expectations (as the Georgia high school example) often tend to reify this simplistic binary. The binary, of course, ignores the complicated nuances of privacy practices and contextualized understandings of identity performance.

Expectations of Privacy

In the physical world, visibly marked cues such as closed doors and crowded spaces delineate expectations of privacy. Online, however, cues that might delineate such expectations often are rendered invisible or are more open to interpretation. This does not mean they disappear completely; it just makes things more complicated. Just as the physical world has architecture that helps us dictate privacy norms (e.g., gendered bathrooms with stalls, doors, locks, and so forth that dictate how the space is to be used, by whom, and with what degree of privacy), the online world has its own architecture in the form of code. Lawrence Lessig (1999) has proposed that the architecture of the Internet (i.e., the code) is one of the most important modes of online regulation. Code essentially dictates what we can and cannot do on any given website or app. For example, some websites require you to create an account, a log-in name, and a password before you can access the information. This is the architecture of the site as determined by the code. Other websites might allow you to leave comments, but they do not enable you to upload a video or embed an image with your comment. Again, this is the architecture of the site and is the intentional coding design decision. Much like the architecture of the physical world, the architecture of a website provides context cues about our expectations of privacy. If a website requires you to log in before leaving a comment, you probably are more aware that your comment is linked to an online identity or account, and thus you will have different expectations of privacy than you will have if the site allows you to leave an anonymous comment without creating an account. If you post something to your Facebook profile, you should be aware that it is more visible than if you share the same information in a private Facebook message to a friend. The message feels more private than a post, but of course it is still accessible to people working at Facebook, reminding us that the same information can be simultaneously private (from the perspective of social privacy) and remain accessible in other contexts. It is the dualistic nature of online information as both private and public that makes online interactions, disclosure, and expectations so capricious.

The complexity of understanding privacy online is due in part to the fact that cues aren't always neatly distinct or visible. The architecture of platforms means that we are not always aware of who has access to online information in the same way we might be in the physical world. Five characteristics of networked publics that render the spaces distinct from the physical world have been identified by boyd (2010): online information is persistent, searchable, replicable, scalable, and locatable. This makes it particularly difficult to assess expectations of privacy and to express different identities in delineated contexts. These dynamics lead to what boyd describes as "context collapse"—moments and practices in which social, spatial, and temporal boundaries converge, often in invisible, unpredictable, and uncontrollable ways. Again, this is not wholly unprecedented or unique to the virtual world, as boundaries certainly collide in the physical world as well, yet the delineations and effects can be more subtle or even invisible online. Additionally, we often have less control of the contexts and visibility of information when we are online.

As an example of context collapse in the physical world, consider what happens when a student on a date runs into a teacher or when a mother overhears her daughter having an intimate conversation with friends in her bedroom. In each of these examples, an individual is articulating and expressing a particular identity in a particular context and the unanticipated presence of someone outside of that context disrupts the social setting and expectations. However, in the physical world we often are aware when these distinct contexts overlap and can adjust our sense of identity and behavior accordingly—for example, we see our teacher and adjust our behavior, or we hear our mother and decide to whisper or change the subject. When we experience context collapses online, they can be more complicated because it is be easier for our audiences to remain unknown and invisible. And because our interactions are archivable and searchable, it can be more difficult to imagine all current and future audiences. When we share something online, we have an intended or imagined audience in mind (Marwick and boyd 2010), yet the information persists and can be replicated and accessed in contexts other than the one we intended and imagined. The complications of identity performance and privacy expectations are disrupted and amplified to some degree when our interactions and disclosures are tracked, saved, and replicated in different contexts.

Degrees of Visibility

If privacy is not a binary and the concepts are blurry, how then do we manage and negotiate privacy norms online? One way to conceptualize online privacy is to shift the conversation away from private and public and instead to think about degrees of visibility. Research indicates that while young people (and adults) understand that social network sites are not entirely private, they still often interact on the sites as though they are private (Barnes 2006). This is in part because they have reasonable expectations that their quotidian interactions and conversations are not of interest to most people. Likewise, they assume that what they are sharing is contained and interpreted within a particular context. When online, individuals have a sense of whom they expect their audience to be on any given site, and act according to the norms of that particular audience and space.

Problems arise, however, when contextual expectations are breached. The legal and communication scholar Helen Nissenbaum (2004) refers to this understanding of privacy as "contextual integrity." She argues that within any context or sphere there are always two complementary and normative expectations at play: norms of appropriateness (what is appropriate to share in a specific context) and norms of flow, or distribution (what is appropriate to transfer or share from one party to another). Together these normative frameworks structure expectations and practices of contextual integrity. Nissenbaum argues that complaints of privacy violations are justifiable when norms of appropriate sharing or appropriate distribution are breached. The idea of contextual integrity is particularly productive when analyzing teens' privacy strategies because teens and adult society often have different understandings and expectations of the social contexts in which young people disclose information, perform identities, and communicate with one another. Social norms are not only powerful strategies for influencing behaviors, but they are also contextually bound and constantly contested; for that reason, they are often open to multiple interpretations and understandings. If we are to understand how young people conceptualize online identity and negotiate expectations of privacy, we must first and foremost understand their social expectations and norms. As I'll explain, norms vary between different social groups and are significantly influenced by identification, subject position, and localized practices. It is not as simple as "young people think of privacy as X"; rather, we must consider how different social groups create and police norms differently. Only then can we have a more nuanced conversation about the consequences of visible online identities and privacy expectations.

Nissenbaum's concept of contextual integrity is incredibly useful, though I think we can go a step further and consider expectations of visibility that also speak to the integrity of contextual specificity. In addition to competing understandings of context and norms between teens and adults, young people's expectations of visibility are also increasingly at odds with the architecture of particular social media platforms. Sites such as Facebook frequently change how information is aggregated, publicized, and accessed within and beyond the site. Much like boyd's (2008) analysis of the introduction of the news feed to Facebook, changes in the platform itself can breach users' expectations of the context and visibility in which information is shared. As will be further addressed later in this chapter, this was the case when Facebook made Likes more visible. Participants didn't expect their Likes to be private; however, they became upset when the context and visibility of their actions were altered and heightened.

Youth desire, seek, and expect some control over the visibility of these interactions. What is concerning, particularly for low-income youth, is the extent to which their practices are scrutinized, pathologized, trivialized, and criminalized within popular imagination and the law (as discussed in chapter 2). The Internet opens up new opportunities for young people to participate in networked publics—that is, "to see and be seen, to socialize, and to feel as if they have the freedoms to explore a world beyond the heavily constrained one shaped by parents and school" (boyd 2014, pp. 201–202). However, harm-driven expectations that are perpetuated via increasingly negative media and adult attention will serve to further silence and marginalize teens' voices and practices. Rather than risk scrutiny, they may choose to speak and engage in more insular and private spaces that are disconnected from the more public spaces and platforms in society. As was further discussed in chapter 5, low-income young people in particular are likely to miss out on opportunities for networking, promoting their creative work, voicing their experiences, and participating in networked publics. The reasons are complex, but we need to pay attention to the ways adult expectations, as well as the architecture and policies of social media platforms, monitor and regulate young people's expectations of visibility and of what consequences.

Networked Visibility

I often hear both adults and teens repeat some iteration of "If you're careful about what you share online, then you have nothing to worry about." As has been noted, this attitude falsely constructs privacy as an individual decision and strategy. It neglects to take into consideration how our behaviors and interactions are networked and how the *visibility of our social networks* reveal a lot about us that we cannot control. Further, it reduces a complex issue—identity expression and speech—to an issue of mere individual responsibility, and thus dismisses the questions of ethics and boundaries altogether. What is absent from these discourses and narratives is the extent to which our online networks—that is, to whom we are connected—inadvertently reveal a lot of seemingly private information about us. Alarmingly, users of social media platforms have little knowledge of or control over what their *networks* make visible and thus reveal about their identities, associations, and interactions, yet networks themselves generate, augment, and manage visibilities.

To illustrate how networked identities mitigate visibility, I conduct an exercise each semester with undergraduate students enrolled in my Digital Media and Society course. I choose a friend from my own Facebook network, then view his or her friends. I take a screen grab of their friend list, capturing twelve random friends in their list (my friend's image and name are not revealed). I then show the screen grab to my students and ask them what they can infer about my friend from twelve of their friends.[3] At first students are a bit uncomfortable or reluctant, but with a little prodding they start articulating their assumptions. "Well, most everyone is black, so maybe the person is black." Others will use names to make assumptions: "Well, it seems a lot of people have Spanish-sounding names, so maybe the person is from Mexico or an immigrant." Others will take note of their age: "There's a lot of pictures of kids and families, so maybe the person is in their thirties or forties." I showed screenshots of twelve friends of one of my gay friends, and it did not take long for a student to accurately guess the friend was a white gay male in his thirties. Students have been able to accurately identify which friends are Muslim and which are Jewish. Others will identify where people work or where they received their education and take guesses about the person's occupation and education level. One student noted that one of my friends had friends from all over the country and guessed that the friend might have moved around a lot. Sure enough, the friend was a professor who had lived in four states in seven years. I've had students accurately guess a friend's industry—social work, news reporter, and teacher—on the basis of the friend's connections. Interestingly, students even make assumptions about political affiliations and ideologies, even in the absence of overt clues. One student accurately commented: "All their friends are white, and kinda look alike. A lot of them have kids or pictures with their partner or spouse. I don't know, it just makes me think she's a conservative white woman." And this assumption was eerily accurate.

Students are amazed they are able to so accurately identify so much information about someone on the basis of only twelve photos from their public Facebook connections. Occasionally they will guess something inaccurate, for example, assuming a person is a college student when in fact the person is a 50-something professor. And occasionally they are not able to make many assumptions at all. However, the wrong assumptions are just as significant, maybe for some even more significant, than accurate guesses. Regardless of the confirmed accuracy, our list of visible connections serves to reveal aspects of our identities and networks. This is a matter of privacy that extends beyond the kinds of information we deliberately choose to reveal about ourselves online. These assumptions can be used to make decisions about us in a variety of contexts that are beyond our control and without our consent or even knowledge. But this is the nature of networked privacy: we can exert *some* control over the information we intentionally choose to share online, however, we have limited control over what our social *networks* reveal about us. Networked visibility makes evident that we cannot reduce privacy to that of individual responsibility, but rather privacy itself is networked.

Similarly, we need to avoid couching privacy within a debate of "hiding" information. As Daniel Solove notes (2007, p. 764), constructing privacy in terms of hiding information "myopically views privacy as a form of concealment or secrecy" and ignores the complexity of privacy as a concept that is also about agency, transparency, control, context, and disclosure. My in-class exercise reveals the extent to which privacy is networked, but also the extent to which privacy far exceeds concerns of hiding "bad" information. Clearly, there is nothing wrong with being a Muslim, or pregnant, or gay, or black. However, these aspects of our identities can lead to blatant or unintentional forms of discrimination. Those who argue that we can and should be the only ones responsible for our own privacy speak from a highly privileged and protected subject position. The need for greater privacy protection is not merely about the ability for us to hide bad information about ourselves. It is imperative that privacy be understood within the context of a society that values, privileges, and protects some identities—or rather devalues, exploits, and discriminates against some identities—more than others. While we do have an individual responsibility to be careful what we share online, understandings of online privacy must evolve to encompass the public and networked nature of visibility, power, and privilege.

Deliberate Disassociation

What is important to note for marginalized youth, is the extent to which their localized and racialized identities, interests, and communicative practices—in other words, their cultural capital—is often misinterpreted, policed, and decontextualized within white hegemonic society (Carter 2003; Giroux 2009; Mendoza-Denton 2008). Because teens navigate different social contexts that include differentiations across age, class, and ethnic boundaries, it can be difficult for marginalized teens to simultaneously manage privacy and fit in with the "right" group. One way this is played out among marginalized young people is via a practice of disassociation; that is, some participants employ deliberate strategies to disassociate themselves from peers whose identities could lead to negative (adult) assumptions about their practices and preferences.

For example, Miguel and his twin brother Marcus (14 years old, undocumented Mexican immigrants) explained that they were anxious about an informal reunion with friends from elementary school because "whenever me and my friend check them on Facebook, they're all, like, ghetto and stuff, and I'm nowhere near that." Countless times throughout the study students explained the ways they attempted to distinguish themselves from peers they perceived of as "ghetto," a word used by virtually all participants—regardless of ethnicity—to primarily describe black peers and Mexican-Americans who were "too loud," were "trashy," or tried to "act hard" and "start fights." These perceptions are embedded within the broader racialized and geographical context of Freeway High and go beyond their use of social media and are outside the scope of this chapter. Nonetheless, their anxieties about race, class, and reputation were heightened, articulated, and made visible in online spaces.

Jack (17 years old, white), an upwardly mobile senior, explained that he blocked people who used "made-up names" on Facebook. While browsing his Facebook one afternoon, he pointed out a Facebook user with a made-up nickname. "See, there we go, Jamie Suckafree (notwitdabullshit)—that's a ghetto name. People are starting to do it on Facebook. I don't even know who that is. See, that's why I blocked that person." There is even an entire Tumblr page dedicated to "ghetto Facebook names." As you can imagine, the page mocks not just the names but the users as well, and includes many derogatory assumptions based on the users' ethnicities. As the trend of creating "ghetto" Facebook names became more popular during the time of our study, it was not uncommon for participants to explain they had blocked or unfriended such people. They often explained it was because the profiles were "annoying" or because they "didn't know that person any-more." However, as Marcus and Miguel also explained, they were anxious about being associated with such people. In a networked society, our rela-tionships are made visible and reveal information about us that can be taken out of context and thus used against us. Some participants blocked and unfriended people with whom they did not want to be publicly associ-ated. Their anxiety was rooted in a concern that adults and other peers would jump to conclusions or make assumptions about them on the basis of their peers. The legitimate concern served to police their relationships, as well as expectations and performances of (often racialized) identities. Although Miguel, Marcus, and Jack were concerned about how others might perceive such connections, and understandably so, there is nothing inherently wrong or risky about connecting with peers who express identi-ties in these ways. The use of false names can also be read through a lens of visibility strategies that made it more difficult to search and identify those teens' profiles. But Miguel, Marcus, and Jack were aware of the extent to which others might make assumptions about them on the basis of these visible connections—assumptions they did not want others to make. At a time when more than three fourths of employers use digital media to screen and monitor employees (Webb 2014), strategies of deliberate disassociation and self-censorship might prove beneficial; the visibility of their connec-tions and practices open up opportunities for discrimination based on misunderstandings of cultural and social capital.

In and of itself, self-censorship is not a bad strategy either. Social norms often dictate that we regulate what we say and how we act in particular spaces and with particular audiences. As with the previous discussion of identity, we intentionally and unintentionally articulate different identities within different contexts. Such norms serve a purpose and can be beneficial in creating and maintaining environments of respect, professionalism, and so forth. However, social norms also speak to normative values, expecta-tions, and assumptions that ought to be continually called into question. Not all norms are beneficial, for example, gender norms can serve to limit how comfortable individuals feel expressing particular interests (e.g., a little boy is not "supposed" to play with princess dolls). For young people, social network sites are often considered peer-driven spaces for socializing. Yet when adults and authority figures surveil their practices, it opens up oppor-tunities for their behaviors to be misinterpreted. Gabriela (16 years old, Mexican-American) expressed anxiety about how her online profiles might be interpreted by adults, specifically future employers or college admissions offices:

I just don't know what they're actually looking for. So, is something wrong with what I post? [Are they going to think] "Oh, this person likes this type of music, or they look like this," and then judge me? So, it worries me. It concerns me that something I posted isn't what they want or something.

Undoubtedly we should encourage young people to think critically about the kinds of information they share online, and even with whom they visibly connect online, but we should also be wary of rhetoric that penalizes young people for expressing themselves in ways that challenge or disrupt adult expectations of appropriate identity expression and peer connections.

None of the participants I got to know used "ghetto" names on Facebook, yet the practice was not uncommon, particularly for black and Hispanic peers. How might such names be interpreted by employers? What assumptions might adults make about teens that choose to express their identities in such a way? What about teens who do not articulate such identities but are connected with peers who do? The practices are situated within a context of peer relationships, as well as a particular racial and ethnic identity. Miguel and Marcus expressed anxiety and ambiguity about the ways they interacted with "ghetto" friends and were trying to navigate their own identities and friendships. Practices of deliberate disassociation can be an effective strategy for negotiating identities, however when social norms enact power and put pressure on youth to disconnect or self-censor, we need to make sure we are critically questioning the normative values of such assumptions and practices.

Unintentional Visibility

Facebook has changed the social media landscape in a lot of ways. As the most popular social network site, with 1.39 billion monthly active users as of December 31, 2014 (Facebook Newsroom, 2015), it has the power to shape social media norms. The architecture has undergone a lot of changes in its first eleven years; these changes directly influence conceptions of privacy and identity by shaping our understanding of "sharing." In the early days of Facebook, sharing was understood as something that was done between and among friends. However, the increasingly commercialized and public aspects of Facebook have broadened the concept of sharing beyond just interpersonal relationships and has been expanded to indicate a more public and commercial sense of sharing. On page 54 of her 2013 book *The Culture of Connectivity*, José van Dijck explains that "Facebook wants its preferred meaning of sharing, implying complete openness and maximum exchange of data with third parties, to become the 'shared norm.'" It is in the financial interest of Facebook to encapsulate the meaning of sharing within an economic framework that allows the platform to capitalize on users' sociality.

Facebook's archival nature, combined with the increasing publicness of interactions, works to create a visible and seemingly static understanding of identity. The social network site has become a portal to many other websites and apps—from shopping, to news, to games, and more—which works to create a persistent and semi-cohesive online identity. The architecture and the norms work together to attempt to create "one identity" across the web (van Dijck 2013b). Ivan Montiel (2012) argues that Google has also encouraged users to construct one consistent identity, which he refers to as "persistent identity." As Google has created and acquired different apps and services (among them Google+, YouTube, Vidmaker, Softcard, and Android), it has also created one portal that allows users access to all their expanded services using only one log-in, one profile, and one password. Beyond merely streamlining users' experiences and aiding in convenience, it also shapes social norms and expectations of identity, visibility, and privacy. The commercial impetus that underpins corporate acquisitions and pushes for a unified identity across platforms is often incompatible with users' social practices and preferences on the sites.

The push toward a persistent and cohesive identity is contradictory to the way young people have historically constructed communities and identities—both online and offline. For example, since the 1990s blogs have been popular spaces for youth to play with different modes of identity, to participate in disconnected online communities, to engage and communicate with strangers, and to experiment with different interests and networks. Until recently, norms dictated that interactions could be pseudonymous and disconnected from offline embodied identities (as was the case for Regina, mentioned earlier in this chapter). It was not too difficult to create different and disconnected profiles that articulated different identities and then to pop in and out of different networks. These practices and platforms were reflective of and embedded in the evolving and experimental states of identity construction, particularly for adolescents. However, Facebook has increasingly rendered identities and interactions public and visible in a way that not all young people appreciate or are even able to understand. As I reveal, participants in this book tend to find the archival and public nature of Facebook to be oppositional to the more fluid and strategic nature of their communication practices and expressions of their identities. These differences in expectations are clearly articulated by exploring young people's reactions to a change in Facebook's architecture.

Public Liking

In 2010, Facebook changed its interface with the introduction of the Like button. As described by Facebook, the Like button is designed to "give positive feedback and connect with things you care about." Initially users could Like pages run by commercial entities such as brands, celebrities, musicians, TV shows, and corporate restaurants. They served as a way for users to express interest in something and articulate particular aspects of their identities via their profile pages. The Like button is also one feature that Facebook uses to determine what users see in their news feeds. Although Likes were never private, they initially functioned in a more private manner. For example, you could Like a band or a celebrity, but this information was not published in your news feed. In order to know that your friend had Liked a band or a television show, you would have to click on your friend's profile page and then view her Likes section to see all the things she had liked. Later the Like feature was added to users' individual posts and photos; it became a way to acknowledge your friends' updates without having to leave an actual comment. Initially these interactions were visible on the individual updates, but they were still not publicized or made visible in the news feed.

However, in 2011 Facebook began publishing Likes in users' news feeds, so you could easily and unintentionally see what your friends had been doing on the site and beyond.[4] Rather than going to your friend's page to see that Sarah had Liked Mark's post about his vacation, your news feed would publish a story alerting you that "Sarah Likes Mark's photo album Vacation at the Beach." This interface also pushed popular content (i.e., a post that has received a lot of likes or comments) to the top of your news feed. This meant that if a lot of your connections were engaging with Mark's vacation album it was more likely to show up at the top of your feed (even if it was not recent or new). This architectural design and interface functioned to heighten the visibility of particular posts and interactions among your Facebook network. If that post was someone announcing a new job, then that might be a positive feature for the user (i.e., the network was made aware of the big announcement and the individual received a lot of validation and praise). However, if the post receiving a lot of attention within the network was derogatory, gossipy, or controversial (as determined by the peer groups included), this could have a negative effect on the user and their network because it continued to draw attention to something that might be causing strife within different social circles.

Cassandra (18 years old, biracial) explained how the publishing of Likes (the new feature that had just been introduced during the week of the following conversation) created problems in her group of friends.

Cassandra: Before you could see who Liked so and so's picture, but it never told you on the news feed who Likes so and so's picture. If you went to someone's picture and looked at all the Likes you could see who Liked it, but now in the news feed it's, like, yesterday I saw this girl Liked this boy's picture and she has a boyfriend and she Liked this boy's picture and it said "Kara Liked Devonte's picture." Ten minutes later it said "Devonte Likes Kara's picture." I guess they haven't seen the new Facebook but, this girl has a boyfriend and they started Liking each other's pictures back and forth every 10 minutes and the boyfriend was, like, "What the hell?" Usually you wouldn't—for instance—that girl's boyfriend wouldn't go to Devonte's profile and check all his pictures to see if his girlfriend Liked it, but now it says it on the news feed so he can just automatically see that.

Q: So he did say "What the hell?" Where did he say that? On Facebook?

Cassandra: Yeah. He wrote on her wall and he was, like, "Why are you liking all these guy's pictures?" She was, like, "What?" They figured out finally and they were talking about it but that's just crazy.

Q: You just noticed it?

Cassandra: It was the first thing I saw when I logged on, it was at the top. I just ignored it after that. It was just crazy because you couldn't have saw that before, but the whole news feed said "Kara Liked Devonte's photo" and then "Devonte Liked Kara's photo"—it was, like, for 15 photos.

Q: Wow. That is definitely something. Do you feel like you don't want to get involved in that?

Cassandra: No. I don't care. I wasn't going to say anything or anything—everyone could already see it because he posted it on her wall—he didn't message her "What the hell?" — he wrote "What the hell?" on her wall.

Q: Why would Kara's boyfriend write about that on her wall instead of calling her?

Cassandra :   I think that's just the kid coming out in him. I don't know. I would think someone more mature and older would just message their girlfriend and be, like, "I just saw you Liked — you had a picture Like war with this random guy." He just wanted to put her—I guess just, like, put her out there and let everyone know that he saw it and he's doing something about it—you know?

Q: Does that happen a lot?

Cassandra : Oh, yeah.

Cassandra went on to discuss other examples about how people used Facebook to deliberately cause problems or air grievances in a public space: "People do that a lot on Facebook—put business out there that nobody cares about. I don't even know—just dumb things. … That's the only reason I don't like Facebook."

As the interaction between Devonte and Kara demonstrated, publicizing Likes added an additional dimension to the ways Facebook broadcasted information to users' news feeds. Devonte and Kara probably were aware that their Likes weren't private, but, as Cassandra explained, Kara's boyfriend was unlikely to have noticed the Likes before the change in Facebook's interface. Even if Kara's boyfriend had noticed that she had Liked Devonte's photos, it may not have been interpreted in the same way were it not for the timing, which Facebook rendered visible. In other words, seeing that Kara has Liked a lot of photos is one thing, but seeing that Kara had Liked a lot of photos in a short time span was interpreted differently. The changes in Facebook's interface and algorithms changed the context in which users could Like information by rendering their pseudo-private interactions highly visible. One student explained: "We all creep on each other's Facebooks, but you're not supposed to let people know that. But Liking something really old is kinda embarrassing. … Other people now see it too, it makes it obvious you were creeping." The public nature of Liking something and the intentional ways it gets publicized to mutual friends disrupted participants' expectations of how to appropriately interact on Facebook and challenged their taken for granted understandings of social norms.

Invisible Algorithms and Misunderstood Intentions

Facebook's algorithms fail to account for the overall sentiment of the popular and trending posts. Just because a post receives a lot of interaction from people in one's network, does not necessarily mean users want to see the post. Furthermore, publicizing Likes on the news feed can have other privacy implications that disrupt expectations of visibility and context. For example, you might be cautious about sharing and commenting on an overtly political post. However, if you Like a news story that has been posted to another friend's wall, or you leave a comment on an organization's post, those comments and Likes are made visible to the broader community. These seemingly private interactions—Liking a story about marriage equality, for example—can inadvertently reveal information about you that you did not intend to share on Facebook. In this way, connecting with a friend or Liking something posted by an organization can feel semi-private, it is an interaction between you and an individual post; however, the information is often made visible on the site and in a context that is not visible to you or easily understood. This is because Facebook's terms state that once you Like something, you have "consented" to Liking all future posts from that organization, what Sandvig (2014) refers to as "Like recycling." Like recycling is also how ads are generated in your feed; they appear to be endorsed by your friends, but the process is a bit more invisible and deceptive. The visibility of your interactions is determined by invisible algorithms, not your intentions. For example, let's say Sarah's friend posts a rant about a local senator and provides a link to a news story from Fox. If Sarah Likes her friend's rant, both of their other friends might see future ads in their news feed saying "Sarah Likes Fox News." In context, what Sarah was Liking was her friend's rant about the senator, but her Like is re-appropriated and shared in a completely different context stripped of her original intent.

This is also problematic because of the multiple levels of publicness and privacy levels that are operating on Facebook at any given time. For example, Jada (16 years old, black) kept her Facebook mostly private, meaning the only ones who could see what she posted were people she had added to her network (i.e., people she has friended). However, others in her network could choose to make their posts or profiles public.[5] This means that what she chose to post on her profile should only be visible to select friends, but her *actions* on Facebook were public and were shared with everyone to whom she was connected, including friends of friends and family members she kept on a restricted list. When Jada Liked a photo posted by a friend with a public profile, her Like and comment became visible to everyone in her network, despite her own privacy settings. This was also true of all Pages that she interacted with—for example Comedy Central—because Pages have more open privacy settings than she did. In other words, the more public settings override her restrictive private settings. Van Dijck (2013a, pp. 49–50) explains: "All features added to Facebook have resulted in mostly invisible algorithms and protocols that, to a great degree, control the 'visibility of friends, news, items, or ideas. … Facebook's interface foregrounds the need for users to be connected, but partly hides the site's mechanisms for sharing users' data with others." The differences between privacy settings—Jada's in comparison with Comedy Central's—can have detrimental effects in terms of disclosure, identity, and privacy. Most the teens I got to know were cautious of what kind of information they deliberately shared on Facebook (and other social media platforms) such as what photos they posted, where they checked-in, the language they used (for example, many chose not to cuss), etc. However, they did not give as much critical and deliberate thought to everything they actually *did* on the site. Clicking Like feels more like a private action than re-sharing the story. Although the Like is intended to be somewhat public—a way to acknowledge a joke for example—participants did not intend for the interaction to be broadcast to their entire network (as demonstrated by Kara and Devonte's "Like war"). According to boyd (2014, p. 57), "There's a big difference between being *in* public and *being* public. Teens want to gather in public environments to socialize, but they don't necessarily want every vocalized expression to be publicized. Yet, because being in a networked public—unlike gathering with friends in a public park—often makes interactions more visible to adults, mere participation in social media can blur these two dynamics."

Consider Michelle, an 18-year-old biracial lesbian. Before coming out to her family, she employed different privacy strategies on Facebook that would allow her to connect with and communicate with her friends, while also ensuring that particular family members did not find out that she identified as a lesbian. She did this by creating lists that restricted the kinds of information family members could see, such as photos that she posted to Facebook. However, because Facebook renders interactions visible, and because others in her network had different privacy settings than she did, Michelle's seemingly private conversations and Likes can inadvertently reveal information about her sexuality. For example, she might Like another friend's post or leave a comment on a news story that could unintentionally reveal something about her sexuality that she intended to keep private. Because these interactions feel private, she understandably believed these interactions were contained to that specific friend or that isolated news story, however because of "Like recycling" her actions were reappropriated in a different context and had the potential to reveal information about her identity she did not expect to share with her entire Facebook network. Individuals can only exert limited control and agency over what is revealed about them via Facebook. Regardless of what they deliberately choose to share on Facebook, the public nature of their interactions, combined with "Like recycling" makes it increasingly easy for someone to infer users' ideologies, sexuality, religious affiliations, politics, and so forth, even if they do not deliberately reveal this information on their own posts and profiles. Michelle and other teens are increasingly aware of the fact that they have limited control over what their networks reveal about them; they are increasingly frustrated by changes in Facebook's interface, and as a result are limiting their use of Facebook in favor of other social media platforms.

Further complications are added by the fact that Facebook does not make it easy to see your own Likes, nor is it easy to un-Like something once you have Liked it. Unlike your list of friends, which you can fairly easily access and manage (e.g., unfriend someone to whom you no longer wish to be connected), it is much more difficult to see every page and organization and story and post and photo you have Liked. Your name and image will show up in your friend's news feeds ("Sarah Likes Fox News") without your explicit knowledge, and those same ads are not showing up in your own news feed or on your own profile. In fact, Facebook makes it exceptionally difficult to see and manage how your name and account are used across the platform and the opt-out options are not easily accessed either. Participants were mostly unaware that when they see ads with friends' endorsements, these "endorsements' may not have been explicit or intentional. Further, when they Like a funny joke or meme, they typically do not pay much attention to the organization or page that initially shared the joke. For example, as one organization documented, people who Liked the conservative group For America later had their name associated with a post arguing that "Obamacare must go!" Those users were upset that Liking one story was a license to endorse something completely unrelated later (DesMarais 2012).

From an everyday social norm understanding of Facebook, Liking one post by an organization is not typically understood as consent to support and promote every future post from that organization. In other words, there is a disparity between how teens (and adults) conceptualize their interactions on Facebook and how Facebook understands privacy and social norms. What I am advocating for is a better and more accessible way for users to manage their Likes. Facebook could be more transparent about how Likes are publicized across the site and offer easier and more accessible options for un-Liking something. The platform could provide users with a greater knowledge of and control over how their names are used in other people's news feeds. Just because someone Liked a news story from five years ago, it should not mean that that users' identity should be forever linked to the organization or brand.

Resistance Strategies

Some participants embraced the changes to Facebook's interface, policies, and algorithms and others were unaware or more apathetic about them. However, many young people in this study were bothered by these changes and resisted the move toward a public, consistent, and converged identity. Undoubtedly there are a lot of reasons why teens may be using Facebook less frequently, but I believe one reason has to do with their expectations to perform more fluid, ephemeral, and disconnected online identities. Facebook connects disparate social networks—from childhood, high school, work, family, church, etc.—into one space and collapses those contexts. The platform does not consider the different ways people interact with different groups, the fluid nature of identity, or the variation in social norms that fluctuate across different contexts. In other words, the interface ignores the "contextual integrity" of how young people intend to interact and share information. Rather than attempting to manage one cohesive and acceptable identity, some young people are choosing to use different social networks to articulate different aspects of their identities and connect with different communities.

I consistently hear young people explain that they are reluctant to express opinions on Facebook. A young black female explained to me: "If I post something that I don't think is a big deal, someone is going to make it political. Or, like, read into it or something. Then, like, there's people on my Facebook fighting with each other and they don't even know each other. I see this all the time. No, I just don't even post stuff anymore, it's not worth it." Time and time again, young people explained that they preferred not to post personal information or opinions on Facebook because they could be misinterpreted or used to start fights between the different networks on their Facebook. How then do young people manage their interests, passions, identities, and networks online? If you were to look at Facebook, one might mistakenly jump to the conclusion that young people don't use social networks to express opinions or beliefs. Much of what you may see are inside jokes, silly videos, and humorous memes being passed around and shared. You will see a lot of people making plans, posting photos of their friends, or discussing quotidian social interactions. However, while teens (like adults) do these things, there is a lot more going on via social media than there may seem to be at first glance.

When I first met Gabriela, she used Facebook daily but expressed ambiguity about the site. She had deleted it from the home screen of her phone and removed the bookmark from the browser on her laptop. She explained that she checked Facebook a lot out of habit, but then found that she was often "frustrated, annoyed, and bored" with what she saw. "I think Facebook is kind of dying but slowly." Instead, she preferred to use Twitter and Tumblr for different purposes. This allowed Gabriela to tap into different online communities, use different accounts for different purposes, and maintain relationships in a more private way. For example, Gabriela and her boyfriend shared a Tumblr account that was just for the two of them—no one else had the link. While she and her boyfriend also sent text messages throughout the day, she said she liked Tumblr because they could share images and song lyrics and quotes with each other: "Like, if I saw a picture that reminded me of him, I'd re-blog it and he could see it later." Tumblr was a way for Gabriela and her boyfriend to foster intimacy and communicate, but in a more private way than Facebook typically afforded.

Additionally, Gabriela used two Twitter accounts—one for friends and one for following musicians. When asked what she liked about Twitter, she explained: "It's kind of becoming the new Facebook a little bit. But not that many people really like it. And so, I just like what I do. I basically just post whatever's on my mind just rapidly. It goes faster. And so, people don't have to follow you. If they want to follow you then they know that they're just going to see it. And on Facebook it's not like that." Twitter does not require a reciprocal relationship. Gabriela liked that people could choose to follow her if they wanted, but she did not have to also see their posts. Other students expressed similar attitudes. Antonio (17 years old, Mexican-American) explained: "If people don't want to see what I post, then just don't follow me." This is quite different form the norms of Facebook. Breaking off a connection—unfriending someone—has a lot of social implications that speak to the nature of the friendship. It can cause a lot of problems within groups of friends and is imbued with different meanings and interpretations that are not conveyed on Twitter. Additionally, Facebook's Terms of Service explicitly prohibit users from creating multiple accounts. Rather than creating different accounts for different purposes, Facebook users are expected to negotiate complicated and ever-changing privacy settings.

Tumblr and Twitter streamline privacy management by allowing users, and even encouraging them, to create different profiles and different accounts. This allows young people to not only keep their networks separate (the equivalent of performing different identities in different public spaces and contexts in the physical world), but also invites experimentation. Young people can explore different interests and articulate different identities within the same platform, but via different accounts. Tumblr in particular affords anonymity and exploration. "By providing an outlet where people can be anonymous and detached from their actions," Montiel argues (2012, p. 24), "users are able to make mistakes and experiment." Particularly for young people, who are caught between and betwixt different subject positions, identities, roles, and imagined selves, the ability to experiment is significant and valuable. Tumblr provides a space for young people to express themselves without the same risks that have become common on Facebook. To reiterate Gabriela's quote from the beginning of the chapter: "Everyone keeps their Tumblr private usually because they post, like, actually what they're going through or what they feel." The community-driven and personal aspects of Tumblr facilitated anonymity and experimentation that was not feasible on a site such as Facebook.

Additionally, the private nature of Tumblr afforded Gabriela and other young people the freedom to express themselves, but without a concern for their reputation. Gabriela continued: "I tend to stop caring about what people think and so I post what I feel. If I get sad then I post what I'm sad about. I have trouble saying things out loud. I have an idea how to say it in my head, so I write it on Tumblr. It helps me process my thoughts." In terms of identity and privacy, Gabriela's comment that she "stops caring what people think" speaks to some teens' preference for platforms that invite personal expression in spaces that are more or less invisible to their peers, but afford visibility within a different context. Gabriela chose to express herself on Tumblr because she valued the feedback she received from the community. She enjoyed processing her emotions via writing and on a blog. However, unlike on Facebook, the expressions did not become part of her online identity repertoire. The public and publicized nature of Facebook encourages young people to consciously construct identities for the approval of one's network. Whereas Tumblr, as a more private blog, encourages individuals to express themselves for the sake of expression and connection, rather than as part of reputation management.

Conclusion

Returning to a framework of visibility, discussions of privacy are often couched in harm-driven expectations about the risks of making personal information overly accessible. Understandably adults worry that young people might intentionally or inadvertently reveal too much information about themselves. Personal information opens up opportunities for misinterpretation and has the potential to harm future opportunities. Certainly we are justified as a society to be concerned about what kinds of information young people are sharing, with whom, in what spaces, and for what purposes. However, we need to also call into question who is deliberately and intentionally accessing information about young people, in what spaces, and for what purposes. The burden of responsibility should not lie solely on the shoulders of young people. That is, while they have a responsibility to be smart about what they share online, and while educators and parents ought to help young people make smart decisions about what they share online, we need to also question how those with power are using digital media to surveil and exploit young people's online practices.

In a lot of ways, media panics about predators and privacy have been effective in educating young people about the risks of oversharing. In 2013, research reveals, 60 percent of teen Facebook users kept their profiles private (Madden et al. 2013). Likewise, qualitative research continually indicates that young people employ various strategies for managing and maintaining their privacy (boyd 2014; Marwick and boyd 2010; Vickery 2014). My conversations with and observations of teens suggest that the overwhelming majority took some measure to protect their privacy and were aware of the risks involved in oversharing online. And, as has already been noted in this chapter, young people employ different and deliberate strategies to maintain privacy within certain spaces and keep information from certain audiences.

However, if we frame sharing and visibility only as a risk—and an individual responsibility—we miss valuable opportunities to help young people construct positive online identities. More and more often, young people explain to me that they are no longer using Facebook, have little to no interest in LinkedIn, use Twitter for entertainment but not for networking, and keep their Instagram and Tumblr accounts completely private. College seniors who are about to enter the workforce tell me they are reluctant to create digital portfolios and construct a positive online identity. They consider these deliberate disassociation practices to be smart strategies for protecting their privacy, and they are correct. However, I am concerned that the privacy pendulum has swung too far in the direction of protection. I see evidence that young people are so concerned with minimizing risks that they are likely to miss out on the opportunities that can also accompany visibility (see chapter 5). Such practices of hiding, self-censorship, and opting out risk further marginalizing the voices and experiences of non-dominant youth.

Reflecting on her own online privacy strategies, Inara (17 years old, Mexican-American) explained: "Sometimes I really don't care. I'm a grownup. I think I should be allowed to say what I want to say, and not have people judge me." Inara voiced frustration that she could not use online spaces to express herself in the ways she preferred; instead she had to constantly negotiate her intended audience with potential imagined audiences. While this was not a bad strategy in and of itself, for Inara and others like her this often meant just not posting or sharing anything in a public space in the first place. In other words, it was easier to remain hidden than to negotiate visibility. In an age of increasing surveillance, it is no wonder young people (and adults) are cautious about creating public online identities. In 2015, an Illinois law made it legal for school administrators to access students' social media sites; since then, administrators have gone so far as to require students to share passwords with administrators (Schwarz 2015). Schools in north Texas (and probably elsewhere) employ police officers to actively monitor all forms of communication that are transmitted over the school's Wi-Fi (source: author's personal communication with school district). This is, of course, in addition to other modes of surveillance in which schools block students' and faculty's access to websites, apps, and services (as discussed in chapter 3). This blatant surveillance further reinforces differences in power, access, and transparency. Those with the least amount of social capital and power are often subjected to greater modes of surveillance. For example, minimum wage workers are more likely to be subjected to drug testing before employment than are educated white-collar workers (Gilliom 2001). In response to the Illinois bill, Kade Crockford, director for the Massachusetts American Civil Liberties Union, said: "You have to think about the school-to-prison pipeline—who will be affected by this legislation, who will be arrested in school as a result of information discovered by administrators on their phones? It's kids of color, poor kids, kids with intellectual and learning disabilities. That's what we see across the country" (Koebler 2015). Crockford is absolutely correct: the Internet opens up new modes for increased surveillance, particularly of those without power. That is why marginalized young people are seeking out spaces that afford more privacy, more ephemeral forms of communication, anonymity, and disconnectedness, which are powerful and effective tools for evading surveillance. Snapchat and private Instagram accounts provide safer opportunities for exploration, experimentation, and peer interactions without the prying eyes of administrators, employers, and law enforcement. At the same time, the invisibility of their interactions and practices also serves to reify their already marginalized and often silenced subject positions, experiences, and concerns. The Internet and social media afford young people opportunities to participate in networked publics. It affords opportunities for teens to network with those with power, to organize for social change, to share their unique experiences. However, these opportunities can be severely limited by harm-driven expectations that perpetuate fears and heightened risks associated with sharing. As the law professor Samuel Bagenstos cautions (2013, p.14), we need to be "especially concerned that social equality is threatened when one class of people—defined by wealth or income—systematically gives up the choice to engage in those activities that are especially important to defining and understanding the self." Digital media are important for "defining and understanding the self," yet self-censorship and practices of disconnectedness can paradoxically protect privacy and evade surveillance while disproportionately further marginalizing non-dominant populations.

Real social change in protecting young people online will not occur until adult society quits playing "gotcha" with young people's privacy practices, and instead respects the contextual integrity of young people's practices and preferences. Like adults, young people need spaces for inter-personal and private communication *and* spaces for networking and public participation. They need spaces where they feel safe to express unique identities—identities that adults and society may find concerning. But they also need spaces to participate as citizens and engage in public discourse about their concerns and experiences. And they need adults to help them understand the difference, to help them navigate different levels of visibility.

Lastly, we need platform policies and architecture that respect the differences in these spaces; we need policies and interfaces that aim to not only profit from teens' participation, but also strive to understand and respect their unique practices and expectations. Because young people have begun to abandon Facebook, and because other platforms have become more popular, it may seem odd that I have spent so much time analyzing Facebook in this chapter. However, Facebook is the social network site with the longest history, and through it we can analyze how changes in architecture and business models affect discourses of risk, visibility, and privacy. Despite its waning popularity—or perhaps because of its waning popularity among young people—we can learn a lot about how teens' preferences, expectations, and practices shape and are shaped by commercial platforms that structure their engagement. For all its ills and benefits, Facebook has provided us with great insight into the tenuous relationship among commercial platforms, young people's practices, and expectations of visibility and risk. I worry about self-censorship and disconnected practices that further silence and marginalize those already occupying positions of disadvantage in our society. Understandings of privacy must balance strategies for protection with strategies for helping young people embrace visible networked opportunities.

7 (Dis)Connected Pathways: Expectations, Goals, and Opportunities

There are so many challenges out there, and I feel that school hasn't prepared them with everything they need to know to succeed. I want to prepare them for the real world. ... I think the after-school club fills in some of those gaps that the school doesn't prepare them for, because getting out into the real world is tough.

Mr. Lopez (teacher and mentor to after-school media clubs)

Throughout this book, I have primarily focused on how policies and practices at school have exacerbated risks for young people or missed chances to create more equitable opportunities for marginalized and low-income students. In this chapter, I also consider technology classes and after-school clubs as examples of how teachers, schools, and policies can help students manage the costs and benefits of risks associated with digital media. As I will demonstrate, Mr. Lopez, the Tech Apps teacher, intentionally incorporated media technology into his courses, which served as working models of how learning can look when opportunity-driven expectations are at the forefront of students' and teachers' approaches to media use at school. However, there remain other systemic barriers—material and cultural— that block connections to more equitable pathways. The move toward opportunity-driven expectations of student media use can be situated within a broader optimistic view that considers the positive relationship between technology and social change. However, I also worry about discourses that celebrate the democratic potential of digital media to create new pathways for future success, yet overlook the very material, cultural, and social constraints that prevent those most in need from actually benefitting from the very interventions designed to close those participation gaps.

One approach that aims to instate a balance between opportunity-driven expectations and an awareness of the risks and barriers that inhibit more equitable outcomes, is the *connected learning model* that was developed by the collaborative and interdisciplinary Connected Learning Research Network (Ito et al. 2012). On the basis of international research in many different learning environments, Ito et al. explain connected learning as an approach to education that "advocates for broadened access to learning that is socially embedded, interest-driven, and oriented toward educational, economic, or political opportunity." "Connected learning," they continue, "is realized when a young person is able to pursue a personal interest or passion with the support of friends and caring adults, and is in turn able to link this learning and interest to academic achievement, career success or civic engagement. This model is based on evidence that the most resilient, adaptive, and effective learning involves individual interests as well as social support to overcome adversity and provide recognition."

As is illustrated in figure 7.1, connected learning involves three properties of learning experiences: production-centered, shared purpose, and openly networked. Further, four design principles structure the connected learning environments: everyone can participate, learning happens by doing, the challenge is constant, and everything is interconnected. Together these contexts, properties, and design principles make up the connected learning approach that Ito et al. argue supports and sustains learning that engages young people in beneficial and equitable ways.

The connected learning approach is intentionally focused on alleviating economic and educational gaps. However, as I will demonstrate, risk structures choices in seemingly individualized ways that are actually deeply embedded within social contexts that limit the autonomy of choices. Because Freeway High's student population included many students from low-income backgrounds, first-generation immigrants, and families without college backgrounds or experiences, the school and students faced many challenges to equitable learning opportunities. Many students were academically disengaged and struggled to maintain interest in school for a variety of reasons including language barriers, family obligations such as caring for siblings, financial hardships, and precarious and nomadic home lives. Additionally, many students came from families that did not have experience with college and thus they were often navigating unfamiliar pathways without much home guidance or connections to expanded social capital. For example, Anna (18 years old, Mexican-American) had mentioned wanting to go to college but had not applied yet. When asked if she was planning to apply to college, she responded as follows.

Anna: I don't even know. I haven't even looked really at all. I don't know what I'm going to do so I don't know where to look for a school. I don't

Connected learning knits together three crucial contexts for learning:

Peer-supported   In their everyday exchanges with peers and friends, young people are contributing, sharing and giving feedback in inclusive social experiences that are fluid and highly engaging.

Interest-powered   When a subject is personally interesting and relevant, learners achieve much higher-order learning outcomes.

Academically oriented   Learners flourish and realize their potential when they can connect their interests and social engagement to academic studies, civic engagement, and career opportunity.

Core properties of connected learning experiences include:

Production-centered   Digital tools provide opportunities for producing and creating a wide variety of media, knowledge, and cultural content in experimental and active ways.

Shared purpose   Social media and web-based communities provide unprecedented opportunities for cross-generational and cross-cultural learning and connection to unfold and thrive around common goals and interests.

Openly networked   Online platforms and digital tools can make learning resources abundant, accessible, and visible across all learner settings.

Design principles inform the intentional connecting of learning environments:

Everyone can participate   Experiences invite participation and provide many different ways for individuals and groups to contribute.

Learning happens by doing   Learning is experiential and part of the pursuit of meaningful activities and projects.

Challenge is constant   Interest or cultivation of an interest creates both a "need to know" and a "need to share."

Everyone is interconnected   Young people are provided with multiple learning contexts for engaging in connected learning—contexts in which they receive immediate feedback on progress, have access to tools for planning and reflection, and are given opportunities for mastery of specialist language and practices.

New media amplifies opportunities for connected learning by:

Fostering engagement and self-expression   Interactive, immersive, and personalized technologies provide responsive feedback, support a diversity of learning styles and literacy, and pace learning according to individual needs.

Increasing accessibility to knowledge and learning experience   Through online search, educational resources, and communities of expertise and interest, young people can easily access information and find relationships that support self-directed and interest-driven learning.

Expanding social supports for interests   Through social media, young people can form relationships with peers and caring adults that are centered on interests, expertise, and future opportunity in areas of interest.

Expanding diversity and building capacity   New media networks empower marginalized and noninstitutionalized groups and cultures to have voice, mobilize, organize, and build economic capacity.

Figure 7.1

A framework for connected learning. Source: Ito et al. 2013 (licensed under a Creative Commons Attribution-Noncommercial-No Derivative Works 3.0 United States License).

know what I'm looking for. I'm totally out of it. It doesn't help that my parents are totally not on track of anything that we're doing.

Q: Do your parents not really talk about it?

Anna: They always are encouraging me. Like, "Yeah, you keep your grades because you can get scholarships and go to college." I'm, like, "Do y'all even know how to apply for a scholarship? Because I don't. And y'all ain't much help."

Anna, like many other students at Freeway High, had aspirations of attending university or pursuing a middle-class career, yet her expectations, like those of many other students at Freeway, were often unrealistic. Despite the connected efforts of some of the courses and clubs at Freeway, students still did not have access to the material resources nor the social and cultural capital at home that would allow them to navigate these unfamiliar future pathways. Significantly, I do not want to imply that these shortcomings were the fault of individuals, instead the disconnects highlight systemic inequities and broken connections between education, home, and the labor market. Sonia Livingstone and Julian Sefton-Green poignantly articulate this observation in their book *The Class* (2016, p. 251): "Connecting learning across school and home might seem beneficial for everyone, but given the different resources that families can call on, in practice it opens the door to socioeconomic inequalities. Further, shifting the burden of responsibility for children's learning from school to (also) home compounds already-heightened parental anxieties over children's increasingly uncertain educational and employment prospects."

Freeway High provided college-readiness workshops that helped students find and apply for scholarships. Yet the workshops often competed with other activities that students were already invested or interested in, such as band or the media clubs. Despite the many challenges, Freeway High was striving to find ways to be more relevant to students' needs. This was evident from the many after-school clubs, vocational programs, and other resources aimed at supporting marginalized populations. Yet the success of such strategies varied within different student populations and often benefited those who already had advantageous access to networks of social and cultural capital. Students who were already at a disadvantage experienced marginal benefits but still faced systematic barriers that inhibited access to equitable opportunities.

Learning and Future (Dis)Connections

One somewhat successful approach to engaging students, which is the focus of this chapter, was that taken by Mr. Lopez's technology courses and after-school clubs, which fit with many aspects of the connected learning model. As will be discussed, Mr. Lopez's pedagogy had proved effective with many students at Freeway High and was credited with helping marginalized students graduate and find their passions. However, despite some success stories (including those of Javier and Gabriela addressed in this chapter), some students still faced structural and discursive barriers that prevented them from overcoming material and environmental challenges. The connected learning model not only provides a useful lens for exploring vital connections within students' learning ecologies but also allows us to consider the disconnections that inhibit opportunities. At a glance, it stands to reason that schools ought to connect to home life in ways that amplify opportunities. Yet for many working-class families this connection presented an additional burden of responsibility that families were not equipped to provide for a variety of reasons including precarious immigrant status, financial challenges, and unfamiliarity with middle-class habitus[1] and norms (Bourdieu 1990). Sergio's and Selena's stories will highlight that there was a disparity between some students' expectations about future opportunities (in the technology and media industries) and their home life and the school's capacity to prepare students for those positions. As I address through the stories of four teens at Freeway—Sergio, Javier, Gabriela, and Selena—the expectations about digital media literacy, skills, and opportunities tend to be contradictory and unstable: the school as an institution develops and employs particular expectations of technology, education, and goals, but students and their families have diverse expectations and make meaning out of their practices in ways that do not necessarily align with their future-oriented goals or the labor market. Students who did not have the advantages of diverse social networks and cultural capital were the least likely to reap the benefits of connected learning approaches.

If technology and media are to serve as interventions in the lives of marginalized young people or if media are to partially provide pathways to future successes, we must consider the role technology plays within the wider socially connected context of young people's lives. Further, we must consider how young people's expectations of their own futures are supported (or not) by the expectations of their peers, schools, adults, and the labor market of the creative media industries. Young people's expectations of their future—as well as the ways in which they make meaning out of their own practices—often differ from the expectations of the adults in their lives and the ways social institutions map out future opportunities. In order for their expectations to come to fruition, they need adults and institutions to actively support—as well as shape—their opportunity-driven expectations. They also need expanded access to economic and cultural capital that expansive social networks provide more privileged and assimilated students.

What the lives of the four young people addressed in this chapter reveal is the importance of making and supporting significant connections between different influences and spaces of their lives—but also the importance of connecting their expectations to real-world opportunities, which are often missing. There is a disparity between the aspirations of young people, educational expectations, and employment options supported by precarious and uncertain labor markets. Building upon the connected learning model, I analyze the connections or disconnections between six key areas of the students' lives: academic, peers, home life, adults, interests, and extracurricular activities as related to each students' self-described short-term or long-term career goals (figure 7.2). *Peers* refers to the teen's closest and most influential friends; *academic* refers to their formal educational environments and curricula at school; *home* refers to the support for and capacity to learn at home (access to the technology, resources, books, software, etc. necessary to learn at home); *adults* refers to parents, guardians, and/or other adult role models in their social networks that the teen trusts; *interests* refers to the teen's personal passions, hobbies, curiosities, and activities; *extracurricular* refers to their informal learning spaces and activities (clubs, sports, band, church, etc.). Career *goals* are representative of a student's self-identified and articulated short-term and long-term aspirations, expectations, and future career options. Students obviously had important life goals that transcended careers and economic aspirations— such as marriage, children, hobbies, and so forth; however, for the purpose of this analysis, goals are couched within a market-driven understanding of students' career expectations, desires, and options.

In figure 7.2, the size of each sphere is representative of its influence on the participant and his or her goals (i.e., a large peer sphere and small adult sphere indicate that the participant's goals are largely influenced by their peers, and not as influenced by the adults in their life). In an ideal world, all six areas would both connect to and support a student's career goals *and* there would be strong connections between each of the six nodes. Likewise, each sphere would be similar in size, as all six areas would influence one another and support the student's aspirations, expectations, and goals. The

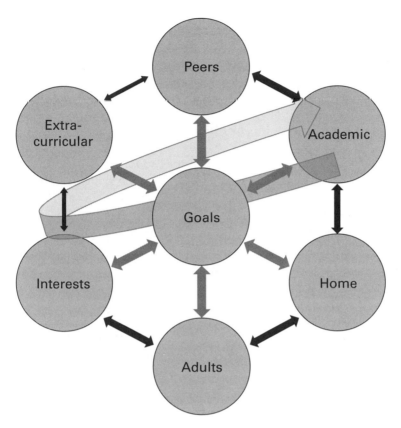

Figure 7.2
A model of an ideal learning ecology.

length of the arrows indicates the quality or strength of the connections; a short arrow is indicative of a weak connection, a long arrow signifies a strong connection, and a missing arrow denotes a broken or missing connection. The elliptical arrow represents the importance of connecting a teen's interests and extracurricular activities with their formal learning environment (i.e., academics) and goals, and vice versa. In the ideal model the formal learning spaces are both supported by and supporting the student's informal learning spaces at school and connecting to the labor market.

Through an analysis of the connections or disconnections between media technology and other aspects of teens' lives, I am able to avoid a technologically deterministic approach and instead situationally consider the ways in which technology and learning are socially situated and constructed within the broader lives of teens. Only when goals, the labor market, and learning ecologies are connected and supported can digital media literacy truly serve as an effective pathway to economic, civic, and social opportunities for equality. I do not mean to imply that the most important value of digital literacy is economic success or career opportunities. I hope the rest of the book has demonstrated the social, civic, educational, and personal value of practicing and connecting digital media literacies. The Digital Media Club and the Cinematic Arts Project were both designed in part to help marginalized students forge pathways to economic success. The focus of this chapter is on how the students' learning ecologies in relation to digital media helped connect them with future career opportunities. Through an examination of Mr. Lopez's classes, the after-school media clubs, and four select students involved in the programs, this chapter explores the complicated and unequal connections between risk, education, expectations, digital media, and future (economic) opportunities.

Integrating Media in the Classroom

As has been noted, many teachers' (and the school's) policies are ones of unacceptable use that do not provide students opportunities to use technology responsibility. There were exceptions though, particularly (and unsurprisingly) in the technology-focused courses. Through an analysis of Mr. Lopez's acceptable use of technology approaches, I briefly consider what can be gained when media are incorporated as a connected aspect of the formal learning environment. Mr. Lopez aimed to integrate students' personal media technologies into the classrooms in innovative ways, yet their efforts were inhibited via fears and policies of panic that tried to minimize risks without a respectful balance of opportunities.

Beyond focusing on media as the driving force, Mr. Lopez's pedagogical approaches were centered on project-based learning. Rather than merely teaching students how to do something, his courses challenged students to solve problems and to create something together. As has been noted, many students at Freeway High did not have access to high-quality or reliable Internet access outside of school, even those who did were unlikely to have access to expensive proprietary software or expensive camera equipment. So for some students this was the first time they had the freedom and opportunity to mess around with software and equipment. Through their experiences in the technology courses, some students discovered a previously unknown passion for digital media, film, photography, video games, graphic design, and digital music.

Media Production as Risk Intervention

Aware of the challenges his students faced at school and home, Mr. Lopez deliberately constructed his classes as a student-focused safe space that could serve as an opportunity for marginalized students to find a niche and support, particularly for those at risk of dropping or failing out of school. He did this by incorporating and validating students' personal interests into their assignments, but also by helping them make connections between their other courses and their technology course. In other words, by helping them stay motivated in their technology classes, he was actually able to help them engage with their other courses as well, and thus hopefully do better in school all around. As a Mexican-American filmmaker and educator, Mr. Lopez personally identified with and related to many of the students in his classes: "I see myself in them. I know what they are going through. I'm here because I want them to know people like us, we can succeed." Many of his students viewed him as a mentor and role model, which was iterated in practically every interview with his students. Devan (19 years old, black) was a recent graduate of Freeway High and explained the personal importance of Mr. Lopez's class:

In my freshman year I was bad. I didn't know what I wanted to do. The cool thing about this is that I wanted to get to Tech Apps, so I could get it done so I could go to Video Tech next. It made me happier because I was doing the stuff that brought my mood up which made me work harder in the other classes. It's a weird concept, but since this made me so much happier because I could use my imagination, rather than just have my head in a book all day, I could go to my math class and get it done so I could get to film. My grades drastically improved. Without this I'd have been in a different situation. I don't think I'd be here [as a high school graduate or mentor] today, if it weren't for Mr. Lopez and his courses.

Devan's story resonated with a lot of Mr. Lopez's students who agreed that incorporating technology and media into the school day provided motivation to do well in other classes. Just as athletes are required to keep minimum grades in order to compete in athletic competitions at school, Mr. Lopez planned field trips and excursions around town for his students, and, just as with athletics, he required passing grades in order for students to participate in the excursions. Sports has been shown to provide intrinsic motivation (fear of failure) and extrinsic motivation (a dedicated commitment to the sport and the team) that can help motivate athletes to do well in school (Simons, Van Rheenen, and Covington 1999). In a similar way, the technology courses provided both intrinsic and extrinsic motivation for marginalized students to do well in school, not just in the courses they were interested in, but other classes as well.

As another example, Jasmine (16 years old, multiracial) was highly engaged in her media classes and was an active member of the after-school Cinematic Art Project. However, she was only moderately engaged in her more traditional courses. Her grandparents (with whom she occasionally lived during the study) insisted she keep her grades up, something that was a struggle for her, but they made it a requirement for her continued participation in the Cinematic Arts Project. She explained that project-based learning helped her apply what she was learning across different topics.

Jasmine: To me, project-based learning is basically giving us a project that gives us the whole core of classes, like math, science, history and English. Because English you have to write the script. Math you have to know the time and break down how much batteries you need and how much time you want the camera and all that stuff. Geography—you have to go out location scouting. People think we don't learn by that — "Oh, they're just doing projects. You don't learn anything." You do learn a lot.

Q: You feel like you learn a lot?

Jasmine: Oh yeah. That's probably the only reason I'm doing good in my math class—because we do so much in Video Tech. We do so much projects now, I'm, like, "Yeah. I get that." Also, some people do help me with my math.

Q: Do you feel like the stuff you learn in video tech or video apps applies to other classes or helps you learn in other classes?

Jasmine: It kind of comes together. It helps you learn about life too—how to manage your time, how to solve problems, and when you can just say no to some things.

Q: What do you mean by that?

Jasmine: Like, you have a whole bunch of projects and somebody comes to you and says, "Can you do this for me?" It's, like, "I can't have all this."

Jasmine pointed out many important aspects of connected learning. First, is that project-based learning helped her to make connections between her other courses. As a low to moderately engaged student, finding ways to apply what she was learning in math to a project she cared about helped her to focus on the courses she did not enjoy much. Also, as her comment highlighted, project-based learning provided opportunities to develop life skills that were applicable beyond formal educational settings. At the end of her film project, I asked Jasmine what was the most important thing she had learned through the experience. I had expected her answer to reflect on the filmmaking process, but instead her answer surprised me: "Communication, learning how to communicate with people. It can be really frustrating, you have to tell people exactly what you want and be specific, people don't listen or get it always." Jasmine's answer was similar to the answers of many other students in the clubs and classes who reflected on the ways the projects helped them learn to work together, manage their time, and follow through on long-term goals. Project-based learning, of course, does not have to be contained to technology-focused courses nor do the projects necessarily have to incorporate technology; yet the use of technology enabled students to seek out information, solve problems, and creatively contribute in ways that were more consistent with their informal and out-of-school modes of learning. There were, of course, risks associated with their practices, as have been discussed throughout the book, but students and teachers such as Mr. Lopez balanced these risks with opportunities in beneficial ways.

Filling in Gaps: The Role of After-School Media Clubs and Interest-Driven Learning

As part of a broader trend in the United States, Freeway High has two different tracks for students: college-prep and vocational. The vocational track has the well-intentioned goal of preparing students for non-college pathways after high school graduation, yet it has been heavily scrutinized and criticized because it often "replicate[s] inequality along lines of race and social class and contribute[s] to the intergenerational transmission of social and economic capital" (Oakes 2005, p. xi). Tracking aims to ensure that students who are presumed to be college-bound (as determined by a combination of factors, including test scores, grade-point averages, parents' educational backgrounds, economics, and student interests) are guided to enroll in more math and science courses, including Advanced Placement (AP) courses and college dual-credit courses.[2] Students who are not presumed to be college-bound are advised to take skill-based courses, to take fewer math and science courses, and not to take AP courses. Vocational education focuses on intense specialization, "interpreted by the public schools to mean the provision of an education, that would best meet individuals' future needs and thus train them to play their specialized roles in industrial America" (ibid., p. 33). My purpose here is not to conduct a larger examination or critique of tracking, although it merits further academic research,[3] but rather to contextualize the after-school media clubs within the larger ecology of Freeway High.

After-school activities were a large part of student life at Freeway High.[4] The majority of participants in this study were involved in at least one after-school activity, although some students' participation was more limited (less involved) because of part-time jobs, sibling care, restrictive transportation, or other home obligations. The school's vocational tracks, such as automotive technology, metal tech (carpentry, plumbing, welding, etc.), fashion merchandising, construction, and culinary arts/hospitality were supported via coursework that aimed to help students develop specialized skill sets. They also were supported via after-school clubs that offered students opportunities to further pursue their interests and develop necessary skills. The college-bound tracks focused on Advanced Placement courses and advanced math and science courses, many of which were pre-requisites for more advanced courses they took in the final years of high school. They also were supported with clubs that focused on leadership opportunities, debate team, business club, service committees, and tutoring, which were aimed at bettering a students' college resume and preparedness. Activities such as band, orchestra, theater, and athletics tended to attract a diverse population of students from both vocational and college tracks.

The media technology courses and after-school media clubs occupied a more liminal space than the traditionally established college and vocational tracks. Per state regulations, students were required to take a minimum of one computer course in order to graduate. The technology courses tended to either be focused on computer science, which required advanced math pre-requisites that many students on career paths did not have (thus these courses were essentially limited to college-bound students). The other traditional technology option was a more basic audio/visual (A/V) course, which prepared students for entry-level technical (non-creative arts) careers. Yet the design-oriented creative digital media courses and video game courses attracted creative students who were not exclusively interested in technical careers and approached media and technology as an art, rather than a technical skill. These courses were not typically part of the broader college-bound track, but served as an elective for college-bound students who were not interested in computer science.[5] In this way, the courses attracted students from both college and career tracks.

For some students, the course merely fulfilled an elective requirement. However, for many of the students in the courses, it became a passion, something they were interested in and wanted to further pursue. This is how the after-school Digital Media Club was developed—students in Mr. Lopez's courses wanted to continue to pursue creative media design and production projects outside of the formal classroom. Students in the Digital Media Club were interested in the creative aspects of media production, but their interest did not fall along the computer science or A/V technical dichotomy of other courses and clubs. Recognizing an opportunity to fill in a gap in the options of after-school clubs, as well as an opportunity to serve and mentor marginalized young people, Mr. Lopez worked with the students to get the Digital Media Club approved as an officially supported and recognized club at Freeway High. He explained:

I want to give them a place to come and actually apply their skills. Most of them are going to be looking for jobs and they already are looking for jobs or some are looking to go to college. I want to be able to, from a personal standpoint, give them all the skills they need to go and be successful. There are so many challenges out there and I feel that school hasn't prepared them with everything they need to know to succeed. I want to prepare them for the real world. ... I think the after-school club fills in some of those gaps that the school doesn't prepare them for, because getting out into the real world is tough. ... But also the club is fun, I want them to learn in a fun way and projects are a great way to do that.

Although open to any student, the Digital Media Club attracted students caught between the institutional structures of the school: students who were on a vocational track because they did not believe college was an option for them (due to immigration status, economic constraints, or familial obligations), but who were not interested in the other vocational tracks available at Freeway. These students found the club to be a creative outlet that fit their personalities, interests, and goals. There were some college-bound students in the club, however, a large number of the students were classified by the school as "at risk." Many of the club's participants were academically disengaged for a variety of reasons (e.g., language barriers, unstable home lives, academically behind due to relocations or family obligations, economic struggles). For some the consequences of behavioral issues had caused them to fall behind in school, which contributed to further disengagement. Thus, as Mr. Lopez's quotation iterates, the club filled in a gap and served students who did not neatly fit into the college-bound and vocational tracks offered at school. And, as Mr. Lopez noted, he strived to teach students the real life skills necessary for succeeding after high school; skills that middle-class students tend to learn at home and via peer networks (Lareau 2003), but that marginalized students may not have access to in the same ways.

Students joined the club for a variety of reasons, but the overall motivation could be classified as what Ito et al. (2010) refer to as "interest-driven participation."[6] The students had a desire or curiosity to further explore an interest related to digital media and production. Some students joined via the encouragement of peers or teachers, while others joined to gain access to equipment such as cameras, microphones and other recording gear they did not have access to at home. Still, others joined in order to gain access to the computers themselves and the array of software, which was otherwise unavailable to many of the students outside of the school's computer labs. The students in the Digital Media Club had mixed aspirations: a select few expected to go to a four-year university, others were interested in a two-year degree from a community college, and many expected to enter the work force full-time after graduation. As will be discussed through the four case studies in this chapter, their post-graduation expectations were often unclear, and at times unrealistic.

The Digital Media Club and the Cinematic Arts Project differed from the formal learning environment in several ways that influenced what was learned, how, and by whom. Mr. Lopez strived to incorporate peer learning and personal interests into the formal classroom, but the after-school clubs were better equipped to facilitate this mode of learning to a greater degree. Learning with and via digital media enables a shift from the teacher as primary means of instruction, and allows students to learn in other ways, which was evidenced in the clubs. Mr. Lopez was present, but was not often the primary means of instruction in the classroom; instead students often preferred to rely on computer tutorials, peer-to-peer learning, and autonomous messing around with software and the technologies.[7] Through weekly observations and interviews, it became clear that students enjoyed figuring out how to do things on their own.[8] With the time and flexibility afforded in the after-school clubs, students could mess around with technology until they figured out how to do what they were attempting to learn.

The Cinematic Arts Project was started by a group of Digital Media Club participants who were primarily interested in working on collaborative film projects; it met at the same time and in the same lab as the Digital Media Club, but functioned as a satellite organization specializing in film production. It was in its second year at the time of this study. In the first year, only Freeway High students and teachers were involved, but in the second year it expanded to include two other high schools from the school district. The students wrote, shot, produced, edited, and directed a short narrative film, which they submitted to an international film festival. In

2010 the film was selected for inclusion in the festival, but in 2011 their film was not accepted. Additionally, members of the Cinematic Arts Project (including Javier, discussed later in this chapter) also submitted personal films they had produced separately from the official club project. These students capitalized upon the expertise of the teachers and mentors in the club, as well as the school's equipment and other resources to create personal projects; two of the personal film projects that were produced in the clubs were accepted and screened at an international film festival the year of this study.

The Cinematic Arts Project also produced a "behind-the scenes" film, a short documentary, and webisodes for the website, which were produced by members of the club's publicity team. The teams all worked in collaboration with mentors, teachers, and volunteers from the local film community on collaborative film projects. The club met several times a week for many hours at a time, as well as on weekends, in order to finish the films in time to submit to local and international festivals. The students gained real world experience producing films, working together, fundraising, and publicizing the films; they screened their films at local events as a way to raise funds. The mentors and teachers were well connected within the local film community, which enabled students to gain access to resources and expertise. The students involved with the project were dedicated, ambitious, and creative; many viewed the project as a professional and entrepreneurial opportunity rather than a school project or hobby (see chapter 5).

Motivations and Incentives for Participation

If all of this is sounding positive, it's because it is. The well-intentioned clubs and dedicated teachers and mentors undoubtedly had a positive influence in the lives of the students involved with the club; this is evident from countless stories like that of Devan, who attributed academic success and even the ability to graduate to the help of Mr. Lopez and the media clubs. Research demonstrates that after-school programs, such as the Digital Media Club and the Cinematic Arts Project, can have positive developmental outcomes in the lives of young people (Daud and Carruthers 2008; Nicholson, Collins, and Holmer 2004), particularly for economically disadvantaged or marginalized young people (Mahoney, Parente, and Zigler 2009). I do not want to appear dismissive of their efforts and the successes of the clubs; however, in order to experience long term and meaningful benefits it is not enough for young people to merely join a program, but rather they must become psychologically engaged. Research unsurprisingly evidences that individuals who are engaged learn more than disengaged individuals (Gottfried, Fleming, and Gottfried 1998). Engagement is the result of many factors, not least of which intrinsic and extrinsic motivation. I do not think we can overlook the role of motivation in shaping young people's engagement and participation with media and technology. We must also consider how opportunity and motivation are also mediated and regulated via other aspects of students' lives.

For the young people mentioned in this book, learning about digital media was constructed as both a means to an end as well as a goal in and of itself. And while the club was accomplishing a lot of good, we need to step back and take a more holistic approach to understanding the role of both digital media and education as risk intervention strategies. Scholars and practitioners are increasingly aware that media and technology in and of themselves are not solutions to any given problem and research demonstrates that not all media practices are equally valued by students or educational institutions (Sims 2014). As was noted earlier, such an assumption is technologically determinist and ignores the cultural, material, and economic context in which individuals access, use, and make meaning through and with technology. Such expectations ignore the extent to which learning happens within social contexts and the ways in which sociality mediates attitudes, meaning, and uses of technology. Alongside the many positive interventions and success stories, we need to evaluate outcomes and experiences critically in order to understand what the clubs accomplished and as a way to identify disconnects between expectations, aspirations, and actual industry opportunities.

The clubs, as well-intentioned as they were, also have the potential to reproduce the very inequalities they strive to alleviate; there were missed opportunities for fostering the deeper, more critical, and democratic digital literacies required for full participation in a digital and participatory culture. Those concerns are where I now turn my attention, as will be analyzed through an examination of four case studies: those of Sergio, Javier, Selena, and Gabriela. All four students had an interest in and expectations of perusing media as a career option, which allows us to analyze how media fit heuristically within the different nodes of their lives.

Career or College? Expectations of Future Opportunities for Sergio and Javier

Sergio (18 years old, Mexican-American) and Javier (18 years old, Mexican immigrant) were both seniors who were heavily invested in the Cinematic Arts Project at Freeway High. They developed a friendship as part of the

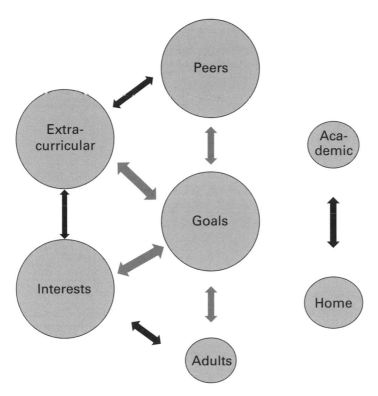

Figure 7.3
Sergio's learning ecology.

club and worked together on several film projects both in and out of school. Both Sergio and Javier aspired to work in the film industry after graduating high school and both were moderately academically engaged, but in different ways. However, Sergio and Javier's expectations for how to pursue a film career differed in significant ways.

Figures 7.3 and 7.4 illustrate Sergio's and Javier's learning ecologies. At first glance, it may appear as though the young men had similar goals and opportunities; however, their expectations of how to make connections to pursue and achieve their goals meant they followed two different—and unequal—pathways after high school.

Although Sergio earned relatively good grades and strove to do well in school, as a first-generation immigrant student whose parents had a middle school and high school education he did not view college as the most viable option after high school. When asked if his parents had helped prepare him for college of a career after graduation, Sergio responded:

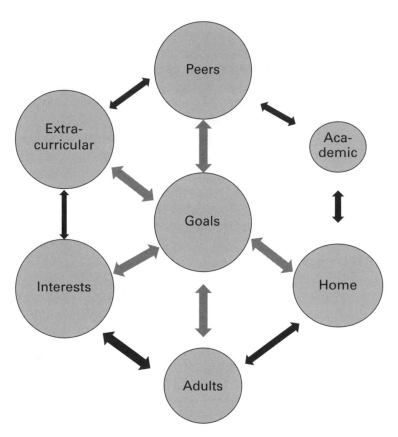

Figure 7.4
Javier's learning ecology.

They haven't really helped me in any other way, just a roof above my head, food, and stuff like that. But, like, I mean, 'cause they're from Mexico, they don't really know how everything works here, in America, so they can't really help me out with that as much as other people can. … 'Cause all my dad ever applies to is construction 'cause that's all he knows 'cause he doesn't have a high school degree or college degree, nor does my mom so all she knows how to do is, like, janitorial stuff, so that's all she applies to.

As the son of immigrant parents, Sergio was navigating unfamiliar pathways. The opportunities available to him at Freeway were helping him develop valuable skill sets, but Sergio's family lacked the connections and social capital necessary to develop viable future options. As the model of his learning ecology illustrates, there were disconnections between his academic engagement, resources at home, social network, and opportunities for a career in the film industry. Javier, on the hand, had emigrated from Mexico with his parents and an older sister at the age of 14. His father was the Spanish teacher at Freeway and his mother occasionally worked as a musician. His father had graduated from college in Mexico and his sister was currently pursuing a college degree in film in Mexico. The differences in Sergio's and Javier's family situations influenced their own expectations and shaped their perspectives of creative digital media career options.

Like many immigrant families, Sergio lived in a multi-generational home with his extended family. He had emigrated from Mexico with his mother and his older siblings when he was only two years old. His parents were still married; however his father had lived in Mexico separated from the rest of the family for the past 16 years. In fact, Sergio had met his father only a few times, most recently on a trip to Mexico when he was 15 years old. Sergio's mother was effectively a single mother who had raised her four children in the US. Sergio and his mother shared a converted one room garage bedroom that was attached to his sister and brother-in-law's home; his two younger nieces and a nephew also shared the home. He had an older brother and sister who also lived nearby.

Sergio's family had one outdated computer in the home, which was shared by all seven family members. He did not have a mobile phone, but he often borrowed a Wi-Fi-enabled iPod Touch from his friend Antonio (17 years old, Mexican-American). Although the iPod provided a way for Sergio to stay connected to his peers and a way to watch videos and search the Internet, it limited the kinds of media he could create. When it came to producing media he preferred to hang out after school in the media club, which provided him access to his friends, as well as to expensive media editing software and high-quality computers.

Sergio's mother had a high school education, and was enrolled in English classes at a church during the time of the study; his father had quit pursing formal education after middle school in order to earn money for the family. The only person in Sergio's family to have gone to college was his older brother, who had attended a local community college for one year before deciding to work full time. However, despite a lack of educational role models at home, Sergio could be described as moderately academically engaged. He cared about his studies and knew how to get work done quickly to pass his classes and have more free time for filmmaking. He enjoyed reading and math, was full of curiosity, enjoyed learning, and shared a mutual respect with most of his teachers.

However, what really excited Sergio was filmmaking. Often sacrificing sleep and other responsibilities to work on film, Sergio spent nearly all of his out-of-school time (and a lot of his in-school time) working on film projects with peers. He considered his interest to be more than a mere hobby, and referred to filmmaking as his "work." He took a lot of pride in what he created, but he was also quite critical of himself. He compared his work to professional films and was always striving to make his own films better and more professional. Rather than seeing it as merely an outlet for self-expression or a hobby he shared with friends, Sergio deliberately invested time in his film projects, expecting that they would pay off financially in the future. This investment often came at the expense of other academic work and grades. He considered his participation in the Cinematic Arts Project as training for the post-graduation workforce: "Right now I'm doing things like writing scripts and making movie so I can build up a portfolio and then submit it to, like, places. And probably have my potential first part-time job in a film industry company or something like that." His assumption that he would submit his portfolio to "like, places" is indicative of his own unfamiliarity with navigating a creative career path.

Javier's interest in film was similar to Sergio's in that he too aspired to be a professional filmmaker and invoked a discourse of professionalization when discussing his films: "I think projects like [the ones we do in the Cinematic Arts Project] help me to be artistically more mature because you're working with other people that know about what you're doing and you have this big responsibility because now it's not, 'Ah, I'm just doing my short film, whatever.' It's professional, it's good work." Javier's family was more upwardly mobile than Sergio's. His mother struggled to find consistent work in the United States, so the family lived primarily off his father's teaching salary. They lived in a two-bedroom apartment just around the corner from the school. Javier had access to the family's shared Internet-enabled computer. Like Sergio, he did not have a mobile phone. He spent much of his leisure time at home watching foreign and amateur films on YouTube. Javier was a mature teen who was quick to engage in philosophical conversations about politics and the world. Well liked by his teachers and peers, he was looked up to by many of the students in the clubs. He had established himself as a peer expert within the space, and other students often came to him for help with their own projects. He was simultaneously balancing school work, projects for the clubs, his own personal projects, and collaborating on films and scripts with his peers. Javier invested more time in film than in school. He did not consider grades very important, valuing creativity and personal expression above more traditional academic courses and rigor.

Javier admitted to staying up much too late working on film projects. Toward the end of the spring semester, some members of the film club had failed to edit the "behind the scenes" footage for a short film they were working on; Javier took on the extra workload. He recalled this as follows.

Javier: So, I had to edit it in one night. I really didn't sleep at all, and I didn't come to school because I had to do that.

Q: So you stayed at home?

Javier: Yeah. Finally, I had to sleep.

Q: So, did you have software at home to do it then?

Javier: No. I borrowed a computer. I needed ten minutes of behind the scenes footage. And when I did it, it was, like, really intense. It was so much work. I think it sounds hard, and it is really hard, and it is a lot of work, and it is a lot of time that you have to spend, and you get really tired, but I think you can manage that because of the passion that you have. When you have that dream of film, "I want to do it. I want to do it." That's what helps you do it because if you don't have the backup it's hard to do it. Sometimes it gets really, really hard.

As this quotation demonstrates, Javier's passion for film sometimes took a toll on his school work and physical health. He was often tired when I met with him, but he felt his investments were worth the sacrifices. His school work often suffered, but he maintained passing grades so he could continue to fully participate in the after-school activities.

Although Sergio was somewhat more invested in academics and cared more about his grades than Javier, it was Javier who expected to go to college, not Sergio. Javier intended to move back to Mexico, take a year off of school to work on films, and then apply to the university where his sister was currently pursuing a film degree. Sergio, on the other hand, did not consider college to be a viable option, despite the fact that he had decent grades, enjoyed learning, and had friends who were college-bound. He would occasionally talk about trying to go to the University of Southern California (USC), but had not made plans to apply, had not taken the SAT,[9] had not filled out FAFSA forms,[10] and had not attended any of the college readiness workshops offered by the school. In fact, he missed one of the college-readiness workshops because he was too busy working on a film for the Cinematic Arts Project. Even though he occasionally mentioned college, it was not a realistic expectation (especially an expensive, highly competitive, out-of-state private school such as USC), nor was he actively pursuing steps to achieve this aspiration. In actuality, Sergio was anxious and even felt pressured to get a job and start earning money after graduation. He was connected to peers with larger social networks and access to greater capital; thus his answers reflected middle-class aspirations, but he did not appear to give any real consideration to applying to colleges. Sergio viewed his digital media courses and the after-school club as vocational training, rather than as academic pursuits. In contrast, Javier, who was not particularly academically engaged, considered his digital media courses and the club to be an investment in his academic and career future.

For students who were disengaged with formal learning environments, it seemed creative digital media production and the club provided a potentially alternative pathway to success and career opportunities. Many of these students navigated a daily situation with unstable financial resources and unreliable or nonexistent peer and familial networks (as potential sources of social and cultural capital). Despite these situations, many students still engaged in robust and deeply fulfilling connected learning environments facilitated through their participation with media production and digital media networks. In this way, motivation for future-driven success influenced participants' engagement in the clubs and learning about digital media. Identification as an artist and producer, combined with a recognition that digital media was more than just a hobby, shaped opportunities for learning and participation, which are key elements for sustained motivation (Dawes, and Larsen 2011). Digital media were constructed not just as tools for media production but also as opportunities for future success.

Although Sergio and Javier constructed similar narratives about the value of media production in their lives, the college-bound versus vocational expectations had different influences on their future-oriented aspirations. They both valued digital media and film, but they imbued their practices with differing meanings. Having watched his older sister successfully graduate from Freeway and be admitted to film school in Mexico, Javier considered digital media and filmmaking to be a means to an end— college and later a career. He presumed that his average grades would not hold him back from pursuing a degree in the creative arts, and thus he invested the majority of his time, intellectual curiosity, and creativity into film.

Sergio on the other hand, strived to earn decent grades to make his mother proud, but did not make the connection that his grades could help him continue a post-high school education. Rather, for Sergio, developing better digital media and film skills was the ultimate goal. He approached his media classes and experiences in the club as a pathway to a future career without the need for additional education. Though he valued the creative process, he also viewed his experiences within a vocational context. This is not surprising when contextualized within the broader culture of Freeway, which encouraged and prepared students for vocational training. Sergio's career-oriented aspirations were not problematic in and of themselves. However, unlike more traditional and established vocational tracks, the digital media industry offers fewer employment opportunities for high school graduates. At present there aren't pathways to career opportunities in digital and creative media that are as well established and structurally supported as the pathways in other vocational tracks (automotive, hospitality, HVAC, and so on.). Thus, Sergio's goals and interest in creative media as part of a vocational track becomes problematic when those pathways to future opportunities are disconnected from and not fully supported by the institutions in which they are embedded.

Notably, there were missing connections between student expectations, after-school clubs, and career opportunities. Sergio probably could have been a candidate for the college-bound track. As a student with decent grades from a first-generation minority household, there were scholarship opportunities available to him. However, his limited access to social capital, combined with a school that presumed his vocational aspirations, he accepted these expectations of his own future. But unfortunately he chose a vocation that is not largely supported by the precarious and unstable film and creative media industry. We see the reproduction of inequity when low-income students' ideal future aspirations do not meet reality and when their future expectations are not actively supported by nor valued in society. The connected learning model prescribes connections between students' existing spheres of influence within their learning ecology, yet remains disconnected from the larger systems that structure future opportunities. To a certain degree, the model privileges academic pathways to success (e.g., higher education), and does not alleviate barriers that preclude students from viable career options outside of pursuing a college degree. What I mean by this is that the connections between personal interests and education (both formal and informal) are crucial (as the model iterates), but there remain systematic inequities that preclude students from pursuing practical career options in the absence of higher education. Social media potentially could provide opportunities for students to expand their social networks and access to social capital—thus alleviating opportunity gaps—yet policies and harm-driven curricula inhibited these connections. As has been noted, unlike more established vocational tracks (e.g., automotive industry, hospitality), there are few career options in the creative media fields outside of attaining a college degree (and even then they remain unstable and limited). As such, the connected model still privileges higher education as the preferred career pathway. A missing node needs to be connections to economic opportunities via vocational pathways.

Further, the Digital Media Club and Cinematic Arts Project unintentionally—and perhaps problematically—began to attract other students who were on the vocational track. Or, more accurately, students on the college-bound track were less invested in the club and were even dropping out of it. For example, Jack (17 years old, white) was the son of two college-educated parents; his mother worked in the tech industry and his father worked for the state. He and his friends were on the college-bound track and were on the golf team together. Jack was a talented filmmaker whose short film won an award at a local festival. In an at-home interview, his mother expressed support for Jack's interest in film and said she was glad he had found something about which he was passionate. However, despite his interest in film and media, and despite external and family validation for his talent and creativity, he dropped out of the film club the following semester. He explained that the reason for this seemingly unexpected decision was that he "didn't feel like part of the team" and didn't fit in with the other members. He also mentioned feeling alienated when the other students would start speaking Spanish, a language he didn't understand. From my observations of the Cinematic Arts Project, it was apparent that Jack was on friendly terms with everyone in the club but didn't socialize with the other members outside of the club. Further, because he was on the college-bound track, he was taking different classes than the majority of the clubs' members.

The social aspects of the media and film clubs mediated the students' experiences, their expectations, and the values they attached to their own practices. Although Jack enjoyed creative media production, he valued it as a hobby and a personally meaningful interest, rather than as a necessary component of his future success. Jack expected to go to college and was actively pursuing many different interests, film merely being one of them.[11] Even though the Tech Apps class appealed to students on both tracks, over time the Digital Media Club and the Cinematic Arts Project increasingly attracted marginalized students—misfits who were not involved in a lot of other clubs[12]—and students who were on the vocational track. Others in the school began to perceive the clubs as vocational. One explanation was that middle-class students, unlike many low-income students, could hang out together at someone's home and utilize home computers for the same kinds of activities that low-income students utilized in the clubs. For example, Jada (16 years old, black) and her friends would make music videos together on the weekends, using their phones, home computers, and unrestricted access to YouTube (see chapter 5). What was unfortunate was the expectation that the Digital Media Club and Cinematic Arts Project should fit within a college or vocational framework imposed by the school. Arguably, digital media production should also be valued as an outlet for creativity, self-expression, empowerment, social change, and socialization—much in the same way that we view traditional literacy and writing. Students who are good writers do not necessarily join poetry clubs, a school newspaper, or creative writing clubs as a manifestation of vocational or college aspirations; rather, they may do so in order to express ideas, identity, and creativity with peers. In a similar way, the media clubs could have served the needs and met the expectations of both college-bound and vocational-track students, whose desires and goals were diverse and for whom the clubs would be meaningful in different ways.

Sergio's and Javier's stories illustrate the importance for young people to not only find a passion and support for one's interests, but also to find a way to navigate systems that will support long-term goals and career expectations. Two years after graduation, Sergio was working in a retail job to help financially support his mother. He had taken some film classes at a community college at night, but his education was moving slowly. He maintained an interest in film; however, despite his high school aspirations and expectations, he had faced many difficulties in pursuing film without the institutional support of the school. In the two years since graduation, he had casually collaborated on one film project with his girlfriend and a former mentor from the film club; they had made a short music video based on the popular Harlem Shake meme.[13] He had not completely abandoned his film goals, but he was considering earning an Associate's degree to further his retail career. The vocational-track courses at Freeway High prepared marginalized students with interests in the creative industries neither for higher education nor for jobs. The career expectations and aspirations of marginalized vocational-track students remained disconnected from realistic potential opportunities available in the current labor market.[14]

Javier, on the other hand, succeeded not through navigating local opportunities and pathways but by returning to his homeland only four years after leaving it. He went back to Mexico after graduation to live with his sister (two years older than he) and work on films. She was already socially connected and established there as a film student, and Javier was able to collaborate on projects with her and her friends. In contrast with challenges Sergio faced in the United States, Javier was able to capitalize on his sister's connections, resources, and knowledge of social structures. After taking a year off, he joined his sister in film school in Guadalajara, where he was still perusing a film degree at the time of writing. Sergio had the emotional support of his family, but he did not have the structural and social support that Javier's family offered. For example, Javier talked about applying to private film schools in the US, but had been advised by his parents to pursue an education in Mexico, which was an economically wise decision to save money. Although the Cinematic Arts Project and Digital Media Club provided Javier and Sergio with skill sets, opportunities, and personally meaningful experiences that were valuable in their own rights, they were unable to help Sergio overcome the barriers and challenges he faced as a low-income high-barrier immigrant in the US. There were too many disconnections between his expectations of the future and the school's ability to prepare him for the structural barriers he faced after graduation. This serves as an explicit example of how overly focusing on individualized risk often comes at the expense of opportunity. How might Sergio's experiences and expectations been different had federal, state, and local policies been driven by expectations of opportunity rather than harm? What if the school had invested more effort, resources, curriculum, and policies in creating equitable opportunities for marginalized students rather than policing technology in an effort to eradicate risk? As was noted throughout the first part of the book, rules and policies may reduce some risks—exposure to inappropriate content and people—but they also exacerbate other risks—namely social and economic inequities.

Gabriela: Competing Expectations of the Well-Connected

When I first met Gabriela (16 years old, Mexican-American), in the fall of her tenth-grade year of high school, she had dreams of traveling the world to take photographs. She was also contemplating getting into wedding photography or portraits, but was mostly interested in nature, architecture, and candid photography. Through her enrollment in the Tech Apps courses and her involvement in the Digital Media Club, she was learning how to use photo-editing software, as well as how to do web design. She enjoyed "playing with photos" and liked to digitally manipulate her images.

The adults in Gabriela's life valued her interests and talent and were mostly supportive of her aspirations. For example, her uncle—a

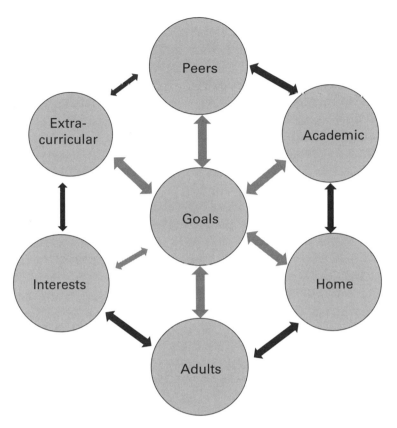

Figure 7.5
Gabriela's learning ecology.

semi-professional photographer—helped her purchase her first camera. Gabriela had limited mobility options, since her home was located in a disconnected suburb that was not well served by local transportation. However, she and her father shared a close relationship, and he would often drive her downtown to take photographs on the weekends. She enjoyed candidly photographing the busier scenes of the city life—people strolling among the city skyline, bikers crossing the city's river on one of its many unique bridges, or dogs playing in the parks. Her home life was unusual but loving and stable. Her working-class parents were divorced but were cohabitating after several years of living apart. Gabriela and her 12-year-old sister shared the master bedroom, and each of her parents occupied one of the guest rooms. Gabriela's side of the room was plastered with photos she had taken, photos taken by her uncle, and images torn from magazines.

Practically every inch of the wall was covered in photos, art, and bulletin boards with pictures of her friends. It was obvious that photography was a passion.

Gabriela was respectful of her parents' desires for her; she did her best to follow her parents' rules and meet their expectations. Her parents saw education as important to Gabriela's future and made it clear that they expected her to earn good grades, and for the most part she did. One afternoon she told me that her latest history grade hadn't been very good, and I asked her what she was going to do about it. She replied: "When my grades go down, I know I can usually fix them on my own. I get help from the teacher after school and catch up. But if I couldn't [handle it], well, yeah, I would tell my parents. They have friends who could tutor me; they help me and my sister in school however they can." Gabriela was a good student who surrounded herself with friends who also cared about earning good grades and doing well in school. She and her friends discussed their grades, expected to go to college, and supported one another academically.

The different nodes in Gabriela's life were well supported and connected. For the most part she enjoyed school, or at the very least knew how to do school well. She found outlets and support for her creative interests in after-school activities and involvement in the Digital Media Club. She shared a mutual respect for many of the adults in her life who were able to offer her emotional and material support. Her working-class parents strived to provide the best for their daughters and saw media and technology as an investment in their future; each member of the family had their own mobile phone and personal computer and their home had gaming consoles, two televisions, music, books, and a high-speed Internet connection. Her father explained that he viewed technology as an investment in his daughters' academic futures and also thought it brought the family together; they enjoyed playing video games together or having family movie nights on the weekends.

Although her father—who sold and installed window and door screens—was supportive of her interests, he nonetheless worried that Gabriela needed a more "stable career option" than he believed photography would provide. While encouraging her to pursue photography as a hobby, he wanted her to consider nursing. Gabriela was ambivalent about nursing; she told me she was considering it just to please her parents. Her mother did custodial work at a local hospital and occasionally took Gabriela to work with her so she could see what the hospital environment was like. Neither of her parents had more than a high school education; they had emigrated from Mexico in their twenties, and had worked hard to provide a stable life for

Gabriela and her sister. Hoping that Gabriela would have more financial stability than they had had growing up, they understandably worried about her pursuing a creative career. Their concerns were valid and their expectations were reasonably influenced by their own class position—that is, pursuing a creative career comes with many risks that privileged families are more equipped to support than working-class families (which often do not have a "safety net" of financial savings or a well-connected social network to fall back on if a creative career fails). However, during my time with Gabriela, she only ever got excited about her post-graduation options when discussing photography and art. Nursing was always discussed in terms of something "she was supposed to do" because it guaranteed more financial stability and upward mobility than photography. She was torn between her own passions, talent, and aspirations and her parents' expectations, advice, and desires for her life. Gabriela was facing an internal crisis regarding her future decisions and pathways.

In comparison with many of the other students involved in the Digital Media Club, Gabriela was not as marginalized as many of the other first-generation immigrant young people. Although her parents were divorced, they still lived together, and both played active roles in her life. Though they did not have money for college, they had provided Gabriela with the support she needed to explore her interests, goals, and academics. Her parents were connected to upwardly mobile friends with more social capital that Gabriela could tap into for advice and support. Though she often spoke Spanish in the home, both of her parents spoke English at work. Her peer group consisted of assimilated Mexicans who were college-bound.[15] In other words, she and her family were upwardly mobile and connected to middle-class society in ways that many other marginalized immigrant families at Freeway were not. However, despite her positive academic disposition, good grades, academically supportive peer group, and future-oriented aspirations, her parents feared that Gabriela was at risk of facing financial hardships if she pursued a career in the creative arts. They did not want their daughter to struggle with the same financial hardships they had faced; understandably they viewed a career in the medical field as a more secure and less risky career option than photography.

Through her enrollment in the Tech Apps course and her participation in the Digital Media Club, Gabriela discovered a career pathway that connected her creative interests to her parents' class expectations: advertising and graphic design. Through his connections in the local community, Mr. Lopez arranged an opportunity for students in the Digital Media Club to tour the local advertising office of a major national tech company. The students learned about the creative and business sides of advertising and had an opportunity to meet with working professionals at the company. During our final meeting, Gabriela told me—with a huge smile on her face—that she had decided to pursue a career in advertising, with a focus on graphic design because it combined her love of photography and images with a more stable career path than photography alone. This was by far the most excited discussion of her future goals I had ever heard from Gabriela. With help from Mr. Lopez and the Digital Media Club, Gabriela put together an online photography portfolio and landed a summer internship with a local advertising agency and gained professional experience working alongside media professionals.

In the eight months I spent with Gabriela, I saw her interest in photography evolve from a passion to an identification that allowed her to explore new career paths. It is worth speculating about the extent to which her father's desires for his daughter were gendered: he wanted her to achieve a stable career (as a nurse, but not a doctor) without disrupting traditional gender norms and expectations (which professional photography would have challenged). Advertising provided a compromise between stability and gendered expectations—and Gabriela assured me that her father was supportive of her new career aspirations. Although her new career path fit with her father's gendered expectations (almost half of those in the advertising industry are women), it is important to note that the advertising industry is still overwhelming white (80 percent)—Hispanics account for only 10 percent of the industry (Grillo 2015; Labor force statistics 2014), and thus advertising is not a typical career path for a minority student such as Gabriela. However, through the connections and opportunities that the Digital Media Club provided, and with her parents' support, Gabriela was able to explore options she had not previously identified or cultivated on her own. A year after the study ended, I followed up with Gabriela via Instagram, and later email. She was living with a relative in Florida and enrolled in classes at a community college.

Connected learning across all nodes of her learning ecology helped Gabriela establish and seek realistic expectations that were structurally supported and valued. Significantly, though, her family was better connected and more upwardly mobile than many of the immigrant families in the study, which undoubtedly played a role in helping her navigate a pathway to success. School played an integral role in helping Gabriela navigate pathways that connected her interests and goals, but her family also took on the responsibility of helping to create these pathways. Understandings of risk and opportunity position these choices as individualized, but class position structures options in inequitable ways. Gabriela's family was able to shape her options in beneficial ways that are not afforded all students. Mentors such as Mr. Lopez (among other teachers at school) encouraged Gabriela to enroll in AP courses and to consider college as a stepping stone to future success. Additionally, her assimilated parents and extended family helped provide Gabriela with the social and cultural capital she needed to negotiate her expectations with the structural and material reality of achieving her goals. The different nodes of Gabriela's life—academic, familial, peers, home, extracurricular, and personal interests—were actively connected with one another and intentionally supported her expectations and goals in realistic ways. Similar to Javier's story, the connections between Gabriela's home, academic, and personal interests were also privileged within and supported by higher education (as a pathway to a career) more than they would have been within the creative industry without a college degree.

Broken Connections: Selena's Disengaged Expectations

Selena (17 years old, Mexican-American) was a senior who described herself as "goth."[16] With long hair dyed black, baggy jeans, multiple piercings, dark red lipstick, heavy eyeliner, and heavy-metal-band T-shirts, Selena intentionally presented herself as unapproachable. "I like dark things," she told me. "Like, I was writing vampire fiction way before *Twilight*, but, like, the evil kind, not this sparkly shit." She explained that her family was "weird": "My mom, she's chola[17] and my dad's a headbanger, I don't know how they ended up together. My [21-year-old] brother, he's all tatted up.[18] My [older] sister, she's a real mess, like, maybe bipolar or something. And my little sister, she's evil [laughs], nah, but she's always trying to get me in trouble, yo." She identified herself and her friends as "ghetto" but not in the "fake" way other students at her school did. Unlike many of the students at Freeway who used the term pejoratively, Selena perceived the label "ghetto" as a more accurate description of where she had come from and had lived. Having divorced parents, she had moved back and forth between central and west Texas multiple times, either with her single mother or with her father (who was in west Texas with his other family). She described the west Texas town as particularly "ghetto" because of poverty, drugs, gangs, crime, and fights. She had been sent from Freeway High to an alternative school for fighting. She presented herself as "tough," but believed that she did so out of necessity rather than an expression of a chosen identity. She explained: "All these people here [at Freeway], they

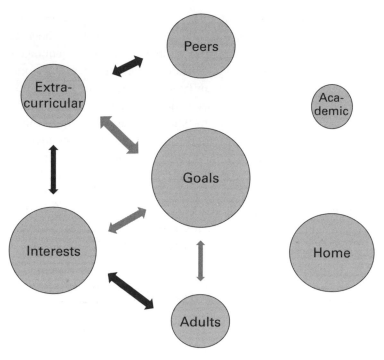

Figure 7.6
Selena's learning ecology.

act hard, but then you go to their house and their parents are married and
they have their own room and they have this happy little life. No, like,
that's not ghetto. Me? I know ghetto." In a school with a large immigrant
and low-income population of students whose situations were in many
ways similar to Selena's, she still struggled to fit in with her peers, whom
she perceived as superficial.

Selena was struggling with school and home life and had little support
from friends or family members. Although she had a few friends at school,
she spent most of her social time with older friends who had dropped out
of high school. Her mother was currently unemployed, and despite the fact
that she had many years of experience and an Associate's degree she was
struggling to find work. Her father was in west Texas and had limited contact with Selena at the time of the study. Neither of Selena's parents nor any
of her older siblings had graduated from high school, although her older
sister had earned a GED certificate after dropping out of high school. Her
brother made ends meet through unstable jobs that often required him to
move. In view of the careers and the financial instability of her family,

Selena had low expectations about her own future, and to a certain extent assumed she would follow a path similar to those of her family members and friends—one with bouts of unemployment, low income, unsteady work, and financial stress and struggles.

Selena's disposition toward formal education can best be described as disengaged—she frequently cut class, had a history of getting into fights, described school as boring, and often missed assignments and failed to do homework. She described tenuous relationships with many of her teachers and expressed little interest in earning good grades. She enjoyed reading, and thus English was one class she found tolerable; however, she expressed frustration that her English teacher didn't allow her more freedom to choose her own books for class or to express more stylistic creativity in her writing. She believed that she was intellectually capable of doing well in school but frequently admitted that she lacked the motivation and resiliency to complete school assignments as well as she should.

Outside of school Selena was curious. She explored personal interests and enjoyed teaching herself new skills. For example, when I visited Selena in the two-bedroom apartment she shared with six other people (her mother, her younger sister, her older brother, his girlfriend, and their two children), she played an Evanescence[19] song for me on her keyboard. Impressed, I asked how long she had been playing and who had taught her how to play. She told me that at the age of 13 she had taught herself how to play on her little sister's Barbie keyboard just by listening to the Evanescence song and watching YouTube videos. Her uncle later gave her his old keyboard for Christmas so she could expand her skills and interest beyond what the limited Barbie keyboard offered. At the time of the study she had taught herself about fifteen songs that way.

Additionally, although Selena did not tend to enjoy writing for school, she wrote several short stories on her own outside of school. With limited disposable income and limited mobility, she spent a lot of time in her room (which technically she shared with her little sister, but her little sister frequently slept on the couch in the living room with her mother, so Selena had some sense of privacy at night). In her bedroom was an outdated computer that was not connected to the Internet. When I visited the home, Selena explained that the reason she had not been writing much was that the mouse on her computer had broken and she could not figure out how to open and access her files without a mouse. She was hoping to find a new mouse soon and was hoping she would start writing again more when she did.[20] In the meantime, she had been writing in a note pad by hand, but she was frustrated that she could not access and edit the stories she had already started. She also kept a sketchbook in which she liked to sketch the covers of her favorite CDs, fairies, and people's faces. She did not share her writings with me, but she proudly showed me several drawings. She had talent for music, drawing, and sketching. In other words, she was creatively curious and a motivated learner when given the right circumstances.

When not at school, Selena and her friends often hung out at local parks, where they would smoke, drink, and just "chill." She used these opportunities—both at home and with friends—to write poetry, short stories, and screenplays. Her mother was aware of her interest in writing and expressed pride when I asked her about her daughter's writing. However, her friends expressed more ambiguous attitudes that fluctuated between supporting her and distracting her. "My friends, yeah, they tell me 'You are different, you can actually graduate, 'cause you're smart.' But then when we're hanging out they be like 'Stop working; let's go do something.'" Her friends frequently tempted and convinced her to skip school and the after-school Digital Media Club.

I met Selena through her participation in the Digital Media Club, which differed from the participation of many of her peers and the other students in this book. Although her participation was still in principle voluntary, Selena was earning credit for a course she had previously failed; she needed the credit in order to graduate. Mr. Lopez was required to record her time and her activities in the club and was trying to "stay on top of her" so she could earn credit for the elective course she had previously failed. When I first met her, she was a semi-regular participant in the club. Though by no means the most popular student there, she had found her niche, and she hung out with a few of the other students. She reported that friendship was one of her motivations for coming to the club, along with having access to the computers and software. She spent most of her club time taking and editing photos, but also liked to listen to music or mess around with graphic design software.

As the semester continued, Selena's participation in the Digital Media Club waned. By the end of the study she had quit coming altogether. When I asked her why she was not coming to the club as often as she had, she explained that she was disappointed that her script had not been selected for the Cinematic Arts Project. Every student in the club was given an opportunity to submit a script, after which the teachers and the adult mentors selected one script that members of the Cinematic Arts Project would collaboratively produce that academic year. As we continued talking, Selena admitted that her script was only half done, and that its unfinished state was probably the reason it wasn't selected, although she felt it was good.

It became evident through the time I spent with Selena that she was a self-motivated learner, but only so long as she maintained interest in a topic and only if she saw an immediate payoff for her efforts. Often she lacked the resiliency—or time—to follow through on projects. In one interview she briefly explained her growing frustration with participating in the Digital Media Club:

Selena: The fact that I'm doing editing in school is what throws off my motivation.

Q: How come?

Selena: I don't like school.

Q: You just don't like school?

Selena: No.

Q: So, would you pick it [video editing] up again maybe when you're not having to do it for school?

Selena: Actually, yeah. Probably in college I probably will. Or if I ever just decide to go and make my own movie by myself, then, yeah, I'll probably try to do it.

Q: So, you enjoy script writing and editing so long as it's not for school?

Selena: Yeah. Pretty much. And also all the stuff that Mr. Lopez used to have me working on was stuff that I didn't like doing. Put it this way: If it's something that I recorded, that I wrote, that I did, then I will edit it. I can edit it. I can do everything on it. But if it's somebody else's stuff that I don't find interesting, I'm not into it. I can't do it.

Q: So it needs to be yours?

Selena: Yes. It needs to be mine. I don't like it whenever he has me doing other people's stuff.

Q: Does he let you do your own stuff in there?

Selena: Yeah. But right now how they're having that whole Cinematic Arts Project thing. Everybody's so preoccupied with that. They're always using the cameras. And lately right now I'm just focused on graduating. So, that's one of the other reasons why I'm trying not to get distracted by this. I just want to graduate.

The club became the only space with the potential to support Selena's preferred style of learning, creativity, interests, and goals. However, even then she struggled with lack of motivation, resiliency, and competing interests and goals.

Selena's comments also revealed her own unrealistic and non-situated expectations about her future. She occasionally mentioned wanting to attend community college, even though she adamantly disliked school. She liked learning and hoped college would be more interesting. However, she did not seek funding, attend any college readiness workshops, or seek help in navigating the college application system. Going to college was something she spoke of but not something she actively tried to do. She also unrealistically mentioned wanting to make a professional movie on her own, something that is not a realistic expectation and reveals her own misunderstandings about the nature of the film industry and the collaborative aspects of filmmaking.

As Jada noted in a comment quoted earlier in this chapter, filmmaking is an inherently collaborative process, and Selena struggled to work with others. I point this out not to criticize Selena's aspirations, but rather to highlight the disparity between her expectations and the avenues and hurdles she needed to navigate in order to make her expectations a reality. Mr. Lopez strived to help her, and he deserves much credit for trying to help her graduate, yet there were many other material and structural barriers that prohibited her from identifying and creating a pathway to a stable future.

In a preliminary study, Nickki Pearce Dawes and Reed Larsen (2011) found that motivation develops when individuals cultivate personal connections to a program's activities and goals. They situated their research within a broader context of psychological literature that focuses on theories of motivation, including interest theory and self-determination theory (SDT). Interest theory suggests involvement must be personally meaningful for individuals. From a psychological perspective, interest is defined as "focused attention, increased cognitive functioning, persistence and affective involvement" (Hidi 2000, p. 312). Similarly, SDT supposes that sustainable engagement must be integrated into one's sense of self and identity. Dawes and Larsen (2011, p. 260) claim that the highest level of engagement is achieved when individuals internalize goals "driven by three basic universal psychological needs of the self: competence, autonomy, and relatedness." Creative projects facilitated by her Tech Apps course and the Digital Media Club provided Selena with extrinsic motivation—graduation—but she was unable to sustain the intrinsic motivation necessary to overcome challenges and setbacks.

Further, although Selena reported that she usually enjoyed her time in the Digital Media Club, it nonetheless competed for her time and took her away from her out-of-school friends. To compensate, she would often skip school to hang out with those friends, then try to come back to the club later in the day when classes were over. Thus, neither her peers in the club nor her out-of-school friends provided the support and encouragement she needed to meaningfully invest in her pursuit of digital media and writing projects. Despite skipping school and the club, Selena continued to meet with me for a while, sometimes off campus and sometimes after school hours. Selena deliberately presented herself as tough and unapproachable, yet she was a likeable person. She opened up with me about many of her personal struggles and was honest about her own shortcomings. From an outside adult perspective, it appeared to me that Selena's tough attitude was a way to fit in with her peers and a facade intended to distance herself from peers at school. The more time we spent together, the more apparent it was that Selena was fighting an uphill battle to succeed. Her disinterest appeared to me to be a defense mechanism—if she had low expectations, she would not be disappointed.

If we examine Selena's interest in and experience with creativity and digital media, it is easy to identify how missing connections failed to support her goals. She faced severe economic challenges and instability that contributed to her stress. She lacked familial adult role models who could have helped her to build resiliency and to overcome frustrations when she did not accomplish what she was trying to do. There were few academic classes that supported her autonomous learning style and creative interests. Although catering to students' unique learning styles is a challenge— particularly in low-income schools with larger classrooms and fewer teachers—self-identified didactic learners such as Selena need guidance on developing resiliency and perseverance. Because she had struggled academically and did not exhibit a lot of motivation, her attitude could be misinterpreted as uninterested. However, Selena actually enjoyed learning, but not in the rigid ways the majority of her courses were designed. Her courses left little room for the incorporation of personal interest, self-guided learning, and outlets for creativity. As a result, when she became frustrated she was more likely to quit than to overcome challenges. We can see how the autonomous and creative atmosphere of the Digital Media Club's informal learning environment motivated Selena more than her formal academic courses did; the space served as a potential intervention in her precarious pathways to future success. But the motivation and opportunities were not enough to help her navigate the systematic, familial, and material barriers in her life.

Although Selena continued to meet with me for a while after she began skipping school and the club, eventually that too stopped. She would cancel appointments on me, and eventually I decided to stop trying; I didn't want to be one more source of stress or pressure in her life. If she wanted to reinitiate contact with me, she knew how. I don't even know if Selena graduated from high school; I suspect she may not have, in view of how frequently she was skipping school and the club (which she needed for credit). However, I am hopeful that someone else in her life or at school provided her with the support she needed to accomplish that major milestone; she would have been the first from her family to graduate, and we can only speculate what opportunities that would have afforded her.

Conclusion: What Are the Significant (Dis)Connections?

Javier's and Gabriela's stories fit within a traditional market-driven narrative of upward mobility and economic opportunities, whereas Sergio's and Selena's stories are a lot messier. All four stories can help us identify what connections are necessary for helping young people navigate future pathways of opportunity—or, more precisely, what missed connections emerge as crucial for creating opportunities.

The biggest differences in the stories concern the roles of and the (dis) connections between peers, academic, adults, and home. Javier, Sergio, and Gabriela all had peer networks that supported their goals and/or their interests and academic pursuits. Selena, on the other hand, lacked peer support of her goals, interests, and academic pursuits.

Much has been written about the effect of peer groups on teens' academic performance, motivation, engagement, and self-efficacy; studies have found that peer networks and a sense of belonging are important for supporting (or detracting from) academic success (Goodenow and Grady 1993; Hymel, Comfort, Schonert-Reichl, and McDougall 1996; Juvonen, Espinoza, and Knifsend 2012; Wentzel 2005).

Additionally, for Sergio and Selena (and to a certain extent for Javier) there was a disparity between their interests and academics and their home life. They did not have access to the resources and the material capital necessary for their home life to play a significant role in supporting their goals. Sergio and Selena did not have access to technology that would have enhanced their personal interests as well as their academic pursuits. Likewise, in comparison with the parents of Javier and Gabriela, their parents were not as well connected or equipped to help with homework or creative media production. Their home lives afforded them less access to social networks that could have provided more diverse and resourceful social capital.

Further, what is abundantly clear in Javier's and Gabriela's cases is the extent to which each node actively supported their academic goals and the labor market. While Selena and Sergio found some spaces and influences that supported their goals, there were disconnects between academics and their goals, their home life and their goals, and the adults in their lives and their goals. For Selena, there also were disconnects between her peers and her goals. I do not identify these disconnects as a way to demonstrate deficiencies or failures on the parts of Selena and Sergio, but rather to draw attention to the structural and systematic barriers that shaped their connections, or lack thereof.

The connected learning model helps us to identify essential connections and can illuminate disconnections that detract from academic success and learning. Yet the model does not necessarily connect to alternative pathways of success outside of higher education. The creative media and technology industries in particular still privilege college as the preferred pathway. Sergio's story in particular highlights how connections between formal education and personal interests do not necessarily lead to a pathway that connects career aspirations to economic opportunities. Arguably Sergio was a candidate for higher education, but despite the connections this was not an expectation he had of himself. In the absence of higher education he was left to navigate precarious opportunities and was unable to work his way into the creative industry. His academic and informal education did not accurately manage his expectations or help him connect long-term goals to his interests and skills.

Notably absent from the ecologies of all four students' (even Gabriela, who was well connected and supported) was a supported connection between (a) personal interests, extracurricular activities, and goals, and (b) academics (i.e., the elliptical arrow in the ideal model). On the one hand, this further highlights the significance of the informal learning environments in helping students map out pathways that support their goals and expectations. But on the other, it accentuates and emphasizes a missing connection: academics must significantly support the informal learning spaces and personal interests of marginalized young people (and vice versa). As Sergio's story demonstrates, there do not (yet) exist clear pathways for attaining social capital and economic stability in the creative industries outside of (a) academic pathways and/or (b) well-connected social networks that students' can tap into for social capital. In the absence of higher education or connections in the industry, it remains difficult for students to connect their interests and informal learning nodes to their aspirations and goals. Hence the importance of helping students make greater connections between the informal and the formal learning environments, so that they are able to tap into other interests, skill sets, networks, knowledges, and capitals that create multiple pathways for attaining their goals.

Schools, as a democratic space to create more equitable opportunities, are in a unique position to help students tap into greater networks of resources and capital. They ought to be expected to help students manage risks and alleviate burdens of responsibility that are otherwise displaced onto families and the home. To a certain degree, Mr. Lopez was helping students make connections within the larger creative industry and community; he introduced them to working professionals, encouraged collaboration within and beyond the school, and aimed to equip students with the efficacy and confidence to participate in public spaces beyond the school. However, there were still barriers that made it challenging for students to cultivate ongoing relationships, networks, and resources. Merely meeting a professional does not provide students with access to resources and capital; rather, those relationships must be cultivated over time through mentorship, trust, and reciprocity.

This is where I see opportunities for digital media to alleviate gaps in inequitable distributions of resources and opportunities. Young people's participation in networked publics provide opportunities for youth, regardless of social class and home life, to make connections beyond their immediate spheres of influence. Online they can connect and share with peers and adults, amateurs and professionals, in ways that are not easily feasible in offline social networks. But of course teens need incentives, support, and guidance in identifying and maintaining those relationships, which is where education, teachers, and policies can intentionally and deliberately contribute to more equitable opportunities.

Conclusion: Opportunity-Driven Expectations

If the potential of connection is to outweigh the appeal of disconnection in the future, we must directly address the risk-averse fears and self-protective practices that stand in the way of rethinking society in the digital age.
Sonia Livingstone and Julian Sefton-Green (2016, pp. 252–253)

I briefly want to return to the three stories at the beginning of the book: a fictional episode of *Law & Order SVU* in which a teen girl was shamed for texting a nude photo, the news story of Megan Meier, who hanged herself as a result of bullying on MySpace, and the story of the teen twins Marcus and Miguel, who spent much of their free time playing video games. Each of these stories is about teens and digital media, and here I want to further complicate the ways in which each story portrays the relationship between youth and risk in the digital world. Common to all three stories are elements of youth who are constructed as at risk in familiar ways: as vulnerable to threats of sex, abuse, bullies, isolation, and addiction. All these concerns are embedded within historical fears and harm-driven expectations that have been fueled by popular media narratives, news stories, and policies about young people's digital media practices.

In the *Law & Order* episode on sexting and abuse, risk avoidance was presented as an individualized responsibility. The girl was physically and emotionally punished for expressing her sexuality, and thus the episode quite literally depicted her sexuality as harmful. Eventually her boyfriend was arrested for physically beating her, but the entire episode overly focused on the role of technology as the culprit of harm, rather than an abusive partner. Essentially it failed to take into consideration the role of consent by not addressing nor punishing the teens who knowingly distributed the girl's image without her permission; collective social responsibility for managing risk and harm was effectively erased from the narrative. Though the episode raised some provocative questions as to how the law should address teen sexting, it nonetheless perpetuated a dualistic understanding of privacy by essentially saying "if teens don't want anyone to see something, they should not have been doing it in the first place." Such rhetoric creates an easy avenue for blaming teens for their own victimization. In this case, the rhetoric failed to acknowledge the contextual integrity in which the photo was produced and distributed. The narrative served to reify a binary understanding of public and private that ignored the networked social context of young people's communicative practices.

The suicide of Megan Meier is a particularly interesting example of how teens, technology, and risk are discursively produced. Although the case became a watershed moment that projected cyberbullying to the forefront of public conversation, even leading to new laws, the case was not actually about *teens*. Rather, it was about an *adult* who bullied a teen. As tragic as Megan's story was, it also illustrated the ways in which young people are often used as scapegoats for larger societal problems. Bullying and cyberbullying are not mere "youth" problems, yet policies frequently aim to regulate "youth" problems when they are actually embedded within larger social and adult issues as well. Megan's story highlighted how risk narratives can reify boundaries between youth and adult in ways that overlook the fluidity of youth as a discursive construct, and miss the nuances of risk and opportunity that do not fit within a neatly contained binary of youth/adult or risk/opportunity.

The story of Marcus and Miguel, like so many of the stories in this book, is not typically represented in the news or in narrative fiction, or reflected in policies. Their experiences simultaneously demonstrated how risks are inevitable, but are accompanied by beneficial opportunities as well. The risky behaviors of talking to strangers and spending a lot of time playing games actually revealed the social benefits of technology for marginalized teens. The story of Marcus and Miguel probably was less thematically familiar than the *Law & Order* episode or the story of Megan Meier. For one thing, discourses of risk are often gendered—Marcus and Miguel's story probably would be interpreted differently had they been two 14-year-old girls meeting and connecting with strangers online, rather than two boys. Stories of girls at risk (via technology) more typically dominate fictional narratives, but also news stories about teens at risk. As was explored earlier, this stems from a long fearful history in which girls and girls' sexuality are discursively constructed as innocent, vulnerable, and in need of (adult) protection. Stories about girls (but not necessarily their actual experiences or voices) often dominate many narratives of risk, policy, and popular culture. Because boys are typically discursively constructed in more agentive and assertive ways, and therefore not as likely to viewed as vulnerable or incapable; the risks they take are less likely to incite a media panic.

Yet beyond the gendered construction of their experiences, Marcus and Miguel's classed position also rendered their experiences less visible. The experiences of working-class and poor young people are often silenced, marginalized, or erased from public concern. The ways in which low-income and immigrant youth navigate the digital contours of their daily lives differ from the ways in which their middle-class peers do so, as a result, they encounter unique and differentiated risks that must also demand attention and protection. But far too often their stories, ingenuity, opportunities, needs, and anxieties are silenced by the louder, more familiar, privileged concerns of the middle class. It is imperative that we produce more inclusive narratives, expectations, and policies that take into account the diverse ways different populations aim to capitalize on the benefits of their digital media practices.

From Disconnections to Connections

My goal has been for the stories told and the research described in this book to contribute to a more nuanced understanding of how expectations of risk, technology, and youth shape policies, opportunities, and young people's lived experiences. I have aimed to expand the analytic lens beyond historical fears and harm-driven expectations to also incorporate the risks and opportunities that are subsumed within popular discourses of risk. What I have tried to make clear are the ways in which harm-driven expectations perpetuate disconnections in society. I want to briefly return to the primary disconnects introduced at the beginning of the book as a way to pose an alternative model based on opportunity-driven expectations and connections.

The current harm-driven model of approaching the relationships between risks, youth, and technology is built upon fearful misunderstandings, broken connections, and missed opportunities. The actual everyday lived experiences of marginalized young people are rarely incorporated into popular imaginaries of young people today. This is evident in the "digital native" and "digital generation" rhetoric that expects all young people to be well connected. It assumes that young people innately know how to use media, and disregards the necessity of intentionally helping teens develop skill sets and critical digital literacies required for participation in networked publics. Further, it ignores the unique barriers that inhibit some marginalized young people from confidently and safely participating in a networked digital world. Within the current model of harm-driven expectations, we see discourses of risk that devalue the ways young people make meaning out of their own mediated practices. Their practices are overlooked or dismissed within adult-centric institutions. And many narratives, policies, and practices overly focus on the role of technology as an agent of social change; they presume that new technologies are inherently harmful. Harm-driven expectations lead to the creation of policies and practices that aim to regulate and control technology, rather than to understand the broader context in which technology plays a role in young people's learning ecologies. The harm-driven model amplifies the voices of the privileged at the expense of the marginalized, values protection over empowerment, and tries to control technology—and, by extension, youth—in ways that further alienate young people from equitable opportunities.

Ultimately I have argued for a shift in the way we approach technology, and in what we expect of young people, of media, of schools, and of policies. Rather than aiming to control technology or young people, and rather than expecting harm (and therefore aiming to protect), what if we were to expect opportunity? What if we were to approach policies and practices and systems from the perspective of how risky opportunities can benefit young people individually and society collectively? How can digital media alleviate burdens that create barriers for the most vulnerable in society? How can adults, schools, and laws not only protect young people, but also *empower* them to become citizens who participate in the creation of their own mediated cultures, opportunities, and networked publics? That is, what if we were to approach technology from expectations of opportunity, rather than harm? Rather than the model of disconnections that was presented in the introduction (figure I.2), I'm proposing a model of connections, as illustrated in figure 8.1.

Here we move away from a focus on media panics, and instead we focus on a relationship between lived experiences and mediated representations of youth. If young people are more accurately, holistically, and inclusively represented, heard, and validated in media, then their stories and experiences can positively influence policy and design. Not only can laws protect young people, they can empower young people and the adult institutions that serve them to play active roles in the development and influence of technology in young people's lives. Thus, the second aspect is a mutual and symbiotic relationship between young people's digital media practices and those of educational institutions. With opportunity-driven expectations, both young people and educational institutions recognize the expertise and experiences of the other and would work together to create curriculum, policies platforms, and opportunities that would protect and validate young

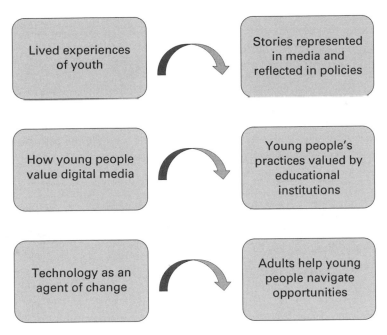

Figure 8.1
Connections that contribute to opportunity-driven expectations.

people's values. Finally, if we stop focusing so much on technology as a source of concern, and instead focus on young people's lived experiences with technology, we may privilege young people as agentive, rather than as passive victims who are harmed by technology. This shift also facilitates opportunities for young people and adults to work and learn and play and explore the digital world together.

Although participation gaps are closing as more young people are afforded opportunities to develop critical digital literacies, we know that young people's media ecologies—and therefore their participation in networked publics—remain unequal. I addressed some of the explanations and barriers that inhibit marginalized young people from fully participating, networking, and visibly sharing online in chapter 5. Participatory cultures afford new opportunities for young people to play active roles in their own ecologies, and that includes opportunities to co-create and co-design spaces that serve their unique needs. While I am critical of platforms that exploit and capitalize on young people's practices, I am cautiously optimistic of hybrid models that profit in ways that respect young people's preferences, expectations, and practices. But that can happen only if young people are equipped with the tools to create their own spaces and are empowered to view themselves as citizens and agents of change, rather than mere consumers or as vulnerable and passive victims.

When marginalized young people are empowered and trusted not only to create media but also to network, collaborate, deliberate, and organize within networked publics, the benefits are simultaneously individualized and collective. The opportunities require an approach to literacies that expands our constructions of young people beyond that of consumers to embrace understandings of young people as citizens. It must identify and acknowledge that all learning and media ecologies are not created equal, and that the experiences of marginalized young people demand attention and representation alongside their better-connected peers. Only when their stories are incorporated and validated can we begin to write policies that enhance equity and opportunity for all. This requires us to listen to, learn from, and value the perspectives of youth, to see their practices through a lens of survival, ingenuity, and creativity. Adults and institutions must value their expertise and unique generational practices rather than merely criticize or dismiss practices that we do not initially understand. Not until adults learn and respect the ways marginalized young people value media in their lives, the ways they make meaning out of their practices, and the ways they manage and negotiate risk and opportunity will adult institutions be able to implement policies and practices that truly serve their needs. This, of course, means relinquishing control and allowing young people to have opportunities to co-create spaces alongside and within educational institutions, policies, and law.

What Should We Be Worried About?

I am worried about the current generation of young people not merely as individuals, but as a collective population who are disadvantaged by current structural, material, and systematic inequalities. I am worried that fear is a driving force that aims to protect the privileged at the expense of the vulnerable. I am worried that we are creating systems that benefit some and disadvantage others. I fear that adult-controlled platforms undermine young people's practices in the name of profit. And I am alarmed that when we aim to control young people, we miss out on opportunities to instead guide teens as co-creators and fellow citizens. I know that we have work to do to bridge the gaps between young people's expectations and the realities of navigating current opportunities and future pathways.

In sum, I have tried to demonstrate that ultimately what we should be worried about are inequities related to *regulation, access, control, participation*, *visibility*, and *opportunity*. Although these concerns are inter-related and overlap, each has been given attention in its respective chapter. First, regulations (addressed in chapter 2) play a fundamental role in shaping practices. While I am critical of many of the policies that have attempted to regulate young people's online practices, I am not suggesting that all policies that regulate and protect minors are inherently negative. Instead, I am arguing for a more nuanced *evidence-based* approach that moves beyond sensational fear-based stories and panics about individualized risk. Policies must be written and enacted in such a way that they take into consideration the collective nature and responsibility of risk in networked media, and in such a way that they not only reflect the concerns of the market or the most privileged but also rely on research that investigates the unintended consequences that policies have for marginalized and disadvantaged populations. Such an approach brings me to my next two concerns: access and control.

Concerns about access (as addressed in chapter 3) are often couched in conversations about digital divides—that is, about who does and who doesn't have access to high-quality technology. Those concerns are valid, and although the gaps have been largely eradicated we know we still have work to do. However, I am concerned not only about access to *technology* (that is, hardware and software), but also about access to *content*—that is, about policies and rules that limit teens' access to online discursive spaces, learning ecologies, communities, and networked publics. I believe that we do young people a grave disservice when we make decisions about what is and is not valuable and educational on the basis of limited adult-centric understandings and values. I have tried to demonstrate that we should not block all potentially objectionable content at the expense of access to beneficial content. We must equip teens—and the adults in their lives—with tools and literacies for safely navigating potentially risky content.

Both regulation and access can be summed up as battles for control (as addressed in chapter 4). Certainly adults and adult institutions have a responsibility to protect young people. However, as has been demonstrated throughout this book, negotiations of control can operate alongside— rather than in opposition to—discourses of trust and responsibility. Without doubt many parents negotiate a balance between control and trust, and between constraint and responsibility with their children. In the same ways, schools must find ways to allow students opportunities to earn trust, responsibilities, and privileges so as to not only minimize harm but also maximize benefits. The argument then comes full circle to the role of policies that can empower institutions and equip schools, rather than exert control.

Further, as was addressed in part II of the book, I am concerned about unequal modes of participation, about structures that inhibit pathways to success, and about commercial platforms that fail to take into account young people's preferences and strategies for maintaining visibility and privacy. We have an obligation to marginalized young people to identify barriers that inhibit their capacity for developing the network, social, and digital literacies necessary for visibly participating in networked publics (as addressed in chapter 5). Schools must work alongside institutions, policies, and the industry to understand how to create more equitable pathways for opportunity, success, and upward mobility (addressed in chapter 7). And we have an obligation not only to help young people navigate unintentional and intentional visibility in networked publics, but to also listen to and validate their own preferences and practices, rather than dismiss or exploit them (examined in chapter 6). While it is heuristically beneficial to address each of these concerns individually, and to address the discourses of risk separate from opportunity-driven expectations, I have aimed to demonstrate the integral and symbiotic relationship between discourses of risk—that is, harm-driven expectations—and the lived experiences of youth. Only when we transfer our expectations from harm to opportunity— and expand our concern beyond the most privileged—can we begin to create just policies and equitable opportunities.

Looking Ahead

The risk industry is pervasive and it shapes expectations, but it can change. It is my hope that opportunity-driven expectations of both youth and technology will be driven by a deliberate dedication to creating a more just digital and material world for young people. Imagine if all the time, energy, and money spent passing restrictive policies were instead invested in creating platforms that enabled young people and educators to manage and navigate risks via other modes of regulation. Instead of primarily investing research funds in identifying the harms of digital media, we must invest more funds in understanding how platforms, education, curriculum, and opportunities can help young people explore, learn, cultivate, and invest in meaningful participation and the acquisition of greater social and cultural capital. Policy makers and educators must work together to develop policies and curriculum that enable, educate, and empower teachers to incorporate technology in innovative ways. Schools and parents need to help young people develop mutually beneficial social norms—norms of respect, of boundary setting, of healthy habits, of self-efficacy, and of critical awareness. These norms simultaneously reduce risk and enhance opportunities for civic engagement and beneficial online participation. Imagine what we could accomplish by working together—as researchers, policy makers, educators, and young people—to bridge divides between education and the industry in a way that helped create new pathways for young people to succeed. This takes work. It takes money. It takes a dedication to protect and empower those on the margins of society. But it benefits us all when we recognize that managing risk is not an individual responsibility, but a mutually beneficial collective goal and obligation.

Much of the research discussed in this book is critical of current systems, but I hope it is also encouraging. I believe that we can do better, and that we owe it to the next generation to do better, and I fully expect that we can create more equitable opportunities for young people. I was constantly impressed and inspired by the resourcefulness, imagination, and cleverness of the young people I got to know during this project. I want to be explicitly clear that their shortcomings were attributable to structures and systems that inhibited them from achieving their goals. When we as a society work together to create policies and practices that respect and value the experiences of young people—*all* young people—and embrace technology for the better, I expect we will begin to create more equitable opportunities and pathways for all young people. But this must be a deliberate and intentional goal—one that values democracy, justice, and equity above the myth of meritocracy, profit, and control.

Memories of many of the young people I met at Freeway High will stay with me for many years to come. I was struck by their passion, their creativity, and their talent, as well as by the ways in which they were able to exhibit these with and through digital media. I will remember Gabriela's beautiful images of downtown and Javier's short film that used a mime to reflect upon identity. I'll remember Selena playing her keyboard for me so I could hear the Evanescence songs she had taught herself. However, I will also remember my disappointment when Sergio told me he wasn't applying to college. I'll remember Jasmine telling me she only wanted to try for her associate's degree because she did not think getting a bachelor's degree would be possible for her. While I want to be cautious not to overly insert my own middle-class, highly educated, and white privileged values into my interpretations of their choices, I could not help but feel a bit of disappointment. Here were two talented, dedicated, passionate, and driven students who still did not think a four-year degree was attainable. But more so, they were ill-equipped to navigate career paths without the social benefits of a university degree. This speaks to institutional and systemic problems that are much more complex than the role of digital media in these teens' lives. Yet I cannot help but wonder how schools might better leverage the potential of digital media to create more equitable futures.

A truly networked classroom would embrace the opportunities and wealth of information afforded by digital media. With digital media, students have the power to take an active role in helping to create and mold learning environments. In other words, education can move beyond traditional models that rely on teacher-to-student transmission of knowledge. With the right tools and support, schools can instead equip and empower students to contribute to knowledge formation and discovery. Douglas Thomas and John Seely Brown (2011, p. 52) refer to this as a *collective learning environment*. They define collectives as "a collection of people, skills, and talent that produces a result greater than the sum of its parts. ... Collectives are not solely defined by shared intention, action, or purpose (though these elements may exist and often do). Rather, they are defined by an active engagement with the process of learning." Digital media provide students and teachers access to collectives of limitless knowledge that are not bound by physical or geographical constraints. Digital literacy education moves beyond merely teaching students how to use tools, but rather allows students to contribute to the learning processes. Networked classrooms could and should empower students to harness the wealth of information available to them via the Internet and mobile devices.

During my time at Freeway High, I met students who had created impressive online portfolios of their work and accomplishments, students who had created their own YouTube channels, and students who were harnessing the potential of digital media to create online professional identities. Yet, for the most part, these were more middle-class and college-bound students. They had the social and cultural capital outside of school to appreciate the significance of their online endeavors in a different context. What role should schools play in all of this? Beyond helping students create online portfolios or manage positive digital footprints, how else might schools create networked classrooms that integrate digital literacies into broader conceptualizations of citizenship? "If the potential of connection is to outweigh the appeal of disconnection in the future," Livingstone and Sefton-Green (2016, pp. 252–253) argue, "we must directly address the risk-averse fears and self-protective practices that stand in the way of rethinking society in the digital age."

For the teens in this book, career pathways were presented in a dichotomous manner (college pathways or vocational tracks) that erased the role society played in creating and limiting those options; there were significant disconnections between students' expectations and choices and the opportunities and realities of the labor market. In many ways, spaces such as the after-school clubs helped students legitimize their interests and practices in personally validating ways that valued self-expression and media production outside of the marketplace. However, at the same time, the practices and spaces were presented as pathways to career and economic opportunities that created the illusion of choices that were not readily accessible to marginalized students. As a society, we need to rethink the role of higher education as the preferred pathway to economic security, especially in light of rising tuition costs and the burden of student debt. Schools need to be acutely aware of the ways well-intentioned vocational tracks create expectations of opportunities that can actually exacerbate and reproduce the very inequalities they aim to alleviate. The connected learning model is a step in the right direction; it moves away from fear-based discourses that construe young people as passive and technology as a threat. But we need to carefully consider and continue to research how schools can connect young people to pathways for economic, social, and civic opportunities.

Social inequities far expand issues related to digital media and are indicative of greater systemic and historical problems within the education system and society writ large. Yet I believe that digital media tools and literacies can provide an opportunity for schools to contribute to learning, participation, and opportunities. It is my hope that this research identifies a need for schools, policies, and youth-serving organizations to rethink their role in shaping young people's media and learning ecologies. At the same time, I have tried to highlight teens' innovative, responsible, and creative digital media practices. Young people's digital media practices and cultures will continue to evolve outside of school; however, they should also continue to evolve alongside education. I was inspired by many of the students at Freeway High. I was also inspired and encouraged by teachers, such as Mr. Lopez, who was actively helping students explore opportunities and to push the boundaries of their current social and economic positions. I am confident that over time schools will continue to evolve, embrace change, and harness the potentials of digital media in order to create more equitable futures for students. Alongside other scholars, it is my goal to contribute to emerging research that will produce more productive and positive expectations about young people and digital media. But we have to stop worrying about risks as inherently harmful and instead embrace risky opportunities together.

Appendix A: Participants and Methodologies

This book came about as part of the Digital Edge project, led by Principal Investigator S. Craig Watkins. The Digital Edge is part of the Connected Learning Research Network and is supported by the John D. and Catherine T. MacArthur Foundation. Broadly speaking, the goal of The Digital Edge is to more fully understand teens' media ecologies, as well as the informal and formal learning environments in which they engage and interact. The research for this book was gathered as part of that project, along with the support of graduate students at the University of Texas: Andres Lombana Bermudez, Alexander Cho, Jennifer Noble, Vivian Shaw, and Adam Williams III.

It has been suggested that networked technologies provide new opportunities for learning, both in scope and nature, which provide opportunities for new skills, as well as compliment traditional modes of learning (Sefton-Green 2004). However, research demonstrates that it can be difficult to assess how teens are learning and what is being learned via new technologies. Quantitative approaches help map ownership and access but are less suited for contributing to more nuanced understandings of teens' motivation, skills, and learning with technologies. One way at understanding nuance and peculiarities is through in-depth qualitative approaches, which observe and build relationships with teens over a substantial amount of time. It is in this vein that this particular project enters into a growing body of research dedicated to assessing and contributing to a deeper understanding of how young people engage with digital technologies for the purpose, or with the outcome, of learning.

In accordance with a media ecologies framework, the researchers in this study conducted ethnographic research that utilized a multi-methodological approach intended to analyze how teens and schools incorporated digital media into their learning ecologies and everyday lives. The project was conducted throughout an entire academic year in order to build trusting relationships with the participants. Although the larger project addressed issues of risk to a certain degree (e.g., by asking teens about their perspectives and experiences with issues such as privacy and bullying), risk remained more peripheral to the overall Digital Edge project. Thus, this book is my distinct contribution to that project; it is unique in that it explicitly considers how policies, teens, and schools construct, manage, and negotiate risks associated with digital media and how expectations manage those risks. Because this book came out of a larger research study (The Digital Edge), I rely on data I personally collected as well as data collected from the entire research team.

The methodology, as will be further described, included qualitative in-depth one-on-one interviews (both unstructured and semi-structured) with students, parents/guardians, teachers, and mentors; focus groups in which several students participated; observations conducted in the after-school digital media clubs and in three elective technology classes; policy analyses related to media technologies; textual analysis of students' digital communication (Facebook, Tumblr, text messages, etc.); and participant-generated data contributions, such as journals, maps, and photos produced by the participants themselves. Together the data gathered through these different approaches provided an in-depth and nuanced understanding of the ways digital media functioned in participants' learning and media ecologies.

Recruitment of Participants

Mr. Lopez, the Tech Apps teacher and head of the Digital Media Club and the Cinematic Arts Project, initially helped recruit participants. He introduced us to students from his classes whom he thought might be interested in the project. We also held two recruitment meetings after school in order to explain the project goals and expected time commitment. We asked interested students to return the consent and assent forms (signed by a legal guardian) to Mr. Lopez. From there we used a snowball approach wherein we asked students if they had any friends whom they thought would like to participate. This allowed us to recruit diverse participants, some of whom were directly connected to the digital media classes and clubs, as well as friends who were less interested in digital media production. Because the participants shared their lives and stories with us, our "data" are really best described as collections of stories, which have informed the ethnography. As compensation for their time and commitment, participants received $150 in December and another $150 in May if they continued to participate.

Descriptions of Participants

The participants were 19 students between the ages of 14 and 19 years. Nine were female:

Gabriela—16 years old, Mexican-American
Jada—16 years old, black
Selena—17 years old, Mexican-American
Jasmine—16 years old, multiracial (black, white, and Native American)
Amina—17 years old, East African
Cassandra—18 years old, biracial (black and white)
Anna—18 years old, Mexican-American
Inara—17 years old, Mexican-American
Michelle—18 years old, biracial (black and white)

Ten were male:

Javier—18 years old, Mexican
Sergio—18 years old, Mexican-American
Identical twins Miguel and Marcus—14 years old, undocumented
    Mexican immigrants
Kyle—18 years old, white
Michael—18 years old, black
Antonio—17 years old, Mexican-American
Diego—16 years old, Mexican-American
Alberto—18 years old, Mexican-American
Jack—17 years old, white

We also worked with an alumnus of Freeway High who served as a mentor in the after-school clubs, Devan (19 years old, black). We conducted interviews with the principal and other teachers, but worked most closely with Mr. Lopez (the Tech Apps teacher and head of the Digital Media Club and the Cinematic Arts Project) and Mr. Warren (the Video Game Production teacher).

Interviews

Participants were matched with a member of the research team on the basis of common interests and similar demographics. For example, we typically matched female students with female researchers and when possible paired researchers and participants of similar ethnic identities and sexualities. Participants met one-on-one with a member from the research team on a weekly basis. The weekly meetings lasted between 30 and 60 minutes.

Meetings usually took place in a classroom, a hallway, or a lab after school. However, some weeks it was more convenient for students to meet at a coffee shop, in someone's home, or at a restaurant. Because of the transportation and time constraints some students faced, we were willing to meet them in a space that was accessible and comfortable for them. The weekly meetings were conducted from mid October 2011 through early May 2012. A few follow-up interviews via email were conducted a year or more after the completion of the project. One female participant (Selena) dropped out of the study in the spring, and one male participant (Michael) joined the study during the spring semester. However, all other participants met with their respective team members weekly over the entire course of the project. This allowed us time to build trust and a rapport with students.

Interviews provide personal accounts of media interactions, routines, and perspectives, which allow for individuals to discuss media within the broader context of their lives. Quality interviews privilege participants first as individuals within particular social structures and roles (families, workers, friends, parents, etc.), and audiences or users as a secondary role always already intersecting with other social positions (Yin 2009; Livingstone 2003). The project employed both semi-structured and unstructured styles of interviewing in order to analyze how teens, teachers, mentors, and parents/guardians thought about identity, family, school, media, technology, learning, and risk. These topics brought up many intersectionalities, such as race, gender, and class, which we also addressed accordingly. Individual members of the research team met one-on-one with respective students approximately once a week for about an hour at a time. I also casually hung out with participants who participated in the after-school clubs regularly (in addition to individual meetings).

For consistency and comparative purposes the team developed semi-structured, open-ended interview protocols, which were developed around particular topics (e.g., friends, family, school, social network sites, mobile phones, future plans, and so on). Alongside semi-structured, open-ended interviews, the study also designed time for unstructured interviews based on participants' personal interests, hobbies, activities, and passions. The semi-structured protocols provided a starting point for conversations with participants (and ensured the team was gathering similar information about participants), but conversations often deviated from the protocols in order to further discuss topics and interests that were uniquely related to respective participants. Unstructured interviews, on the other hand, were planned or spontaneous interviews that focused on a topic or theme related to respective participants. They did not follow a set of questions, nor were they applicable to all participants. Instead, they were as a way to further discuss or follow-up on particular topics that had come up in earlier interviews or observations.

For ethnography, data collection is an iterative process in which researchers constantly refine a hypothesis and "must go back and collect more cultural data, analyze it, formulate new hypotheses, and then repeat these stages over and over again" (Spradley 1979, p. 94). Thus, in both the semi-structured and the unstructured interviews the team used different question strategies to gather information and to clarify understandings of participants' responses. Drawing from Spradley (1979), different question strategies were employed, such as: descriptive questions (e.g., "Tell me about your after-school routine" or "What do you like about Tumblr?"), structural questions (i.e., asking participants to explain answers, asking the same question in different ways, and providing participants with context to get a more in-depth response), as well as contrast (and contrast clarifying) questions (e.g., "What is the difference between sending a text message and a Facebook message?" or "You seem to have implied your band friends are different from your film friends, if so, can you explain the differences to me?"). Because most interviews lasted about an hour, there was time to ask follow-up questions and visit topics that organically came up (these were in addition to questions from the semi-structured interview protocols we developed). The unstructured interviews occurred spontaneously, such as while walking to the interviewing room, but also emerged during semi-structured interviews. Often they were based on themes or topics which emerged between individual members of the research team and participants over the course of the study.

As an example, while reviewing field notes from semi-structured interviews related to home, school, and her friends, I noted that Jada often referenced an interest in fashion. In separate interviews she told me she enjoyed watching *E!* because of the fashion trends, she told me how her grandmother taught her how to sew, and how she joined the Business Club because of an interest in fashion merchandising. Thus, after reviewing my field notes related to Jada I discovered the importance of fashion in her life. In following semi-structured interview protocols I always tried to incorporate questions about fashion in order to understand how her interest in fashion was or was not related to other topics such as, her mobile phone and social media use, career goals, and peer relationships. Jada is just one example; for other participants I also found ways to incorporate questions related to their personal interests or experiences. According to Spradley

(1979), this mode of research is consistent with ethnographic studies. He contends that it is only after the researcher has gathered cultural data that she can begin to formulate a hypothesis (e.g., fashion was part of Jada's identity).

While the broader research questions driving the study focus on media, technology, and modes of learning and engagement, the interviews were structured in such a way as to get to know participants as students, sons/ daughters, friends, and peers (rather than merely as media producers/ consumers). That is, the first few protocols and meetings with participants focused on their school life, home life, friends, hobbies, general media use, and interests (i.e., not just media interests but also their participation with band or sports or their interest in fashion, cooking, etc.). Of course digital media were a part of these initial interviews, but mostly to the extent to which participants discussed media in relation to other aspects of their lives. Having established rapport and relationships with participants, later protocols more explicitly focused on (digital) media such as social network sites, video games, film production, and mobile technologies. In the course of eight months the team conducted more than 250 individual interviews with teen participants. Additionally, we also conducted several ad hoc spontaneous focus groups with groups of friends and two formal focus groups (one focused on their favorite media and media in the home and the other was only with senior participants as a way to discuss post-graduation plans).

Home Visits

The team conducted eighteen in-home interviews with at least one parent or guardian of the participants. The participants chose which parent or guardian they wanted us to interview, in some cases more than one parent or guardian was present. To the degree that parents/guardians were comfortable the interviews were conducted in English. However, three of the parent interviews were conducted in Spanish by a research team member who was a native Spanish speaker. The interviews helped gain a broader and deeper understanding of the participants' home life—socioeconomic status, living situation, parent/child interactions—as well as an opportunity to observe media in the home. To the degree to which participants' parents/ guardians were comfortable, individual team members also got tours of participants' homes and bedrooms, which allowed opportunities to further observe media (e.g. books, magazines) and technology in the home (e.g., placement, up-to-date equipment, number of computers/TVs, etc.). The interviews with parents or guardians lasted from about ninety minutes to two hours and focused on the parent or guardian's use of technology at home and work (when applicable) and attitudes about their child's use of technology at home and for school. We also asked questions about their thoughts on education in general, and Freeway High specifically, household regulation of technology, and the importance of media and technology to their child's future goals and plans.

School and After-School Observations

During the fall semester of 2011 the Digital Media Club met at least three times a week; at least one member of the research team observed the space almost every time the club met. During the fall semester I personally observed the club on a weekly basis, often just hanging out with members before or after I met up with participants for individual interviews. During the spring semester the club met more sporadically because of the film project. Nonetheless, I was on the Freeway campus at least once a week to observe the after-school space regardless if there were official meetings or not. This provided me with contextual information about how the spaces functioned, what the students were working on, and allowed me to more informally hang out with participants who were in the space. As a team, we attended a home football game on a Friday night. This was a way to understand the culture of the school (football is very important to high school life in Texas) and to observe several participants in the band, on the dance, team, and on the field. Some members of the team also attended a pep rally and film screening.

By being at the school regularly, I also had the chance to get to know some of the participants' friends who were also in the clubs, which provided me with contextual information about participants' peer groups and affiliations. Lastly, in order to contextualize what students told me during interviews, as well as to gain a more in-depth perspective of how digital media functioned at Freeway, I also observed Mr. Lopez's technology application class five times during the fall 2011 semester. This provided more insight into how the class was structured as well as allowed me to observe participants working on projects in a more formal learning environment. Throughout the book I draw from my personal fields notes in order to inform my analysis. At times, I also draw from the insights and field notes written up by other members of the Digital Edge team. Members of the team met regularly to compare notes, work on interview protocols, and discuss findings and queries. The frequent meetings and group interpretations were an integral aspect of the iterative nature of ethnography and have contributed to my analyses in this book.

Policy Analysis

In addition to participant data, I also conducted analyses of federal, state, and school policies. I traced the history of federal policies regulating Internet use in an American context and conducted a discursive analysis of the ways risk has been mobilized via federal policies that are related to the Internet and youth. I was primarily looking at how digital media and youth have been discursively constructed within policies. As part of my analysis, I considered the relationship between policies and digital literacies. Digital literacies are essential for combating and avoiding risky situations and encounters online (Livingstone, Haddon, Görzig, Ólafsson, et al. 2011). Therefore, in addition to federal policies I also analyzed Freeway High's Informational Technology (IT) policies and curriculum guidelines. I specifically focused on the ways Freeway High's policies and curriculum enable or inhibit students' and teachers' development of digital literacies. Freeway High's policy and curriculum analysis comes from reading the school district's policies, which included justifications for procedures and rules. Additionally, I drew from field notes based on conversations with Mr. Lopez and Mr. Warren. They informed my analysis since both teachers were in contact with members of the school board. Conversations with the teachers helped to contextualize the school's attitudes, understanding, and justification for its technology policies.

Digital Media Communication

In order to gain a more nuanced understanding of how participants utilized and engaged with digital technologies, they shared content from their personal digital communication with individual members of the team. For example, they walked team members through different aspects of their Facebook, such as their profiles and privacy settings. This allowed participants a chance to show what they liked and disliked about a particular site, how they used it, and with whom they communicated. It also allowed an opportunity to observe the language and aesthetic choices participants used on social media sites, as well as how they and their peers used different media and spaces. The communication and data shared during these sessions helped to situate technology and media within a broader context of participants' social and educational lives. It also provided insight into how participants interacted in such spaces and was used to generate more perceptive interview questions—in this way the method was an iterative process in which interviews, observations, and textual analysis were used to inform future protocols and interviews.

Taking a cue from collaborative ethnographic practices (Foley 2002) participants also generated data they shared with individual team members. For example, in order to show us other aspects of their lives participants took photos of their home, social, school, and work lives using a disposable camera that we provided for them. After we had the film developed, participants shared their photos and explained more about why they took the photos. They were also asked to keep a journal about their media use. This was not as successful as had hoped (in retrospect it was discovered that it felt too much like homework, so they were not enthusiastic about the project), but for those participants who did keep journals the accounts provided more insight into their media attitudes and use and provided a jumping off point for future interviews.

Coding and Analysis

With the permission of the students and their guardians, all of the semi-structured (and some of our unstructured) one-on-one interviews were recorded using small audio recorders. The recorders were about three inches long and were not obtrusive (could easily be placed on the other side of the table or even on an empty chair out of sight); we believe the presence of the recorders did not inhibit students' candidness or comfort disclosing information during recorded sessions. We did not find many discrepancies between what was said "on record" and what was said during non-recorded sessions; in other words, we do not have reason to believe the presence of the recorder significantly changed the nature of the interviews. Informal conversations were also recorded when hanging out in the after-school clubs (always with the consent of students). The team met regularly to share field notes, which were also stored and shared via a secure and private online site. Additionally, recorded interviews were conducted with mentors in the after-school clubs, as well as with the teachers, Mr. Lopez and Mr. Warren. The team used a professional transcription service to have all of the recorded interviews transcribed (this included interviews with participants, focus groups, teachers, and parents or guardians). With the exception of three parent interviews, which were conducted in Spanish, all of the interviews were transcribed in English.

To analyze transcripts and field notes, the team used an open access, cross platform application called Dedoose, which is designed for analyzing qualitative and multi-method research. All transcripts were uploaded to Dedoose, then excerpts were created and coded according to a code tree the research team collaboratively developed. The coding process was iterative and required a lot of tweaking as the project continued. The codes rendered data searchable and also allowed for easier identification of trends. Dedoose made it possible to search literally thousands of pages of transcripts in order to analyze data related to particular topics of interest for this book. Some of the codes that were used to pull data for this project included: risk, social network sites, mobile phones, peer networks, school, home life, media production, literacy, socio-economic status, and privacy.

Grounded Theory Approach

I analyzed data gathered from participants (i.e., interviews) in conjunction with my field notes, which were based on observations that were conducted in the formal learning environment, the after-school clubs, and participants' homes. The analysis is also greatly indebted to the invaluable input of the Digital Edge team. We met regularly to discuss findings and theories, which have intricately worked their way into my analysis in this book. Additionally, I want to acknowledge that what we as researchers call data, are really our constructions of other people's constructions of reality (Geertz 1973). Thus I hope that by including what Clifford Geertz refers to as "thick descriptions," I have provided context and depth for my analysis. I have largely employed a grounded theory approach to analysis insofar as the trends, hypotheses, and findings emerged over the course of the eight-month study and were used to develop theories. This is in contrast to approaches that initially develop and test hypotheses, which are determined before the research is conducted. Charmaz (2006, p. 2) writes: "Stated simply, grounded theory methods consist of systematic, yet flexible guidelines for collecting and analyzing qualitative data to construct theories 'grounded' in the data themselves. ... Data form the foundation of our theory and our analysis of these data generates the concepts we construct." As was mentioned, ethnography is an iterative process in which hypotheses must be constantly revisited and refined. For that reason, my analysis involved reading, coding, and analyzing initial interviews and field notes and then identifying emergent themes and trends. From there I often went back to participants—and other members of the research team—to "test" the hypotheses, that is, to check that what I thought I had identified matched the participants' (and other researchers') perspectives.

Grounded theory as a method emerged from Barney Glaser and Anselm Strauss (1967), two sociologists who studied dying patients in hospitals. My method of analysis draws from the Glaser and Strauss insofar as I engaged in simultaneous data collection and analysis, constructed analytical codes and categories for data (that were not derived from preconceived deduced hypotheses), and the majority of my literature review developed alongside and after analysis. As a team, our analysis relied on early coding of transcripts and field notes in order to inform questions. Because my overall emphasis is on risk as a social construct, throughout the entire process I employed discursive analysis to understand how risks were mobilized and enacted via policies and schools, as well as the ways participants negotiated and resisted risk (discourses).

In order to get at these large questions of risk, I drew from Yin (2009) in that I started with small questions based on emerging themes and codes and then gathered data which addressed those questions. From there I repeated the process in order to develop broader questions which were the focus of each chapter. The analysis is presented from a theory-building approach (ibid.) in which each chapter contributes to a part of the theoretical argument being made about risk, regulation, teens, and digital media.

Validity

I spent approximately an hour a week with these young people on a one-to-one basis, consequently I developed a highly personal, and at times intimate, relationship them. One criticism of qualitative interviewing as a method, especially with young people, is the concern that they will want to please the researchers, that is, that they will answer questions how they think the researcher wants them to answer (Mitchell 2002). I would like to note that I do not have reason to believe this was the case with the participants in this study. During our time together they were open and at times chose to make themselves vulnerable. This was true of the teens I worked with, and the teens that worked with other members of the research team. They often shared information beyond what was asked or expected; they did not always present themselves in the best light, but rather appeared candid and honest in interviews.

Furthermore, I have reason to believe that participants confirmed the trustworthiness of their relationships with me. Gabriela explicitly told me: "I don't usually like talking about myself, adults just say 'Oh, how are you?'

and I don't know what to say. But with you it's different. I like specific questions, and it's fun to talk to you." Similarly, Jasmine once said: "I don't trust most adults; well I don't mean you, of course." During weeks when we were unable to meet, the students were often the ones to text me and ask when we could meet again. They were respectful of my time as I strived to be of theirs. At the end of the study participants remarked how much they had enjoyed our meetings and asked to stay in touch with me. I share this as evidence of the intimate and trusted relationship I developed with participants, which I hope bears credence to the validity of my data and analysis.

Lastly, one of the challenging, yet dynamic aspects of ethnography is the degree to which everything is always evolving. During my time with these young people they experienced many changes, including breakups, new living situations, moves, new jobs, changes in access to technology, and changes in aspirations and career paths. Within ethnography there is a tendency to want to create a linear narrative around participants' identities and experiences—but again, the data here is really a collection of ever evolving stories that participants shared over time. As a disclaimer, I want to note that their lives were constantly changing, along with how they constructed their identities. I have tried to provide context when necessary so as to provide a clearer and more nuanced picture of their lives, identities, and experiences.

Appendix B: Theorizing Risk

In this book I am less concerned with identifying, quantifying, and calculating the risks young people encounter online, but rather my focus is on *how* risks and anxieties are constructed and mobilized within society; thus it is important that I explain what is meant by the concept risk. The notion of risk is used to describe a lot of different behaviors, practices, and situations from the mundane to the serious. If you start to pay attention you realize how often we interject concepts of risk into our everyday lives to the extent that they often fade into the background. For example, we may leave for work early on a rainy day because traffic will be slow and we do not want to "risk being late," we may drive slower because we do not want to "risk getting into an accident," and of course we all wear seatbelts to "reduce our risk of injury" in the event we do get into an accident. This simple example demonstrates how our lives are regulated through an awareness of risk as well as the different nodes which contribute to regulation: self-regulation based on experiences (e.g., leaving early so we are not late), expert opinions and data (e.g., statistical data demonstrates rain increases the likelihood of a car accident), and institutional enforcement through laws and policies (e.g., the state requires drivers to wear a seatbelt). For that reason, the meaning and the regulation of risk must be historically and contextually situated.

The meaning of the word "risk" has changed throughout history. Most commentators link the concept of risk with pre-modern maritime ventures related to dangers associated with sea voyages. "At that time," according to Luhmann (1993, p. 226), "risk designated the possibility of an objective danger, an act of God, a force majeure, a tempest or other peril of the sea that could not be imputed to wrongful conduct." In this way risk was considered to be something beyond human control and therefore outside of human blame or responsibility. However, changes in meanings of risk accompany the emergence of modernity towards the end of the seventeenth century and gaining momentum in the eighteenth century.

Modernist notions of risk are often associated with models of insurance based on probabilities and chance in which risks can be "good" (i.e., gain) or bad" (i.e., loss) (Douglas 1992). However, by the end of the twentieth century notions of risk as neutral—that is, with the potential for good and bad outcomes—tend to be lost. According to Lupton (1999, p. 8), "Risk is now generally used to relate only to negative or undesirable outcomes, not positive outcomes. ... In everyday lay people's language, risk tends to be used to refer almost exclusively to a threat, hazard, danger or harm." Lupton goes on to note that probability is less important in colloquial uses of risk. In fact we tend to conflate notions of risk and uncertainty and employ notions of risk to describe unfortunate events even when the probability of harm is not likely or even estimable. Lupton and others (Short 1984; Douglas 1985, Skolbekken 1995) suggest the proliferation of risk in expert discourses has contributed to an increased awareness and adaption of risk in society.

What society determines is a risk and what, where, and who gets labeled as "risky" have significant implications for how we think about identity, ourselves, others, institutions, and governments. For the purpose of this book it is important to consider how technology and youth are constructed as risk and of what consequence. There are different epistemological and theoretical approaches to studying and conceptualizing risk. On one end of the epistemological continuum is the cognitive scientific perspective commonly found in fields such as engineering, statistics, psychology, and economics. This approach views risks as objectively identifiable threats or hazards that can be measured independently of social and cultural processes (Bradbury 1989). Researchers taking up this approach ask key questions such as "what risks exist and how should we manage them?" While they acknowledge risks sometimes get distorted or biased through social frameworks (often blaming lay people's biased or misunderstood perception), this approach fails to ask how risks get constructed in the first place. (Lupton 1999).

Sociocultural Approaches

A sociocultural perspective of risk emphasizes what is omitted from a cognitive scientific approach: the social and cultural contexts in which risk is understood and negotiated. This approach has been adopted in disciplines such as cultural anthropology, philosophy, sociology, and technology

studies. Within the sociocultural perspective there are (at least) three primary approaches: cultural/symbolic, "risk society," and governmentality
theorists who draw from Foucault's theories. The first two, cultural/symbolic
and "risk society," are associated with a weak constructionist perspective
which recognizes risk as an objective hazard or threat that is inevitably
mediated through social and cultural processes (and can never be known in
isolation from these processes). The cultural/symbolic approach (largely
influenced by the work of the anthropologist Mary Douglas) focuses on
how notions of risk delineate boundaries between self and Other. Important questions include "Why are some dangers selected as risks and others
are not? How does risk operate as a symbolic boundary measure?" and
"What is the situated context of risk?" (Lupton 1999, p. 35).

Also drawing from the weak constructionist perspective is the "risk
society" approach associated with the sociologists Anthony Giddens
(1991) and Ulrich Beck (1992), who build on Marxist critical theory.
Beck (p. 21) defines risk as "a systematic way of dealing with hazards and
insecurities induced and introduced by modernization itself." He continues: "In the risk society the unknown and unintended consequences come
to be a dominant force in history and society. They can be changed, mag-
nified, dramatized or minimized within knowledge, and to that extent
they are particularly open to social definition and construction." This
approach has been taken up by media scholars and sociologists studying
youth, the Internet, and risks. For example, in her influential book *Children and the Internet*, Sonia Livingstone (2009) applies three aspects of the
risk society—the identification, intensification, and individualization of
risk—to studying the relationship between media, policy, children, and
the Internet.

The Governmentality Approach

A third approach, and the one I largely draw from to structure my research,
applies Foucault's (1991) perspective of governmentality to notions of risk.
Research employing this perspective argues that what we understand to be
a risk is always already historically, socially, and politically constructed.
According to Lupton (1999, p. 114), Foucauldian perspectives focus on "the
ways in which the discourses, strategies, practices and institutions around a
phenomenon such as risk serve to bring it into being, to construct it as a
phenomenon. It is argued that it is only through these discourses, strategies, practices and institutions that we come to know risk." Thus the key
question is not what risk is or how it is identified and measured, but rather

how is risk constructed in a particular context and at a particular historical moment?

Governmentality can be viewed as institutions which (attempt to) regulate citizens' interaction with and relationship to potentially harmful or undesirable incidents (i.e., risks). Like Beck and Giddens, Foucault also believes expert knowledge plays an important role in shaping the ways in which populations are surveyed, compared and trained to conform to social norms. Disciplinary power and regulation is achieved through surveillance, monitoring, observation, and measurement of bodies and subjects. "From this perspective," Lupton writes (1999, p. 87), "risk may be understood as a governmental strategy of regulatory power by which populations and individuals are monitored and managed through the goals of neo-liberalism. Risk is governed via a heterogeneous network of interactive actors, institutions, knowledges and practices." It is easy to observe the role of governmentality in the lives of children and teens. Institutions readily monitor, surveil, test, compare, and train youth populations; such practices are justified within neoliberal goals of self-regulation and productivity. Thus my approach is to understand the ways risks are constructed and mobilized as a regulatory force in young people's digital lives.

Notes

Introduction

1. The story continued with the creation of a fake blog called "Megan Had It Coming." The blog turned out to be a hoax authored by trolls. See Vickery 2008 for more information.

2. Pseudonyms are used to protect the privacy of all the participants in this book.

3. *Minecraft* is a popular computer game that allows players to build three-dimensional constructions out of blocks. Within the game players can explore, gather resources, and engage in combat with other players. The game has different modes (e.g., survival, creative, adventure, and spectacular) and involves many different characters, worlds, and quests. Players can also generate their own content and create maps for other players to download.

4. This is known as *cultivation theory*. It states that "massive exposure to television's reconstructed realities can result in perceptions of reality very different from what they might be if viewers watched less television" (Cohen and Weimann 2000, p. 99). For more information about the origins of cultivation theory, see Gerbner and Gross 1976.

5. Season 10, episode 6, November 11, 2008.

6. See appendix B for a fuller discussion of how risk is theorized.

7. This can be due to restricted access, to supervision and surveillance that discourages messing around, play, or to learning via experimentation, as well as to an increased focus on completing tasks (paying bills, looking for jobs, reading local news, etc.), rather than leisurely activities (Jenkins et al. 2006). There are also cultural variables, such as research that has found that libraries are often male-centric spaces in which women may not feel comfortable (Straubhaar et al. 2012).

8. Such as the incompatibility between Flash media and the iPhone.

9. For more on participatory cultures, see chapter 5 and Jenkins et al. 2009.

10. See appendix A for further explanation of the methodologies and analysis.

11. The Principal Investigator of the Digital Edge project is S. Craig Watkins. I was a member of the research team that conducted the ethnographic research. Our team spanned three disciplines—media studies, sociology, and information studies—and was made up of myself, Andres Lombana Bermudez, Alexander Cho, Jennifer Noble, Vivian Shaw, and Adam Williams III, all of whom were at the University of Texas at Austin at the time of data collection. Broadly speaking, the goal of the project is to more fully understand teens' media ecologies and the informal and formal learning environments in which they engage and interact. The project focused on families, students, and a high school facing significant social, familial, financial, and educational instabilities and challenges, thus it addresses issues of digital and educational equity. While risks were a peripheral aspect of The Digital Edge project, my unique contribution specifically focuses on the role of risk and other regulatory constraints in structuring teens' digital media practices and opportunities. This project was supported and funded by the John D. and Catherine T. MacArthur Foundation as part of the collaborative Connected Learning Research Network (CLRN), an interdisciplinary and international research network "dedicated to understanding the opportunities and risks afforded by today's changing media ecology, as well as building new learning environments that support effective learning and education equity" (Connected Learning Research Network 2012).

12. Hanna, Rohm, and Crittenden (2011, p. 271) go so far as to refer to Web 1.0 as a "passive model." In discussing Web 2.0, they emphasize how traditional media brands can capitalize on the participation of "consumers" rather than as users or citizens.

13. Ellison and boyd explain (and I concur) that "'social network sites' is more accurate than 'social networks' (which is a sociological term of one's social relationships), 'social networking' (which evokes a practice of actively seeking connections and also happens offline), 'online social networks' (one's online connections more generally) or 'social networking sites (which emphasized connecting to new people)" (2013, p. 158). They emphasize the "role of the network (as a noun) as opposed to the practice of networking (as a verb)" (ibid., p. 159).

14. Nextdoor is a website and app that allows neighbors to privately connect online for the purpose of discussing and sharing information pertinent to their neighborhood.

Chapter 1

1. For fuller discussions, see the introduction to Rainie and Wellman 2012, chapter 1 of McChesney 2013, and Marvin 1988.

2. Mods and rockers were two opposing youth subcultures in Britain in the 1960s whose identities were structured around musical genres. Rockers favored rock 'n' roll; mods favored soul, R&B, or ska.

3. The notion that a generation can be defined by its use of technology has been criticized for being technologically deterministic. See Buckingham 2006.

Chapter 2

1. See boyd 2014; Cassell and Cramer 2008; Clark 2012; Finkelhor 2011; Livingstone 2008; Livingstone, Haddon, Gorzig, and Ólafsson 2011; Madden et al. 2013; Watkins 2009.

2. See appendix B.

3. "Obscenity" is difficult to legally define, but is determined by whether the work depicts or describes, in a patently offensive way, sexual conduct or excretory functions specifically defined by applicable state law, and whether the work, taken as a whole, lacks serious literary, artistic, political, or scientific value. "Pornography" is a more limited term; it refers to the erotic content of books, magazines, films, and recordings. Obscenity includes pornography, but may also include nude dancing, sexually oriented commercial telephone messages, and scatological comedy routines. US courts have had difficulty determining what is obscene. This problem has serious implications: if an act or an item is deemed obscene, it is not protected by the First Amendment; however, indecent and erotic materials are granted legal protection.

4. Free speech includes both the right to speak and the right to have access to speech. Denying access to content via censorship has historically been considered a violation of the First Amendment rights.

5. Usenet was a network for the discussion of particular topics and the sharing of files via newsgroups. Bulletin-board systems were a pre-World Wide Web form of communication in which users could upload images and files to "bulletin boards" for other users to download and view.

6. One reason, for example, is that Rimm's sample only included self-proclaimed "adult" BBSs (which required proof of age and a credit card payment) and a select group of Usenet newsgroups. In addition to a non-representative sample, Hoffman and Novak (1995) argue the study was misleading because Rimm did not disclose how he counted images or classified "pornography" (for example, in a data table he labeled supermodels as pornographic). Post (1995) points out that Usenet groups totaled 11.5 percent of Internet traffic at the time of the study and only 3 percent were associated with newsgroups containing pornographic imagery. He more accurately concluded that less than 0.5 percent (3 percent of 11.5 percent) of messages on the Internet were associated with newsgroups that contained pornography (and many of the messages in these "pornographic" newsgroups were text files that may not accurately be classified as sexually explicit). Although we do not have such data about sexual explicitness in the remaining 88.5 percent of the non-Usenet traffic on the Internet, it is fair to say that only a small percentage of pornographic imagery, relative to non-pornographic content, was available in the Usenet

newsgroups, which account for only a small percentage of the overall Internet (Mullin 1996).

7. For a detailed account of how the Rimm Study fueled a porn panic, see Mike Godwin's 2003 book *Cyber Rights: Defending Free Speech in the Digital Age*.

8. This double standard of allowing images of male nipples but not images of female nipples is still enacted within various social media policies today, including those of Instagram (Kleeman 2015) and Facebook (Esco 2014).

9. Kuipers (2006) compared Internet regulation in the United States with that in the Netherlands and found that the US was more likely to enforce legal regulations that restricted minors' access. The Netherlands adopted normative community standards, which were enforced by social norms, by parents, and via educational curriculum and initiatives. This is an example of the ways in which technologies are socially constructed and regulated in different ways. In the US, sexual content is regulated by law, although such regulation often competes with values such as free speech. In the Netherlands, the value of free speech outweighs heavy legal regulation, and protection takes the form of education, parental responsibility, and normative community standards of practice.

10. The MPAA is an example of an industry regulating itself through a voluntary rating system: films are rated G, PG, PG-13, and R on the basis of content. This is in lieu of government regulation, which is complicated by protections of speech. Similarly, the television industry self-regulates through the technological implementation of the v-chip, which enables parents to block shows they deem objectionable or inappropriate. Both of these are examples of industry self-regulation rather than direct government regulation and laws.

11. *To Catch a Predator* was a reality-style television series, hosted by Chris Hansen, that aired as a segment of the program *NBC Dateline* from 2004 to 2007. It also aired in the United Kingdom, in Australia, in New Zealand, and in Portugal. A spinoff book by Chris Hansen, titled *To Catch a Predator: Protecting Your Kids from Online Enemies Already in Your Home*, was published in 2007.

12. Mobile phones in particular allow children a way to get out of threatening situations and allow parents a way to more quickly get in touch with their children if something goes wrong. Other factors leading to a decline in missing children is more aggressive searches for and prosecution and supervision of predators (also enhanced by technology), as well as response systems such as the Amber Alert (also enhanced by the availability of technology). He also notes that technology changes the way kids take risks (more likely online at home than in public); this puts more distance between children and strangers who are looking to harm a child.

13. This is merely a correlational relationship, and we cannot attribute a decrease in crimes to the Internet. Other social and educational programs aimed at curbing risky behaviors are likely contributors. The point is merely to demonstrate the

disproportionate and inverse relationship that as crimes and risky behaviors have decreased, fears about the Internet exacerbating risk have increased.

14. The Protecting Children Act also addressed continuing concerns about pornography by amending the Communications Act of 1934 to prevent video service providers from offering child pornography.

15. The coining of the term "cyberbullying" is often credited to Bill Belsey, a Canadian educator and anti-bullying activist who founded the website cyberbullying.ca (Bauman 2011). Belsey claims to have coined the term after moderating a bullying prevention site in which youth specifically discussed online bullying. But according to the *Oxford English Dictionary* the term was coined by Christopher Bantick in 1998 in an article published in the *Canberra Times* (Bauman 2011). Research by Sheri Bauman (2011) reveals that the word was first used in 1995 in a *New York Times* article about cyberaddiction. The word appears to have originated organically and simultaneously in different places, but it was consistently used to describe harassment or bullying that took place in online spaces. The term began generating attention among youth scholars, educators, and within the medical community around 2006, which is when it began to enter public conversation and discourse (ibid.). Hindjua and Patchin (2009) coined the term "cyberbullicide" to refer to cyberbullying that leads to suicide.

16. For discussions of post-structuralism, power, and language, see Barthes 1972; Eco 1976; Foucault 1970.

17. Forty-six of the fifty states had passed anti-bullying laws by 2010. The exceptions were Hawaii, Michigan, South Dakota, and Montana (Baumann 2015).

18. See *Tinker v. Des Moines Independent Community School District* (1969), which ruled that students' speech rights could be restricted only if they "substantially interfered with the work of the school or impinged upon the rights of other students." *Bethel School District v. Fraser* (1986) found that schools could censor vulgar and offensive language when it "undermined the school's basic educational mission" (p. 684). *Morse v. Frederick* (2007) banned a student's speech at an off-campus event sponsored by the school. The latter "effectively expanded school authority beyond the campus to outside events sanctioned by the school, thereby continuing the post-*Tinker* trend of limiting student speech rights" (King 2010, p. 869).

19. Lori Drew was originally convicted of "misuse" of computer technology under the Computer Fraud and Abuse Act. The conviction was later overturned (Steinhauer 2008; Zetter 2009).

20. For a few examples, see Bluestein and Turner 2012; Stein 2010; Thevenot 2014. This was also the plot of a 2012 Lifetime movie titled *Sexting in Suburbia*, in which a mom took legal action against her daughter's school after her daughter killed herself as a result of bullying.

21. The 2009 Student Internet Safety Act should not be confused with the Internet Safety Act of the same year, which proposed that all ISPs and Wi-Fi providers, public and private, keep records and make them available to the police for at least two years.

22. Sexting first reached the attention of the general public in 2009, when a scandal in rural Pennsylvania made national news (Searcey 2009) and was the subject of a 2012 Lifetime show titled "My Life is a Lifetime Movie" (Baker 2012). Around that time, CosmoGirl.com and the National Campaign to Prevent Teen and Unplanned Pregnancy conducted a survey of teen sexting that falsely linked sexting to the risk of pregnancy (Sex and Tech 2008).

23. This case is particularly complex and widespread. For a detailed account and analysis, see *The Atlantic*'s article "Why Kids Sext" (Rosin 2014).

24. Via state laws regulating age of sexual consent.

25. Examples include the invasive procedures welfare recipients are subjected to, stop-and-frisk laws that target people of color, and electronic surveillance and monitoring of former prisoners.

Chapter 3

1. 101 pregnancies per 1,000 girls, whereas the national rate is 84 (Bridges 2008).

2. 62 births per 1,000 girls ages 15–19, whereas the national rate is 41 (Bridges 2008).

3. This can result in what is known as the "echo chamber" effect. It is both intentional (we seek out information that supports our beliefs) and unintentional (search engines and social network sites use algorithms to learn our preferences and show us results that support our perceived beliefs). See Pariser 2011 for more information about the "filter bubble" and Sunstein 2009 for more information about "echo chambers."

4. For more information on how information spreads (or "goes viral") online, see Jenkins, Ford, and Green 2013 or Nahon and Hemsley 2013.

5. I deliberately omit his name here so as not to further link his name to this false accusation.

6. The analysis for this section relies on an analysis of district wide policies that were made available to me by Freeway's principal and in interviews with teachers and students. CSD is a pseudonym.

7. The exception to this was the Tech Apps teacher, Mr. Lopez, whose students noted he often encouraged them to look information up online using resources,

such as Google. Mr. Lopez's courses and approach are discussed in greater detail in later chapters.

8. See appendix A for more detailed information about participants' ethnic identities.

9. For other advanced search tips, see Widder 2014 and Rheingold 2012.

10. The Children's Online Privacy Protection Act prohibits the collection of data for the purpose of advertisements for children under the age of 13, but does not protect older students, such as the participants in this study.

11. We did not speak with every student or teacher at Freeway High. It is possible that some classes were going online together to learn about and contribute to conversations about racial injustice. However, our conversations with students and teachers didn't seem to indicate that that had been done.

Chapter 4

1. In interviews, several parents complained about having to leave work to come to school to get their child's phone, which the parent wanted the child to have so as to be in contact after school.

2. See appendix A for more detailed information about students' ethnic identities.

3. After the 1999 Columbine High School shooting and the attacks of 9/11, parents urged schools to lift restrictions that completely banned students from bringing mobile devices to school (Trump 2009).

4. For examples of the coverage this study received and some of the misleading headlines that appeared, see Doward 2015; Kottasova 2015; Mobile phone bans lead … 2015; Singal 2015; Mobile phone bans "improve" … 2015; Taibi 2015; Barnwell 2016.

5. Of course, this app is also problematically ripe for enticing students as consumers so it can track their preferences and collect their data for marketing purposes.

6. "FOMO" dates back to 2000 but didn't come into widespread vernacular use until about ten years later (Schreckinger 2014).

7. There is a lot of controversy and debate about the effects of television on physical health. Although some dated studies (many of them conducted under technologically determinist assumptions) show a negative correlation between more television watching and less healthy lifestyles (Dietz and Gortmaker 1985; Robinson 1999), most doctors agree that television is merely one factor that can potentially influence health. Other variables, including income, geography, ethnicity, changes in urban transportation, genetics, access to healthy affordable food, and education level

significantly influence the physical health of children and teens (Anderson and Butcher 2006; Childhood obesity causes, n.d.; Maes, Neale, and Eaves 1997).

8. For more on the shifting norms of mobile phone etiquette in public, see Rainie and Zickuhr 2015.

9. See the introduction for further discussion of Ito et al.'s (2010) interest-driven and friendship-driven genres of participation.

10. See, for example, "Bored kids, busy parents" (http://www.parentfurther.com. php53-8.dfw1-2.websitetestlink.com/resources/enewsletter/archive/bored-busy); "Boredom" (https://www.positivediscipline.com/articles/boredom); "11 survival tips for summer boredom" (http://fun.familyeducation.com/slideshow/activities/66335.html); "Ideas for bored kids" (https://www.pinterest.com/ksilvan/ideas-for-bored-kids/); "I'm bored: How to deal with your child's boredom" (http://www.handinhandparenting.org/article/im-bored-how-to-deal-with-your-childs-boredom/); "How to deal with a bored kid" (http://time.com/3919836/parenting-bored-children/).

Chapter 5

1. For a further explanation of how participatory culture and commercial culture work in tandem, see Wesch 2008.

2. Founded in 2000, DeviantArt is an online community that showcases various forms of user-made artwork and provides a platform for artists to discuss and critique work. It also includes resources such as tutorials, journals, and portfolios. As of 2013, the site had more than 25 million users and more than 246 million submissions.

3. E! (the Entertainment Network) and BET (the Black Entertainment Network) both feature celebrity news and gossip, red-carpet events, celebrity interviews, and talk shows.

4. The rapper Drake was popular with students at Freeway at the time of the study.

5. On the hybrid economies that emerge in participatory cultures between bottom-up amateur media makers and top-down corporate commercial media cultures, see Jenkins, Ford, and Green 2013.

6. Throughout this chapter I intentionally avoid referring to their creative media content and projects as "work." This is a deliberate strategy intended to resist market-driven approaches and values to young people's media production.

7. Here I intentionally make an exception and use the word "work," rather than "projects," "productions," or "creative media content," to draw attention to the labor involved in media creations.

Chapter 6

1. A judge dismissed the suit against the school district, but upheld the lawsuit against the individual administrator who found and shared the photo. At the time of writing, it is unclear what the outcome of the suit was.

2. For more about the psychology of identity, see Goffman 1959.

3. This may seem similar to the Georgia high school example I criticized. However, it is important to note that I only use the public profile pictures of the friends and do not share any information that is kept behind privacy walls (that would otherwise only be visible to friends). Facebook users typically choose a profile picture knowing it is visible to strangers and is accessible to anyone regardless of friend status. Additionally, Facebook users can control who can view their friends; if a user hides their friends then they are never included in this experiment. I only take screen grabs from friends who have made their entire friend list public. I also include a screen grab of twelve of my own friends, thus rendering myself equally as vulnerable in this experiment. Further, I do not reveal the name or identity of my friend and my goal is not to shame or embarrass. I am comfortable that I have not shared information or photos that breach contextual integrity of a public profile picture.

4. Starting in April 2010, users could Like information on sites outside of Facebook. This means that "when the user clicks the Like button on a site, a story appears in the user's friends' News Feed with a link back to the website" ("Like Button," Facebook Developers, May 2011). For example, if you Liked an article about college football on ESPN's website, a link to the article on ESPN's website would appear in your friends' news feeds with a caption that you had Liked the article. You did not have to deliberately post the article to your Facebook for your friends to know you had Liked it. From your friends' perspective, it appeared as though you had intentionally re-shared the article through your Facebook feed.

5. Public is the default for "Pages," which are typically representative of an organization or group, rather than an individual; but it is an option for individuals and individual posts.

Chapter 7

1. The term *habitus* refers to individuals' construction of class dispositions, histories, schemata, and perspectives. See Bourdieu 1990 for more on the relationship between habitus, taste, and class dispositions.

2. Freeway High offered twenty AP courses, and approximately 25 percent of students took at least one AP course, but only 10 percent took an AP math course. Approximately 5 percent of students were in a Gifted/Talented program.

3. A full discussion of how the tracks at Freeway High supported future pathways to success, or not, is outside the scope of this project. For more information about this topic, see Watkins et al. 2017.

4. Much has been written about the role and value of after-school activities, particularly in the lives of marginalized students. See Daud and Carruthers 2008; Newman et al. 2000; Nicholson, Collins, and Holmer 2004; Rhodes 2004; Shann 2001.

5. After my time in the field, I followed up with the school district. I was informed that the state of Texas was re-working its pathways to include more technology-focused and design-focused options that would fit within a college-bound track, but that they would not be implemented for several years.

6. For further explanation, see the introduction to this book.

7. See Ito et al. 2010 for more about "messing around" as a mode of learning.

8. In her research on YouTube and youth, Patricia Lange offers a critique and further investigation of the "self-taught" narrative espoused by many of the participants in her study. Although young people often articulate and believe that they have taught themselves how to create and edit media, Lange noted that over time participants contradicted themselves by acknowledging the role of parents, peers, and teachers in helping them learn new skills and literacies. She makes the case that even "self-taught" learning happens through "socially encoded forms of knowledge" (2014, p. 191), such as online tutorials and instruction manuals. Further, young people use the term "self-taught" to refer to any form of knowledge acquisition that takes place outside of school and formal learning, thus often overlooking the other modes of informal learning that have contributed to their knowledge and skills.

9. The Scholastic Aptitude Test is required for admission to most colleges in the US.

10. The Free Application for Federal Student Aid is an application for college grants and scholarships from the federal government.

11. In a follow-up interview almost a year later, Jack expressed an interest in attending a top-ranked public university to major in business or finance; he seemed to have lost interest in filmmaking entirely.

12. The one exception seemed to be band, in which several members of the media clubs were also involved.

13. Harlem Shake was a video meme in which people replicated short comedic videos that were accompanied by the song "Harlem Shake." It spread quickly, thousands of videos being uploaded to YouTube every day at the height of its popularity in 2013 (Wood 2013).

14. For more about the assimilation trajectories of creative immigrant young people, see Bermudez 2015.

15. At one point, Gabriela's father expressed concern that she was hanging out with the "wrong kind of Mexicans." This caused strife between Gabriela and her father for a time. However, after getting in trouble with her new group of friends at a party, Gabriela reconnected with her former friends. She negotiated her Mexican-American identity in many different ways. For example, she preferred to listen to traditional Mexican music, which her father hated because he associated it with drugs, gangs, violence, and high school dropouts. After exploring different peer groups, Gabriela explained that she actually felt more comfortable around her upwardly mobile and assimilated (immigrant) peers. She was learning how to negotiate her identity in many different ways and sought the advice of her father regularly.

16. *Goth* (short for "gothic") describes a subculture and fashion style marked by dark clothing and makeup (for males and females), often with a fascination for morbid interest and styles.

17. *Chola* is a slang word used to stereotypically describe people in the US of Latin American descent, usually Mexican, who are low-income, tough, and often associated with gangs. It often refers to fashion—dark red lip liner, dark eye makeup, piercings, lots of gold jewelry, straightened and gelled, hair, and so forth (Calderon-Douglass 2015). To my knowledge, Selena's mother was not associated with a gang; rather, Selena was referring to her mother's identification with the fashion subculture.

18. "Tatted up" means "covered in tattoos."

19. Evanescence is a popular American rock band featuring a female lead pianist and singer, Amy Lee.

20. Full disclosure: After the home visit I gave Selena an old mouse I no longer needed.

References

Abernathy, J. 1995. Net censorship: Alternatives gain momentum. *PC World* 13 (9): 54–55.

Ahuja, M. 2013. Teens are spending more time consuming media, on mobile devices. *Washington Post*, March 13. https://www.washingtonpost.com/postlive/teens-are-spending-more-time-consuming-media-on-mobile-devices/2013/03/12/309bb242-8689-11e2-98a3-b3db6b9ac586_story.html

Ally, M., ed. 2009. *Mobile Learning: Transforming the Delivery of Education and Training*. AU Press.

Anderson, D. R. 1998. Educational television is not an oxymoron. *Annals of the American Academy of Political and Social Science* 557 (1): 24–38.

Anderson, P. M., and K. F. Butcher. 2006. Childhood obesity: Trends and potential causes. *Future of Children* 16 (1): 19–45.

Armstrong, C., and S. I. Fontaine. 1989. The power of naming: Names that create and define the discipline. *WPA: Writing Program Administration* 13 (1–2): 5–14.

Attwood, F. 2002. Reading porn: The paradigm shift in pornography research. *Sexualities* 5 (1): 91–105.

Aufderheide, P. 1997. Media literacy: From a report of the national leadership conference on media literacy. In *Media Literacy in the Information Age*, ed. R. Kubey. Transaction.

Azzam, A. M. 2007. Why students drop out. *Educational Leadership* 64 (7): 91–93.

Bagenstos, S. R. 2013. Employment law and social equality. *Michigan Law Review* 112 (2).

Baker, P. 2001. Moral panic and alternative identity construction in Usenet. *Journal of Computer-Mediated Communication* 7 (1).

Baker, R. L. 2012. Tunhannock "sexting" scandal to air on Lifetime TV tonight. *Times Tribune*, November 28. http://thetimes-tribune.com/news/tunhannock-sexting-scandal-to-air-on-lifetime-tv-tonight-1.1409387

Barnard, J. 2015. Internet use to drive 1.4% increase in media consumption in 2015. http://www.zenithoptimedia.com/internet-use-drive-1-4-increase-media-consumption-2015/

Barnes, S. 2006. A privacy paradox: Social networking in the United States. *First Monday* 11 (9). http://firstmonday.org/article/view/1394/1312.

Barnes, S. 2014. The 50 best "ripped from the headlines" *Law & Order* episodes, ranked.   http://flavorwire.com/484828/the-50-best-ripped-from-the-headlines-law-order-episodes-ranked

Barnwell, P. 2016. Do smartphones have a place in the classroom? *The Atlantic*, April 27.   http://www.theatlantic.com/education/archive/2016/04/do-smartphones-have-a-place-in-the-classroom/480231/

Barthes, R. 1972. *Mythologies*. Hill and Wang.

Bauman, Z. 1991. *Modernity and Ambivalence*. Polity Press.

Bauman, S. 2011. *Cyberbullying: What Counselors Need to Know*. American Counseling Association.

Baumann, L. 2015. Gov. Bullock signs Montana anti-bullying bill into law. *Great Falls Tribune*, April 21. http://www.greatfallstribune.com/story/news/local/2015/04/21/gov-bullock-signs-montana-anti-bullying-bill-law/26145567/

Bawden, D. 2008. Origins and Concepts of Digital Literacy. In *Digital Literacies: Concepts, Policies, and Practices*, ed. C. Lankshear and M. Knobel. Peter Lang.

Bawden, D., and L. Robinson. 2009. The dark side of information: Overload, anxiety and other paradoxes and pathologies. *Journal of Information Science* 35 (2): 180–191.

Baym, N. 2010. *Personal Connections in the Digital Age*. Polity Press.

Beck, U. 1992. *Risk Society: Towards a New Modernity*. SAGE.

Begos, J. D. 1987. The diaries of adolescent girls. *Women's Studies International Forum* 10 (1): 69–74.

Beland, L., and R. Murphy. 2015. Ill Communication: Technology, Distraction & Student Performance. Discussion Paper No 1350, Centre for Economic Performance Education and Skills Programme. http://cep.lse.ac.uk/pubs/download/dp1350.pdf

Bell, V. 2010. Don't touch that dial!: A history of media technology scares, from the printing press to Facebook. http://www.slate.com/articles/health_and_science/science/2010/02/dont_touch_that_dial.html

Bennet, W. L., C. Wells, and D. Freelon. 2011. Communicating civic engagement: Contrasting models of citizenship in the youth Web sphere. *Journal of Communication* 61: 835–856.

Bennett, S., K. Maton, and L. Kervin. 2008. The "digital natives" debate: A critical review of the evidence. *British Journal of Educational Technology* 39 (5): 775–786.

Bethel School District v. Fraser, 478 U.S. 675, 677–78 (1986).

Belton, T., and E. Priyadharshini. 2007. Boredom and schooling: A cross-disciplinary exploration. *Cambridge Journal of Education* 37 (4): 579–595.

Berman, J. 2002. Statement. http://www.copacommission.org/report/statements/berman.shtml

Bermudez, A. A. L. 2015. Networked and Disconnected: Latino/Hispanic Immigrant Youths, Digital Media, and Assimilation into the U.S. Doctoral dissertation, University of Texas.

Billieuz, J., M. Van der Linden, M. D. D'Acremon, G. Ceschi, and A. Zermatten. 2007. Does impulsivity relate to perceived dependence on and actual use of the mobile phone? *Applied Cognitive Psychology* 21: 527–537.

Bissler, D. L., and J. L. Conners, eds. 2012. *The Harms of Crime Media: Essays on the Perpetuation of Racism, Sexism and Class Stereotypes*. McFarland.

Blackburn, B. 2016. Malfunctioning heater leads to Fort Worth toddler's death. WFAA TV, Dallas. http://www.wfaa.com/news/local/tarrant-county/malfunctioning-heater-leads-to-fort-worth-toddlers-death/187970848

Bloustein, G. 2003. *Girl Making: A Cross-Cultural Ethnography on the Process of Growing Up Female*. Berghahn Books.

Bluestein, G., and D. Turner. 2012. School cyberbullying victims fight back in lawsuits. *HuffPost Education*, April 26. http://www.huffingtonpost.com/2012/04/26/school-cyberbullying-vict_n_1457918.html

Borland, J. 2003. RIAA sues 261 file swappers. http://www.cnet.com/news/riaa-sues-261-file-swappers/

Botelho, G. 2012. *Seventeen* magazine vows not to alter images, to "celebrate every kind of beauty." CNN, July 6. http://www.cnn.com/2012/07/05/us/seventeen-photoshopping/

Bourdieu, P. 1990. *The Logic of Practice*. Stanford University Press.

Boyar, R., D. Levine, and N. Zensius. 2011. *TECHsex USA: Youth Sexuality and Reproductive Health in the Digital Age*. ISIS, Inc.

boyd, d. 2007a. Why youth heart social network sites: the role of networked publics in teenage social life. In *Youth, Identity, and Digital Media*, ed. D. Buckingham. MIT Press.

boyd, d. 2007b. Information access in a networked world. http://www.danah.org/papers/talks/Pearson2007.html

boyd, d. 2008. Facebook's "privacy trainwreck": Exposure, invasion, and social convergence. *Convergence* 14 (1): 13–20.

boyd, d. 2010a. Social network sites as networked publics: Affordances, dynamics, and implications. In *A Networked Self: Identity, Community, and Culture on Social Network Sites*, ed. Z. Papacharissi. Routledge.

boyd, d. 2010b. Privacy, publicity, and visibility. http://www.danah.org/papers/talks/2010/TechFest2010.html

boyd, d. 2011. White flight in networked publics? How race and class shaped American teen engagement with MySpace and Facebook. In *Race After the Internet*, ed. L. Nakamura and P. Chow-Whit. Routledge.

boyd, d. 2014. *It's Complicated: The Social Lives of Networked Teens*. Yale University Press.

boyd, d., and N. Ellison. 2007. Social network sites: Definition, history, and scholarship. *Journal of Computer-Mediated Communication* 13 (2): 210–230.

Bradbury, J. 1989. The policy implications of differing concepts of risk. *Science, Technology & Human Values* 14 (4): 380–399.

Brader, A., and A. Luke. 2013. Reengaging marginalized youth through digital music production: Performance, audience and evaluation. *Pedagogies* 8 (3): 197–214.

Bridges, E. 2008. Texas' youth: focus on sexual and reproductive health. http://www.advocatesforyouth.org/publications/publications-a-z/641-texas-youth-focus-on-sexual-and-reproductive-health.

Broderick, R. 2013. 9 teenage suicides in the last year were linked to cyber-bullying on social network Ask.fm. BuzzFeed News. http://www.buzzfeed.com/ryanhatesthis/a-ninth-teenager-since-last-september-has-committed-suicide#.bd9MKQmrj

Brody, J. E. 2015. Screen addiction is taking a toll on children. http://well.blogs.nytimes.com/2015/07/06/screen-addiction-is-taking-a-toll-on-children/?_r=0

Brosseau, K. 2013. Cell phone addictions cause anxiety and stress. KFVS TV, Cape Girardeau, Missouri. http://www.kfvs12.com/story/23419627/cell-phone-addictions-cause-anxiety-and-stress

Brown, J. D., J. R. Steele, and K. Walsh-Childers, eds. 2011. *Sexual Teens, Sexual Media: Investigating Media's Influence on Adolescent Sexuality*. Routledge.

Bruce, C. 1997. *The Seven Faces of Information Literacy*. Auslib.

Bryant, C. 2010. Adolescence, pornography, and harm. *Youth Studies Australia* 29 (1): 18–26.

Bryner, J. 2014. Teen sexting still rampant, study reveals. Live Science. http://www.livescience.com/20955-teen-sexting-prevalence.html

Buckingham, D. 1993. *Children Talking Television: The Making of Television Literacy.* Falmer.

Buckingham, D. 2003. *Media Education: Literacy, Learning, and Contemporary Culture.* Polity Press.

Buckingham, D. 2006. Is there a digital generation? In *Digital Generations: Children, Young people, and New Media,* ed. D. Buckingham and R. Willett. Erlbaum.

Buckingham, D. 2007. Digital media literacies: Rethinking media education in the age of the Internet. *Research in Comparative and International Education* 2: 43–55.

Buckingham, D. 2008. Introducing identity. In *Youth, Identity, and Digital Media,* ed. D. Buckingham. MIT Press.

Bullock, H. E., K. F. Wyche, and W. R. Williams. 2002. Media images of the poor. *Journal of Social Issues* 57 (2): 229–246.

Bullying and LGBT Youth. 2009. Report for Mental Health America. http://www .mentalhealthamerica.net/bullying-and-gay-youth

Burchell, G. 1996. Liberal government and techniques of the self. In *Foucault and Political Reason: Liberalism, Neo-Liberalism and Rationalities of Government,* ed. A. Barry, T. Osborne, and N. Rose. UCL Press.

Burgress, J., and J. Green. 2009. *YouTube.* Polity Press.

Burkus, D. 2014. The creative benefits of boredom. *Harvard Business Review,* September 9. https://hbr.org/2014/09/the-creative-benefits-of-boredom/

Burns, A. 2008. Select issues with new media theories of citizen journalism. *Media/ Culture Journal* 11 (1). http://journal.media-culture.org.au/index.php/mcjournal/ article/viewArticle/30

Butler, J. 1990. *Gender Trouble.* Routledge.

Calderón-Douglass, B. 2015. The folk feminist struggle behind chola fashion trends. *Vice,* April 13. http://www.vice.com/read/the-history-of-the-chola-456

Campbell, S. W., and Y. S. Park. 2008. Social implications of mobile telephony: The rise of personal communication society. *Sociology Compass* 2 (2): 371–387.

Carey, J. W. 1989. *Communication as Culture: Essays on Media and Society.* Unwin Hyman.

Carral, H. L. 2015. Stop saying technology is causing social isolation. *HuffPost Tech.* http://www.huffingtonpost.com/hector-l-carral/stop-saying-technology-is-causing -social-isolation_b_8425688.html

Carter, P. 2003. "Black" cultural capital, status positioning, and schooling conflicts for low-income African American youth. *Social Problems* 50 (1): 136–155.

Carter, S. P., K. Greenberg, and M. Walker. 2016. The Impact of Computer Usage on Academic Performance: Evidence from a Randomized Trial at the United States Military Academy. Working Paper 2016.02, School Effectiveness & Inequality Initiative, National Bureau of Economic Research.

Cassell, J., and M. Cramer. 2008. High tech or high risk: Moral panics about girls online. In *Digital Youth, Innovation, and the Unexpected*, ed. T. McPherson. MIT Press.

Castel, Robert. 1991. From dangerousness to risk. In *The Foucault Effect: Studies in Governmentality*, ed. G. Burchell, C. Gordon, and P. Miller. Harvester Wheatsheaf.

Castells, M. 2007. *Mobile Communication and Society*. MIT Press.

Catalano, R. F., K. P. Haggerty, S. Oesterle, C. B. Fleming, and D. Hawkins. 2004. The importance of bonding to school for healthy development: Findings from the Social Development Research Group. *Journal of School Health* 74 (7): 252–261.

Charmaz, K. 2006. *Constructing Grounded Theory: A Practical Guide through Qualitative Analysis*. SAGE.

Chau, C. 2010. YouTube as a Participatory Culture. *New Directions for Youth Development* (128), winter: 65–74.

Chemaly, S. 2014. There's no comparing male and female harassment online. *Time* September 9. http://time.com/3305466/male-female-harassment-online/

Childhood obesity causes and consequences. n.d. Centers for Disease Control and Prevention, Washington. http://www.cdc.gov/obesity/childhood/causes.html

Children's Internet Protection Act (2000).

Child Online Protection Act (1998).

Clark, L. S. 2013. *The Parent App: Understanding Families in the Digital Age*. Oxford University Press.

Cobb, S. 1976. Social support as a moderator of life stress. *Psychosomatic Medicine* 38 (5): 300–314.

Cohen, S. 1972. *Folk Devils and Moral Panics: Creation of Mods and Rockers*. Paladin.

Cohen, P., and P. Ainley. 2000. In the country of the blind?: Youth studies and cultural studies in Britain. *Journal of Youth Studies* 3 (1): 79–85.

Cohen, J., and N. Solomon. 1995. How *Time* magazine promoted a cyberhoax. *Media Beat,* July 19. http://www.fair.org/media-beat/950719.html

Cohen, J., and G. Weimann. 2000. Cultivation revisited: Some genres have some effects on some viewers. *Communication Reports* 13 (2): 99–114.

Collins, M. C. 2009. Ripped from the headlines: The use of real crime in *Law & Order* episodes. *Journal of the Institute of Justice and International Studies* 9: 88–97.

Common Sense census: Media use by tweens and teens. 2010. Common Sense Media. https://www.commonsensemedia.org/research/the-common-sense-census -media-use-by-tweens-and-teens

Communications Decency Act. 1996. Title V of the Telecommunications Act of 1996.

Congressional Record. 2009. Proceedings and Debates of the 111th Congress, 1st Session, Issue: Vol. 155, No. 89, June 15. https://www.congress.gov/crec/2009/06/15/ CREC-2009-06-15.pdf

Cooper, A., and E. L. Smith. 2011. Homicide Trends in the United States, 1980-2008. U.S. Department of Justice, Office of Justice Programs, Bureau of Justice Statistics. http://www.bjs.gov/content/pub/pdf/htus8008.pdf

Cramer, M., and G. R. Hayes. 2010. Acceptable use of technology in school: Risks, policies, and promises. *Pervasive Computing* 9 (3): 37–44.

Culp-Ressler, T. 2013. Abstinence-only course in Texas tells kids that having sex makes them like a chewed-up piece of gum. *Think Progress*. http://thinkprogress.org/ health/2013/11/07/2910611/texas-sex-chewed-gum/

Daud, R., and C. Carruthers. 2008. Outcome study of an after-school program for youth in a high-risk environment. *Journal of Parks and Recreation Administration* 26 (2): 95–114.

David-Ferdon, C., and M. F. Hertz. 2007. Electronic media, violence, and adolescents: An emerging public health problem. *Journal of Adolescent Health* 41 (6 suppl. 1): S1–S5.

Dawes, N. P., and R. Larson. 2011. How youth get engaged: Grounded-theory research on motivational development in organized youth programs. *Developmental Psychology* 47 (1): 259–269.

de Certeau, M. 1984. *The Practice of Everyday Life*. University of California Press.

de Souza e Silva, A., and J. Frith. 2012. *Mobile Interfaces In Public Spaces: Locational Privacy, Control, and Urban Sociability*. Routledge.

Dean, M. 1997. Sociology after society. In *Sociology after Postmodernism*, ed. D. Owen. SAGE.

Dean, M. 1999. Risk, calculable and incalculable. In *Risk and Sociocultural Theory: New Directions and Perspectives*, ed. D. Lupton. Cambridge University Press.

Deleting Online Predators Act. 2006.

DesMarais, C. 2012. Facebook likes cause embarrassing posts. *Techlicious*, July 18. http://www.techlicious.com/blog/facebook-may-be-posting-controversial-messages -on-your-behalf/.

Dietz, W. H., Jr., and S. L. Gortmaker. 1985. Do we fatten our children at the television set? Obesity and television viewing in children and adolescents. *Pediatrics* 75 (5): 807–812.

DiMaggio, P., E. Hargittai, C. Celeste, and S. Shafer. 2004. Digital inequality: From unequal access to differentiated use. In *Social Inequality*, ed. K. Neckerman. Russell Sage Foundation.

Diversity in Media Ownership. 2015. Free Press. http://www.freepress.net/diversity-media-ownership

Dixon, T. L., and K. B. Maddox. 2005. Skin tone, crime news, and social reality judgements: Priming the stereotype of the dark and dangerous black criminal. *Journal of Applied Social Psychology* 35 (8): 1555–1570.

Dodson, L., R. Albelda, D. S. Coronado, and M. Mtshali. 2012. *How Youth Are Put at Risk by Parents' Low-Wage Jobs*. Center for Social Policy, University of Massachusetts.

Dominick, J. R. 1999. Who do you think you are? Personal home pages and self-presentation on the World Wide Web. *Journalism & Mass Communication Quarterly* 76 (4): 646–658.

Donlin, M. 2011. The Protecting Children in the 21st Century Act, a re-introduction. *Inside the School*, November 9. http://www.insidetheschool.com/articles/the-protecting-children-in-the-21st-century-act-%E2%80%93-a-re-introduction/

Doward, J. 2015. Schools that ban mobile phones see better academic results. *The Guardian*, May 16. http://www.theguardian.com/education/2015/may/16/schools-mobile-phones-academic-results

Douglas, M. 1985. *Risk Acceptability According to the Social Sciences*. Russell Sage Foundation.

Douglas, M. 1992. *Risk and Blame: Essays in Cultural Theory*. Routledge.

Drunk Driving Prevention. 1983. http://www.adcouncil.org/Our-Campaigns/The-Classics/Drunk-Driving-Prevention

Duggan, M. 2014. Online harassment. Pew Research Center. http://www.pewinternet.org/2014/10/22/part-1-experiencing-online-harassment/

Earnheardt, A. C., and P. M. Haridakis. 2008. Exploring fandom and motives for viewing televised sports. In *Sports Mania: Essays on Fandom in the 21st Century*, ed. L. Hugenberg, P. Haridakis, and A. Earnheardt. McFarland.

Eco, U. 1976. *A Theory of Semiotics*. Indiana University Press.

Ehrlich, B. 2013. Trayvon Martin: How social media became the biggest protest. MTV News, July 15. http://www.mtv.com/news/1710582/trayvon-martin-social-media-protest/

Eisenberg, M. E., L. H. Bearinger, R. E. Sieving, C. Swain, and M. D. Resnick. 2004. Parents' beliefs about condoms and oral contraceptives: Are they medically accurate? *Perspectives on Sexual and Reproductive Health* 36 (2): 50–57.

Eisenstein, E. 1983. *The Printing Revolution in Early Modern Europe*. Cambridge University Press.

Eiserei, T. 2015. How predators use online games to lure children. WFAA TV, Dallas, July 24. http://www.wfaa.com/story/news/crime/2015/07/22/predators-using-online -games-to-lure-children/30549729/

Elkind, D. 2007. *The Hurried Child: Growing Up Too Fast Too Soon*, 25th Anniversary Edition. Da Capo.

Ellison, N. B., and d. boyd. 2013. Sociality through social network sites. In *The Oxford Handbook of Internet Studies*, ed. W. Dutton. Oxford University Press.

Elmer-DeWitt, P. 1995. On a screen near you: Cyberporn. *Time*, July 3: 38–45.

Elmer-Dewitt, P. 2015. Finding Marty Rimm. *Fortune*, July 1. http://fortune .com/2015/07/01/cyberporn-time-marty-rimm/.

Esco, L. 2014. Facebook wages war on the nipple. *Huffington Post Entertainment*. http://www.huffingtonpost.com/lina-esco/facebook-war-on-nipples_b _4548832.html.

Ewald, F. 1991. Insurance and risk. In *The Foucault Effect*, ed. G. Burchell, C. Gordon and P. Miller. University of Chicago Press.

FCC Releases Order Updating Children's Internet Protection Act. 2011. *Funds for Learning*, August 17. http://www.fundsforlearning.com/release/2011/08/fcc-releases -order-updating-children%E2%80%99s-internet-protection-act

Fabos, B. 2004. *Wrong Turn on the Information Superhighway: Education and the Commercialization of the Internet*. Teachers College Press.

Facebook Newsroom. 2015. http://newsroom.fb.com/company-info/.

Faith, M. S., N. Berman, M. Heo, A. Pietrobelli, D. Gallagher, L. H. Epstein, M. T. Eiden, and D. B. Allison. 2001. Effects of contingent television on physical activity and television viewing in obese children. *Pediatrics* 107 (5): 1043–1048.

Fass, P. 1977. *The Damned and the Beautiful: American Youth in the 1920's*. Oxford University Press.

Felipe, J. P. 2015. Put down your damn cell phones. *Inside Higher Ed*. https:// www.insidehighered.com/views/2015/12/21/colleges-need-teach-healthy-digital -boundaries-essay?utm_content=buffera74b3&utm_medium=social&utm_source =facebook&utm_campaign=IHEbuffer

Fernandes-Alcantara, A. L. 2013. Runaway and Homeless Youth: Demographics and Programs. *Congressional Research Service (CRS) Report for Congress* . http://www.nchcw .org/uploads/7/5/3/3/7533556/crs_2013_rhya_history_and_lit_review.pdf

Ferry, B. 2009. Using mobile phones to enhance teacher learning in environmental education. In *New Technologies, New Pedagogies: Mobile Learning in Higher Education*, ed. J. Herrington et al. Faculty of Education, University of Wollongong.

Festinger, L. 1957. *A Theory of Cognitive Dissonance*. Stanford University Press.

Fields, L. 2014. Police bust Virginia sexting ring involving more than 100 teens. ABC News, April 5. http://abcnews.go.com/US/police-bust-virginia-sexting-ring-involving -100-teens/story?id=23208357

Finkelhor, D. 2011. The Internet, Youth Safety, and the Problem of "Juvenoia". Report published by Crimes Against Children Research Center. http://www.unh.edu/ ccrc/pdf/Juvenoia%20paper.pdf.

Finkelhor, D. 2013. Five myths about missing children. *Washington Post*, May 10. https://www.washingtonpost.com/opinions/five-myths-about-missing-children/ 2013/05/10/efee398c-b8b4-11e2-aa9e-a02b765ff0ea_story.html

Finn, J. D., and D. A. Rock. 1997. Academic success among students at risk for school failure. *Journal of Applied Psychology* 82 (2): 221–234.

Fiore, F. 2011. Teen Makes Digital Record of Arlington Graves. *Los Angeles Times*, April 26. http://articles.latimes.com/2011/apr/26/nation/la-na-arlington-graves -20110427

Firestone, L. 2012. Is Social Media to Blame for the Rise in Narcissism? Huffington Post. http://www.huffingtonpost.com/lisa-firestone/facebook-narcissism_b_1905073 .html

Fisch, S. M. 2004. *Children's Learning from Educational Television: Sesame Street and Beyond*. Routledge.

Foley, D. E. 2002. Critical ethnography: The reflexive turn. *International Journal of Qualitative Studies in Education* 15 (5): 469–490.

Foucault, M. 1970. *The Order of Things*. Vintage.

Foucault, M. 1980. *Power/Knowledge*. Harvester.

Foucault, M. 1991. Governmentality (lecture given at the College de France in February 1978). In *The Foucault Effect: Studies in Governmentality*, ed. G. Burchell, C. Gordon and P. Miller. University of Chicago Press.

Fox, N. J. 1999. Postmodern reflections on "risk," "hazards," and life choice. In *Risk and Sociocultural Theory: New Directions and Perspectives*, ed. D. Lupton. Cambridge University Press.

Franks, M. A. 2015. Privacy and Privilege. Presentation at International Congress on Privacy, University of Passau, Germany.

Frechette, J. 2006. Cyber-censorship or cyber-literacy? Envisioning cyber-learning through media education. In *Digital Generations*, ed. D. Buckingham and R. Willett. Erlbaum.

Freedland, J. 2013. From Memory to Sexuality, the Digital Age Is Changing Us Completely. *The Guardian*, June 21. http://www.theguardian.com/commentisfree/2013/jun/21/memory-sexuality-digital-age-changing-human

Friedersdor, C. 2014. Working mom arrested for letting her 9-year-old play alone at park. *The Atlantic*. http://www.theatlantic.com/national/archive/2014/07/arrested-for-letting-a-9-year-old-play-at-the-park-alone/374436/

Fueyo, J. M. 1988. Technical Literacy versus Critical Literacy in Adult Basic Education. *Journal of Education* 170 (1): 107–118.

Gabriel, F. 2013. *Deconstructing Youth: Youth Discourses at the Limits of Sense*. Palgrave Macmillan.

Gabriel, F. 2014. Sexting, Selfies and Self-Harm: Young people, social media and the performance of self-development. *Media International Australia* (151): 104–112.

Garty, L. 2016. Online friendships "equally as potent" for teenagers, Murdoch Uni researcher finds. ABC News, May 3. http://www.abc.net.au/news/2016-05-03/online-friends-equally-potent-teenagers-murdoch-university-study/7380810

Gasper, K., and B. L. Middlewood. 2007. Approaching novel thoughts: Understanding why elation and boredom promote associative thought more than distress and relaxation. *Journal of Experimental Social Psychology* 52: 50–57.

Geertz, C. 1973. *The Interpretation of Cultures: Selected Essays*. Basic Books.

Gerbner, G., and L. Gross. 1976. Living with television: The violence profile. *Journal of Communication* 26: 173–199.

German, M. 2005. Behind the lone terrorists, a pack mentality. *Washington Post*. http://www.washingtonpost.com/wp-dyn/content/article/2005/06/04/AR2005060400147.html.

Giddens, A. 1991. *The Consequences of Modernity*. Stanford University Press.

Gilens, M. 1996. Race and poverty in America: Public misperceptions and the American news media. *Public Opinion Quarterly* 60 (4): 515–541.

Gilliom, J. 2001. *Overseers of the Poor*. University of Chicago Press.

Gilmor, D. 2008. Principles for a New Media Literacy. Media Re: Public, Side Papers. Berkman Center for Internet and Society at Harvard University. http://

cyber.law.harvard.edu/sites/cyber.law.harvard.edu/files/Principles%20for%20a%20
New%20Media%20Literacy_MR.pdf

Girous, H. A. 1996. *Fugitive Cultures: Race, Violence, and Youth.* Routledge.

Giroux, H. A. 2000. *Stealing Innocence: Corporate Culture's War on Children.* Palgrave.

Giroux, H. A. 2009. *Youth in a Suspect Society: Democracy or Disposability?* Palgrave Macmillan.

Giroux, H. A. 2015. Selfie culture in the age of corporate and state surveillance. *Third Text* 29 (3): 155–164.

Giroux, H. A., and A. N. Penna. 1979. Social education in the classroom: The dynamics of the hidden curriculum. *Theory and Research in Social Education* 7 (1): 21–42.

Gladwell, M. 2000. *The Tipping Point: How Little Things Can Make A Big Difference.* Little, Brown.

Glaser, B. G., and A. L. Strauss. 1967. *The Discovery of Grounded Theory.* Aldine.

Godwin, M. 2003. *Cyber Rights: Defending Free Speech in the Digital Age.* MIT Press.

Goffman, E. 1959. *The Presentation of Self in Everyday Life.* Anchor Books.

González, T. 2012. Keeping Kids in Schools: Restorative Justice, Punitive Discipline, and the School to Prison Pipeline. *Journal of Law & Education* 41 (2): 282–335.

Goodenow, C., and K. E. Grady. 1993. The relationship of school belonging and friends' values to academic motivation among urban adolescent students. *Journal of Experimental Education* 62 (1): 60–71.

Google CEO on privacy. 2010. *Huffington Post,* March 18. http://www.huffingtonpost
.com/2009/12/07/google-ceo-on-privacy-if_n_383105.html

Goldstein, A. 2002. Like a sieve: The Child Internet Protection Act and ineffective filters in libraries. *Fordham Intellectual Property, Media and Entertainment Law Journal* 12 (4): 1187–1202.

Goodson, I., and J. M. Mangan. 1996. Computer Literacy as Ideology. *British Journal of Sociology of Education* 17 (1): 65–79.

Gottfried, A. E., J. S. Fleming, and A. W. Gottfried. 1998. Role of cognitively stimulating home environment in children', academic intrinsic motivation: A longitudinal study. *Child Development* 69: 1148–1460.

Graeff, E., M. Stempeck, and E. Zuckerman. 2014. The battle of "Trayvon Martin": Mapping a media controversy online and off-line. *First Monday* 19 (2). http://firstmonday.org/article/view/4947/3821

Gray, H. 1995. *Watching Race: Television and the Struggle for Blackness.* University of Minnesota Press.

Gray, M. L. 2009. *Out in the Country: Youth, Media, and Queer Visibility in Rural America*. NYU Press.

Green, N. 2003. Outwardly Mobile: Young People and Mobile Technologies. In *Machines That Become Us: The Social Context of Personal Communication Technology*, ed. J. Katz. Transaction.

Gregoire, C. 2015. Study links selfies to narcissism and psychopathy. *HuffPost Science*, January 12. http://www.huffingtonpost.com/2015/01/12/selfies-narcissism -psychopathy_n_6429358.html

Grillo, G. 2015. The advertising industry needs diverse leadership to thrive. *Advertising Age*, April 23. http://adage.com/article/agency-viewpoint/advertising-industry -diverse-leadership-thrive/297998/

Gurak, L. J. 2001. *Cyberliteracy: Navigating the Internet with Awareness*. Yale University Press.

Gutierrez, K., P. Z. Morales, and D. C. Martinez. 2009. Re-mediating literacy: Culture, difference, and learning for students from nondominant communities. *Review of Research in Education* 33: 213–245.

Hall, G. S. 1904. *Adolescence*. Appleton.

Hall, L. 2015. I gave my students iPads—then wished I could take them back. *Washington Post*. https://www.washingtonpost.com/opinions/i-gave-my-students -ipads--then-wished-i-could-take-them-back/2015/12/02/a1bc8272-818f-11e5-a7c a-6ab6ec20f839_story.html

Hanna, R., A. Rohm, and V. L. Crittenden. 2011. We're all connected: The power of the social media ecosystem. *Business Horizons* 54: 265–273.

Hargittai, E., and G. Walejko. 2008. The participation divide: Content creation and sharing in the digital age. *Information Communication and Society* 11 (2): 239–256.

Harlan, M. A., C. Bruce, and M. Lupton. 2012. Teen content creators: Experiences of using information to learn. *Library Trends* 60 (3): 569–587.

Hall, S. 1997. The work of representation. In *Representation: Cultural Representations AND Signifying Practice*, ed. S. Hall. SAGE.

Harvard Alcohol Project. 1988. Center for Health Communication. Harvard School of Public Health. http://www.hsph.harvard.edu/chc/harvard-alcohol-project/

Hasinoff, A. A. 2012. Should teens have the right to sext? Privacy, consent, and social media. In *Communication in Question: Competing Perspectives on Controversial Issues in Communication Studies*, ed. J. Greenberg and C. Elliot. Thomson Nelson.

Hasinoff, A. A. 2015. *Sexting Panic: Rethinking Criminalization, Privacy, and Consent*. University of Illinois Press.

Hastings, K. 2009. Teenager commits suicide after 'sexting' a nude photo to her boyfriend made her life a misery. *Daily Mail*. http://www.dailymail.co.uk/tvshowbiz/article-1161112/Teenager-commits-suicide-sexting-nude-photo-boyfriend-life-misery.html

Hebdige, Dick. 1979. *Subculture: The Meaning of Style*. Routledge.

Heid, M. 2014. You Asked: Is Hot Yoga Good for You—and for Weight Loss? *Time* 9 (July). http://time.com/2967716/you-asked-is-hot-yoga-good-for-you-and-for-weight-loss/

Heins, M. 2001. Not. In *Front of the Children: "Indecency," Censorship, and the Innocence of Youth*. Hill & Wang.

Hemp, P. 2009. Death by Information Overload. *Harvard Business Review*. https://hbr.org/2009/09/death-by-information-overload

Henley, J. 2013. Are teenagers really careless about privacy online? The Guardian, October 21. http://www.theguardian.com/technology/2013/oct/21/teenagers-careless-about-online-privacy

Hertz, M. F., and C. David-Ferdon. 2008. *Electronic Media and Youth Violence: A CDC Issue Brief for Educators and Caregivers*. Centers for Disease Control.

Hidi, S. 2000. An interest researcher's perspective: The effects of extrinsic and intrinsic factors on motivation. In *Intrinsic and Extrinsic Motivation: The Search for Optimal Motivation and Performance*, ed. C. Sansone and J. Harackiewicz. Academic Press.

Hier, S. P. 2008. Thinking beyond moral panic: Risk, responsibility, and the politics of moralization. *Theoretical Criminology* 12 (2): 173–190.

Hinduja, S., and J. W. Patchin. 2008. Personal information of adolescents on the Internet: A quantitative content analysis of MySpace. *Journal of Adolescence* 31 (1): 125–146.

Hinjuja, S., and J. W. Patchin. 2009. *Bullying Beyond the Schoolyard: Preventing and Responding to Cyberbullying*. SAGE.

Himma, K. E. 2007. The concept of information overload: A preliminary step in understanding the nature of a harmful information-related condition. *Ethics and Information Technology* 9: 259–272.

Hine, C. 2000. *Virtual Ethnography*. SAGE.

HIV, Other STD, and Pregnancy Prevention Education in Public Secondary Schools—45 states, 2008–2010. 2012. Centers for Disease Control and Prevention. http://www.cdc.gov/mmwr/preview/mmwrhtml/mm6113a2.htm

Hobbs, R. 2006. Multiple visions of multimedia literacy: Emerging areas of synthesis. In *International Handbook of Literacy and Technology*, volume 2, ed. M. McKenna, L. D. Labbo, R. D. Keiffer, and D. Reinking. Erlbaum.

Hobbs, R. 1998. The seven great debates in the media literacy movement. *Journal of Communication* 48 (1): 16–32.

Hoffman, D. L., and T. P. Novak. 1995. A detailed analysis of the conceptual, logical, and methodological flaws in the article: "Marketing pornography on the information superhighway. In *Cyberspace Crime*, ed. D. S. Wal. Ashgate.

Hofstetter, C. R., D. Barker, J. T. Smith, G. M. Zarl, and T. A. Ingrassia. 1999. Information, misinformation, and political talk radio. *Political Research Quarterly* 52 (2): 353–369.

Holland, D. Lachiotte, W. Jr., Skinner, D. and Cain, C. 1998. *Identity and Agency in Cultural Worlds*. Harvard University Press.

Holloway, S. L., and G. Valentine. 2003. *Cyberkids: Children in the Information Age*. RoutledgeFalmer.

Hollywood Diversity Report. Flipping the Script. 2015. http://www.bunchecenter .ucla.edu/wp-content/uploads/2015/02/2015-Hollywood-Diversity-Report-2-25-15 .pdf

hooks, b. 1992. *Black Looks: Race and Representation*. South End.

HoSang. D. 2006. Beyond policy: Race, ideology, and the re-imagining of youth. In *Beyond Resistance! Youth Activism and Community Change*, ed. S. Ginwright, P. Noguera, and J. Cammarota. Routledge.

Horowitz, B. 2006. Creators, synthesizers, and consumers." Elatable blog, February 15. http://www.elatable.com/blog/?p=5

Horst, H. A. 2010. Families. In M. Ito, S. Baumer, M. Bittanti, d. boyd, R. Cody, et al., *Hanging Out, Messing Around, and Geeking Out: Kids Living and Learning with New Media*. MIT Press.

Huizenga, J., W. Admiraal, S. Akkerman, and G. ten Dam. 2009. Mobile game-based learning in secondary education: Engagement, motivation and learning in a mobile city game. *Journal of Computer Assisted Learning* 25 (4): 332–344.

Hunber, J. H. 1992. Inscribing the self in the heart of the family: Diaries and girlhood in late-Victorian America. *American Quarterly* 44 (1): 51–81.

Hunt, A. 2003. Risk and moralization in everyday life. In *Risk and Morality*, ed. R. Ericson and A. Doyle. University of Toronto Press.

Hunt, E. 2016. Online harassment of women at risk of becoming 'established norm', study finds. *The Guardian*. http://www.theguardian.com/lifeandstyle/2016/mar/08/ online-harassment-of-women-at-risk-of-becoming-established-norm-study

Hutchby, I. 2001. Technologies, texts and affordances. *Sociology* 35 (2): 441–456.

Hymel, S., C. Comfort, K. Schonert-Reichl, and P. McDougall. 1996. Academic failure and school dropout: The influence of peers. In *Social Motivation: Understanding Children's Adjustment*, ed. J. Juvonen and K. Wentzel. Cambridge University Press.

Ingraham, C. 2015. There's never been a safer time to be a kid in America. *Washington Post.* https://www.washingtonpost.com/news/wonk/wp/2015/04/14/theres-never-been-a-safer-time-to-be-a-kid-in-america/

Ison, A., A. Hayes, S. Robinson, and J. Jamieson. 2004. Txt Me: Supporting Disengaged Youth Using Mobile Technologies. Australian Flexible Learning Framework.

Ito, M. 2005. Mobile phones, Japanese youth, and the re-placement of social contact. In *Mobile Communications: Renegotiation of the Social Sphere*, ed. R. Ling and P. Pedersen. Springer.

Ito, M. 2008. Introduction. In *Networked Publics*, ed. K. Vernelis. MIT Press.

Ito, M., S. Baumer, M. Bittanti. d. boyd, R. Cody, et al. 2010. *Hanging Out, Messing Around, and Geeking Out: Kids Living and Learning with New Media*. MIT Press.

Ito, M., K. Gutierrez, S. Livingstone, B. Penuel, J. Rhodes, K. Salen, J. Schor, J. Sefton-Green, and S. C. Watkins. 2012. Connected learning: An agenda for research and design. *DML Research Hub*, December 31. http://dmlhub.net/publications/connected-learning-agenda-for-research-and-design/

Iyamba, N. 2012. Stairs among leading causes of injury, death for kids. https://www.ksl.com/?sid=19560857

Jackson, S., and S. Scott. 1999. Risk anxiety and the social construction of childhood. In *Risk and Sociocultural Theory: New Directions and Perspectives*, ed. D. Lupton. Cambridge University Press.

Jenkins, H. 1992. *Textual Poachers: Television Fans and Participatory Culture*. Routledge.

Jenkins, H. 200. *Convergence Culture: Where Old and New Media Collide*. NYU Press.

Jenkins, H. 2007. Reconsidering digital immigrants. Confessions of an Aca-Fan blog. http://henryjenkins.org/2007/12/reconsidering_digital_immigran.html

Jenkins, H., S. Ford, and J. Green. 2013. *Spreadable Media: Creating Value and Meaning in a Networked Culture*. New York University Press.

Jenkins, H., M. Ito, and d. boyd. 2016. *Participatory Culture in a Networked Era: A Conversation on Youth, Learning, Commerce, and Politics*. Polity.

Jenkins, H., R. Purushotma, M. Weigel, K. Clinton, and A. Robinson. 2009. *Confronting the Challenges of Participatory Culture: Media Education for the 21st Century*. MIT Press.

Jensen, G. H. 2009. Introduction to the Puer/Puerella archetype. In *Perpetual Adolescence*, ed. S. Porterfield, K. Polette, and T. Baumlin. State University of New York Press.

Jones, J. 2015. The book test. http://dmlcentral.net/the-book-test/

Judge tosses part of lawsuit over Facebook bikini photo. 2013. WSB TV, Atlanta, October 10. http://m.wsbtv.com/news/news/local/judge-tosses-part-lawsuit-over-facebook-bikini-pho/nbLX3/

Jurgenson, N. 2013. Victim blaming: How not to teach students about privacy. *Cyberology*, June 27. https://thesocietypages.org/cyborgology/2013/06/27/victim-blaming-how-not-to-teach-students-about-privacy/

Julien, H., and S. Barker. 2009. How high school students find and evaluate scientific information: A basis for information literacy skills development. *Library & Information Science Research* 31 (1): 12–17.

Jurkowitz, M., and N. Vogt. 2013. On Twitter: Anger greets the Zimmerman verdict. Pew Research Center. http://www.pewresearch.org/fact-tank/2013/07/17/on-twitter-anger-greets-the-zimmerman-verdict/

Juvonen, J., G. Espinoza, and C. Knifsend. 2012. The role of peer relationships in student academic and extracurricular engagement. In *Handbook of Research on Student Engagement*, ed. S. Christenson, A. Reschly, and C. Wylie. Springer.

Kaiser Family Foundation. 2010. Generation M^2: Media in the lives of 8- to 18-year-olds. https://kaiserfamilyfoundation.files.wordpress.com/2013/04/8010.pdf

Kalmus, V., P. Runnel, and A. Siibak. 2009. Opportunities and benefits online. In *Kids Online: Opportunities and Risks for Children*, ed. S. Livingstone and L. Haddon. Policy Press.

Kanuga, M., and W. D. Rosenfeld. 2004. Adolescent sexuality and the Internet: The good, the bad, the URL. *Journal of Pediatric and Adolescent Gynecology* 17 (2): 117–124.

Kaplan, A. M., and M. Haenlein. 2010. Users of the world, unite! The challenges and opportunities of social media. *Business Horizons* 53: 59–68.

Karaian, J. 2015. We now spend more than eight hours a day consuming media. *Quartz*, June 1. http://qz.com/416416/we-now-spend-more-than-eight-hours-a-day-consuming-media/

Katz, J. E. 2006. *Magic in the Air: Mobile Communication and the Transformation of Social Life*. Transaction.

Kearney, M. C. 2006. *Girls Make Media*. Routledge.

Keating, F. 2014. Selfies linked to narcissism, addiction, and mental illness, say scientists. *International Business Times*, March 23. http://www.ibtimes.co.uk/selfies-linked-narcissism-addiction-mental-illness-say-scientists-1441480

Kellner, D. 1998. Multiple literacies and critical pedagogy in a multicultural society. *Educational Theory* 48 (1): 103–122.

Kelly, P. 2000. The dangerousness of youth-at-risk: The possibilities of surveillance and intervention in uncertain times. *Journal of Adolescence* 23: 463–476.

Kelly, P. 2001. Youth at risk: Processes of individualization and responsibilization in the risk society. *Discourse* 22 (1): 23–33.

Kelly, P. 2003. Growing up as risky business?: Risks, surveillance, and the institutionalized mistrust of youth. *Journal of Youth Studies* 6 (2): 165–180.

Kendrick, W. 1987. *The Secret Museum: Pornography in Modern Culture*. University of California Press.

Keohane, J. 2010. The crime wave in our heads." *Dallas Morning News*, March 26. http://www.dallasnews.com/opinion/sunday-commentary/20100326-Joe-Keohane-The-crime-wave-762.ece

Khuffash, R. 2014. The 1% rule and why it still matters. *Medium*, April 1. https://medium.com/@ramykhuffash/the-1-rule-and-why-it-still-matters-ba0e40bbbffb#.e4e9k680v

Killoran, E. 2012. Internet rumors, gossip and misinformation: People only want to read what they already believe. *International Business Times*, April 28. http://www.ibtimes.com/internet-rumors-gossip-and-misinformation-people-only-want-read-what-they-already-believe-693614

Kincaid, J. R. 1992. *Child-Loving: The Erotic Child and Victorian Culture*. Routledge.

King, A. V. 2010. Constitutionality of cyberbullying laws: Keeping the online playground safe for both teens and free speech. *Vanderbilt Law Review* 63 (3): 845–884.

Kleeman, S. 2015. Instagram finally revealed the reason it banned nipples—It's Apple. *Tech.Mic*, October 1. https://mic.com/articles/126137/instagram-banned-nipples-because-of-apple#.87eOgcIsn

Knorr, C. 2010. Talking about "sexting." *Common Sense Media*, November 19. https://www.commonsensemedia.org/blog/talking-about-sexting

Koebler, J. 2015. Illinois says rule-breaking students must give teachers their Facebook passwords. *Motherboard*, January 20. http://motherboard.vice.com/read/illinois-says-students-have-to-give-up-facebook-passwords-or-face-prosecution

Kohler, P. K., L. E. Manhart, and W. E. Lafferty. 2008. Abstinence-only and comprehensive sex education and the initiation of sexual activity and teen pregnancy. *Journal of Adolescent Health* 42 (4): 344–351.

Kolb, L. 2008. *Toys to Tools: Connecting Student Cell Phones to Education*. International Society for Technology in Education.

Kottasova, I. 2015. Kids do a lot better when schools ban smartphones. *CNN Money*, May 18. http://money.cnn.com/2015/05/18/technology/smartphones-schools-ban/

Kraut, R., S. Kiesler, B. Boneva, J. Cummings, V. Helgeson, and A. Crawford. 2002. Internet paradox revisited. *Journal of Social Issues* 58 (1): 49–74.

Kravets, D. 2009. Cyberbullying bill gets chilly reception. *Wired*, September 30. http://www.wired.com/2009/09/cyberbullyingbill/

Kuipers, G. 2006. The social construction of digital danger: Debating, defusing, and inflating the moral dangers of online humor and pornography in the Netherland and the United States. *New Media & Society* 8 (3): 379–400.

Labor force statistics from the current population survey. Bureau of Labor Statistics, US Department of Labor. http://www.bls.gov/cps/cpsaat18.htm

Lange, P. G. 2014. *Kids on YouTube: Technical Identities and Digital Literacies*. Left Coast.

Lange, P. G., and M. Ito. 2010. Creative productions. In M. Ito, S. Baumer, M. Bittanti, d. boyd, R. Cody, et al., *Hanging Out, Messing Around, and Geeking Out: Kids Living and Learning with New Media*. MIT Press.

Lareau, A. 2003. *Unequal Childhoods: Class, Race, and Family Life*. University of California Press.

Lave, J., and E. Wegner. 1991. *Situated Learning: Legitimate Peripheral Participation*. Cambridge University Press.

Lee, D. 2013. Boston bombing: How internet detective got it very wrong. *BBC News*, April 19. http://www.bbc.com/news/technology-22214511

Lee, V. E., and D. T. Burkam. 2003. Dropping out of high school: The role of school organization and structure. *American Educational Research Journal* 40 (2): 353–393.

Lenhart, A. 2007. Cyberbullying. Pew Research Center. http://www.pewinternet.org/2007/06/27/cyberbullying/

Lenhart, A. 2009. Teens and sexting. Pew Research Center. http://www.pewinternet.org/files/old-media/Files/Reports/2009/PIP_Teens_and_Sexting.pdf

Lenhart, A. 2012. Teens and online video. Pew Research Center. http://www.pewinternet.org/files/old-media/Files/Reports/2012/PIP_Teens_and_online_video.pdf

Lenhart, A. 2015. Teens, social media & technology overview 2015. Pew Internet Research Center. http://www.pewinternet.org/2015/04/09/teens-social-media-technology-2015/

Lenhart, A., M. Madden, and P. Hitlin. 2005. Teens and technology: Youth are lead-ing the transition to a fully wired and mobile nation. Pew Internet & American Life Project. http://www.pewinternet.org/files/old-media/Files/Reports/2005/PIP_Teens _Tech_July2005web.pdf.pdf

Lesser, G. S. 1974. *Children and Television: Lessons from Sesame Street*. Random House.

Lessig, L. 2006. *Code and Other Laws of Cyberspace, Version 2.0*. Basic Books.

Lessig, L. 2008. *Remix: Making Art and Commerce Thrive in the Hybrid Economy*. Penguin.

Lievrouw, L. 2006. New media design and development: Diffusion of innovations v. social shaping of technology. In *Handbook of New Media* (updated student edition), ed. L. Lievrouw and S. Livingstone. SAGE.

Light, B., M. Griffiths, and S. Lincoln. 2012. Connect and create: Young people, YouTube, and graffiti communities. *Continuum* 26 (3): 343–355.

Ling, R. 2010. *New Tech, New Ties: How Mobile Communication Reshapes Social Cohesion*. MIT Press.

Livingstone, S. 2003. The changing nature of audience: From the mass audience to the interactive media user. In *Companion to Media Studies*, ed. A. Valdivia. Blackwell.

Livingstone, S. 2004. Media literacy and the challenge of new information and communication technologies. *Communication Review* 1 (7): 3–14.

Livingstone, S. 2008. Taking risky opportunities in youthful content creation: Teenagers' use of social networking sites for intimacy, privacy and self-expression. *New Media & Society* 10 (3): 393–411.

Livingstone, S. 2009. *Children and the Internet*. Polity.

Livingstone, S., L. Haddon, A. Görzig, K. Ólafsson, et al. 2011. Risk and Safety on the Internet: The perspectives of European children. http://www2.lse.ac.uk/media@lse/ research/EUKidsOnline/EUKidsII%20(200911)/EUKidsOnlineIIReports/ D4FullFindings.pdf.

Livingstone, S., and J. Sefton-Green. 2016. *The Class: Living and Learning in the Digital Age*. NYU Press.

Livingstone, S., E. Van Couvering, and N. Thumim. 2005. *Adult Media Literacy: A Review of the Research Literature*. Ofcom.

Locating the School-to-Prison Pipeline. ACLU Fact Sheet. https://www.aclu.org/fact -sheet/what-school-prison-pipeline

Long-term strategic vision would help ensure targeting of E-rate funds to highest-priority. 2009) U.S. Government Accountably Office. Report to Congressional Requesters (GAO-09–253 FCC's E-rate Program).

Luhmann, N. 1993. *Risk: A Sociological Theory*. Aldine de Gruyter.

Lumby, C., and N. Funnell. 2011. Between heat and light: The opportunity in moral panics. *Crime, Media, Culture* 7 (3): 277–291.

Lupton, D. 1999. *Risk: Key Ideas*. Routledge.

Lyons, L. 2004. Most teens associate school with boredom, fatigue. Gallup.com, June 8. http://www.gallup.com/poll/11893/most-teens-associate-school-boredom -fatigue.aspx

Maag, C. 2007. A Hoax Turned Fatal Draws Anger but No Charges. *New York Times*, November 28. http://www.nytimes.com/2007/11/28/us/28hoax.html?_r=1&oref =slogin

MacLaggan, C. 2014. In Texas, less progress on reducing teen pregnancy. *Texas Tribune*, July 6. http://www.texastribune.org/2014/07/06/teen-births-texas/

Mackay, H., and G. Gillespie. 1992. Extending the social shaping of technology approach: Ideology and appropriation. *Social Studies of Science* 22 (4): 685–716.

Madden, M., A. Lenhart, S. Cortesi, U. Gasser, M. Duggan, A. Smith, and M. Beaton. 2013. Teens, social media, and privacy. Pew Research Center. http://www .pewinternet.org/2013/05/21/teens-social-media-and-privacy/.

Madrigal, A. G. 2013. #BostonBombing: The anatomy of a misinformation disaster. *The Atlantic*, April 19. http://www.theatlantic.com/technology/archive/2013/04/ -bostonbombing-the-anatomy-of-a-misinformation-disaster/275155/

Maes, H. H., M. C. Neale, and L. J. Eaves. 1997. *Behavior Genetics* 27 (4): 325–351.

Mahoney, J. L., M. E. Parented, and E. F. Zigler. 2009. Afterschool programs in America: Origins, growth, popularity, and politics. *Journal of Youth Development* 4 (3): 26–44.

Malik, S. 2002. *Representing Black Britain: Black and Asian Images on Television*. SAGE.

Mann, S., and R. Cadman. 2014. Does being bored make us more creative? *Creativity Research Journal* 26 (2): 165–173.

Manovich, L. 2009. The practice of everyday (media) life: From mass consumption to mass cultural production? *Critical Inquiry* 35 (2): n.p. http://www.jstor.org/ stable/10.1086/596645

Marron, D. 2015. Every single word spoken. Tumblr. http://everysinglewordspoken .tumblr.com/

Martinez, G., J. Abma, and C. Copen. 2010. *Educating teenagers about sex in the United States. Data brief*. U.S. Department of Health and Human Services, Centers for Disease Control and Prevention.

Marvin, C. 1988. *When Old Technologies Were New: Thinking about Electric Communication in the Late Nineteenth Century.* Oxford University Press.

Marwick, A. 2008. To catch a predator? The MySpace moral panic. *First Monday* 13 (6). http://firstmonday.org/htbin/cgiwrap/bin/ojs/index.php/fm/article/view/2152/1966.

Marwick, A., and d. boyd. 2010. I tweet honestly, I tweet passionately: Twitter users, context collapse, and the imagined audience. *New Media & Society* 12 (1): 114–133.

Mastro, D. E. 2009. Racial/ethnic stereotyping and the media. In *The SAGE Handbook of Media Processes and Effects*, ed. R. Nabi and M. Oliver. SAGE.

Mazzarella, S. R. 2003. Constructing YOUTH: Media, youth, and the politics of representation. In *A Companion to Media Studies*, ed. A. Valdivia. Blackwell.

Mazzarella, S. R., and N. O. Pecora. 2007. Girls in crisis: Newspaper coverage of adolescent girls. *Journal of Communication Inquiry* 31: 6–27.

McChesney, R. W. 2013. *Digital Disconnect: How Capitalism Is Turning the Internet Against Democracy.* New Press.

McGhee, P. E., and T. Frueh. 1980. Television viewing and the learning of sex-role stereotypes. *Sex Roles* 6 (2): 179–188.

McGrath, J. 2004. Abstinence-only adolescent education: Ineffective, unpopular, and unconstitutional. *University of San Francisco Law Review* 38: 665–700.

McLaughlin, J. H. 2012. Explore the First Amendment rights of teens in relationship to sexting and censorship. *University of Michigan Journal of Law Reform* 45 (2): 315–350.

McPherson, K. 2006. Wikis and literacy development. *Teacher Librarian* 34 (1): 67–69.

McRobbie, Angela. 1990. Settling accounts with subcultures: A feminist critique. In *On Record: Rock, Pop, and the Written Word*, ed. S. Frith and A. Goodwin. Pantheon Books.

McRobbie, Angela, and Sarah Thorton. 1995. Rethinking "moral panic" for multi-mediated social worlds. *British Journal of Sociology* 46 (4): 559–574.

Meares, T. 1997. Drugs: It's a question of connections. Paper 475, Faculty Scholarship Series, Yale Law School. http://digitalcommons.law.yale.edu/fss_papers/475?utm_source=digitalcommons.law.yale.edu%2Ffss_papers%2F475&utm_medium=PDF&utm_campaign=PDFCoverPages

Megan Meier Cyberbullying Prevention Act (2009). 111th Congress, 1st Session, H.R. 1966.

Mendoza-Denton, N. 2008. *Homegirls: Languages and Cultural Practices among Latina Youth Gangs*. Blackwell.

Mercer, K. 1990. Black art and the burden of representation. *Third Text* 4 (10): 61–78.

Michels, S. 2008. Prosecutors bringing charges under law inspired by Megan Meier suicide. ABC News, December 24. http://abcnews.go.com/TheLaw/story?id=6520260

Miles, A. 2007. Network Literacy: the new path to knowledge. *Screen Education* 45 (autumn): 24–30.

Miller, D. 2013. "What is social media?"—a definition. Global Social Media Impact Study. http://blogs.ucl.ac.uk/global-social-media/2013/05/01/what-is-social-media-a -definition/

Miller, H. 1995. The presentation of self in electronic life: Goffman on the Internet. Paper presented at Embodied Knowledge and Virtual Space Conference, Goldsmiths College, University of London. http://web.ntu.ac.uk/soc/psych/miller/goffman/htm

Mitchell, C. 2002. *Researching Children's Popular Culture*. Routledge.

Mitchell, K. J., D. Finkelhor, L. M. Jones, and J. Wolak. 2012. Prevalence and characteristics of youth sexting: A national study. *Pediatrics* 129 (1): 13–20.

Mobile phone bans "improve school exam results." 2015. BBC News, May 17. http://www.bbc.com/news/education-32771253

Mobile phone bans lead to rise in student test scores. 2015. *UT News*, May 18. http://news.utexas.edu/2015/05/18/mobile-phone-bans-lead-to-rise-in-student-test-scores.

Moessner, C. 2007. Cyberbullying. *Harris Interactive Trends & Tudes* 6 (4): n.p.

Montiel, I. 2012. The transition towards persistent identities. *Science in Society Review*, spring: 24–26.

Morley, D. 2006. Unanswered questions in audience research. *Communication Review* 9: 101–121.

Morse v. Frederick, 551 U.S. 393 (2007).

Mullin, D. I. 1996. The First Amendment and the Web: The Internet porn panic and restricting indecency in cyberspace. Presented at Untangling the Web (conference sponsored by the Librarians Association of the University of California, Santa Barbara, and Friends of the UCSB Library).

Murphy, S. 2010. How kids are immune to information overload. *Live Science*. http://www.livescience.com/11099-kids-immune-information-overload.html

Nahon, K., and J. Hemsley. 2013. *Going Viral*. Polity.

Nardini, M. L., and R. L. Antes. 1991. An at-risk assessment: Teachers rate their students on academic skills and behavior. *Clearing House* 65: 56–62.

Nationwide Children's Hospital. 2010. Choking is a leading cause of injury and death among children." *Science Daily*. https://www.sciencedaily.com/releases/2010/02/100226212559.htm

NCAC Staff. 2013. The First Amendment in schools: A resource guide. http://ncac.org/resource/first-amendment-in-schools/

Negra, D., and Z. Asava. 2013. Race and cinema. http://www.oxfordbibliographies.com/view/document/obo-9780199791286/obo-9780199791286-0127.xml

Nett, U. E., T. Goetz, and L. M. Daniels. 2010. What to do when feeling bored? Students' strategies for coping with boredom. *Learning and Individual Differences* 20: 626–638.

Newman, S. A., J. A. Fox, E. A. Flynn, and W. Christeson. 2000. American's After-School Choice: The Prime Time for Juvenile Crime, or Youth Enrichment and Achievement. Report published by Fight Crime: Invest in Kids.

Nicholson, H. J., C. Collins, and H. Holmer. 2004. Youth as people: The protective aspects of youth development in after-school settings. *Annals of the American Academy of Political and Social Science* 591 (1): 55–71.

Nielsen. 2015. The Total Audience Report: Q4 2014. http://www.nielsen.com/us/en/insights/reports/2015/the-total-audience-report-q4-2014.html

Nissenbaum, H. 2004. Privacy as contextual integrity. *Washington Law Review* 79 (1): 119–158.

Oakes, J. 2005. *Keeping Track: How Schools Structure Inequality*, second edition. Yale University Press.

Oblinger, D. G., and J. L. Oblinger, eds. 2005. *Educating the Net Generation*. Educase.

O'Brien, M. 2009. The tactics of mobile phone in the school-based practices of young people. *Anthropology in Action* 16 (1): 30–40.

Odem, M. E. 1995. *Delinquent Daughters: Protecting and Policing Adolescent Female Sexuality in the United States, 1885–1920*. University of North Carolina Press.

Olfman, S. 2008. *The Sexualization of Childhood*. ABC-CLIO.

Oliver, M. B. 2003. African American men as "criminal and dangerous": Implications of media portrayals of crime on the "criminalization" of African American men. *Journal of African American Studies* 7 (2): 3–18.

O'Malley, P. 1992. Risk, power and crime prevention. *Economy and Society* 21 (3): 252–275.

O'Reilly, T. 2005. What is Web 2.0? http://www.oreillynet.com/pub/a/oreilly/tim/news/2005/09/30/what-is-web-20.html

O'Rourke, J. 2013. Lifetime move directory: Ripped from the headlines. *Crushable.* http://www.crushable.com/2013/12/29/entertainment/lifetime-movie-reviews-headlines-new-current-events-movies/

Owens, E. W., R. Behun, J. C. Manning, and R. C. Reid. 2012. The impact of internet pornography on adolescents: A review of the research. *Sexual Addiction & Compulsivity* 19 (1–2): 99–122.

Pariser, E. 2011. *The Filter Bubble: How the New Personalized Web Is Changing What We Read and How We Think.* Penguin.

Parker, J. K. 2010. *Teaching Tech-Savvy Kids: Bringing Digital Media into the Classroom, Grades 5–12.* Corwin.

Patchin, J. W., and S. Hinduja. 2006. Bullies move beyond the schoolyard: A preliminary look at cyberbullying. *Youth Violence and Juvenile Justice* 4 (2): 148–169.

Patton, R. 2014. E-rate modernization: it just goes to show … . Cisco Blogs, Nobember 20. http://blogs.cisco.com/education/e-rate-modernization-it-just-goes-to-show

Paul, A. M. 2013. You'll never learn! students can't resist multitasking, and it's impairing their memory. *Slate,* May 3. http://www.slate.com/articles/health_and_science/science/2013/05/multitasking_while_studying_divided_attention_and_technological_gadgets.html

Pearson, G. 1983. *Hooligan: A History of Respectable Fears.* Macmillan.

Peetsma, T. T. D. 2000. Future time perspective as a predictor of school investment. *Scandinavian Journal of Educational Research* 44 (2): 177–192.

Peffley, M., T. Shields, and B. Williams. 1996. The intersection of race and crime in television news stories: An experimental study. *Political Communication* 13 (3): 309–327.

Pekrun, R., T. Goetz, L. Daniels, R. H. Stupnisky, and P. Raymond. 2010. Boredom in achievement settings: Exploring control-value antecedents and performance outcomes of a neglected emotion. *Journal of Educational Psychology* 102 (3): 531–549.

Perkins, A. 2014. Should employers restrict personal device use in the workplace? http://www.commonplaces.com/blog/should-employers-restrict-personal-device-use-in-the-workplace/

Perrin, A., and M. Duggan. 2015. American's internet access: 2000–2015. http://www.pewinternet.org/files/2015/06/2015-06-26_internet-usage-across-demographics-discover_FINAL.pdf

Peters, J. D. 1999. *Speaking into the Air: A History of the Idea of Communication.* University of Chicago Press.

Pew Research Center. 2013. A quarter of teens mostly access the internet using their cell phones. http://www.pewresearch.org/daily-number/a-quarter-of-teens-mostly -access-the-internet-using-their-cell-phones/

Phillips, S. 2011. Teens sleeping with cell phones: A clear and present danger. *Psych Central.* http://blogs.psychcentral.com/healing-together/2010/12/teens-sleeping -with-cell-phones-a-clear-and-present-danger/

Pokin, S. 2007. A real person, a real death. *St. Louis Post-Dispatch*, November 19. http://www.stltoday.com/suburban-journals/stcharles/news/stevepokin/pokin -around-a-real-person-a-real-death/article_511f32a2-ebd1-5568-8a1a-b2218cc60135 .html

Popham, W. J. 1999. Why standardized tests don't measure educational quality. *Educational Leadership* 56 (6): 8–15.

Post, D. G. 1995. A preliminary discussion of methodological peculiarities in the Rimm study of pornography on the "Information Superhighway." Georgetown University Law Center, published as part of 'The Cyberporn Debate', eLab: Research for a Digital World. Available: http://elab.vanderbilt.edu/research/topics/cyberporn/ david.post.htm

Prensky, M. 2001. Digital natives, digital immigrants. *On the Horizon* 9 (5): 1–6.

Prensky, M. 2005. Listen to the natives. *Educational Leadership* 63 (4): 8–13.

Prensky, M. 2008. Turning on the lights. *Educational Leadership* 65 (6): 40–45.

President's Commission on Obscenity and Pornography. 1970. *Report.* Government Printing Office.

Protecting Children in the 21st Century Act (2007).

Przybylski, A. K., K. Murayama, C. R. DeHaan, and V. Gladwell. 2013. Motivational, emotional, and behavioral correlates of fear of missing out. *Computers in Human Behavior* 29 (4): 1841–1848.

Puchko, K. 2014. The most embarrassing statistics about women in Hollywood. Cinemablend.com. http://www.cinemablend.com/new/Most-Embarrassing-Statistics -About-Women-Hollywood-67381.html

Quittner, J. 1996. Free speech for the Net: A panel of federal judges overturns the Communications Decency Act. *Time*, June 24: 56–58.

Radford, B. 2006. Predator panic: Reality check on sex offenders. Live Science, May 16. http://www.livescience.com/othernews/060516_predator_panic.html

Rainie, L. 2010. Networked Creators: How users of social media have changed the ecology of information. Paper delivered at VALA Libraries Conference, Melbourne.

Rainie, L., and B. Wellman. 2012. *Networked: The New Social Operating System*. MIT Press.

Rainie, L., and K. Zickuhr. 2015. Americans' views on mobile etiquette. Pew Research Center. http://www.pewinternet.org/2015/08/26/americans-views-on-mobile-etiquette/

Raynes-Goldie, K., and L. Walker. 2008. Our space: Online civic engagement tools for youth. In *Civic Life Online: Learning How Digital Media Can Engage Youth*, ed. W. Bennett. MIT Press.

Reagle, J. 2015. Following the Jonses: FOMO and conspicuous sociality. *First Monday* 20 (10). http://firstmonday.org/ojs/index.php/fm/article/view/6064/4996

Reese, S. D., O. H. Grandy, and A. E. Grant. 2001. *Framing Public Life: Perspectives on Media and Our Understanding of the Social World*. Routledge.

Rheingold, H. 1995. Would-be censors base arguments on bogus research. The Well. http://www.well.com/~hlr/tomorrow/cyberporn.html

Rheingold, H. 2012. *NetSmart: How to Thrive Online*. MIT Press.

Rheingold, H. 2013. Participative pedagogy for a literacy of literacies. In *The Participatory Cultures Handbook*, ed. A. Delwiche and J. Henderson. Routledge.

Rhodes, J. E. 2004. The critical ingredient: Caring youth-staff relationships in after-school settings. *New Directions for Youth Development* (101): 145–161.

Rimm, M. 1995. Marketing pornography on the information superhighway. *Georgetown Law Journal* 83 (5): 1849–1934.

Ringrose, J. 2006. A new universal mean girl: Examining the discursive construction and social regulation of a new feminine pathology. *Feminism & Psychology* 16 (4): 405–424.

Rios, V. M. 2006. The hyper-criminalization of Black and Latino male youth in the era of mass incarceration. *Souls* 8 (2): 40–54.

Ripley, A. 2013. Bored to death. https://newrepublic.com/article/115928/twitter-shows-epidemic-school-boredom

Roberts, D. F., U. G. Foehr, V. J. Rideout, and M. Brodie. 1999. *Kids and Media @ the New Millennium*. Kaiser Family Foundation.

Robertson, M. R. 2015. 500 Hours of video uploaded to YouTube every minute [forecast]. ReelSEO, November 13. http://www.reelseo.com/hours-minute-uploaded-youtube/

Robinson, T. N. 1999. Reducing children's television viewing to prevent obesity: A randomized controlled study. *Journal of the American Medical Association* 282 (16): 1561–1567.

Rosen, L. 2006. Adolescents in MySpace: Identity formation, friendship and sexual predators. http://www.csudh.edu/psych/lrosen.htm

Rosin, H. 2014. Why kids sext. *The Atlantic*, November. http://www.theatlantic.com/magazine/archive/2014/11/why-kids-sext/380798/

Rubin, A., S. M. Sawyer, and H. Taye. 2015. The top social media platforms' efforts to control cyber-harassment. *Socially Aware*, August 31. http://www.sociallyawareblog.com/2015/08/31/the-top-social-media-platforms-efforts-to-control-cyber-harassment/

Rudra, G. 2013. Bikini-clad student sues Georgia high school for circulating image. ABC News, June 24. http://abcnews.go.com/US/bikini-clad-student-sues-georgia-high-school-circulating/story?id=19467058

Ryan, R. M., and E. L. Deci. 2000. Self-determination theory and the facilitation of intrinsic motivation, social development, and well-being. *American Psychologist* 55: 68–78.

Sacco, D. T., K. Silbaugh, F. Corredor, J. Casey, and D. Doherty. 2012. *An Overview of State Anti-Bullying Legislation and Other Related Laws*. Kinder & Braver World Project.

Sacks, P. 1999. *Standardized Minds: The High Price of America's Testing Culture and What We Can Do to Change It*. Da Capo.

Sandvig, C. 2014. Corrupt personalization. Social Media Collective Research Blog, June 26. http://socialmediacollective.org/2014/06/26/corrupt-personalization/

Saul, D. J. 2014. 3 million teens leave Facebook in 3 years: The 2014 Facebook demographic report. iStrategy Labs. http://istrategylabs.com/2014/01/3-million-teens-leave-facebook-in-3-years-the-2014-facebook-demographic-report/

Saxena, S. 2004. *Breaking News: The Craft and Technology of Online Journalism*. Tate McGraw-Hill.

Scheidt, L. A. 2006. Adolescent diary weblogs and the unseen audience. In *Digital Generations: Children, Young People, and New Media*, ed. D. Buckingham and R. Willett. Erlbaum.

Schofield, J., and A. Davidson. 2002. *Bringing the Internet to School: Lessons from an Urban District*. Jossey-Bass.

Scholz, T. 2008. Market ideology and the myths of Web 2.0. *First Monday* 13 (2). http://firstmonday.org/ojs/index.php/fm/article/viewArticle/2138/1945

Schramm, W., J. Lyle, and E. B. Parker. 1961. *Television in the Lives of Our Children.* Stanford University Press.

Schreckinger, B. 2014. The Home of FOMO. *Boston,* August. http://www .bostonmagazine.com/news/article/2014/07/29/fomo-history/

Schwarz, J. 2015. Schools can require students to hand over their social media passwords under Illinois law. *Washington Post* GovBeat blog, January 22. http://www .washingtonpost.com/blogs/govbeat/wp/2015/01/22/schools-can-require-students -to-hand-over-their-social-media-passwords-under-illinois-law/.

Scott, S., S. Jackson, and K. Backett-Milburn. 1998. Swings and roundabouts: Risk anxiety and the everyday worlds of children. *Sociology* 32 (4): 689–705.

Searcey, D. 2009. A lawyer, some teens and a fight over "sexting." *Wall Street Journal,* April 21. http://www.wsj.com/articles/SB124026115528336397

Sefton-Green. 2004. Literature review in informal learning with technology outside school. *Performing Arts* 7 (7): 1–23.

Sefton-Green, J. 2013. *Learning at Not-School.* MIT Press.

Sex and Tech. Results from a survey of teens and young adults (2008). The National Campaign to Prevent Teen and Unplanned Pregnancy. Washington, DC. http:// thenationalcampaign.org/resource/sex-and-tech

Shade, L. R. 2011. Surveilling the girl via the third and networked screen. In *Mediated Girlhoods: New Explorations of Girls' Media Culture,* ed. M. Kearney. Peter Lang.

Shann, M. H. 2001. Students' use of time outside of school: A case for after school programs for urban middle school youth. *Urban Review* 33 (4): 339–356.

Short, J. 1984. The social fabric at risk: Toward the social transformation of risk analysis. *American Sociological Review* 49: 711–725.

Simons, H. D., D. Van Rheenen, and M. V. Covington. 1999. Academic motivation and the student athlete. *Journal of College Student Development* 40 (2): 151–161.

Sims, C. 1988. Schools responding to beeper, tool of today's drug dealer, by banning it. *New York Times,* September 25. http://www.nytimes.com/1988/09/25/us/schools -responding-to-beeper-tool-of-today-s-drug-dealer-by-banning-it.html

Sims, C. 2014. From differentiated use to differentiating practices: Negotiation the production of privileged identities. *Information Communication and Society* 17 (6): 670–682.

Singal, J. 2015. New research suggests de Blasio's unbanning of cell phones in NYC schools may have been a bad idea. *New York,* May 21. http://nymag.com/scienceofus/ 2015/05/downside-of-allowing-cell-phones-in-schools.html

Skenazy, L. 2009. *Free-Range Kids: How to Raise Safe, Self-Reliant Children (without Going Nuts with Worry)*. Wiley.

Skolbekken, J. A. 1995. The risk epidemic in medical journals. *Social Science & Medicine* 40 (3): 291–305.

Smith, B. J. 1944. The First 100 Years: In the Beginning … . National Amateur Press Association. http://www.amateurpress.org/ajhist/begin.htm

Smith, M. D. 2014. How Trayvon Martin's death launched a new generation of black activism. *The Nation*, August 27. http://www.thenation.com/article/how-trayvon -martins-death-launched-new-generation-black-activism/

Smith, A. 2015. U.S. smartphone use in 2015. Pew Research Center. http://www .pewinternet.org/2015/04/01/us-smartphone-use-in-2015/

Solomon, J. 2003. FBI tied McVeigh to supremacist plotters. *Seattle PI*. http://www .seattlepi.com/national/article/FBI-tied-McVeigh-to-supremacist-plotters-1107464 .php.

Solove, D. J. 2007. *The Future of Reputation: Gossip, Rumor, and Privacy on the Internet.* Yale University Press.

Spigel, L. 1992. *Making Room for TV: Television and the Family Idea in Postwar America.* University of Chicago Press.

Spradley, J. P. 1979. *The Ethnographic Interview*. Wadsworth, Thomson Learning.

Springhall, J. 1998. *Youth, Popular Culture, and Moral Panics: Penny Gafts to Gangsta Rap, 1830–1996*. Macmillan.

Stahl, B. C. 2006. On the difference of equality of information, misinformation, and disinformation: A critical research perspective. *Informing Science Journal* 9: 83–96.

Stammer, L. B., and C. Hall. 1995. Terror in Oklahoma City: American Muslims feel sting of accusations in bombing's wake. *Los Angeles Times*, April 22. http:// articles.latimes.com/1995-04-22/news/mn-57460_1_oklahoma-city-bombing

Stein, S. 2010. Parents defend 12 year-old's bullying, sue school. *Jezebel*, July 1. http://jezebel.com/5577513/parents-defend-12-year-olds-bullying-sue-school

Steinhauer, J. 2008. Verdict in MySpace suicide case. *New York Times*, November 26. http://www.nytimes.com/2008/11/27/us/27myspace.html

Stephens, K. K., and J. L. Ford. 2016. Unintended consequences of a strategically ambiguous organizational policy selectively restricting mobile devices use at work. *Mobile Media & Communication* 4 (2): 186–204.

Stern, S. R. 1999. Adolescent girls' expressions on Web home pages: Spirited, sombre, and self-conscious sites. *Convergence* 5 (4): 22–41.

Straubhaar, J. Spence, J., Tufekci, Z., and Lentz, R. G., eds. 2012. *Inequity in the Technopolis: Race, Class, Gender, and the Digital Divide in Austin*. University of Texas Press.

Stuart-Cassel, V., A. Bell, and J. F. Spring. 2011. *Analysis of State Bullying Laws and Policies*. U.S. Department of Education.

Sullivan, B. 2013. Students can't resist distraction for two minutes ... and neither can you. NBC News, May 18. http://www.nbcnews.com/technology/students-cant-resist-distraction-two-minutes-neither-can-you-1C9984270

Sunstein, C. R. 2009. *Going to Extremes: How Like Minds Unite and Divide*. Oxford University Press.

Sunstein, C. R. 2014. *On Rumors: How Falsehoods Spread, Why We Believe Them, and What Can Be Done*. Princeton University Press.

Taibi, C. 2015. The academic case for banning cell phones at school. *Huffington Post*, May 20. http://www.huffingtonpost.com/2015/05/18/whats-working-cell-phone-ban-teens-school_n_7305538.html

Tait, G. 1995. Shaping the "at-risk" youth: Risk, governmentality and the Finn Report. *Discourse* 16 (1): 123–134.

Takao, M., S. Takahashi, and M. Kitamura. 2009. Addictive personality and problematic mobile phone use. *Cyberpsychology & Behavior* 12 (5): 501–507.

Tapscott, D. 1998. *Growing Up Digital: The Rise of the Net Generation*. McGraw-Hill.

Taylor, A. 2005. Phone talk. In *Mobile Communication: Re-Negotiation of the Social Sphere*, ed. R. Ling and P. Pedersen. Springer.

Taylor, J. 2012. Are your children overloaded with information? *Huffington Post*, December 11. http://www.huffingtonpost.com/dr-jim-taylor/information-overload_b_2272263.html

Teen fact sheet 2012. Pew Research Center. http://www.pewinternet.org/fact-sheets/teens-fact-sheet/

te Riele, Kitty. 2006. Youth "at risk": Further marginalizing the marginalized? *Journal of Education Policy* 21 (2): 129–145.

Texas Health and Safety Code ex. 85.007. Educational materials for minors. http://www.statutes.legis.state.tx.us/Docs/HS/htm/HS.85.htm

Texas STD Surveillance Report (2014). Texas Department of State Health Services. https://www.dshs.texas.gov/hivstd/reports/STDSurveillanceReport2014.pdf.

Thevenot, C. G. 2014. Parents sue school district over bullied daughter's suicide. *Las Vegas Review-Journal*, October 21. http://www.reviewjournal.com/news/las-vegas/parents-sue-school-district-over-bullied-daughter-s-suicide

Thiel-Stern, S. 2007. *Instant Identity: Adolescent Girls and the World of Instant Messaging*. Peter Lang.

Thiel-Stern, S. 2014. *From the Dance Hall to Facebook: Teen Girls, Mass Media, and Moral Panic in the United States, 1905–2010*. University of Massachusetts Press.

Thomas, D., and J. S. Brown. 2011. *A New Culture of Learning: Cultivating the Imagination for a World of Constant Change*. CreateSpace.

Thomson, K. 2011. White Supremacist Site MartinLutherKing.org Marks 12th Anniversary. *Huffington Post*, January 16. http://www.huffingtonpost.com/keith -thomson/white-supremacist-site-ma_b_809755.html

Tinker v. Des Moines Independent Community School District, 393 U.S. 503, 504 (1969).

Trenholm, C., B. Devaney, K. Forston, J. Wheeler, and M. Clark. 2007. Impacts of Four Title V, Section 510 Abstinence Education Programs: Final Report. Princeton Mathematica Policy Research. http://www.mathematica-mpr.com/~/ media/publications/PDFs/impactabstinence.pdf

Trump, K. S. 1995. Schools security assessments and crisis preparedness. *Updating School Board Policies* 26 (6): 1–5.

Trump, K. S. 2009. Is it safe to allow cell phones in school? *District Administration*, November. http://www.districtadministration.com/article/it-safe-allow-cell-phones -school

Turkle, S. 1995. *Life on the Screen: Identity in the Age of the Internet*. Simon & Schuster.

Turkle, S. 2011. *Alone Together: Why We Expect More from Technology and Less from Each Other*. Basic Books.

Turrill, D. 2014. The Total Audience Report. Neilsen. http://s1.q4cdn.com/199638165/ files/doc_presentations/2014/The-Total-Audience-Report.pdf

Tyner, K. 1998. *Literacy in a Digital World: Teaching and Learning in the Age of Information*. Erlbaum.

Urbina, I. 2007. Court rejects law limiting online pornography. *New York Times*, March 23. http://www.nytimes.com/2007/03/23/us/23porn.html

van Dijck, J. 2013a. *The Culture of Connectivity: A Critical History of Social Media*. Oxford University Press.

van Dijck, J. 2013b. "You have one identity": Performing the self on Facebook and LinkedIn. *Media Culture & Society* 35 (2): 199–215.

Vickery, J. R. 2008. The Megan Meier MySpace suicide: Exploring the social aspects of convergent media, citizen journalism, and online anonymity and credibility. Presented at International Symposium on Online Journalism, Austin.

Vickery, J. R. 2010. Blogrings as online communities for adolescent girls. In *Girl Wide Web 2.0: Revisiting Girls, the Internet, and the Negotiation of Identity*, ed. S. Mazzarella. Peter Lang.

Vickery, J. R. 2014a. Talk whenever, wherever: How the U.S. mobile phone industry commodifies talk, genders youth mobile practices, and domesticates surveillance. *Journal of Children and Media* 8 (4): 387–403.

Vickery, J. R. 2014b. "I don't have anything to hide, but … ": The challenges and negotiations of social and mobile media privacy for non-dominant youth. *Information Communication and Society* 18 (3): 281–294.

Vitelli, R. 2013. Stress, texting, and being social. *Psychology Today*, December 16. https://www.psychologytoday.com/blog/media-spotlight/201312/stress-texting-and-being-social

Vogel-Walcutt, J. J., L. Fiorella, T. Carper, and S. Schatz. 2011. The definition, assessment, and mitigation of state boredom within education settings: A comprehensive review. *Educational Psychology Review* 24: 89–111.

Walker, K. 2000. "It's difficult to hide it": The presentation of self on Internet homepages. *Qualitative Sociology* 23 (1): 99–120.

Wallin, P. 2009. Bullying: What's the big deal? *PennLive*, February 17. http://www.pennlive.com/bodyandmind/index.ssf/2009/02/bullying_whats_the_big_deal.html

Ward, J. R., ed. 2015. *Real Sister: Stereotypes, Respectability, and Black Women in Reality TV*. Rutgers University Press.

Watkins, S. C. 2009. *The Young and the Digital: What the Migration to Social Network Sites, Games and Anytime, Anywhere Media Means for Our Future*. Beacon.

Watkins, S. C. 2012. Digital divide: Navigating the digital edge. *International Journal of Learning and Media* 3 (2): 1–12.

Watkins, S. C., A. Cho, A. Bermudez, J. Vickery, V. Shaw, and L. Weinzimmer. 2017. *The Digital Edge: The Evolving World of Social, Educational, and Digital Inequality*. New York University Press.

Webb, J. 2014. Should companies monitor their employees' social media? *Wall Street Journal*, October 22. http://www.wsj.com/articles/should-companies-monitor-their-employees-social-media-1399648685

Weeks, L. 2012. Tragedy gives the hoodie a whole new meaning. NPR, March 24. http://www.npr.org/2012/03/24/149245834/tragedy-gives-the-hoodie-a-whole-new-meaning

Weiss, J. 2012. Texas' standardized tests a poor measure of what students learned, UT-Austin professor says. *Dallas Morning News*, August 11. http://www.dallasnews.com/news/education/headlines/20120811-texas-standardized-tests-a-poor-measure-of-what-students-learned-ut-austin-professor-says.ece

Wentzel, K. R. 2005. Peer relationships, motivation, and academic performance at school. In *Handbook of Competence and Motivation*, ed. A. Elliot and C. Dweck. Guilford.

Wesch, M. 2008. An anthropological introduction to YouTube. https://www.youtube.com/watch?v=TPAO-lZ4_hU

Wesch, M. 2009. Participatory media literacy: Why it matters. mediatedcultures.net, January 3. http://mediatedcultures.net/thoughts/192/

Widder, B. 2014. Think you know how to Google? *Digital Trends*, November 9. http://www.digitaltrends.com/computing/the-35-best-google-search-tips-and-tricks/

Winsten, J. 2011. The Designated Driver campaign: Why it worked. *Huffington Post*, March 18. http://www.huffingtonpost.com/jay-winston/designated-driver-campaig_b_405249.html

Withers, G., and M. Batten. 1995. *Programs for At-Risk Youth: A Review of the American, Canadian and British Literature since 1984*. Australian Council for Educational Research.

Wolfgang, M. E. 2002. Victim precipitated criminal homicide. In *Crime and Justice at the Millennium*, ed. R. Silverman et al. Springer Science + Business Media.

Wood, E. 2013. The Harlem Shake has exploded. *YouTube Trends*, February 12. Available: http://web.archive.org/web/20130424074859/http://youtube-trends.blogspot.com.au/2013/02/the-harlem-shake-has-exploded.html

Woollaston, V. 2013. Revealed, what happens in just ONE minute on the internet: 216,000 photos posted, 278,000 Tweets and 1.8m Facebook likes. *Daily Mail*, July 30. http://www.dailymail.co.uk/sciencetech/article-2381188/Revealed-happens-just-ONE-minute-internet-216-000-photos-posted-278-000-Tweets-1-8m-Facebook-likes.html

Yazzie-Mintz, E. 2007. Voices of students on engagement: A report of the 2006 High School Survey of Student Engagement. Center for Evaluation and Education Policy, Indiana University. http://eric.ed.gov/?id=ED495758

Yin, R. K. 2009. *Case Study Research: Design and Methods*, fourth edition. SAGE.

Zetter, K. 2009. Judge acquits Lori Drew in cyberbullying case, overrules jury. *Wired*, July 2. http://www.wired.com/2009/07/drew_court/

Zheng, R. 2006. From WebQuest to virtual learning: A study on students' perception of factors affecting design and development of online learning. In *Teaching and Learning with Virtual Teams*, ed. S. Ferris and S. Godar. Information Science Publishing.

Index